SHELTER IN AFRICA

SHELTER IN AFRICA

edited by Paul Oliver

BARRIE & JENKINS
COMMUNICA - EUROPA

First published 1971 by Barrie & Jenkins Ltd.
24 Highbury Crescent, London N5 1RX

© 1971 by Barrie & Jenkins Ltd.

Paperback edition 1976

SBN 214 20205 4

Printed in Great Britain by
Fletcher & Son Ltd, Norwich

PICTURE CREDITS

As Editor of *Shelter in Africa* I wish to thank the photographers and illustrators listed below who have kindly assisted the contributors and myself with pictures. Except where noted the maps and drawings are by the contributors themselves. Woodcuts and early line blocks are, for Mr. Barrie Biermann's article, from his own collection, and elsewhere from those in my possession.

For their permission to reproduce blocks from their books I am indebted to the following:

Miss Elspeth Huxley and her publishers, Chatto and Windus, for the illustration, page 87*b* from *The Sorcerer's Apprentice*.

Mr. Max Lock and his publishers, Faber and Faber, for the existing and proposed plans for the Sabon Gari, Kaduna, on pages 236 and 237 from *Kaduna 1917. 1967. 2017: A survey and plan of the capital territory for the Government of Northern Nigeria*, 1967, pp. 183–4.

Mr. B. A. W. Trevallion and his publishers, Newman Neame Ltd., for the existing and proposed plan for part of Metropolitan Kano on page 237 from *Metropolitan Kano*; Report on the twenty-year development plan, 1963, p. 60.

Acknowledgements are also due to Aerofilms Limited and the Chief Survey Officer, Government of Ghana, Survey Division, Accra, Ghana, for permission to reproduce the aerial photographs on page 153.

Finally, I owe a special debt of gratitude to Mrs. Stella Swithenbank for permitting me to reproduce the drawings by her late husband, Mr. Ramsey (Michael) Swithenbank, to illustrate Mr. Andrew Rutter's article on Ashanti Vernacular Architecture.

Note. *The illustrations listed below are reproduced by kind permission of the owners, copyright holders or photographers. Copyright obtains on the entire contents of this book; no illustration may be reproduced, except for purposes of review, without the authority of the owner, copyright holder or photographer.*

Peter Alford ANDREWS 126, 127, 129, 130, 136–41
Ian ARCHER 46–8, 49*l*, 49*t*, 50–7
D. M. ARNALL 195*tl*, 195*br*
Barrie BIERMANN 96–105
Thomas L. BLAIR Frontispiece 2, 12, 21*l*, 227–31, 234, 235
John COLLINS 195*tr*, 195*bl*, 196–7
Miles DANBY 36–45
David ETHERTON 173–80, 180, 181*t*, 183*b*, 184–9
Badi FOSTER 219–25
Naigzy GEBREMEDHIN 106–23
Georg GERSTER 180*b*
Guy GERVIS 212–16
GOVERNMENT OF GHANA, SURVEY DIVISION 153*l*, 153*r*
Amancio d'Alpoim GUEDES 200–9, 232, 233
David HICKS 182, 183*t*
Robert HOPEWOOD 192*br*, 198
Anton JANSZ 125, 128, 131–5, 142
Michael LEVIN 143–51
Ronald LEWCOCK 80–95
Max LOCK and Partners 237
Maurice MITCHELL 14*r*
Ralph MTHAWANJI 190–2*bl*, 193
Paul OLIVER 13, 14*b*, 15–20, 21*r*, 24, 49*br*, 164*b*, 166
Andrew F. RUTTER 154, 160–3, 164*t*, 165, 167–8, 170
Friedrich SCHWERDTFEGER Frontispiece 1, 58–78
Ramsey (Michael) SWITHENBANK 155–9, 169
B. A. W. TREVALLION 236
Paul VERITY 11, 26–35

CONTENTS

INTRODUCTION

Paul Oliver

When Olaudah Equiano first came to London, Osterley Park and Syon House were being built; when he returned, a few years later, in 1767, Kenwood was under construction. Olaudah Equiano, called Gustavus Vasa by the British naval officer who bought him in Virginia, was an Ibo from the Benin region of Nigeria. He had been captured as a boy by a raiding party and sold to slavers on the coast. His adventures as a slave in a naval vessel and on the schooner of a Philadelphia trader must have accustomed him to European languages and mode of life. A dozen years after his capture he had purchased his freedom and made his way to England to study the barber's trade. Over thirty years passed from the date of his capture to the publication of his memoirs, during which time he must have witnessed the expansion of London, the building of the British Museum and the speculative houses and squares of Bloomsbury. How he viewed them we can only guess, but when he wrote of the villages of the Ika district on the Niger River where he was born and raised, it was without exaggeration, apology or belittlement.

'In our buildings we study convenience rather than ornament. Each master of a family has a large square piece of ground, surrounded with a moat or fence, or inclosed with a wall made of red earth tempered, which, when dry, is as hard as brick. Within this are his houses to accommodate his family and slaves; which, if numerous, frequently present the appearance of a village. In the middle stands the principal building, appropriated to the sole use of the master, and consisting of two apartments; in one of which he sits in the day with his family, the other is left apart for the reception of his friends. He has besides these a distinct apartment, in which he sleeps, together with his male children. On each side are the apartments of his wives, who have also their separate day and night houses. The habitations of the slaves and their families are distributed throughout the rest of the inclosure. These houses never exceed one story in height; they are always built of wood, or stakes driven into the ground, crossed with wattles, and neatly plastered within and without. The roof is thatched with reeds. Our day houses are left open at the sides; but those in which we sleep are always covered, and plastered in the inside with a composition mixed with cow dung, to keep off the different insects which annoy us during the night. The walls and floors also of these are generally covered with mats. Our beds consist of a platform, raised three or four feet from the ground, on which are laid skins, and different parts of a spungy tree called plantain. Our covering is calico or muslin, the same as our dress. The usual seats are a few logs of wood; but we have benches, which are generally perfumed, to accommodate strangers: those compose the greater part of our household furniture. Houses so constructed and furnished require but little skill to erect them. Every man is a sufficient architect for the purpose. The whole neighbourhood afford their unanimous assistance in building them, and in return receive and expect no other recompense than a feast.'[1]

Today the houses of the Ika region approximate those of the Yoruba and the type that Equiano described has disappeared; across the Niger and east of Onitsha the Ibo still live in houses that are very similar to those that he had known. His account was full enough to give us some evidence of the processes of influence and change which take place when differing peoples are contiguous, and evidence, too, of the persistence of the type in the region of the Niger for the past two centuries. It is, however, singular in having been written by a member of an African culture even if he were one who had been long accustomed to a European way of life. Even d'Avezac-Macaya's careful interrogation of Osifekunde, the Ijebu slave who as a young man had been kidnapped by Ijo raiders some fifty years after Equiano's capture, did not elicit more detailed information on the house forms of his people. Accounts of architecture in Africa before the coming of the Europeans are fragmentary, for the Arabic reports which have been studied and published are usually sketchy when dealing with this subject, and writings from within the African cultures south of the Sahara are virtually non-existent.

To a large extent we have to rely for information on the earlier history of building types in Africa on surviving examples, on deductions from types presently in existence, and from the writings of western explorers, travellers and missionaries. The study of existing buildings is probably less confidently undertaken today than it might have been a few decades ago, for current research bears out what is implicit in the comparison of Equiano's narrative with the forms in his own region today: that the material cultures of African societies are subject to modification and change, which, if slower than in countries which have paid continuing tribute to the vagaries of

Frontispiece 1 *Entrance to a compound, Zaria, Northern Nigeria. The decorative wall pattern is cut into cement plaster.* Frontispiece 2 *Squatter housing, Boghari, Algeria. The buildings are of stone, mud plastered and with matting roofs.*

fashion and style, or which have evolved a professional caste of architects within the community whose personal identities have been stamped upon the buildings which they have designed, are still significant enough to throw doubt on simple conclusions as to the permanence of building form.

Individual personality played a large part in the creation of the picture of African shelter which has been left us by the early travellers. Curiosity, condescension and contempt are to be found in the writings of different traders, voyagers and men of God who, for different reasons, found themselves in contact with African societies. Their own cultural heritage and professional involvement coloured their attitudes and in many instances the conviction that the 'African' was an inferior being meant that only the most superficial descriptions of the building materials and methods of construction were noted. How village organisation or family relationships might be expressed in the physical disposition of the community, or how the use of spaces within and without the buildings might be controlled by social hierarchies or symbolic values were scarcely appreciated, much less examined.

In some respects the spirit of inquiry in the eighteenth century makes some of the reports from this period more valuable, and less obstructed by the attitude of the writer, than many of those in the nineteenth century. Although it was a period of great architectural elegance and sophisticated craftsmanship in the cities, the rural vernacular in most European countries in the eighteenth century was simple and direct: thatched roofs, stone, cob, mud and wattle walls, timber frames, turfs, slates and other found materials were in wide use. The trader could find respect for ingenuity and skill in the employment of rude tools and natural resources, as did Francis Moore, who, in 1733, built a factory with Mandingo labour at Yamyamacunda on the Gambia. He gave a detailed description of the building process, because he 'thought it would be amusing to the Reader, to see how easily the People, whom we call Barbarous, can procure the Conveniences of Life. Here is a House built, with a Hall 40 Foot by 13, two lodging Rooms 20 Feet by 13, and 3 strong Store-houses, without any Iron-work, Trowells, Squares, or Carpenters Rules, and with the smallest Expence to the Company, for I did it with their Servants only, having hired no other help but the man who laid and smooth'd the Clay. And the Inside was not only convenient and free from Vermin, but very clean, and had a cool Look, for the Clay is hard, close, smooth, and takes Whitewash very well.'[2]

Moore made careful drawings of the towns and plantations that he encountered in his travels and left detailed descriptions of other aspects of life in the 'Inland Parts' of Africa. As trader and builder he paid attention to methods and materials in building whereas James Bruce, travelling in Ethiopia in 1770, left a colourful, episodic but vividly descriptive account of his adventures, but was much less informative as to the details of the places where the events occurred. At much the same time Andrew Sparrman, a Swedish naturalist, was travelling in the Dutch colonies of South Africa, observing the Hottentots. He was far more sensitive to the relationship between shelter and mode of life, noting that 'their habitations are as simple as their dress, and equally adapted to the wandering pastoral life they

lead in those parts. In fact, they scarcely merit any other name than that of huts; though not, perhaps, as spacious and eligible as the tents and dwelling-places of the patriarchs, at least they are sufficient for the Hottentot's wants and desires.' From this he drew the moral that 'the great simplicity of them is, perhaps, the reason, why in a Hottentot's craal, or village, the huts are all built exactly alike; and that one meets there with a species of architecture, that does not a little contribute to keep envy from insinuating itself under their roofs'.[3] Sparrman, though finding some features of the Hottentot dwellings uncomfortable, was aware of the advantages afforded to the occupants of a central fire in reducing risk and distributing warmth given that the inconvenience that he felt from the smoke was not shared by those who were 'inured to it from infancy'. He described the arched frame structure of the hut noting that the 'materials for these huts are by no means difficult to be procured; and the manner of putting them together being both neat and inartificial, merits commendation in a Hottentot, and is very suitable to his character'.[4]

Faintly patronising though his account was, Andrew Sparrman was nevertheless attempting to relate the house form to the requirements of the people rather than to assess it on the standards of his own culture. This was a continual problem to the traveller who was inevitably conditioned by the standards of his home countrymen to whom his remarks would be addressed. It was rationalised by John Barrow at the turn of the century by a comparison with familiar vernacular forms: 'The dwelling of a Booshuana,' he wrote, 'is not ill-calculated for the climate. In elegance and solidity it may probably be as good as the *Casae* or first houses that were built in imperial Rome, and may be considered in every respect superior to its construction and in comfort to most of the Irish cabins, into which the miserable peasantry are oft-times obliged to crawl through puddles

Francis Moore. 'Draught of a Pholey Town and Plantation about' from Travels into the Inland Parts of Africa, *1738.*

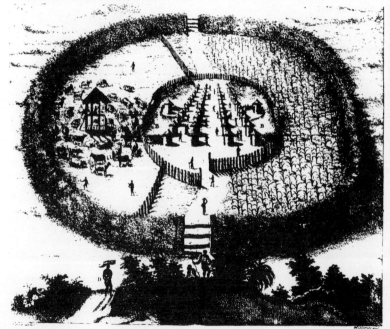

Mungo Park. Village compounds from Travels in the Interior districts of Africa, *1799.* Right: *Georg Schweinfurth. Interior of Ceremonial house from* The Heart of Africa, *1873.*

of water. The hut of a Booshuana is not only raised upon an elevated clay flooring, but the ground of the whole enclosure is so prepared that the water may run off through the gateway; and the whole of their cookery being carried on in this open area, the inside of the dwelling is free from smoke and soot'.[5]

As the adventurers penetrated deeper into the land mass many were enticed by the fame of distant cities. Undoubtedly, expectations of great buildings shaped in the minds of the explorers and made their disappointment the more keen when the African towns did not meet their imagined splendours. It took Rene Caillié a year to reach Timbuktu; he remained there for only a fortnight; 'the city presented,' he wrote, 'nothing but a mass of ill-looking houses built of earth. Nothing was to be seen in all directions but immense plains of quicksand of a yellowish-white colour'.[6] A similar disappointment greeted Hugh Clapperton some four years before, when he reached Kano after a trans-desert trek from Tripoli to Lake Chad. 'At eleven o'clock we entered Kano, the great emporium of the kingdom of Haussa, but I had no sooner passed the gates, than I felt grievously disappointed; for from the flourishing description of it given by the Arabs, I expected to see a city of surprising grandeur: I found, on the contrary, the houses nearly a quarter of a mile from the walls, and in many parts scattered into detached groups, between large stagnant pools of water.' He was provided with a house 'at the south end of the morass, the pestilential exhalations of which, and of the pools of standing water, were increased by the sewers of the houses all opening into the street'.[7]

Sick and uncomfortably housed, Clapperton was nevertheless able to appreciate the atmosphere of Kano's great market; following him in mid-century Dr. Heinrich Barth became 'aware of the great inaccuracy of the little sketch of the town given by Clapperton, who himself pretends only to give an eye-sketch'. He thought it worth his while 'to survey and sketch it more minutely'.[8] Barth was a remarkable explorer, a philosopher and geographer whose energy, acuity of vision and sympathy for the peoples whom he visited made his *Travels in Africa* required reading for the generations of explorers, merchants, military men and missionaries who followed him. Whereas many of his predecessors were interested in the larger buildings and complexes while dismissing the reed huts and one-celled mud buildings that they encountered, Barth paid careful attention to all. He left detailed descriptions of Kano, Katsena and Timbuktu, but also described and drew the simplest forms of shelter. In Múbi, for example, when most of his company were sick and lying 'like so many corpses on the ground' he found himself with 'ample leisure to study minutely the architecture of my residence'. The clay-walled and thatched-roofed hut was about twelve feet in diameter, whose door 'a little elevated from the floor, was three feet high and fifteen inches wide, and not at all adapted for very stout persons. From the wall at the right of the door ran another wall, "garuwel súdo", of the same height but unconnected with the roof, right across the hut in an oblique line, to the length of about six feet, separating one part of the dwelling, and securing to it more privacy'.[9] He went on to describe the internal arrangement of vessels, corn-urn and bed, sketching the utensils and a small footstool, and drawing conclusions as to the reasons for their situation.

It is instructive to compare Barth's writings with those of Sir Richard Burton whose travels in East Africa and the Lake Regions were undertaken only a few years later. Burton was no less detailed in his descriptions but the brilliant, vainglorious, untiring explorer could not entirely suppress his sense of superiority over the subjects of his writings, even when he was making a 'succinct account' of habitations which 'form a curious study and no valueless guide to the nature of the climate and physical conditions to which men are subject'. He viewed with some contempt 'the normal African form, the circular hut described by every traveller in the interior: Dr. Livingstone appears to judge rightly that its circularity is the result of a barbarous deficiency in inventiveness'.[10] But even when he wrote, as he did of the Wak'hutu, that their 'dirty, slovenly villages' were 'an index to the character of the people' he made a careful note of their construction. They had, he said, in one of his favourite

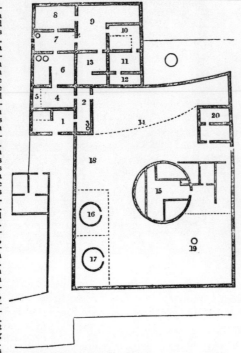

1. Segífa, or "sóro chín-nabe," into which a person coming from the small yard before the house first enters through the principal gate. In the corner there is a spacious clay bench, "dá-gali," raised three feet from the ground. 2. Small open courtyard, with a very fine chédia or caoutchouc-tree (3), in which we had generally a troop of monkeys, while at the bottom a couple of squirrels (*Sciurus*) were living in a hole. 4. A second courtyard with a henhouse (5). 6. Inner segífa, where, in the beginning, the servants loitered, and which was afterwards changed into a simple dining-room. Here generally the water-jars were kept. 7. Small courtyard, with water-jar. 8. Inner room where I used to live, and afterwards, Mr. Vogel. 9. Inner large courtyard, where, in the corner, the kitchen was established. 10. Room with a large claybank, where Mr. Overweg used to recline in the daytime. 11. Bedroom of Mr. Overweg, and afterwards of the Sappers, Corporal Church and Macguire. 12. Small back courtyard. 13. Storeroom. 14. Outer enclosure of great courtyard in the beginning of our residence in Kúkawa. This wall we afterwards pulled down, when we obtained a very large yard for our horses and cattle. We, at times, had six horses and five or six cows. 15. Very large well-built conical hut, with clay wall and thatched roof. In the interior there were two spacious raised claybanks of the kind called dagáli" and "zinzin," and in the background a raised recess, separated by a wall two feet high, for luggage or corn. This hut I occupied during my last stay in Kúkawa after my return from Timbúktu, when I built in front of it a large shed with that sort of coarse mats called síggedí. 16. Hut occupied by Maádi, a liberated slave, first in the service of Mr. Richardson, afterwards in that of Mr. Overweg, and lastly, Mr. Vogel's head servant. Having been wounded in the service of the expedition, a small pension has been granted to him. 17. Hut occupied by another servant. 18. Place for our cattle. 19. A well. The sandy soil, as I have said, obliged us to change the place of our well very often, and we had great trouble in this respect. 20. A clayhouse which, during the latter part of our stay, fell to ruins.

Henry Barth. Plan of his house in Bornu, April 1851, from Travels and Discoveries in North and Central Africa, *1853.*

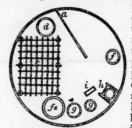

The door, a little elevated above the floor, was three feet high, and fifteen inches wide, and not at all adapted for very stout persons. From the wall at the right of the door (*a*) ran another wall, "gáruwel súdo," of the same height, but unconnected with the roof, right across the hut in an oblique line, to the length of about six feet, separating one part of the dwelling, and securing to it more privacy. In this compartment was the bed (*c*), consisting of a frame made of branches, and spread over pilasters of clay about three feet high. In the most sequestered part of the hut, in the corner formed by the round enclosing wall and the oblique one, at the top of the bed—"kéla kagá," as the Kanúri say—stood the corn-urn (*a*), about six feet high, and, in its largest part, two feet wide, destined to keep a certain provision of corn always at hand; besides this, there was a smaller one (*fe*) at the foot of the bed—"shí kagá." At the side of this smaller urn were two small pedestals of clay (*g*), serving the purpose of a sideboard, in order to place upon them pots or other articles. Then followed the kitchen, "defforíde" (*h*), still under cover of the oblique wall, but exactly on a line with it, so that the smoke might more easily find its way through the door, and consisting of a narrow place enclosed on each side by a low wall, to protect the fire, between which three stones, or rather small clay mounds like fire-bricks, supported the cooking-pot, while a small wooden footstool (*i*) accommodated the industrious landlady when busy with her most important culinary employment. While to all this part of the hut a certain degree of privacy was secured by the oblique wall, a considerable space to the left of the door remained unprotected; and here stood the large water-urn (*f*), which, always remaining in its place, is filled by means of smaller portable urns or pitchers.

Henry Barth. Plan of a Kanuri hut at Múbi, from Travels and Discoveries in North and Central Africa, *1853.*

similies, 'doors little higher than an English pigsty', but he went on to describe their structure as 'a cylindrical framework composed of tall stakes, or the rough trunks of young trees, interwoven with parallel rings of flexible twigs and withies, which are coated inside and outside with puddle of red or grey clay'.[11] His description continued at length, but it bore out Henry Nevinson's observation that Burton 'saw everything clearly, but everything in the flat'. The Wak'hutu villages, Burton stated, 'could scarcely be called permanent; even the death of a chief causes them to be abandoned, and in a few months long grass waves over the circlets of charred sticks and straw'.[12] He saw no reason or virtue in this.

Sir Richard Burton's slightly jaundiced eye was indicative of the viewpoint of many of his successors, a large number of whom shared his prejudices without sharing his sharp perception. In many books were attitudes which justified, in the opinion of their readers, the invasion of Africa by the Europeans. White missionaries and military 'expeditions' alike infiltrated and disrupted indigenous societies with a sense of a divine right to convert the 'barbarians' and take care of the 'children' of 'Darkest Africa'. King Leopold's wily appropriation of the vast region of the Congo basin was followed in the early

'eighties by the annexations of widely dispersed territories by Germany, precipitating the 'Scramble for Africa'. Any doubts as to the morality of carving up the continent by the European powers or of milking its wealth under Colonial rule could be dispelled by such reports as Commander Bacon's of the Royal Navy when he accompanied the expedition against Benin in 1897: 'This was the palaver house, the ju-ju compound. Long sheds ending in raised alters on which were bronze heads with carved tusks stuck into them and carved clubs all smeared with blood. The whole compound smelt of death and corruption. In the centre was an erection of iron hooks for hanging portions of the victim's bodies and near it a well into which the bodies were flung. The streets of the town were filled with the bodies of sacrificed slaves, in front of every house whose owner could afford it was the body of a human being.'[13] Commander Bacon's chilling, sensational description, which was born out by others, Captain Alan Boisdragon for example, contrasted with the descriptions given by Dutch merchants to Olfert Dapper over two centuries before: 'The city has thirty main streets, very straight and each about thirty-six meters wide, with many broad, though somewhat narrower intersecting streets crossing them. The houses are

The 'gutea' house, Southern Sudan.

arranged along them in good order, close to each other as in Europe, decorated with gables and steps and with roofs thatched with palm and banana leaves. Though they are not very high they are usually large and have long corridors inside, especially in the noblemen's houses. These houses have many rooms with walls made of a reddish clay which they know how to smooth by washing and scouring them until they gleam like a mirror.' To the Dutch merchants 'these people are in no way inferior to the Dutch in regard to cleanliness'.[14]

The end of the Boer War also saw the virtual end of the European carving of the African continent. There were disputes between some of the occupying colonial powers over territories and borders, but the partition of Africa was everywhere a fact, with Great Britain and France controlling vast territories and Germany, Portugal, Spain, Italy and Belgium claiming the remainder. Colonial administrations, often governed by incredibly small numbers of men, with minimal military support, set about organising the taxation of their 'possessions'. Sir Harry Johnston, for instance, was expected to administer the whole of Nyasaland on a budget of ten thousand pounds and with the support of one British officer and seventy-five Indian troopers. Though the societies which they technically administered were disrupted by colonial rule direct contact with Europeans was still often extremely limited. Some of the local officials, governors, military officers and the missionaries who rapidly followed them established some kind of rapport with the tribes with whom they were in contact. Though warrior societies and inter-tribal wars, witchcraft and magic, and often, the carving of ritual objects, sculptures and masks were all subject to the repression of the administrators, there were many of the latter who noted in detail the structure of tribal life and published their observations at the end of their 'tours'.

Discussions of the building forms of African peoples and their relation to community life tended to be sketchy in these writings. 'The Kikuyu hut (nyum-ba) is a strong, comfortable, well-built structure, admirably suited to the requirements of its users. It lends itself to the employment of any form of vegetable growth available', wrote W. Scoresby Routledge and Katherine Routledge in 1910. 'Its merits are manifold . . . its chief faults are lack of light, and any means of ventilation beyond the door.'[15] They gave some information on the

preparation of materials and the use of the hut, but their description was less informative than was Burton's of the same type, seventy years before. Burton, for all his gratuitous comparison with a pig-sty, was a more accurate observer and more aware of the specific merits of the *nyum-ba*. 'The door-way resembles the entrance to an English pig-sty, it serves, however, to keep out heat in the hot season, and to keep in smoke and warmth during the rains and the cold weather; the threshold is garnished with a horizontal log or board and defends the interior from inundation. The door is a square of reeds fastened together by bark or cord, and planted upright at night between the wall and two dwarf posts at each side of the entrance; there is generally a smaller and secret door opposite that in use, and jealously closed up except when flight is necessary. In the colder and damper regions there is a second wall and roof outside the first, forming in fact one house within the other.'[16]

A curious anomaly had developed: the travellers of the eighteenth and early nineteenth century often left more accurate and detailed studies of the forms of shelter they encountered than did their successors in the period of Colonial administration who, in many cases, had a score or more years of direct contact with the African peoples. In the early writings principles of material resources, of appropriate technologies, of climate control, comfort conditions, durability or ephemerality, permanence or portability according to the nature of the society – these and many others had been delineated. In spite of the growing sophistication of research techniques in the twentieth century there had been no substantial advance in the study of African shelter types; rather, there had been a regression. Even the indefatigable Captain R. S. Rattray in his unsurpassed studies of Ashanti culture in the old Gold Coast, *Ashanti, The Tribes of the Ashanti Hinterland, Ashanti Law and Constitution* and *Religion and Art in Ashanti*, could make no contribution on Ashanti shelter. His extraordinarily thorough analysis of the weaving of *kente* cloths and his descriptions of the *cire-perdue* process of bronze-casting gold weights had no parallel in architecture. Instead, he invited the critic Vernon Blake to comment, but Blake could only say that 'when we eliminate the ornament there remains very little to examine in the architecture of Ashanti. The buildings would seem to possess that open shed-like aspect common to those of easy conditions the tropical world over'.[17] It was an expression of opinion that Bowdich, over a hundred years before, would have been ashamed to share when writing his report on the *Mission to Ashantee*.

Why was so important an aspect of tribal culture as the study of its architecture, let alone its village and town organisation, neglected to this extent? To some degree it may have been due to the persistence of attitudes to the simplicity of many forms of African shelter which Sir Richard Burton could only suppress with difficulty and which was dismissed in a few words in the expendable works of numerous soldiers and missionaries in the years of the 'scramble'. Unconsciously, perhaps, they had assimilated these expressions of disinterest and had accepted that the buildings had no merit as architecture or as art. But this would not account for the rudimentary description of house types made by, for instance, Sir Charles Dundas in his *Kilimanjaro and Its People* published in 1924. Still more conspicuously summary are the four pages that the distinguished anthropologist I. Schapera devoted to their dwellings in his study of some 450 pages, *The Khosian Speaking Peoples of South Africa* which appeared six years later. Schapera was the editor of another work, as large, on *The Bantu-Speaking Peoples of South Africa* which was an 'Ethnological survey' including studies of traditional folklore, music, linguistics and so on by a wide variety of writers, in which only a page was devoted to built forms. Sketchier still was the entry on shelter in her work on the Baganda, *An African People in the Twentieth Century* by Dr. L. P. Mair. 'In the matter of housing, furniture and tools,' she wrote, 'there have been so many changes that the old-fashioned household must be described by itself as something obsolete. The house was built of a framework of elephant grass canes, supported on posts, fastened with a kind of strong creeper or with osiers, and thatched with grass, dry banana-leaves or occasionally papyrus. The floor was strewn with grass.'[18] These brief notes were not born of contempt or outright dismissal by the anthro-

pologists concerned; they were really born of a development in anthropological research which made them seem virtually irrelevant in comparison with the problems that faced the researcher in the field.

Back in 1851 Henry Barth could ride around Kano 'guided by a lad well acquainted with the topography of the town' noting the 'manifold scenes of public and private life' which he beheld from the saddle. 'It was the most animated picture of a little world in itself, so different in external form from all that is seen in European towns, yet so similar in its internal principles.'[19] The difference in the external forms was self-evident whether it was in architecture or in language; it was the realisation that they were far from being similar in their internal principles that changed the course of the literature on African societies. Under the inspiration and guidance of the great Bronislaw Malinowski, who had himself made a lively attack on some of the assumptions of Schapera and Mair in 1938, British anthropology took a very different direction. And though there were many important contributions by anthropologists from many

Street scene in Kano.

Dogon compounds on cliff debris, from the Bandiagara escarpment.

European countries, with Henri Junod's study of the Thonga of South Africa published by the Swiss Romande Mission in 1913 being outstanding, for the most part anthropological research in Africa was dominated by the British school in the period before the Second World War. Social anthropology and 'functional' anthropology led to a study of 'internal principles', the structural systems within African societies which moved far away from shelter. Problems of kinship and lineage, of clan structure and blood brotherhood, of divine kingship and inheritance occupied such field workers as A. R. Radcliffe-Brown and E. E. Evans-Pritchard. Systems of law and constitution, of linguistic structure, of ecology and subsistence economy commanded the attention of others – and still do. So a work on *Igbo Village Affairs* with reference particularly to one village, that of Umueke Abgaja, by M. M. Green, based on his field work in the 'thirties and published in 1947, contained virtually no reference to the form of the village or of its component dwellings. Even studies of witchcraft and magic, of ritual and belief such as *The Springs of Mende Belief and Conduct* by Harris and Sawyer convey little of the organisation of the cult houses and ceremonial buildings in which rituals take place.

Relatively few studies to date have attempted to relate the internal principles, the hidden and abstract systems, with those of the physical form of house and village. In this Marcel Griaule, the eminent French anthropologist and his team, were exceptional. Griaule showed that a complex symbolism governed the layout of the village and the individual dwelling, the cultivation of the fields and by interaction, all other facets of Dogon life. 'The village may be square like the first plot of land cultivated by man, or oval with an opening at one end to represent the world egg broken up by the swelling of the germinating cells. Whatever its shape it is a person and must lie in a north to south direction, the smithy is the head and certain particular shrines the feet. The huts used by the women at their menstrual periods, situated east and west, are the hands; the family homesteads form the chest, and the twin-ness of the whole group is expressed by a foundation shrine in the form of a cone (the male sexual organ) and by a hollowed stone (female organ) on which the fruit of the *Lannea acida* is ground to express the oil.'[20] As in the village, so too the compound: 'the plan of the house, then, represents a man lying on his right side and procreating,' he demonstrated, adding that the same attitude is adopted on the marriage bed as in the position in the grave. 'Thus the same pattern, continually repeated on an ever-expanding scale, leads from man to the cosmos, each stage of the process also representing the whole, while a series of material avatars leads from the world itself to smaller and smaller groupings – district, village, village-section, homestead.'[21]

Griaule's work has been received with some dubiety in certain quarters where it had been noted, particularly in the earlier diagrams which he had used to demonstrate the anthropomorphic principle, that the theoretical and physical organisations did not agree in detail. To the Dogon, thinking in a highly developed symbology, it was the principal that mattered; to the anthropologist in some schools of thought, it was dangerous to act in an interpretative role; the very presence of the anthropologist in the society which he studies alters that society, and his interpretations may alter it still further in the constructs of his own thinking conditioned by his own culture. Fear of flaws through such subjectivity may account for the emphasis on anthropology as a science, statistical, quantifiable, measurable facts in genetics or taxonomy being the only kinds of admissible data, such as exemplified by the work of Carlton S. Coon and the German-American school on the one hand; and the amassing of data on the material culture of a people – such as Barrie Reynold's *Material Culture of the Peoples of the Gwembe Valley* – on the other. In the former building forms are not discussed; in the latter they are matters of report.

It would seem that the most valuable contribution that anthropologists could make to the study of African vernacular architecture would be to show the relationships between their areas of specific study and the buildings, villages, communities and cities in which they take place. Few anthropologists have been trained in architecture and planning; few in the latter disciplines have had the advantages of anthropological training or the fortune and finance to indulge in the field-work which would inform them better on the nature of African societies. A catalogue of material elements in the culture may supply the planner with some information on material resources and local technology, but the reasons why they are deployed in a particular way within a specific house-type, the needs within the society which they may meet in the realisation of the built form or the organisation of the village plan – these are of considerably more importance. Malinowski chided I. Schapera for his assumption that 'the administrator, trader and labour recruiter must be regarded as factors in the tribal life in the same way as are the chief and magician'[22] and his subsequent challenge, *The Dynamics of Culture Change*, was published posthumously. If it has been subjected to criticism since, it nevertheless drew attention to the importance of a methodological approach to the study of societies in transition, under Western influence and in the processes of urbanisation.

Today this is seen as a sociologist's field of study. P. H. Gulliver wrote a paper on 'The Anthropological Study of Complex Urban Societies' and still managed to avoid any mention of the problems of architecture and planning. It appeared in *The African World: A Study of Social Research* a 574-page volume with many distinguished contributors writing on subjects ranging from agriculture to folklore, music and dance. But even 'The Visual Arts' by Roy Sieber had no room for a discussion of architecture in Africa, even at the most superficial level of visual appearances. Understandably, these studies in *The African World* directly reflect the specialisations of the editor and writers, and equally understandably, these are not specialisations in building or architecture. But it is precisely in housing, urbanisation and planning that the most dramatic changes are now taking place. These are areas in which detailed information on the systems and sub-systems of African culture and their inter-action on house-, village- and town-forms would be of the greatest value to those who bear the responsibility of designing for the future. From the eighteenth-century grid-iron plan of Cape Town to the star plan of Dakar's *Plateau*, from the colonial city of Ouagadougou to the proposed development plans for the cities of Nigeria, it is European planning thought which has determined the map of Africa's urban centres. Admittedly, many such decisions were made primarily for the European settlers, but in a large proportion of instances they are for the use of Europeans no longer. The African designers trained in European-styled schools and sharing a westernised environment seldom question the appropriateness of these planning concepts in assuming the role formerly the province of European architects and planners alone. It is by no means unlikely that, with these precedents they too will produce the multi-storied flats of Casablanca, the disciplined rows of inhabited drums of Lusaka or the batteries of Native Townships of Johannesburg which are all the physical results of European decisions on the housing suitable for Africans.

Often the architect seems not to have bothered in the past to question his decisions in the light of the needs of the society for whom he was designing, or the conditions imposed by the environ-

Main entrance to a ksar, *Tinezouline, Draa Valley, Southern Morocco.*

ment – like the designer of the University of Ghana, Legon, who in the 1950's seems not to have questioned whether a patio-styled building type which was apparently inspired by a Hollywood image of a Spanish *estancia* should be suitable for the edge of the tropical rain forest. Yet, when the architect or planner does wish to base his design decisions on social and environmental characteristics of a particular region he has often little on which to draw for reference. Frequently he may initiate his own research in order to equip himself with the necessary information and understanding of the society for whom he is planning, even though he may be untrained for such work and limited in the time and finances available to him. To the anthropologist his reports may be based on insufficient knowledge of technique and based on inadequate sampling, but this is preferable to an approach to design which is based on superficial resemblances. 'In Accra, Ghana, a group of young architects of the Division of Public

Grid-iron planning, Lagos – but it could be one of a score of African cities.

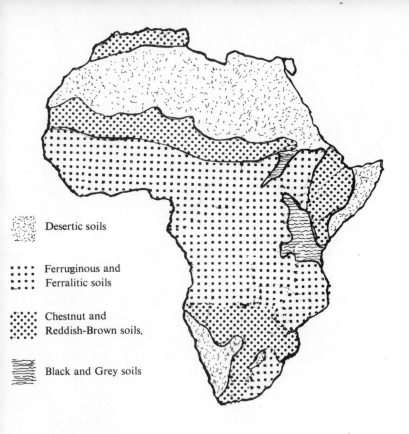

Desertic soils

Ferruginous and
Ferralitic soils

Chestnut and
Reddish-Brown soils,

Black and Grey soils

Soils of Africa.

Rainfall map of Africa.

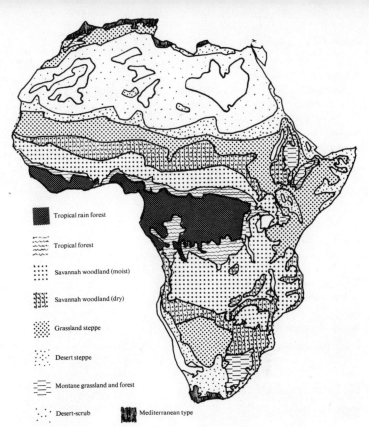

Tropical rain forest

Tropical forest

Savannah woodland (moist)

Savannah woodland (dry)

Grassland steppe

Desert steppe

Montane grassland and forest

Desert-scrub   Mediterranean type

Vegetation map of Africa (after Clarke and Clarke, and other sources).

Population map of Africa (after Stamp, and other sources).

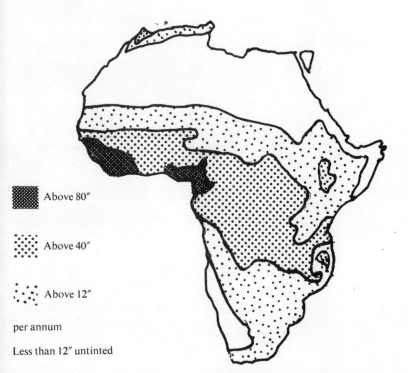

Above 80″

Above 40″

Above 12″

per annum

Less than 12″ untinted

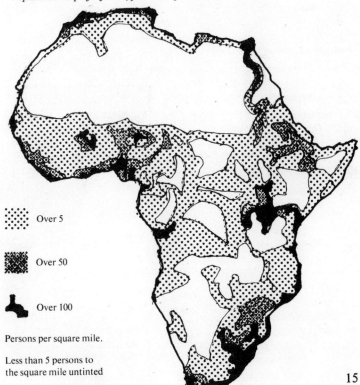

Over 5

Over 50

Over 100

Persons per square mile.

Less than 5 persons to
the square mile untinted

15

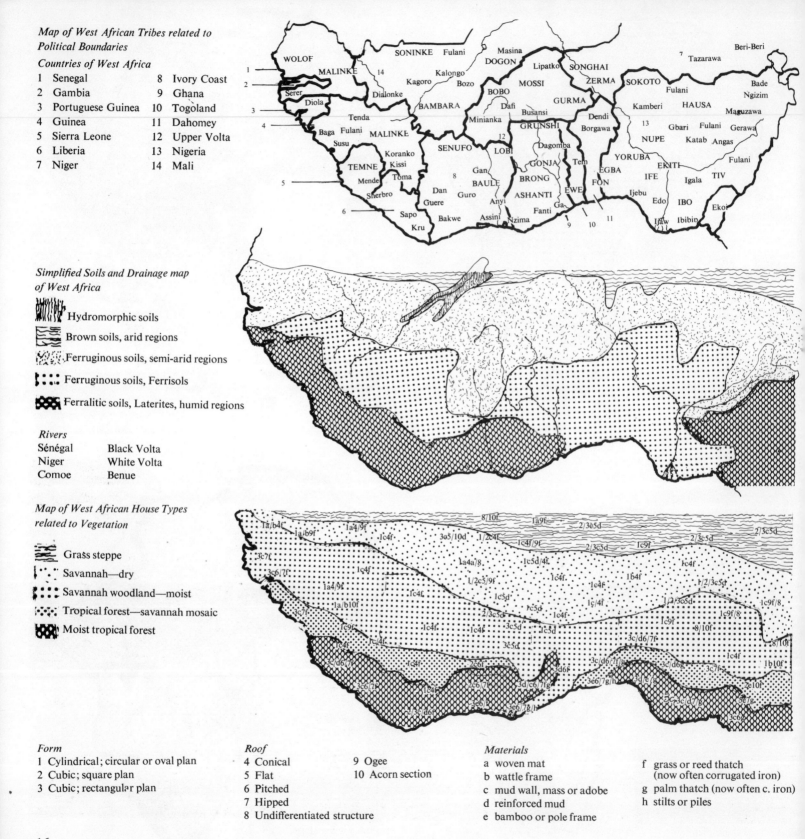

Map of West African Tribes related to Political Boundaries

Countries of West Africa

1	Senegal	8	Ivory Coast
2	Gambia	9	Ghana
3	Portuguese Guinea	10	Togoland
4	Guinea	11	Dahomey
5	Sierra Leone	12	Upper Volta
6	Liberia	13	Nigeria
7	Niger	14	Mali

Simplified Soils and Drainage map of West Africa

- Hydromorphic soils
- Brown soils, arid regions
- Ferruginous soils, semi-arid regions
- Ferruginous soils, Ferrisols
- Ferralitic soils, Laterites, humid regions

Rivers

Sénégal	Black Volta
Niger	White Volta
Comoe	Benue

Map of West African House Types related to Vegetation

- Grass steppe
- Savannah—dry
- Savannah woodland—moist
- Tropical forest—savannah mosaic
- Moist tropical forest

Form
1 Cylindrical; circular or oval plan
2 Cubic; square plan
3 Cubic; rectangular plan

Roof
4 Conical
5 Flat
6 Pitched
7 Hipped
8 Undifferentiated structure
9 Ogee
10 Acorn section

Materials
a woven mat
b wattle frame
c mud wall, mass or adobe
d reinforced mud
e bamboo or pole frame
f grass or reed thatch (now often corrugated iron)
g palm thatch (now often c. iron)
h stilts or piles

Construction,' wrote Myron Goldfinger with unintentional irony, 'have designed the Junior Staff Quarters at Government House in a style responsive to the spirit of North African Architecture. . . . The sharp articulation of the forms, the deep visual penetration of the walls, and the narrow, sun-sheltered areas are typical of many North African villages, such as Tinehir in the stone desert of Morocco. Although typical dwellings are repeated the clustered arrangement of standardized units of alternating heights creates a rich interplay of forms and a complexity of experience.'[23]

But Tinehir in the stone desert of Morocco is not Accra on the humid coast of West Africa, with the rain forest sprawling in lush undergrowth behind the city. North African vernacular on the West African coast – the example not only emphasises the vulnerability of criteria based on visual appearances, it also stresses the disasters inherent in generalisations about Africa. The people, the culture, the climate, the vegetation, the soils, the temperature, the precipitation of rain, even the density of population in the two regions are not comparable. It is perhaps futile to consider Africa as a unity in any sense that is applicable to architecture, but traditionally, and in many ways analytically, Africa is a continental entity over which may be laid maps which correspond only in their outline. In the overlaying of the maps the characteristics of specific regions become apparent.

No map of Africa is more misleading than that with which we are most familiar – the map of political boundaries determined by the peace settlement of 1919 and raggedly maintained through the processes of obtaining independence by the new nations. As the conflicts

Fulani compounds, Northern Nigeria.

in Chad, Nigeria, Congo, Rwanda and elsewhere have borne painful witness neither nationhood nor political boundaries reflect tribal organisation and allegiance. When the tribal map is laid upon the political map the anomalies of the arbitrary boundaries are evident, but even Professor G. P. Murdock's important 'Tribal Map of Africa' draws linear boundaries where none exist.[24] African peoples generally determine frontiers by agreement, and occasionally by natural limits defined by river or mountain range, but in cultures where individuals do not 'own' the land as parcels of property, precise cartography has no relevance. In many regions the same territories are shared by two, three or more tribes, who may be related linguistically. The linguistic map, as drawn by Greenberg and others, may follow the tribal map in broad outline but may show, as in the case of the Negritic–Bantu complex of languages, a spread which embraces Negro Africa and much of the continent south of the Equator.

Seen in detail, as in West Africa, the overlay of political, tribal and linguistic maps creates a cultural picture that is much closer to the distribution of peoples than is the subregional division of Territories and Provinces within National borders. But this is mocked by the nomadic and semi-nomadic peoples such as the Fulani or Touareg whose migratory movements leave only a cloud of amorphous and inaccurate shapes for the cartographer to delineate as best he can. For the cultural map to relate to the subsistence economies of the peoples represented, other essentially physical factors must be considered.

Across the cultural maps which reflect the social organisation and structures of African peoples are those which are conditioned by physical characteristics and natural resources. Prominent among these are the maps of climate, vegetation, soils and water resources which profoundly affect basic economies. It is in this that the most delicate balance between society and environment is discerned, and is mirrored in housing- and plan-forms. The heavy precipitation of rain in the tropical regions, the density of forest growth and the lack of seasonal variation, such as is seen on the West African rain-forest belt, affect profoundly the pattern of daily life, the distribution of villages, the methods of farming and the structures of both the communities and the buildings which house them. Here the availability of hard lateritic soils and broad-leaved palms determines both the materials from which walls and roofs are constructed as well as the forms of cultivation which the land supports. Such conditions contrast dramatically with the distribution of compounds in the savannah regions, which are subject to long periods of sun and sudden, seasonal rains. The land scarcely supports the community for much of the year, but bursts into lush grass landscape for brief periods following the rains. Closer to the desert the towns are dependent upon the straggling loop of the Niger and act as termini for the trans-Ṣaharan camel trains, and more recently, the trucks which keep tenuous contact with the communities beyond the desert.

Such cultural–economic change conditioned by the environment is as important, if totally different in kind, in the dense, wet montane regions of Rwanda as it is in the open country of the veldt. Ultimately, the strongest conditioning factors are climatic, the precipitation of rain or exposure to tropical sun affecting the vegetation that may grow in African soils, the availability of water and the life that

may be sustained. For the African builder the climate adds further constraints in terms of environmental control, with protection from sun and rain, rotting and disintegrating materials, ventilation, temperature ranges from freezing nights to more than a hundred degrees in the desert, all adding to the problems of housing. In some cases they are problems which never have been solved, and with the resources available, could not be; in others they have been effectively and elegantly met. To the member of a tribal society, however, they are often not recognised as problems in the abstract to be subjected to consideration in isolation. For such separation of one element of housing, or indeed of any other aspect of life, is contrary to the close-knit structure of the total society where change in one aspect implies subtle change in every other. This does not mean that social patterns in Africa are not subject to change, nor that house-form and village structure do not change either. But the change is one of subtle response to pressures and environmental factors rather than to the decision of the economist or the planner. It is a process which has been summarised by Christopher Alexander, following a discussion of the Mousgoum hut of the French Cameroun, as one of 'fit'. 'On the one hand,' he wrote, 'the directness of the response to misfit ensures that each failure is corrected as soon as it occurs, and thereby restricts the change to one subsystem at a time. And on the other hand the force of tradition, by resisting needless change, holds steady all the variables not in the relevant subsystem, and prevents those minor disturbances outside the subsystem from taking hold. . . . even the most aimless changes will eventually lead to well-fitting forms, because of the tendency to equilibrium inherent in the organization of the process.'[25]

The foregoing outline of the multiplicity of factors which affect individual cultures, regions, tribes, even single villages and communities must serve to emphasise the importance of case studies rather than of generalised ones. In many societies, however, one or other element tends to be dominant, determining the response of others which go to make up the total life-style of the community. In some instances these may be cultural, being powerfully conditioned by the lineage or kinship pattern of the community; in others the climate, the economy or the natural resources of the region may be the fundamental determinant to which all others are related. But in all cases it is their interaction which ultimately decides the refined form of the house type and community structure, even though the element of choice may have originally decided the germinal shape. Individual cultures have evolved forms as diverse as the great, arrow-head shaped houses of the Bamiliké in the Camerouns to the painted *kraals* of the N'Debele; from the demountable shelters of the pastoral Bantu to the mud cities of the Hausa states; from the troglodyte earth-caves of Matmata to the 'bomb' houses of the Massa. It was of the latter that André Gide wrote of his astonishment that 'the few rare travellers who have spoken of (their) villages and huts have only thought to mention their "strangeness"'. To Gide they were beautiful, 'a beauty so perfect, so accomplished, that it seems natural. No ornament, no superfluity. The pure curve of its line, which is un-

Gorfas at Medenine, Tunisia. Built by the Bedouin as granaries the gorfas are now used by squatters for housing. The mud buildings are arranged around a large oval compound with a single, narrow entrance.

interrupted from base to summit, seems to have been arrived at mathematically, by an ineluctable necessity....'[26] Christopher Alexander's 'good fit'.

In this volume only a handful of house types are considered, representing only a fraction of the unknown number – perhaps five thousand – of peoples of Africa. But it is part of the intention of this second collection of new studies in vernacular architecture to show that the precise relation of shelter to society can only be meaningfully studied by specific examples. In order that they should be to some extent representative, however, the examples chosen illustrate the dominance of one or other feature, and are drawn from varying kinds of ethnic, climatic, environmental and cultural regions. The first of these, a study of the Kababish nomads of the Kordofan of Northern Sudan by Paul Verity, considers a society of rigorous frugality in which personal possessions are minimal, food and drink are, by Western standards, barely sufficient to sustain life and the total economy is centred around the breeding of camels. Among the

Troglodyte dwellings, Matmata, Tunisia. The caves open off a central thermal 'lung' where a well is seen in the foreground.

Massa 'bomb' houses, Northern Cameroon.

camel nomads, stages are measured in waterholes and distances in grazing land in desert regions. The severity of life and the limitations of resources impose controls which have made ultimately, a virtue out of asceticism, and have dictated strict codes of behaviour which for the Kababish, ensure rather than conflict with his freedom.

Whereas the life of the Kababish is largely conditioned by the search for grazing and for water, that of the Toffinou is totally dependent on an abundance of water. Miles Danby's study of the fishing community of Ganvié in Dahomey considers a people whose total economy and way of life centres around the fish of Lake Nokwé. Their houses, raised on stilts, are directly over the water, and through careful farming, and harvesting of the fish by various means, they have effected a skilful balance with the seasonal variations in water level and stock. The stability of their society has nevertheless enabled them to be responsive to changing circumstances in their fishing and their successful equilibrium with the ecology of the region is reflected in the egalitarian nature of their community structure. The introduction of a cash economy has been less disruptive of Ganvié life than it has been among the Nabdam of Nangodi, whom I visited in 1964 and who were the subject of a detailed study by Ian Archer in 1965–66. This sedentary, but fragmented people on the Savannah fringe, were free of a stratified system of caste or class, but were under the chieftaincy of a Grunshi lineage from Upper Volta. A resettlement programme was being considered when I was there, but in the subsequent couple of years the chief had died, better communications had been established and the traditional way of life had already been assailed by increased contact with the Akan communities of the South. Some evidence of this Akan influence was already evident in the buildings of the Naba's compound and related compounds and this has been studied further by Ian Archer.

Significant in the complex of the compounds of the Naba of Nangodi and those of his brothers is the physical demonstration of their family relations. Here, kinship is drawn on the landscape in the organisation of the compounds, an aspect which is to be found in many African communities, and which is central to the theme of Friedrich Schwerdtfeger's study of the Hausa compounds of Zaria. The exterior enrichment of the houses of Sokoto, Kano, Jos, Zaria and other great cities of the Hausa Sultanates are justly celebrated, and their symbolism will be the subject of a paper in a future volume in the series. Most reports on the houses of the region have been confined to speculation on their form based on photographs from the air. Schwerdtfeger's study is uniquely important because it penetrates the screen of absolute privacy traditionally applied to the households of the Hausa. With the help and active co-operation and interest of the Emir of Zaria he measured, and studied in detail, over eighty buildings, details of many of which are here published for the first time. After relating the housing of Zaria to conditions of climate, soils and vegetation, Friedrich Schwerdtfeger discusses the history of the Emirate and shows how the housing in the city has been shaped by it. In particular he shows how lineage and kinship are reflected in the organisation of the houses, and how changes in the family pattern are directly reflected in the erection and use of the buildings.

Zaria is a mud city, its soils being compacted into bricks, and the compound walls being raised above the borrow pits from which the building materials have been excavated. It is also a Muslim city, the Hausa having embraced the Mohammedan religion centuries ago. The penetration of Islam from the north and east into black Africa has been considerable over many centuries. Along the East Coast of Africa this influence has been long and lasting, but the region of the Zanj, the subject of Ronald Lewcock's study, has been subjected to many other cultural influences – Arabic, Persian, even Chinese and Indonesian. The cultural complex of the coastal region assumed a firm character by the thirteenth century when the Swahili Africans, with a strong intermixture of these imported elements, established their trading ports. Whereas the Hausa states assumed their trading role as intermediaries between the desert peoples and North Africa, and the black African cultures of the coastal rain forests, the Swahili of the Zanj maintained their trading position through sea routes. Along the coast the towns were built of many materials, among them stone and coral stone, whose durability has ensured that some clear impressions of the life of these now long-deceased communities of three and four hundred years ago, remains.

There is evidence, as Ronald Lewcock shows, of thatched roofs and timber structures having been used in the Zanj. Except for the rare model, or the technological conservatism which results in a new material being used in a manner more appropriate to its predecessor, there is relatively little evidence of the forms of building in the more ephemeral materials. Whereas the great stone structures of Meroë or Zimbabwe still stand today, perhaps eventually to reveal some of the secrets of their builders and the societies which once peopled them,

The 'cylinder-and-cone' house type, characteristic of hand-moulded or compacted mud architecture, with reed thatch roof.

Rectangular buildings with pitched roofs, typical of the 'carpenter' society. Ashanti.

early buildings in reed or grass, palm branch or bamboo have totally disappeared. Deductions have been made, sometimes unquestioningly, concerning the survivals in the light buildings of the present and their relationship to those of the past. But there is much evidence of innovation and change, adaptation and adjustment, in the recent buildings of which there are records to throw doubt on the persistence of house-forms over many centuries without evolutionary change. The process may be slow, it is true, and the good fit achieved through subtle interaction of needs and resources. Through this process houses of great beauty and purity of form exist today in many tribal societies. But not for long, perhaps. Much has gone that may never be preserved; much else is disappearing. This is central to Barrie Bierrmann's documentation of Indlu – the domed dwellings of the Zulu. In so strongly organised a people, with a considerable military skill in relation to that of the tribes whose lands they invaded, that the Zulu had a rigid hierarchy is not unexpected. This hierarchical structure was precisely expressed in the plan of their settlements and the geometry of their form.

In the examples so far discussed, tented structures, rectangular, carpentered buildings, compounds of cylinder-and-cone cells, combined cylindrical and cubic complexes and pure domes have all been represented. A distribution map of these house-types might show in broad terms the spread of the tent across the desert and steppe regions, or the cylinder/cone dwellings across the savannah and forest regions. But there would be a multitude of pockets where no such forms occurred, and many others which showed mixed types or the incidence of very different kinds of structure. It is evident that even within the same geographic region many house-types may co-exist, depending partly on the movement of peoples, partly on the subsistence economies, partly on preference in the selection of materials from available resources. Naigzy Gebremedhin has selected a group of house-forms from those being built or currently extant in Ethiopia and has shown how these relate to the distribution of peoples, the topography and climate of the country and other factors which have influenced their development. His study proposes a typology of the house-forms for the region and relates this to the economies of the peoples who build them. A number of specific examples shows the range of buildings produced by the Ethiopian peoples and also indicates the possibility of adaptation to suit the requirements of a nation emerging from feudalism.

To conclude this discussion of some of the forms of traditional shelter in Africa, one in particular – the tent of the Arabised Berber of Southern Morocco, the Tekna – is examined in great detail by Peter Alford Andrews. His researches show the minutiae of features by which sub-tribes within the tribal complex are identified, and the range of variation acceptable to the people within the parameters of the tent-form that they use. A structure which may be dismissed somewhat summarily because of its apparent simplicity is seen to have a degree of refinement which custom, use and necessity have determined. Like other indigenous peoples whose cultures have come into contact with that of the West, the Tekna have assimilated certain minor features into their own material possessions, few though they are – manufactured rope or a cardboard suitcase instead of the hair ropes and woven bags of traditional fabrication. Their culture is

under pressure – relatively minor pressure at present but likely to be comparable with that which the Kababish expect within three decades. This is a recurrent theme in all the studies which are devoted to the shelter of peoples building traditional houses from local resources in the face of technological change, western influence, migration, urban settlement and industrial development. The implications of these formidable pressures are examined through a number of examples in the second part of the book.

Taking his cues from the structural anthropologist's view of Lévi-Strauss, which emphasises the inter-action of systems within the construct of the total society, and Christopher Alexander's analysis of the processes of adaptation in the light of culture change, Michael Levin examines the relationship of social structure and house-forms among the BaKosi of West Cameroon. He shows the processes of change in house-form through the traditional creative evolution of the BaKosi village and compares this with the effects of structured change through the implementation of Colonial policies. German rule and missionary zeal changed village form and ended the traditional shrine, but the adaptability of the BaKosi and the comparative ease of transition has not caused traumatic changes in the lives of members of the community to date.

When I was living in Ashanti I was impressed by the vigour of the culture and the strength of traditional mores in a society which was well adjusted to the long exposure to European influence in economy, local administration, bureaucracy and many other sectors. That this was an assimilation based on what Paul Bohannan has termed the 'working misunderstanding' between the African and the British cultures in Ashanti is not to be denied. In *The Dynamics of Culture Change* Bronislaw Malinowski observed that 'the Europeans do not dispense the bounties and benefits of their culture with any less discrimination than the African shows in taking what is offered to him'.[27] Andrew Rutter's study of vernacular architecture in Ashanti shows the degree to which the traditional forms have been retained, the old Ashanti village organisation preserved and the principles by which the relationship of spaces within the houses and between them within the village structure determined. But he also shows the modifications that have taken place through British rule and subsequent Independence and considers the agents of change which are leading to current trends to flamboyance in Ashanti building.

There are many points of contrast between the Akan peoples of the tropical rain forest and the Arabs of the Algerian desert. Not only are their social structures and religions very different, from the role of women in the societies to their attitudes to polite salutations, but their relationships with their respective environments is dissimilar. Whereas the Ashanti live in a fertile, relatively well-watered, abundantly endowed milieu whose luxuriance they fought for, ferociously defended and systematically farmed, the peoples of the Sahara resided in a harsh, dry and inhospitable region, which had to be tamed to be lived in. For some tribes this meant a nomadic, frontierless movement across the face of the desert: Touareg, Reguibat, Bedouin. For others, Arab or Berber, it meant the building of densely clustered *ksour*, desert towns with cliff-like walls, whose thermal control makes them comfortable, and whose design protects the privacy of the women. The use of the ancient *foggara* irrigation network and the concentration near the oases of many *ksour* taps the underground water table of the Saharan region. David Etherton discusses the ways in which life is supported and shelter provided in the regions of Algeria and gives special attention to the Ibadite artificial oases of the Mzab. These, he points out, are by their man-made construction closer to the artificial oases of the oil companies which are dotting the desert and transforming its ancient culture. It is a transformation that still requires government protection for the Mzabites, not only from the companies but from the tourists who pour along their new concrete roads and upset the balance of Mzabite economy.

How damaging such contact may be is illustrated in a study by Ralph Mthawanji, a native of Malawi, of the processes of urbanisation taking place among the peoples of that land-locked country. He summarises the structure of the different tribes in terms of lineage and custom, shows the dependency of the African extended family and the balance maintained through the traditional agricultural base of the kinship village. The introduction of a money economy, though minimal in the form of a small poll-tax, ultimately undermined the stability of the traditional way of life. The effects of the monetisation of the economy on the village, the movement of people and the gradual urbanisation of the various tribes are discussed and Ralph Mthawanji makes suggestions as to how the traditional family and tribal structure could be a constructive base to a planning policy.

Around the Malawian city of Blantyre, as around most African cities today, are to be seen squatter and self-help settlements. In Mocambique these are the *caniços*, the subject of a survey by Amancio d'Alpoim Guedes. He shows the house-forms of the traditional patterns within the rural areas and how the techniques of construction are adapted to the urban environment on arrival in the city limits. As time passes the reed and stick houses are augmented with found materials, and the use of corrugated iron or concrete block, controlled by a tribal pride in the construction, finish and maintenance of the buildings leads to more permanent structures whose appearance is agreeable and whose accommodation is of good standard. The *caniços*, d'Alpoim Guedes emphasises, are not slums, although officially they are considered undesirable. This ambivalence of governmental attitude to the squatter settlement is a commonplace, and the source of much distress and instability in the community. Badi Foster examines attitudes to the inhabitants of the Moroccan *bidonvilles* and their shanty homes, and the 'patterns of encounter' between their population and that of the administrative city. Shanty-town dwellers suffer pressures of unemployment, inadequate services, poor housing and petty bureaucracy. Foster's study shows the importance of social communication within the *bidonville* and the psychological and official attitudes which inhibit the processes of successful urbanisation.

If the *bidonvilles* grow around the cities through the needs of the poor to be near the sources of the cash economy, Koidu, in Sierra Leone, is somewhat different. It is perhaps the most rapidly expanding city in Africa and is situated in a newly opened diamond-mining area. Its inhabitants, legally and illegally, are supported by the mining of diamonds and it is an expensive town in which to live. Because of its explosive growth which has condensed in a few years the whole

problem of urbanisation of Africa, it is a microcosm of the conflicts of interest which arise when western systems and monetary investment are laid over a tribal pattern. The Government, foreign investment and the traditional structure of the indigenous people, the Kono, on whose land Koidu stands, are all under pressure. After seven years there is still no water supply and other services are undependable. Yet housing is the principal permanent investment in Koidu and with the lack of a building industry and the unsuitability of the traditional Kono dwelling for the surplus of wealth in a diamond-mining town, a new vernacular is arising.

Koidu is the subject of rudimentary planning only, and the squatter settlements are contained only by the lines of communication, land ownership and the few services available. Though this volume is primarily a collection of case studies in traditional and urban shelter in Africa and the factors which determine them, Thomas Blair's analysis lays out the problems of the larger issues now confronting African nations in planning strategy. In the face of continual urban expansion and increasing industrialisation the fast-growing cities will become larger still and the makeshift policies that are applied to the *caniços*, the *bidonvilles* or Koidu can only lead to increasing aggravation of the problems that these settlements already face. Thomas Blair summarises some aspects of the traditional African city and the parasitism of the colonial city and examines the problems of that inheritance today. His analysis considers slum rehabilitation and the politics of squatting and considers the principles upon which the housing programmes of African nations depend. The factors that frame growth are seen against the proposals that have been made for such cities as Kano and Kaduna, or for the towns of the Zambian copper belt. He concludes with a statement of the educational problem now facing those who are teaching the new generation of African planners.

The history of the Colonial period in Africa is irreversible, the impact of industry and technology on the Third World inevitable. In the realisation of the growing urbanisation of Africa, planning policies must be clarified and new and effective strategies implemented. But African society and structure is not the mirror of Europe and should not be. Tribalism and nationalism may conflict, Moslem and Christian religions demand very different patterns of behaviour, animism and Hinduism will remain in Africa determining in many ways the structure of life. The extended family preserves the complex of the larger family unit and ensures the care of the aged; tribal structures support the welfare and the mutual dependency of their members: do western-based systems provide better alternatives? In doubt, many African countries have turned to Russia and to China, but not without disillusionment in the bureaucratic processes and authoritarian systems which conflict with traditional self-balancing structures. House-, village- and town-forms have been intimately related to social and community patterns: in the traditional society there is no distinction, and as recent studies in squatter settlements has shown, there is a continued struggle to preserve this inter-dependency.

In the processes of change, which it has been seen, have always applied to African house- and community-forms, the adjustments and modifications have taken place as responses to other alterations in the total system. Now the planners propose structures for cities based on rationalisation of the services and communications. Will their solutions and the new cities that are built and developed have the capacity for responsive change? Will they be sensitively balanced to the eco-system? Will they be environments in which Africans can live in happiness and mutual responsibility? As the examples in this volume may indicate, the problem is an infinitely more subtle one than that of physical planning, and it is to be hoped that those who undertake the master schemes will be aware of it.

NOTES TO INTRODUCTION

[1] EQUIANO, OLAUDAH, *The Interesting Narrative of Olaudah Equiano, or Gustavus Vasa, the African*, London 1789, pp. 10–11.

[2] MOORE, FRANCIS, *Travels into the Inland Parts of Africa*, London 1738, p. 179.

[3] SPARRMAN, ANDREW, *A Voyage to the Cape of Good Hope, 1772–1776*, London, 1785, Vol. 1.

[4] Ibid.

[5] BARROW, JOHN, *Voyage to Cochinchina*, London, 1806.

[6] CAILLIE, RENE, *Travels Through Central Africa to Timbuctoo*, London, 1830.

[7] DENHAM, D., CLAPPERTON, H., and OUDNEY, W. *Travels and Discoveries in Northern and Central Africa in 1822–4*, London, 1826, p. 39.

[8] BARTH, HENRY, *Travels and Discoveries in North and Central Africa*, London, 1857, 1890, pp. 297–8.

[9] Ibid., pp. 479–80.

[10] BURTON, SIR RICHARD, *The Lake Regions of Central Africa Vol. 1*, London, 1860, pp. 121–2.

[11] Ibid., p. 121.

[12] Ibid., p. 122.

[13] BACON, COMMANDER, quoted in Stuart Cloete, *The African Giant*, London, 1956, p. 160.

[14] DAPPER, OLFERT, *Description de l'Afrique*, Amsterdam, 1686.

[15] ROUTLEDGE, W. SCORESBY, and ROUTLEDGE, KATHERINE, *With a Prehistoric People. The Akikuya of British East Africa*, London, 1910, p. 184.

[16] BURTON, op. cit., p. 365.

[17] BLAKE, VERNON, 'The Aesthetic of Ashanti', in RATTRAY, R. S., *Religion and Art in Ashanti*, London, 1927, pp. 380–1.

[18] MAIR, DR. L. P., *An African People in the Twentieth Century*, London, 1934, pp. 107–8.

[19] BARTH, op. cit., p. 291.

[20] GRIAULE, MARCEL, and DIETERLEN, GERMAINE, 'The Dogon', in FORDE, DARYLL, *African Worlds*, London, 1954, pp. 96.

[21] GRIAULE, ibid., p. 97.

[22] MALINOWSKI, BRONISLAW, 'The Anthropology of Changing African Cultures', in MAIR, DR. L. P. (Ed.), *Methods of Study of Culture Contact in Africa*, London, 1938, p. xiii.

[23] GOLDFINGER, MYRON, *Villages in the Sun*, London, 1969, p. 19.

[24] MURDOCK, GEORGE PETER, *Africa, Its Peoples and Their Culture History*, New York, 1959 (accompanying map, 'Tribal Map of Africa').

[25] ALEXANDER, CHRISTOPHER, *Notes on the Synthesis of Form*, Cambridge, Mass., 1964, p. 52.

[26] GIDE, ANDRÉ, *Travels in the Congo* (Trans. BUSSY, DOROTHY), New York, 1929.

[27] MALINOWSKI, BRONISLAW, *The Dynamics of Culture Change*, London, 1942, p. 41.

Low-cost housing in suburban order, Volta Dam Resettlement project, Ghana.

KABABISH NOMADS OF NORTHERN SUDAN

Paul Verity

When your life depends on the rains and the rains fail, a life that is hard becomes even harder. For even the camel cannot exist when the water holes are not refilled after a dry summer. In 1968 the rains were bad and the Kababish tribe suffered greatly; thirty out of every hundred camels died and seventy out of every hundred sheep, cows and goats. In 1969 the rains were worse. The tribesmen with the usual Moslem fataiism face the future with resignation, for it is the will of Allah.

For how much longer can the Bedouin wander freely with his animals across thousands of miles of semi-desert, that to any other people would prove uninhabitable? The Kababish tribe of the Sudan, with whom I spent two months in 1969, although despising the life of the sedentary peoples around them, realise that within thirty years their way of life, which has remained unchanged for one thousand years, will cease.

The Sudan lies south of the first cataract of the Nile, west of the Red Sea and the Abyssinian Highlands, south-east of the Libyan Desert, east of the watershed between the Nile and Lake Chad, north-east of the watershed between the Nile and the Congo, and north of the river forests of Uganda. It is a vast land of nearly a million square miles, the size of Spain, France and Germany together.

The annual rainfall varies from nil in the north to sixty inches in the south, producing a country varying from barren desert to tropical forest. In the desert belt in the north the rocks have been laid bare by erosion. From the sandstone which is the predominant rock, the prevailing north wind is continually rolling grains of quartz sand and building them up into dunes and sandhills which run in the direction of the wind. On the southern edge of the desert regions as far north as latitude 12° north, to the west of the White Nile, is a vast spread of dune; sand now stable, anchored by vegetation nurtured by limited rainfall. The north of the region normally provides excellent grazing for camels. In the centre the plain is covered with dry, parched herbage and such drought-resisting trees and shrubs as are able to survive; in the wet season it produces good crops of millet, sesame, etc. The south of this area, during the rainy season, offers both pasture and a refuge from the fly, to the cattle-owning tribes who spend the dry season near the Bahr-el-Arab to the south.

It is in the north of this area that the nomadic and semi-nomadic tribes are concentrated. Nomadic tribes are sometimes described as primitive peoples who have failed to reach the level of civilisation of villagers and townsmen and thus have adopted a vagrant way of life, making a living by raiding settlements, plundering caravans and continually fighting among themselves. The nomad of the Sudan regards the sedentary man as a toiler, eating only after severe labours, whereas he is a gentleman living on the income from his capital, i.e. his animals. In fact, one of the greatest misfortunes that can overcome a nomad is to become sedentary. The nomad Arab prefers his freedom to the confinement of the town, which soon corrupts the young and undermines the family structure.

There are various forms of nomadism in the Sudan; the Hamitic tribes in the north-east, who move with their animals in the valleys of the Red Sea hills; the cattle breeders of the South Kordofan who have unvarying seasonal movement southward to the Bahr-el-Arab in the dry weather and northward again in the rains. It is, however, the camel Bedouin who are the greatest of the nomads. The largest, and probably the most nomadic of the camel tribes, is the Kababish. This tribe is not homogenous in the sense they are all derived from one family nor that there is any racial difference between them and other nomad tribes; but the several elements that comprise the tribe of perhaps 100,000 people are less contaminated with non-Arab blood than any other tribe in the Sudan. This is accounted for by the fact that for generations before and after the Arab invasion, they have been desert nomads, and their way of life has changed little, since the days when Jacob watered the flocks of Laban, at Haran.

The enormous region of about 48,000 square miles supporting this tribe is the semi-desert, bounded in the south by the line 14° north, by the extent of the grazing in the north, by the Nile in the east, and the Dafur in the west. It cannot be called desert, for as soon as the rain falls, even land that has been dry for several years produces grazing. It is, in the main part, an empty plain dotted with rocky outcrops, few of which reach any great height. The ground is an alternation of sand, gravel and thin grass, broken occasionally by the mushroom-shaped trees. The area is lacerated by *wadis* which occasionally, when the rains are heavy, fill with water drained from the surrounding plains.

As with all camel Bedouin, the life of the Kababish revolves around the needs and lives of their camels. They have no other function than to breed camels, which are their lifeblood; a man's wealth is determined by the number of camels he possesses — his home is made from the hair of the camel, his containers from its skin,

Map of the Northern Sudan including the grazing lands used by the Kababish.

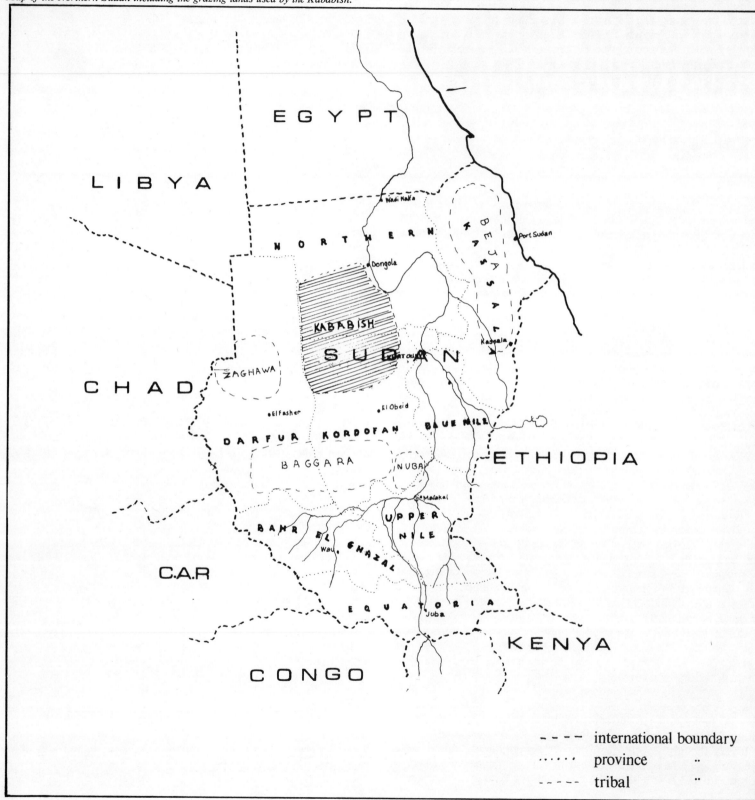

EGYPT

LIBYA

• Wadi Halfa

NORTHERN

BEJA

Port Sudan

• Dongola

KABABISH

SUDAN

Kassala

ZAGHAWA

CHAD

KHARTOUM

• El Fasher

• El Obeid

BLUE NILE

DARFUR

KORDOFAN

BAGGARA

NUBA

ETHIOPIA

• Malakal

C.A.R

BAHR EL GHAZAL

Wau

UPPER NILE

EQUATORIA

Juba

KENYA

CONGO

– – – – international boundary

· · · · · · province   ··

– – – – tribal   ··

26

his food is its meat and milk, his mode of transport its back, his source of income its sale, his increase in wealth its breeding – and he will buy a wife with camels. Thus the life of the nomad is directed to supplying water and grazing for his camels and, in consequence, is regulated by the rainfall and the amount of water available at any time of the year. In the summer the nomad stays near the *wadis*, but in the winter he takes his camels north. As the distances that have to be covered each year to provide grazing for the camels are enormous, the richer families often do not follow the herds. In fact the richer and poorer Kababish may only come together twice in the

The life of the Kababish depends on camels. Camel being milked, the vessel being supported by the right leg.

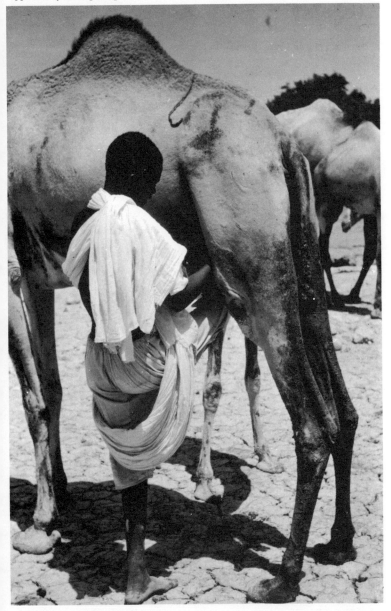

year, a separation made possible because the Kababish do not rely on animals for their main source of food, but on *assida*, ground millet. Other animals, but usually sheep and goats, are also herded to supply milk and some meat when the camels are away from the camp. Thus the household itself will follow the grazing pattern suited to sheep and goats rather to that of the camels. The poorer Bedouin, however, who cannot afford to hire herders to look after their animals, will often graze all their animals together and therefore will not exactly follow the pattern depicted in the chart.

In the summer the Bedu stay near the wells in the south and during the rainy season, from July through September, the camps are near the waterholes, moving from one hole to another. After a heavy rain the scouts are sent out to find the water; if there is good water to be found at any place the camels and the camp will be moved. When the rains have finished the *nushugh*, the annual exodus north, commences. The various sections of the tribe proceed north in a set order, long established by tradition but sometimes changed by the *Nazir* of the tribe to suit the conditions of that year, the distance depending on the rains which govern the extent of the available grazing.

It is not a haphazard wandering but it is as though all the sections of the tribe are drawn up on an immensely long starting line and proceed north-west in a carefully regulated pattern. This is to leave grazing for the return journey. No one may loiter too long in one place or deviate from the course, or he may consume the grazing left behind by another section of the tribe which is farther to the north-west.

The household of a normal Bedouin consists of himself, his wife or wives, children and probably one herdsman. In consequence he is very mobile and can easily move from one waterhole to another during the wet season and transfer his camels to new grazing, just by the packing of his tent and moving his herd. During the *nushugh* he may take part of his family north, or, while he and his male companions go north, he may leave them with a relative's family at the dry season well centres to look after the flocks of sheep and goats.

The mobility of a Sheik's camp is severely restricted, due to its size, for it may contain between sixty and a hundred people. The Sheik is the contact between the Government and the members of his section of the tribe, collecting taxes to the amount stipulated and informing the tribesmen of any government decision. Also, all tribal disputes are brought to the Sheik so that he can pronounce his verdict on them. The placement of the camp during the *kharif*, *darat* and *shita* (or rainy season, post rains and winter seasons), is critical. Its approximate position must be known to the other members of the tribe, and also to government officials, so it will be situated in a well-known place. Furthermore, it will usually be placed near a waterhole, for the sheep and goats need watering every three to four days. This means that it will be some five to six miles from the waterhole, for the grazing close to them is poor, having been eaten previously when the animals have been watered. During the *sayf*, or summer season, the camp is at what is termed its *damar*, the summer grazing ground for the animals. The camp will normally use the same *damar* year after year, so its position is well known.

The camp of the Sheik will usually consist of his four wives;

sometimes more, since he can marry any number of slave women, but only four free women. Each of the Sheik's wives will have a separate tent which is her property (tents are the property of women), all nearly the same, for all wives must be treated equally. The children of each wife will remain with her in the tent, if they are under the age of puberty. Each of the wives will be served by perhaps two families of slaves, young children and women looking after the wives while the male slaves are under the auspices of the Sheik. Slavery was officially abolished in 1934 in the Sudan, but many slaves stayed on with their masters. Ex-slaves are now uncommon among the Kababish except in the El Nurab section of the tribe. As well as slaves the Sheik will probably have retainers. These are men who attach themselves to a particular Sheik and rely on his generosity for food, clothing and favours. In return, depending on their status, they may tend his animals or perform administrative services – but at any time they are free to leave the camp. Their households are the normal nomad arrangement but they are situated near the tents of the Sheik.

Herding camels for watering – part of a herd of a thousand head of camels.

Cycle of Kababish migrations and activities.

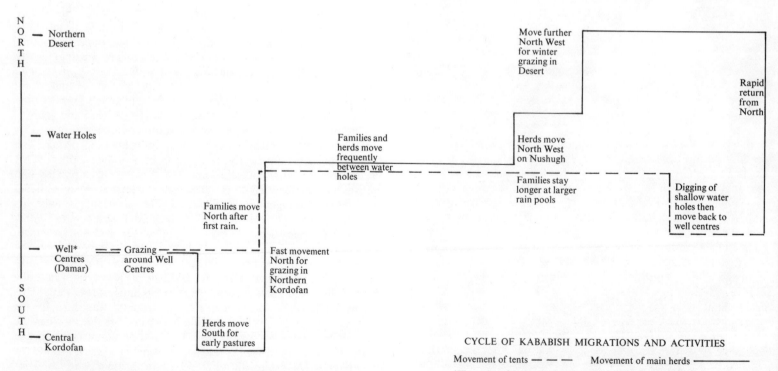

CYCLE OF KABABISH MIGRATIONS AND ACTIVITIES

Movement of tents — — —   Movement of main herds ————

*The centre of the Kababish migration can be considered the Damar since it is the most permanent of their camps, although it is not the geographical centre.

Sheik Ibrahaim-at-Tom on his camel; note tasselled saddle girth.

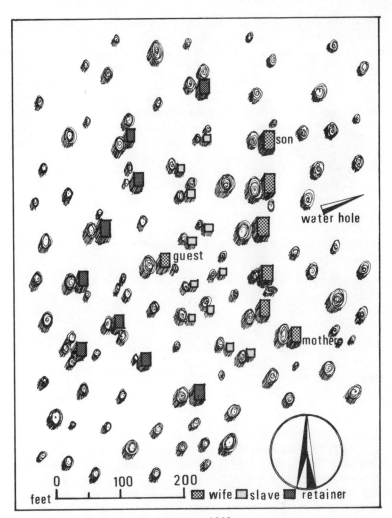

Camp of Sheik Ibrahaim-at-Tom in August 1969.

There will also be guests, either boys who have lost their fathers, who normally perform the duties of herders, or law supplicants, or perhaps just travellers. Herders, hired by the Sheik, will usually be with their animals, but their families may be in the camp. The Sheik's mother may also live in the camp, requiring a separate household, and perhaps the household of a married son of the Sheik may also be present.

The general positioning of the various shelters within the camp during *kharif*, *darat* and *shita* follows a standard pattern that varies slightly depending on the terrain in which the camp is pitched. The following description is based ·on Sheik Ibrahaim-at-Tom's wet season camp in late August. All the tents in the camp faced east towards Mecca and the rising sun. The front line of tents were those of the Sheik's wives, about forty feet apart, in as near a straight line as possible so that no one wife would, by virtue of her position, have precedence over another. Each tent was situated under or next to a tree or bush to provide extra shade from the heat of the sun, for the summer temperature can reach 125° in the shade. The axes of the

tents ran north–south but the main entrances faced east. Thus for most of the day the sun's rays did not penetrate. The Sheik's mother was living in the camp; her tent was situated at the end of the main line and some way ahead of it. A married son was in the camp and had his tent in the main line but at the opposite end to his grandmother. Behind these tents were those of the slaves lying nearly directly behind that tent to which they were assigned, but more important, they were placed near a tree. For the tents of the slaves were so poor that they were partly suspended from the tree, and so thin that without the shrub they would have become intolerably hot. They were placed 150–200 feet behind the main line.

A guest tent which I occupied was situated just behind the tents of the slaves, so I was in a position to call on any slave if the need arose. The tents of the retainers were dispersed around those of the slaves forming a semi-circle, each man having chosen a position that he thought best for the placing of his tent, either because it afforded privacy, or because there was good shade or firewood close at hand.

29

The Nazir *or leader of the Kababish, Sheik Hassan-at-Tom and his advisor. The* Nazir *is one of the few rich Kababish.*

A temporary camp. The slave's tents are frequently supported or suspended from a tree.

Thus the camp was formed in a semi-circle with a radius of perhaps four to five hundred feet.

Except for Hassan-at-Tom, the *Nazir* or leader of the tribe, and a few other Sheiks, few of the Kababish are individually rich. In consequence the variance in size and quality of the dwellings will reflect the prosperity of the households, but the basic construction will always remain the same.

The requirements of a Bedouin shelter are that it should provide a space in which it is cool and protected yet able to catch and trap any cooling breeze. It should provide a modicum of privacy for a man and his wife from the eyes of strangers and also be large enough for the entertaining of visitors. It must protect from the rains and keep a man's few possessions partially dry. But primarily, it must be easy to erect, dismantle and transport.

The moving of a Sheik's camp is a long and time-consuming affair. The camels needed to move the tents are brought from the herds; these animals are fitted with a special saddle for carrying loads. It has the appearance of two inverted **Y**s, lashed about three feet apart and placed over the camel's hump. When everything has been loaded the great train of perhaps a hundred and twenty camels moves off. When a suitable situation for the camp has been found sites for the various tents are picked. The erecting and striking of the tents is done by the slaves and by the women of the household; except for the wives of the Sheik who may be considered as women of the *hareem*, most wives work, and work hard.

A site for the tent having been chosen, the position is worked out with the main entrance facing east and the long axis running north

Kababish tents in line, each sited by a small shade tree.

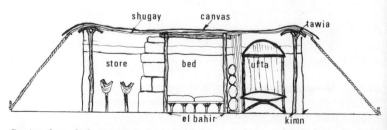

Section through the tent at A–A on the plan.

Mowiwir Camp. The camp has been sited where a few small trees offer a little shade in the desert.

The Sheik's tent. The nahiza *strip passing beneath the* shugay *membrane can be seen, as can the canvas layer and the guy-ropes.*

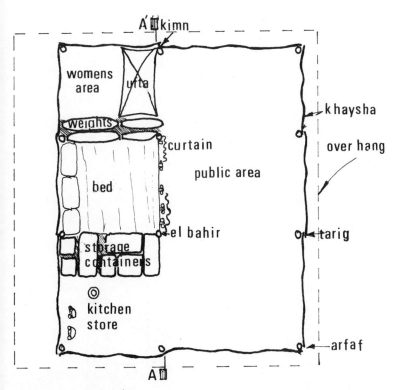

Plan of Sheik Ibrahaim's tent.

and south. The positioning of a tent under, or next to, a tree may necessitate the removal of inconvenient branches. Any extra shade that may be provided by the tree is fully utilised. All grass, small shrubs, stones and other obstructions are removed from the area to be covered by the tent and for several feet around. The ground is then made as level as possible, and finally it is thoroughly brushed. As there is often no carpeting the ground must be made as smooth as possible. An area in front of and just to the right of the tent is reserved for the cooking fire; brushwood is brought and placed in a semi-circle around it, on which the prepared food is placed, out of reach of the dogs. The main covering of the tent, *bayt shugga*, is woven out of camel hair in strips, light brown in colour with a darker brown surround. These strips are made by the women and are so tightly woven that they become completely waterproof. Measuring about three feet, six inches by twenty feet, the strips (*shugga*) are sewn together, four making a covering of some twenty feet by fourteen feet. Normally they have a life-span of four years, one being replaced each year, the oldest due for replacement being placed at the back of the tent.

Supporting poles are placed under the *bayt shugga* which is spread on the ground and these are lifted to an upright position, being placed in holes which have been previously hollowed in the ground. An upright about six feet in height is placed at each of the four corners. These *arfaf* are normally longer at the front of the tent than at the back. Between them on the two longer sides of the tent are placed two further poles (*tarig*), some six feet apart and seven feet from the *arfaf*. About half way along the breadth towards the back of the tent are

31

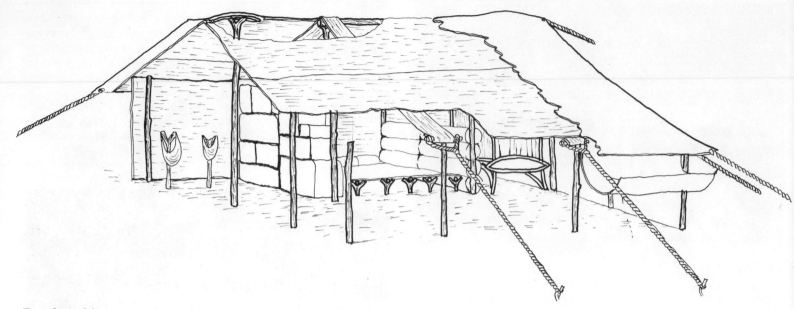

Tent of one of the retainers, showing the tarig *and the raised sections of* khaysha.

placed the main uprights, or *kimn*. About seven feet, six inches long they are located into a curved piece of wood about eighteen inches long, called a *tawia*, on which the tent is supported. Between the *kimn* and in line with the front and back *tarig* are placed two poles, seven feet high. These two poles are forked at the top and carry between them a horizontal ridgepole, the three members together being called *el bahir*. Thin strips of woven camel hair, *nahiza*, about nine inches wide, run the breadth of the tent under the *shugay* (plural of *shugga*). From the *tarig* on one side they run over the ridgepole and then over the *tarig* on the other, continuing about eighteen inches over the *tarig* at the back of the tent and ending in being doubled back on themselves. Through the loops thus formed is passed a piece

of rope; the two ropes join about nine inches from the wood to form a single strand which is then used as a guy rope secured to a stake in the ground. This stake is driven straight down to provide better leverage. When the *nahiza* are tightened they are an additional support for the roof and help to prevent sagging. When the *shugay* are anchored with guy ropes at the four corners and from the centre of each side, a semi-rigid membrane is formed.

It is now quite common to see a layer made from any pieces of canvas that can be obtained and sewn together in the shape of the structure, placed on top of the *shugay* and secured at the corners and centre points. Canvas preserves the *shugay* longer by protecting it in the wet season. In addition the gap between the two membranes has

The Sheik's tent.

Law dispute being heard by the Sheik in the shade of the overhang of his tent, at a daily meeting.

Sheik Mohamed holding a meeting of Kababish tribesmen beneath a shelter suspended between shade trees.

relatives of the Sheik, a Sheik from another part of the tribe, or a government official, the laws of hospitality will be fully extended. Many Bedouin arrive at such times, to talk to the guest or merely to look on and share in the feasting, so the sides of the tent are hung on the guy ropes to provide the greatest area of shade. The guest will sit in the tent, probably on cushions, those next in the line of privilege will sit around him on his carpet, sitting fairly rigidly, and finally the ordinary Bedouin will sit on the sand in an almost regimented position, either crouching on their haunches or sitting cross-legged. A camel — always a female one — will be brought before the guest so

Camels are slaughtered in honour of guests and the whole animal consumed. Here the neck and head of a camel, slung from the branch of a tree, is being skinned.

the effect of acting as insulation, keeping the tent cool in the heat of the summer and warm in the cold weather. The roof has to be securely anchored during the rainy season in particular. Before a rainstorm starts a violent wind builds up, often starting a sandstorm. In fact, despite heavy anchoring it is not uncommon for severe damage to occur because the ropes have given way.

Tied between the upright poles from roof to ground are pieces of woven goat's hair (*khaysha*). One piece will usually cover the gap between two uprights so that any one piece can be moved individually, or a whole side of the tent can be taken away. The back of the tent is covered with one whole piece while the gap between two pieces is the usual form of entrance into the tent. During the hot season it is essential not to bar any prevailing breeze from the tent. The appropriate section of *khaysha* can be lifted up, allowing the passage of breeze from any direction. Other sections are kept down to stop any of the sun's rays from penetrating the tent. The bottom side of the *khaysha*, when lifted, is tied to the guy ropes, thereby providing a greater area covered by shade. Shade is an obsession with the Bedouin as the sun beats down unrelentingly, and one of the prime objects of the tent is to provide it.

The overhang at the back of the tent is extremely important when shade has to be provided and the privacy of the tent maintained. At about seven in the morning, as it begins to get hot, a meeting is held by the Sheik. This takes place on the west side of the tent so that the people are protected from the sun rising in the east by the overhang and the shade cast by it. At this meeting are discussed such things as the location of the camels' grazing, where water is situated and the hearing of any disputes that may have arisen. In the evening at about five o'clock, another meeting takes place, but this time on the reverse side of the tent, the men being protected from the sun by the height of the front. Since these meetings are regular affairs the Sheik will normally keep the side of his tent down, maintaining the privacy of the interior and hiding his wives from prying eyes.

On occasions such as the arrival of special guests, one of the close that they all can see what a fine animal they will be eating and how generous the Sheik is. It will then be slaughtered in front of the guest and the blood drained. The raw intestines are brought to the guest who will then invite everyone to eat with him, with up to twenty persons eating from one plate. As soon as the food has been eaten everyone returns to his place to await more food – this time the cooked meat. The same procedure will take place as before, and will continue until everyone is satisfied. The remains are given to the women and the slaves.

During these feasts the women are not to be seen; they are in the tent hidden behind a screen formed by an *ufta*. A camel equivalent to the *howdah*, the *ufta* is used to transport the wife of a Sheik from one camping ground to another so that she may be comfortable during the journey, and be hidden from the eyes of other men.

The interior of the tent is divided by the *el bahir*. Except perhaps for a rug on the floor, the larger area on the east side is completely unfurnished and in the Sheik's tent is used by him for eating or for public occasions. Between the two poles of the *el bahir* on the west side is the bed, a very large affair about six feet square, on which may sleep the Sheik, one wife and her young children. It is a platform raised about nine inches from the ground, constructed from Y-shaped stakes driven into the ground and poles running east and west, placed between them. On top of these poles are placed smaller pieces of reed or cane, tied together with leather thongs and looking like a bamboo screen. These run north and south, making a strong, fairly pliable bed which can be easily dismantled. A mattress and coverings of some sort are spread on top to provide a modicum of comfort. Often a curtain is hung in front of the bed so that it remains out of sight when the tent is in public use.

To the north of the bed is the *ufta* and all the balancing weights that go with it to keep it stable when the camel is in motion. To the south is a large wall of containers, some metal, some leather, reaching almost from floor to the roof membrane. These contain clothes, cloth and other personal possessions. To the south of this wall is an area in which cooking utensils and the various provisions are stored. The decorations inside the tent are few, but the *ufta* is very decorative, being covered with cowrie shells and much skilful leatherwork. Above the bed are quite often placed two ostrich shells, bound in leather and decorated: a fertility symbol to ensure many children. On the wall above the bed are hung two great leather bags about six feet high, shaped like inverted funnels. They were, and sometimes still are, used for millet bags. The Bedouin will ride south with these bags strapped one on either side of the camel, to the millet growing areas, where they purchase sufficient provisions to last for a year. Now more frequently the Bedouin ride to the small villages bordering the desert to buy their provisions from the merchants who bring supplies to them.

Since, except during the *sayf*, the nomadic way of life necessitates moving camp every two or three weeks, and probably more often, the Bedouin possesses nothing that cannot be moved by two people, and virtually nothing that is not absolutely necessary to his way of life. He has one set of clothes that are worn until there is often hardly sufficient cloth left to cover the loins. Water is so precious that these clothes are rarely washed, it being considered wasteful to clean

clothes except at a waterhole. If a man wants new clothes he will often wait until he needs to buy several items – more millet, *sowut* chewing tobacco or sugar, and he will then sell an animal. The Bedu have a dislike of money, for money means little to them, the sign of wealth being the number of animals possessed. These are never counted – the saying is that if they are all counted they will all die, but the reason is probably that a tax is levied on each animal and, in consequence, no one declares all his stock.

Kababish men. They are wearing their entire clothing, the loops of gathered cloth being opened out to afford some covering at night in the desert cold. High on the upper left arm a knife is worn in a small leather scabbard, handle down for ease of removal. This is the basic tool for skinning, cutting meat and eating.

The Bedu place great value on austerity and asceticism. The harder one's life the less one eats or drinks – and this is minimal. The harder one drives oneself the greater one's esteem. So things of luxury are usually scorned. One would rather sit on the ground than on a seat; one would rather sit upright than sprawl; one must give, not take. Generosity is paramount; one must share what food one has with anyone who is near, which meant that I was short of food, for the curious constantly surrounded me. But these conditions do not apply to the Sheik, for he is an autocrat to whom is afforded all privileges. Despite, or perhaps because of the hardships of their life,

The Kababish are healthy though their lives are rigorous. Older men grow a thin beard and moustache.

the Bedouin are generally very healthy. The usual illnesses are worms ingested from eating uncooked gazelle meat, arthritis from lack of protection during the rainy season, sun blindness and bad backs – the latter being usually slipped discs from riding camels. Disease is almost unknown, for although there are no sanitary appliances the fact that the camp is often moved stops the spread of disease. The desert air is clean and the heat of the sun kills most micro-organisms. Washing is sporadic but occasionally the nomads will wash at a waterhole; otherwise, except during the rains, water costs time and labour to obtain. The usual form of washing is a kind of fumigation: a small charcoal fire is made in a scooped out hollow, on which are sprinkled green twigs of the *kitr* bush. Such fires give off a pleasantly scented smoke in which the Bedouin bathe.

The life of the Bedu offers nothing but hardship for those who partake of it. Everything is at a premium: water, for it is scarce; food, because few variations can survive the heat of the desert for long periods; and possessions, for there is a limit to the number of belongings that can be continually transported from camp to camp, notwithstanding the fact that most of the Bedu are too poor to possess more than the bare essentials for sustaining life. Yet this life gives the Arab what he prizes above everything else – his freedom.

SELECTED BIBLIOGRAPHY

ASAD, TALAL, *The Kababish Arabs*, London, 1970.
DAVIS, R., *The Camel's Back*, London, 1957.
MACMICHAEL, H. A., *Tribes of the Central and Northern Kordofan*, Cambridge, 1912.
SELIGMAN, C. G., and SELIGMAN, B. Z. 'The Kababish, a Sudan Arab Tribe', in *Sudan Notes and Records*, 1920.

Kababish guide. The farther camel bears the Kababish saddle, the nearer is loaded with the guide's few possessions.

GANVIE, DAHOMEY

Miles Danby

For centuries the peoples living along the coast of West Africa have fished in the waters of the Atlantic. In their dugout canoes they have mastered the dangerous surf, to catch all kinds of sea-water fish in their nets. The fishing grounds are well stocked, so there has always been a large surplus for sale to the inhabitants of the coastal towns, and in recent times dried fish in large quantities have been sent to the markets of the interior. Modern economic development has brought the introduction of the deep-sea trawler and refrigerated lorries to take fish fresh to the markets of the large towns, sometimes hundreds of miles from the coast. But still there remain many villages of small houses made from bamboo and the leaves of the palm trees growing on the shore, in which the fishermen practise their craft in the traditional manner. Many of these fishermen, like the Ewe of Ghana and Togo, are itinerant and migrate along the coast with the seasons.

Ganvié, the subject of this study, is a small town of nine to ten thousand inhabitants almost entirely devoted to fishing. It is situated in the Republic of Dahomey 6° north of the Equator and 2° east of Greenwich. It is different from the coastal villages in several ways.

First, it is built in the fishing grounds to which it owes its existence, near the north shore of Lake Nokwé, a lagoon formed behind the sandy coastal strip of Cotonou, the capital of Dahomey. Secondly, it is a comparatively recent settlement having probably been founded about the middle of the nineteenth century. Thirdly, the methods of fishing are very unusual and peculiar to Lake Nokwé itself.

The town of Ganvié is built entirely in the lake and the only means of access is by canoe. The usual approach for a visitor travelling from Cotonou, the capital, is by road as far as Abomey-Calavi (on the main Cotonou–Abomey road) which is the nearest market centre on land to Ganvié; there one must make a journey by canoe for two to three kilometres. All the buildings of the town are on stilts embedded in the bottom of the lake and all communication is on water by canoe.

To understand the development of this remarkable town it is necessary to study the geographical factors of the region which made it possible for settlement to take place in such an unpromising situation. Lake Nokwé is linked to the lagoon of Porto Novo forming one

The edge of Ganvié as it meets Lake Nokwé. In the foreground a complete house is compared with the pole framework of another in course of erection. Some roofs are hipped and others have gable ends, finished in thatch.

During low water, gliding slowly in a canoe through the waterways of Ganvié is an exciting visual experience. The views past the supporting posts of houses in the foreground reveal further waterways, houses, people and canoes, in a moving kaleidescope of light and shade.

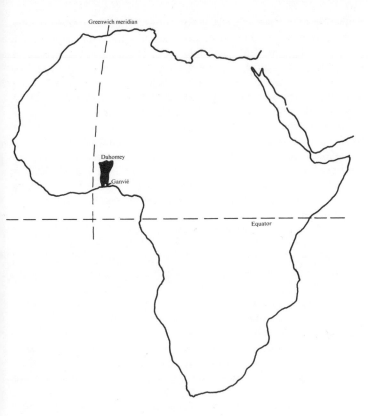

Ganvié: latitude 6° 27′ north; Longitude 2° 15′ east.

The inhabitants of Ganvié are predominantly from the Toffinou tribe. This tribe is of composite origin and is a sub-division of the Adja group of the Beninian culture. The Adja are closely related to the Akan and Ewe of Ghana and also include the Fon and Mahi of Dahomey. The people of the region of the lower Ouémé are known as the Ouémenou and with the Toffinou are usually considered to be part of the Fon grouping. Before the eighteenth century there were very few people in the region of the lower Ouémé, most settlement being to the east of the river. Yoruba families expelled from the Oyo kingdom together with a few settlers from the Allada region then made up the bulk of the population. It was not until the victory of the powerful kingdom of Abomey over its rival, a Ouéménou kingdom with its capital at Zagnanado (which is north of the lower Ouémé at the same latitude as Abomey) at the end of the eighteenth century after nearly two centuries of intermittent warfare, that further settlement took place. After their defeat the Ouéménou emigrated south and re-established themselves on the Sakété plateau near Adjohon.

The situation of Ganvié on Lake Nokwé.

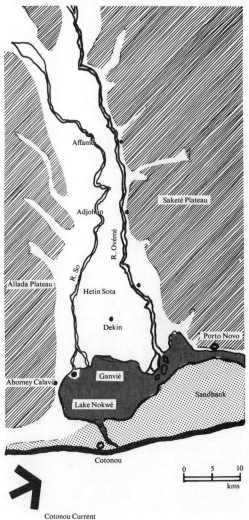

stretch of water which is separated from the sea by a coastal belt of sand on which Cotonou is built. At low water the combined area of Lake Nokwé and Porto Novo lagoon is 150 square kilometres. This bank of sand has been formed by the deposits of the Cotonou current which originates off the eastern end of the Ghanaian coastland and flows most of the year in the direction S.W. to N.E. to W.S.W. to E.N.E. Lake Nokwé is thus in the shadow of this current coast by the plateau of Allada to the west of the valley of the river Ouémé. The waters of the rivers Ouémé and So are prevented from reaching the sea directly by the coastal strip of sand and a lake has resulted. At high water there is a flow to the sea to the east via the lagoon at Lagos in Nigeria and by a channel through the sand bank to the east of Cotonou. Alluvial deposits are also brought by the river Ouémé, forming a delta which is slowly growing and threatens to join the coastal strip and cut off the Porto Novo lagoon.

To the north of the lake lies the valley of the rivers Ouémé and So, twenty kilometres at its widest and narrowing to an average of ten kilometres. This valley has rich alluvial soil but is flooded over a large area during three to four months of the year. To the east and west of the valley are two plateaux, the plateau of Allada and the plateau of Sakété. Their average height is from forty to sixty metres above sea level. The soil is a lateritic clay and has a characteristic red colour which is common to many parts of Africa. Palm nuts are the main crop of the plateau area and are processed locally to make palm oil which is Dahomey's main export.

At high water, the floor level of the houses is elevated above the water, slightly above the eye level of a person seated in a canoe.

The new Fon migration submerged the small groups of Yoruba settlers and eventually assimilated them. The delta area became a zone of refuge for the enemies of the King of Abomey. Further refugees moved west fleeing from the powerful king of Porto Novo.

The Toffinou came from an area to the west and afterwards relations were cut with the Allada plateau because of the marshes and the waters of Lake Nokwé. In this way, the west shore of the lake and the right bank of the river So became a frontier. To the east, the forests of the Sakété plateau were insecure because of sporadic invasion by the Yoruba. It is also probable that slave-raiding both from the east and the west tended to increase the number of refugees and the isolation of the region.

The Ouéménou and Toffinou were thus confined to the valley of the Lower Ouémé, settling on the banks of the rivers and the shores of the lake and practising agriculture on the surrounding marsh areas, which were flooded from three to four months per year. It is surprising that no political entity resulted from so many people of similar origin settling in a relatively confined area. Each large village or group of villages had its own chief but there was no centralised power and therefore no capital. This was the situation at the end of the nineteenth century when the French took over the region as part of their colony of Dahomey and established their capital at Cotonou on the coastal strip due south of Ganvié. This lack of centralisation before the French domination may be due to their social organisation which is fairly typical of refugee communities.

It was remarkably egalitarian in that birth brought no privilege nor any hereditary function or obligation. It was a relatively free society with no class systems or castes. The majority of the male population worked as farmers or fishermen, or both, according to the dictates of season and market. There was, however, considerable social coherence which made it possible for the chiefs to organise communal labour on projects useful to the village, clearance of the forest for cultivation, drainage of the marsh for cultivation and organisation of collective grazing for cattle. There were special rules for the fishermen. A limitation was fixed on the total catch as an attempt to assure the full participation of all in these riches and to safeguard the future of the fisheries. Collective fishing was organised on special fixed dates in certain pools, between the two rivers. Other parts of the rivers were protected and all fishing was forbidden there, in order to maintain reserves for breeding purposes. Certain kinds of traps were prohibited but the open waters of the lake were free of any control. At this time, there were no settlements actually in the lake and no village depended entirely on fishing as Ganvié does today. At the end of the nineteenth century there was a change and for the first time there were settlements in Lake Nokwé consisting of fishing communities, living permanently over the waters of the lake in houses built on stilts.

The ancestors of the present inhabitants of Ganvié probably lived a similar life to the villages on the banks of the river Ouémé where to-day the Ouéménou practise both agriculture and fishing, according to the season. In these villages life is completely related to the rhythm of the flow of the river waters. The river Ouémé is 400 kilometres long and rises in the range of mountains in the north of Dahomey known as the Atakora. The river drains an area of about 45,000 square kilometres, but most of this area in the north consists of impermeable soils which cause a quick run-off during the rainy season from June to October at the source. The waters of the Ouémé rise very quickly during June and by the end of July the river has overflowed its banks. From then until the end of November the plain is inundated and agriculture is impossible as the fields are under water. Owing to the curious contours of the alluvial valley there is a raised embankment on either side of the river which is higher than the plain outside

Bar chart showing the interaction of temperature, rainfall, humidity, seasonal flooding, etc., on the fishing season in Ganvié.

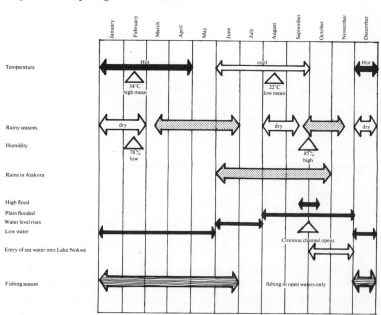

which slopes very gradually to the edge of the plateaux. The houses are built on this embankment as it is the highest possible ground in the area. When the waters start to recede from October onwards the banks are the first sections of land to emerge from the waters, and the houses which are on stilts like the houses of Ganvié stand on dry land until the following rainy season when at the time of highwater in September the waters lap the floors of the houses. During low water, access to these houses is by ladder as the level of the flow is dictated by the height of maximum flood waters above ground level during the rainy season. This varies from fifty centimetres to one metre. The river banks are under water for at least a month, and the plains may be flooded for two to four months. During the flood season life is lethargic and limited. Travel is only by canoe and fishing trips, to collect from traps and lines, take only a few hours a day. Open platforms are constructed for the planting of tomato and pepper seeds which are later planted out as seedlings when the waters start to recede. Other platforms are made to enable cattle to escape the flood from the high points where they have been driven by the rising waters. These are made from bamboo with floating vegetation obtained from the river used as a bed for the cattle and more floating grass is used to feed them. As is often the case in Africa, no milk is produced from the cattle, nor are they used for any sort of work. They are regarded as possessions of prestige and a sort of family capital. Their meat is eaten but not often; usually at social occasions when cattle are ceremoniously slaughtered at marriages and funerals.

When the flood goes down it leaves a mass of floating vegetation, which is an obstacle to immediate cultivation but is a source of organic matter for the soil, which later produces good crops of maize, cassava, tomatoes and other vegetables. Fishing also takes place at this time in the many pools of water left behind. It is very easy to catch the fish and several types of traps and nets are used. Channels are dug to drain the marshy land into the river and these channels are also stocked with fish who swim up from the river attracted by bait made from maize. The fish are then trapped in the channels (*zoudo*) by means of barriers made from palm leaves which prevent their escape back to the river. They breed in the channels and are later caught with traps and nets.

Another method of fishing used in the region of Lower Ouémé is called *aholo*. This is a raft of floating grass and vegetable matter which is anchored with stakes somewhere near the river bank. Fish are attracted to it because of its shade and the maize bait dropped nearby. When a sufficient number of fish has gathered underneath the raft, fishermen carefully surround the fish with mats of bamboo or palm frond dropped vertically at the periphery. The whole affair is gently moved towards the back where the fish are landed with nets. The fishermen must get into the water to do this, so this method can only be used at low water and where the depth is no greater than a man. The method of fish breeding now used by the Toffinou of Ganvié in Lake Nokwé is thought to have been developed from the idea of the *aholo*.

During the last decade of the nineteenth century came the events that caused several villages to abandon agriculture and to rely entirely on fishing. Originally, Lake Nokwé was a completely freshwater lake with its shores a mass of thick forest of mangrove, and

Many canoes have simple decoration in black and white.

the surrounding marshes were covered with bamboo and raffia palm. The only exit to the sea was through the lagoon past Porto Novo, towards Lagos. When the Cotonou channel was first cut about 1895, at the height of the flood from the Ouémé the nature of the water in the lake changed. Between August and November the level of the lake usually rises about one metre to the level of the lower waters of the Ouémé, and when a small channel was made to reduce the flood waters, a torrent of water flowed into the sea. The force of the flow of water widened the channel and the flow increased until the level of the lake dropped appreciably. The water level dropped much more quickly than before the channel was made when the water flowed to the sea past Porto Novo to Lagos. After the water level fell past a certain point, there followed a reverse flow of sea water into the lake and in this way the waters of Lake Nokwé became slightly saline. This presence of salt in the water had far-reaching effects.

Gradually the nature of the plant life on the shores of the lake changed. The forest started to wither and many brush fires occurred. Young plants were spoiled by the salt. It became impossible to grow maize and cassava on the land watered by the lake and the floating vegetation disappeared. Usually the shores of the lake receded. Up to this time the Toffinou had relied on the water of Lake Nokwé for drinking purposes and now the water had become saline they were forced to seek fresh water elsewhere – usually from the wells in the plateau.

The amount of sea water released into the lake was not so great as to make it of high salinity, because the channel does not operate when the lake is at lower water from December to June. Also the channel was not opened every year before 1951. Before this date it took place only at intervals of two to five years and so the degree of salinity must have been very low, particularly as the annual flood waters of the Ouémé must have caused considerable dilution.

It would seem that everything would have been against the Toffinou continuing to inhabit the north shores of the lake – with virtually no agriculture or feed for cattle and no fresh drinking water. However, the salinity in the water did not affect the fishing.

All supplies, except fish, must be brought to Ganvié by canoe from local markets on the shore of the lake.

On festive occasions the main 'streets' or waterways are congested with humanity and canoes.

On the contrary – the changed biological conditions seemed to have made more intensive fishing possible. Also the need for isolation had more or less disappeared as the region of Lower Ouémé was now absorbed into the colony of Dahomey which included the area of the former kingdoms of Abomey and Porto Novo, and peace was firmly established. So there was now no obstacle to the change to complete reliance on fishing because the lake was so rich that the surplus fish could be traded in the markets of the region for maize, cassava and other foods, and of course the essential fresh water which was transported to Ganvié and other settlements in large earthenware jars by canoe.

It is possible that Ganvié was originally in a marsh and that the dying off of the vegetation, and the rise in the level of the lake, gradually produced the present situation of a town built permanently over water. Now there are hundreds of houses built almost entirely of natural materials from the region, which were of course formerly more accessible but are now obtained by trade with the people of the plateau and the delta.

Ganvié is a lively town which has expanded considerably since the beginning of the century when the total population of all the lake villages was estimated at 8–10,000. By 1962 the population had increased to 50,000, with Ganvié at an estimated 9,300 inhabitants. This recent increase was made possible by the development of new ideas in fishing methods and the expansion of markets in the region and in the large towns of Cotonou and Porto Novo. It became the fastest-growing area of Lower Dahomey, which itself is part of a belt of population of a density of about 150 persons per square kilometre, stretching along the West Africa coast from Ivory Coast to Nigeria. By comparison, the population density for Dahomey as a whole is only 20 persons per kilometre.

The fishermen sell their fish to their wives who act as traders, smoking a large proportion for sale or exchange in the local markets. In the season of the biggest catches they trade fish in the urban

markets of Cotonou or Porto Novo and even travel into Nigeria with their wares. The wives in return bring, in exchange, foodstuffs and other goods for consumption and use in Ganvié. The main foods consist of cassava, maize, peppers, palm nuts, haricot beans, tomatoes, palm oil and potatoes. Other local products are palm wine, fresh water (at low water only), *sodabi* (distilled palm wine), firewood, timber and branches used in fish farming. A large proportion of these goods are sold direct from dug-out canoes in the floating market in Ganvié, whereas water is usually taken from house to house, but this is less common because Ganvié itself now has a borehole and the lake water itself is fresh enough to drink at the time of the flood after the impurities have been allowed to settle. With the

The floating market. All the merchants are women, who carry their goods, mostly foodstuffs, in their canoes.

development of a money economy many inhabitants of the plain and the plateaux bring goods by canoe, to sell in the market at Ganvié.

Many of the Ganvié fishermen are now so prosperous that they own land in the plateaux and some even own herds of cattle on the delta islands or in the flood zones behind the river banks. This does not indicate a retreat to dry land but rather a capitalisation of their fishing profits which can be used for exchange and investment purposes when needed. In fact, the fishermen generally enjoy a higher standard of living than the farmers of the region.

The lake provides favourable conditions for fish life, particularly along the north shore. From January to August the depth of the lake varies from one to one and a half metres. The water is rich in micro-organisms which are brought by the rivers during the flood and provide the main source of food for the fish. The salinity, as mentioned before, varies because of the action of the Cotonou channel and has automatically selected certain species and helped to eliminate predators. These biological conditions are ideal for fish-breeding and the Toffinou have developed their own ingenious and sophisticated method. On approaching Ganvié during low water by canoe, it is necessary to navigate carefully past rows of dead branches which emerge vertically from the water. These branches form the fences and hedges of fish plantations and are fixed in the bed of the lake at approximately one metre centres. The species of tree providing the branches is locally known as *niaouli*. The branches, between 1·80 and two metres long, are covered by the flood waters in September and October. The area of water enclosed by the branches varies from the smallest size, which is circular in plan from four to eight metres in diameter, to very large areas rectangular in shape and sometimes several hundred metres square. The general name for such an enclosure is *akadja*, the first type having the particular name *akadjavi* and the large rectangular one being known as *akadjabo*. At flood time the *akadja* retains alluvial deposits and provides a sanctuary where the fish may spawn undisturbed, as the flood waters recede. The slime that gathers on the bed contains algae and micro-organisms which also cover the branches and are the main source of food. The branches also stabilise the water causing the deposit of elements in suspension and as the predators usually prefer running water, they do not penetrate the *akadja* which is really a large trap in which the fish may breed, and later be easily captured. The commonest species of fish attracted to the *akadja* is the *tilapia* which is caught in huge quantities.

The method used depends on the type of *akadja*. The *akadjavi* is fished by the individual owner, who may have the assistance of a son or companion. From his canoe, he throws over it a casting net which is shaped like a truncated cone, open at both ends. The net now circles the *akadja* and is then fixed to the bed with stakes and stones, remaining in a vertical position held by the branches. The fisherman then stands inside the *akadja* and removes the branches one by one, throwing them outside the net. Then the net is carefully closed at the bottom and tightened at the top, so that the fish do not escape, and the whole catch is pulled into the canoe, the *akadjavi* being replaced with as many as possible of the old branches. Four to six catches per year can be made in this way. The *akadjabo* is fished in a similar fashion; it is surrounded with a series of mats joined end to end to form a complete barrier. At one corner a special area, usually circular in shape, is made for the capture and here many traps are set. A group of young fishermen then enter the *akadjobo* and throw the branches outside, at the same time driving the fish into the corner where the traps are raised. Some fish are also caught with nets on the end of poles dragged along the bed at the perimeter of the *akadja*. The *akadja* is then replaced and fishing may take place again in two to three months time. Not all of them are regularly fished; some are held in reserve with a group of *akadjavi* nearby which are periodically stocked from this reserve. Through the years an extraordinary high productivity has been achieved. It has been estimated that fifteen

Beyond the canoe can be seen the branches of an akadjavi *rising from the waters of Lake Nokwé.*

A young fisherman casts his net in the free waters of Lake Nokwé, from his dugout canoe. The net has a fine mesh to catch the ethmalose, *a small fish.*

metric tons of *tilapia* and other species per hectare per year is the average yield from these fish farms in Ganvié.

The total area of water is 15,000 hectares and only 500 hectares are accounted for by the *akadja* method of fish-farming. The remaining open waters are fished by other techniques. A small fish, the *ethmalose*, is caught with a special hand casting-net with a small mesh, thrown from a canoe. Sometimes groups of ten to twenty canoes work together in this way. At night, dragnets up to several hundred metres in length are used in the centre of the lake, when all kinds of fish, and prawns, are caught. In the early morning the people of Ganvié sometimes go fishing *tilapia* with harpoons, spearing them as they come to the surface to breathe. By this variety of means, all the men of Ganvié can take part in the fishing industry, but only relatively rich fishermen can afford the *akadjabo* because it represents a sizeable investment. A hectare of *akadja* requires about 2,000 branches or sixty metric tons in weight, which must be transported by canoe from the local markets like Abomey-Calavi, and after each catch, 30/40% of the branches need replacement.

The activity of fishing is confined only to the men of Ganvié, whereas all trading is carried out by the women, who have economic independence, holding their own accounts and money boxes. The women of the region are in charge of all food processing, buying the raw materials from their husbands, preparing and selling various food made from cassava and maize and wrapped in banana leaves. In Ganvié itself this applies to the drying of fish and prawns for the market. But this economic liberty has not changed the traditional masculine supremacy which is linked to the extended family system and polygamy. Lineage is strictly paternal and the extended family is known as the *khoué*. It is the centre of social and religious life. Young families usually live at the house of the husband and daughters must leave their parental family on marriage. Only men can own land and fishing rights but the daughters may inherit goods and chattels including cattle. Divorce, however, is fairly easy and because of the economic independence of women unhindered by problems of alimony.

Recently there has been a tendency for the younger generation to set up its own independent household away from the *khoué*. This has combined with the relatively new custom of the elder son inheriting fishing concessions to reduce the power of the extended family. The social customs which are thus in a state of transition have naturally affected the layout of the houses in Ganvié. A large extended family comprises all the sons of one father with all their respective wives and children whereas sometimes a son moves to a new house and sets up his own separate establishment with his wife and children.

The basic housing unit in Ganvié is a rectangular structure built of a framework of mangrove or a similar type of timber. This framework consists mainly of vertical poles about 3—4 metres in length which are fixed in the bed of the lake at approximately 50 cm centre and form the perimeter of the rectangular unit. Horizontal poles are then tied to the vertical members with palm fibres to form a horizontal platform which will be the floor of the dwelling. The level of the floor is dictated by the water level at high flood time in September–October and is usually about 1·50 metres above the water level during low water from December to May. The top ends of the

The basic structure of the house before the addition of the thatched roof and walls. A small platform projects all round the roof to take the burden of the thatch, but the palm sticks do not project into the roof, which remains an open space. The jointing is entirely effected by secure lashings with bark withies.

vertical poles are at eaves level and other horizontal poles are tied to the verticals to brace the structure. Further poles are used as rafters and ties to the roof structure which is double-pitched with either gables or hinged ends. It is now necessary to fill in the framework with a floor, roof and wall. The floor is made with palm fronds, small bamboos or other sticks tied close together to the main pole framework which usually spans the shortest distance. Mats are often used as the final interior floor finish.

The roof consists of palm fronds spanning from eaves to the ridge with horizontal ties of the same material forming a structural mat

A house under construction showing the roof partly thatched, and some wall frame panels in position.

Thatched roofs require frequent maintenance and time has revealed the palm leaves used as a base for the grass thatch of this roof.

forming a sort of balcony extending from one or two of the longer sides of the house.

The houses in Ganvié are admirably adapted to provide the best possible comfort conditions from the available materials which are all obtained from the trees and grass of the region. Human comfort depends on the relation between air temperature and relative humidity. Neither of these vary a great deal through the year. As might be expected, the relative humidity is fairly constant and might vary from a mean monthly figure of 78% in February to 85% in September (Cotonou figures). The temperatures by African standards are not too high varying from the highest mean of 34° C in February to the lowest mean of 22° C in August. The humidity is therefore the main problem in obtaining human comfort conditions in Ganvié, and as in all hot–humid countries it is necessary to maintain good circulation of air to allow evaporation of moisture from the skin. The wall construction of the houses

The walls of some buildings have painted decorations. This one has a pattern of squares of strong hues – yellow, red and green.

tied to the pole framework and ready to receive a thick grass thatch finish to keep out the rain and give insulation and shade from the sun. Sometimes, a cantilevered eave structure is made from palm fronds equal to the depth of the thatch to give stability and to facilitate the thatching process. There is no absolute consistency in the design of the roof and some houses have larger spans with thatch fixed vertically to form the gable ends while others with hipped ends have an elegant curve to the ridge, giving a sculptural form to the finished thatch. Palm leaves are also occasionally used together with grass in the thatch.

The walls have a variety of infill panels made from palm or split bamboo. These panels have a vertical finish with horizontal braces and occasional vertical members outside which are tied to the horizontal floor and eaves poles. It is usual for the vertical finish to be to the inside, but some houses have in addition an outside cladding of vertical strips tied together like matting which is often painted in squares and rectangles in simple hues; frequently in the national colours of red, yellow and green. Rectangular door openings are formed in the walls and the door itself is often split bamboo or cane matting, fixed to the head of the frame, which is kept rolled up during the day and dropped at night to close the opening. The house unit always has access to an outside platform where most of the daytime social activity takes place. Nets and traps are repaired there and many vertical poles extend above the platform from which the nets may be hung. The platform is supported on stilts and is made in the same way as the house floor. It is often a separate structure at a slightly lower level than the house floor and may have several house units with access to it. In this case it serves a similar function to a courtyard on dry land, and probably belongs to an extended family. Each building may be divided internally into two or more rooms with each wife having her own room. The newer and separate houses have platforms formed by cantilevering the floor structure outside,

The open platform is used for storage and the repair of fishing nets, traps, water jars and so on, as well as for social life.

The thick thatch roof gives excellent insulation from solar radiation and the wall construction allows a reasonable through ventilation. The two layers of the wall can be seen on either side of the horizontal palm fronds.

allows reasonably good through ventilation, while at the same time providing shade and privacy. It also permits a minimum amount of daylighting to enter the interior. The roof provides an excellent barrier to the main source of heat which is solar radiation from the direct and reflected rays of the sun.

Although there is a fair amount of cloud throughout the year, the solar radiation is nevertheless considerable because of reflection from the water droplets. Thatched roofs are not the best from the point of view of rain penetration and maintenance, but Ganvié does not receive excessive rainfall, the annual figure for Porto Novo being 130 cms compared with 393 for Freetown and 179 for Lagos. Like elsewhere in Africa, the galvanised corrugated iron sheet has been introduced because it is more permanent and requires little or no maintenance. It also is considered to be more modern in spite of the fact that it creates less tolerable comfort conditions because its lack of insulation causes more heat to be radiated into the interior than is the case with a thatched roof.

The dimensions of the buildings in Ganvié are limited by the available size of the materials and their structural qualities. This means that the houses are never more than one room thick which is an advantage for through ventilation, but vertical dimensions are definitely cramped although a few two-storey buildings have been erected by enterprising builders. The smallest building contains fetish objects and is a scaled-down version of a typical house with one side open to view from outside. The layout of the town appears to be haphazard but is governed by the size and manoeuvrability of the dug-out canoe.

The main streets or channels are wide enough to allow the passage of quite a number of canoes without collision, but become very congested on special occasions and market days. The side channels, however, are very narrow and demand very careful navigation be-

tween the supporting poles of houses and the canoes tethered to them or the access ladders.

For most of the year, Ganvié is a three layer town. The bottom layer is the lake itself, a metre or more of water where the fish without whom the town could not exist find shelter, food and the right conditions for breeding, either confined to the still water of the *akadja* or swimming freely in the rest of the lake. The middle layer is the space between the water level and the floor level of the houses which is devoted to the human activities of fishing and transport. The space immediately beneath the houses is used for 'parking' the canoes. The top layer is, of course, the level of the floors of the houses which is dictated by the height of the flood and which is where all social and family life, as well as much work in food preparation and repair of fishing nets and traps, takes place. For a short space of time each year the three-layer town reverts to two layers when the water level rises practically to the level of the houses as a result of the flood of the river Ouémé and a reminder of the rhythm of the rainy season hundreds of miles to the north.

There can be few human settlements where such a close and successful relationship between residence and work has been achieved as in Ganvié and where so much ingenuity has been used in making a complete environment including buildings, canoes and work tools such as fishing traps from a few basic materials limited to local timbers (including palm, bamboo and mangrove) and grasses. Happily, the economic future seems assured as the need for the essential protein of fish is expanding in West Africa because of the population increase and the difficulties of obtaining an adequate meat supply in a climate which encourages the depredation of the tsetse fly. Let us hope that the ecological balance will not be upset in the future by over-production or the introduction of ill-considered techniques.

REFERENCES

GAILLARD, DR., 'Le Lac Nokoué', *Geographie*, No. 17, 1908, pp. 281–4 illus.

'Études sur les lacustres du Bas-Dahomey', *Anthropologie*, No. 18, 1907, pp. 99–125.

KINIFFO, LEOPOLD, 'Une Cité Lacustre', *Bulletin Enseign A.O.F.* 82. Janvier/Mars 1933, pp. 15–18.

MERCIER, PAUL, *Cartes Ethno-demographiques de l'Afrique Occidentales*, Feuilles No. 5 (Togo, Dahomey and W. Nigeria), Dakar I.F.A.N.

'Fon of Dahomey' in *African Worlds* (DARYLL FORDE, Ed.) International Africa Institute and O.U.P., 1954, 210–34.

PELISSIER, P., 'Les Pays du Bas Ouémé du Région Temouin Dahomey Meridional' in *Les Cahiers d'Outremer*, Vol. 15, Nos. 59, 60, 61, Bordeaux, 1962–63.

RECLUS, JEAN-JACQUES ELYSÉE, 'Ouêmé et la lagune de Cotonou' Annuaire de Géographie, 1894, 389–90.

The open platform is often surrounded with buildings on three sides, and with access to the water on the fourth side. It functions like a courtyard on land.

NABDAM COMPOUNDS, NORTHERN GHANA

Ian Archer

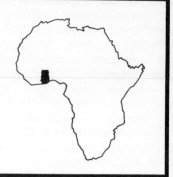

The Nabdam are a small tribe living in north Ghana in the Savannah belt. They are sedentary subsistence farmers living in family compounds consisting of round houses and walled yards built of laterite, and rendered with clay and dung. They may be thatched or occasionally flat roofed. The compound walls are commonly decorated with bold abstract patterns. The people are polygamous with a patrilineal system of inheritance.

It is the purpose of this article to describe the traditional culture of the Nabdam in sufficient detail to discuss the impact of the relatively recent contact that it has made with the more prosperous south, with particular reference to modifications in settlement patterns, and built form.

The Nabdam are members of the Mole Dagbane-speaking peoples, a group of states and tribes which shows considerable cultural uniformity. The history of the very early inhabitants of the northern areas of Ghana is largely lost, but throughout these areas there are myths describing invasions from the north.

Rattray and Fortes believed that five hundred years ago the indigenous inhabitants, the Isala, Vagola and others, had very little political unity, social cohesion consisting of groups of totemic clans

under priests whose influence was spiritual rather than political. They were sedentary people who inherited through the sisters' son.

In contrast, the invaders from the north were, if not Mohammedans, the product of Islam, with military traditions, familiar with the concept of chieftainship and had strong ancestral tradi-

Distribution of Mole-Dagbane speaking peoples

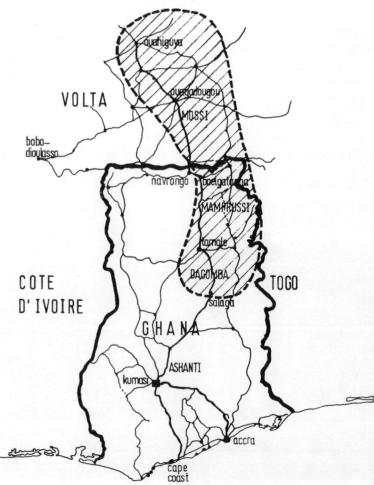

Compound at Bongo

tions protected by patrilineal descent. Because of this, they gave their names and ancestral traditions to the society they invaded, and to some extent were successful in organising the population into states. However, they were small bands of men alone, and by intermarriage, the language, segmented clanship and land customs of the indigenous people remains.

In certain areas myths of origin clearly distinguish between clans who descend from the indigenous people and those descended from the invaders. Two institutions epitomise this social split. One is the office of *Tendaana* (custodian of the earth) held by descendants of the indigenous inhabitants. Their functions are priestly in nature, and their ancestral myths say that they sprang from the earth. This institution is typical of the segmented and homogeneous society of the indigenous people. The other is the office of chief. Their myths of origin suggest a military tradition saying that they came from the north.

The general historical authenticity of these traditions remains in question as there is still the possibility that, as mutual conduct between clans depends so much upon them, these attractive but perhaps too simple explanations of population movement are devices invented for social cohesion.

From time to time, powerful states and confederacies have grown up in the Savannah belt. Today the Nabdam's position has been stabilised by the administration of the British, and later, the State of Ghana, but hitherto, together with other small tribes, the Tallensi, Gorsi and Kussasi, they occupied a no-man's-land between the more politically unified states of Mossi to the north, and Mamprussi to the south. They are in a position where continual warring and population movement has taken place, and their history is consequently complex and difficult to trace. Whether factual or mythical, the traditions that do exist are the framework which shapes their social organisation.

The basic unit of Nabdam society is the minimal lineage, which consists of a man and his children. The maximal lineage consists of an association of people of both sexes comprising all the known

Fetish table, Naba's Compound, Nangodi

descendants of a single known male ancestor in an unbroken male line. Within their lineage, men are supreme in the conduct of lineage affairs and ritual. This is partly because a woman is obliged to marry outside the lineage; she is then separated from her lineage, and is less able to attend the lineage ritual. Furthermore, her children are born outside her own lineage and don't contribute to its continuation.

The maximal lineage is the basic unit of clan structure, a clan consisting of one or more families related by myths of origin, or sometimes with attached lineages related by kinship, through a woman of the authentic male line. The unity of such clans depends upon mutual collaboration in the worship of common ancestors, and the conduct between them is ordered by a mesh of ties and tensions, decided by myths of friendship and feud.

Thus the concept of the Nabdam has no clearly definable border. Kinship and friendship cut across the lineage, the clan structure, and also across tribal structure. The Nabdam are best understood as a people who have more in common with each other in terms of mutual collaboration than with their neighbours, the Tallensi or Gorsi, but this is question of degree. The net of relationships between lineages and clans is sufficiently complex to make the positioning of limits meaningless.

Nangodi and Kongo. Showing distribution of compounds

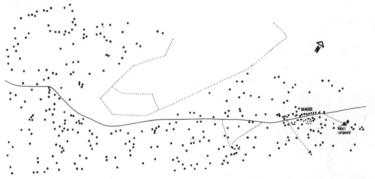

Traditionally, the only social hierarchies were by age. Conduct towards elders went further than mere respect. However, every man was the potential head of his lineage should he live long enough. This social fragmentation goes hand in hand not only with a homogeneous distribution of responsibility and wealth but also accommodated by a highly fragmented settlement pattern. Over areas that are habitable the compounds are evenly distributed, surrounded by their related farming land, and with the exception of recent developments there is little evidence of the concentrations of settlement that are associated with more hierarchical social groups.

When a man dies, his family will usually, in the course of time, split up into its minimal lineages, the eldest son remaining in his father's house, while his brothers will build new compounds. It would not be uncommon for brothers who are close to each other to build adjacent compounds, but they would normally have their own separate compound entrance, indicating mutual, but not essential, co-operation. The compound itself is a loose organisation of laterite round houses and walls, and the amorphous shape is easily broken into and expanded. Furthermore, yearly maintenance is required if

47

they are to withstand the rains, so that unoccupied compounds soon disappear. The built form can thus sensitively respond to expanding and contracting family requirements, and reflects closely the social organisation within.

The topography of north Ghana consists of a monotone of flat plains and gentle slopes of grassland, mapped with gullies which drain to the Volta river system. The forestation becomes sparse as one moves north from the tropical rain forests to the desert. Vegetation is profoundly affected by the marked wet and dry seasons. For six months the ground is arid and bare, with stunted trees occurring uniformly, presenting an unchanging picture. With the monsoons the gullies fill and flood across the land, which springs to life with green grass growing man high.

The Nabdam farm a plateau defined by the Red Volta to the east, the White Volta to the south and the Sissile river to the west, and arbitrarily to the north by the boundary with Upper Volta. The area rises above the plains of Mamprussi and Dagomba, with a more rolling topography and bolder hills of up to five hundred feet in height. It is relatively well drained compared with the plains which become waterlogged during the rains, and arid and useless in the dry season.

Professional minstrels. Parbo's yard. Naba's Compound, Nangodi

Landscape. Bongo

It is at first surprising that the homesteads are not more concentrated about water courses, as some farmers have to travel as much as a mile to collect water. There are remains of settlements built over two hundred years ago close to the main courses of the Volta river system, but it is thought that the spread of population back from the rivers was largely due to a retreat from insect-born diseases like malaria, and sleeping sickness. The relatively high population density in this area compared with that in the plains may in part be explained by the relatively well-drained conditions and hence, some freedom from insect-born diseases. However, the nature of the land, being less subject to erosion, contributes to this in being able to support high-density sedentary farming yielding high protein cereals, compared to the low yield, shifting cultivation typical of the plains. Population densities on the plateau are in the order of five times that on the plains with up to one hundred and seventy people per square mile.

Given the emphasis that the Nabdam put upon the single family economic unit, the nature of the plateau is such that it can support constant sedentary cultivation without lying fallow, and thus can support subsistence level homesteads in an even manner right across its surface.

The basic farming unit, which is to a large extent self-sufficient, is the joint family. This, in its smallest terms, means a man, his wife, children and related older women, but sometimes it means the family head, his brothers, sons and their wives and children.

In the Nangodi area there is a system of markets working on a three-day rota basis, which traditionally was an opportunity for simple barter. Trade specialisation does occur, but traditionally this was no more than a side-line, a man becoming an expert thatcher, builder or leather worker, while farming remained the mainstay of his economy. Division of labour according to sex, age and status is general, but by no means rigid. Mutual co-operation, especially between related families, is common, but is not the rule and depends upon personal relationships.

Each family compound is surrounded first by manured, and then unmanured farmland. Farther removed may be an area devoted to rotational cultivation and fallowing, but the pressing population density has meant that little land is left for this practice. Immediately outside the compound a garden of tobacco, gourds, hibiscus, melon, sweet potatoes and other horticultural crops such as tomatoes and pepper, may be cultivated.

The size of the economic unit, although it is to an extent the result of social and political segmentation, has a basis which is related to farming techniques. Fortes, in his studies of the Tallensi, a neighbouring tribe of the Nabdam, has found that men find it more economic to farm for themselves and break away from the joint family as their children grow. This is partly due to the unexpandable nature of the farm, being surrounded by other land-owners, and partly because there is no economic advantage in farming on a larger scale, using traditional techniques. Primitive farming technique in itself contributes to the segmented nature of land ownership and social structure. The basic pattern of land use is therefore that of the joint family compound occurring in an isolated way in the middle of its related farmland, with land being prepared, manured, seeded, and crops collected in a continuous cycle.

Partly a heritage of times when social tensions were more critical, and when there was a danger from wild animals, is the practice of housing animals within the compound at night. Just inside the entrance of every compound is an animal yard which is demarked from the living quarters by a low wall. Animals are prevented from escaping by wooden bars inserted into holes in laterite piers.

An object of great economic importance, and thus symbolic significance, is the granary. In a small compound this is usually situated between the animal yard and the living areas, and appears on the plan as the hub around which the living areas are radiused. Playing such an important role, especially as grain supplies hover between being insufficient and being at starvation level, the granary becomes an object of status. By saying of brothers living in the same compound that each has his own granary, it is implied that they are running separate economic units, with the status that goes with them. The granary is also the symbol of unity for the joint family: when a joint family breaks up, it is usually on the pretext that the parties require an independent grain supply. In a society of farmers where the fruits of all labour is stored in the granary, and when one's very existence depends upon the proper storage and management of grain, it is not

Laterite entrance piers. Naba's Compound. Nangodi

surprising that the granary becomes the conceptual and physical centre of the farm, and is closely identified with the head of the joint family.

The overwhelming impression of this area is of a long, pervading equilibrium. It becomes meaningless to discuss abstract concepts in terms of the effect that one causes upon another. The idea that one aspect of a culture can be discussed and manipulated against another,

Nabdam Compound, Nangodi

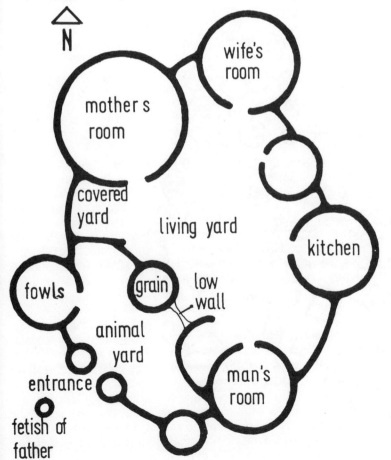

N

wife's room

mother's room

covered yard

living yard

kitchen

fowls

grain

low wall

animal yard

entrance

man's room

fetish of father

Granary. Naba's Compound, Nangodi

which seems so reasonable to the Western mind, has little validity here. For the Nabdam, the essence of existence has been unchanged for five hundred years. Their compounds and farms are not the result of climatic, social and environmental pressures, they are an integral part of the way in which they live. There is no dissociation between the storage function and the symbolic function of the granary. Their ritual ceremonies concerned with ancestors and the earth are no more religious events than they are the mechanisms of inheritance and distribution of resources, and no more these than they are the fabric of social conduct and co-operation.

There has been a long history of limited trade with the Akan States and inevitably, with communications opening with south Ghana, this state of affairs is under attack. The facts of the long and unproductive dry season and of the bare subsistence yield of northern farms have traditionally encouraged the migration south of more adventurous men during the dry season to find work, returning again in March to prepare their farms.

The North has been subjected to a series of 'invasions' from the south – slave raiders, missionaries and the administration of the British. Under the British, arbitrary chiefdoms were set up, with incomes and power, for the purpose of administrative control. Chiefs of this type were hitherto unknown in the area, and compounds of unprecedented size and wealth grew up. One such compound is that of the *Naba* (chief) of Nangodi, Azuri. It appears that there were probably no chiefs, or chiefs of only limited power, before the British came. Some say that the British mistakenly thought the area to belong to a Mamprussi chief at Nalerigu, who then sent his agents to control Nangodi; others say the power came to the Nabdam chiefs directly from the British.

Naba's Compound, Nangodi. Showing building use

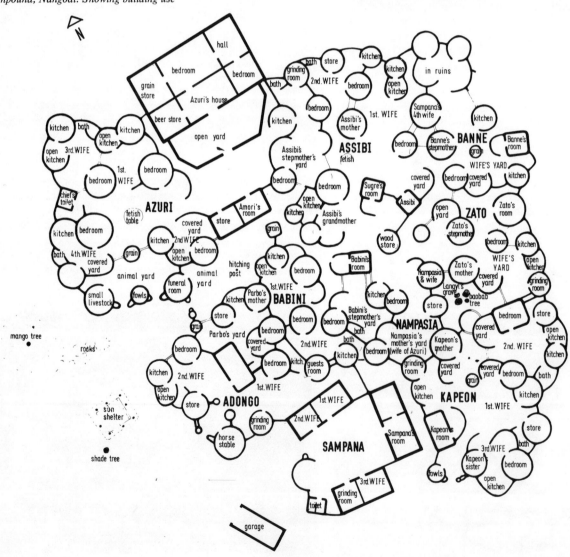

Approach to Naba's Compound, Nangodi

Entrance to Kapeon's Compound. Naba's Compound Nangodi. View from south-east

When the compound was studied in 1965, Azuri had recently died. Hitherto he had lived with his seven brothers, Adongo, Babini, Sampana, Banne, Kapeon, Sugre and Zato, with other members of the same family in another large compound only fifty yards away. Azuri and Adongo were full brothers, as were Sampana and Banne, and all were the sons of Langyil, whose spirit was said to live in a Baobab tree in the centre of the compound, the trunks of which were his arms and chest. The accurate ages of the brothers were not established, but Sugre, Babini and Adongo were obviously older than Sampana and Kapeon, while Zato and Banne were young men with only one wife each. Azuri's son Nampasia, and Sugre's son Assibi, stayed with their wives in the compound as did Azuri's son Amori who was as yet unmarried, and acted as Regent after his father's

death. This is a strikingly large joint family unit, and only makes sense in this area because of the income that the chief received. Furthermore, the inhabitants of the compound are far from typical of Nabdam culture, being in small measure released from the subsistence farming economy.

The same elements that are typical of a Nabdam compound are to be seen here, but without the same organisational clarity. On the south-western side of Azuri's compound, the sub-compounds of Adongo and Kapeon have the most coherence, but at the 'back' of the compound it is impossible to break the traditional Southwest Entrance directly into the sub-compound, neither can the animal yard and granary be articulated with the living spaces in the traditional manner. This is an unusual state of affairs where the fact of the

Naba's Compound, Nangodi. Defining areas of ownership

View across Naba's Compound. Taken from roof of Azuri's mother's internal kitchen. Looking south-east

View from Parbo's covered yard, with Azuri's son Kapeon and Babini

Azuri's second wife's bedroom

government income of the house compensates for the absence of the traditional trappings of independence and for the absence of traditional relationships which are fighting unsuccessfully to exist.

A Nabdam compound, being an amorphous, loosely-organised form is easily expanded to accommodate a growing family. It was evident that the re-building that was being carried out in Babini's sub-compound, because of its constricted position, was causing problems that would not traditionally be experienced.

Sampana had lived in the south for many years, and when he returned north he built a compound closely resembling those built by the Ashanti, with a corrugated aluminium roof. It is probably significant that this compound was almost always empty of people. The sharp definition of inside and outside space does not equal the range of environments produced by the screens, walls and semi-enclosures of the traditional construction, which so aptly accommodates the

complex climate, and the segmented living pattern of the Nabdam. The traditional form of building can be manipulated to create easily a small environ for each wife. The wife will normally decorate the walls of her area by finger-marking the wet rendering as she applies it. Abstract patterns are then applied with vegetable dyes. Sampana's compound had none of this and one felt that the women had been unable to identify with their homes.

Azuri, also, had built himself a rectangular building constructed of sun-dried bricks, cement rendered, with timber rafters and aluminium roof. The comfort conditions in this building were very poor compared with the traditional laterite and thatch round house. But these aluminium-roofed buildings were not the only examples of rectangular forms creeping into use. There were ten other laterite and thatch structures with approximately rectangular plan-forms, and it is probably significant that all of these, with the notable exception of

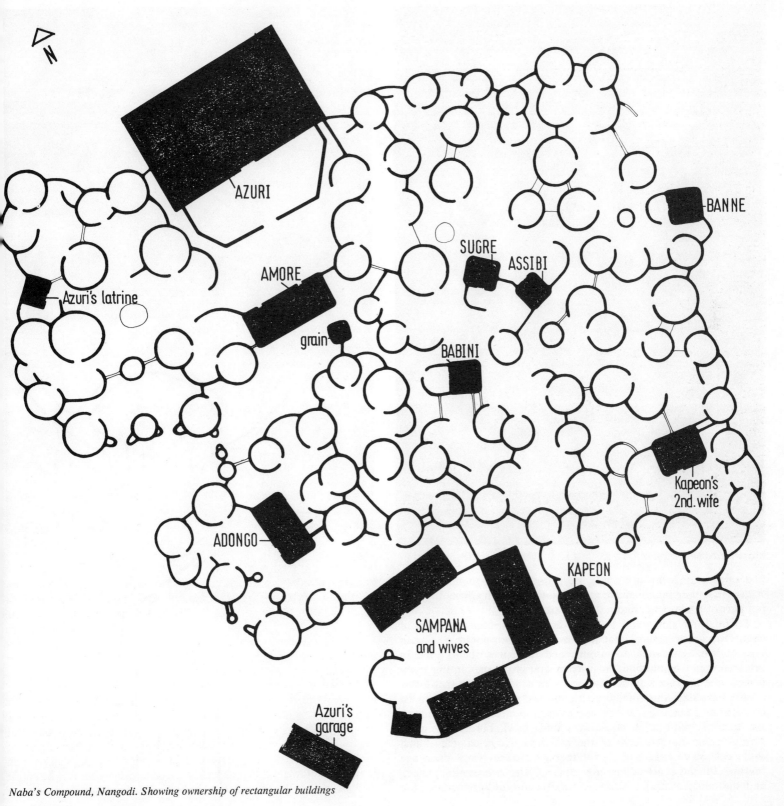

AZURI

BANNE

Azuri's latrine

AMORE

SUGRE

ASSIBI

grain

BABINI

Kapeon's
2nd. wife

ADONGO

KAPEON

SAMPANA
and wives

Azuri's
garage

Naba's Compound, Nangodi. Showing ownership of rectangular buildings

Kapeon's second wife's yard

Azuri's first wife's bedroom
Kapeon's first wife's bedroom

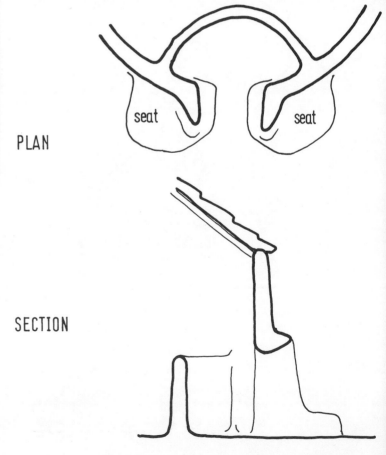

PLAN

SECTION

that of Kapeon's favourite wife, were the personal rooms of men. Although square buildings are not unknown in north Ghana they are not part of traditional building in this area.

To interpret this trend towards the use of rectilinear forms it should be acknowledged that it is easier to incorporate European type bedsteads in such a building, and these were being used in preference to the traditional mat by several of the men in this compound, and also by Kapeon's second wife. It is also true that linear roofing materials, like corrugated aluminium, are more sensibly used on rectilinear buildings, and the increasing availability of such materials to those with surplus resources must inevitably be having its impact upon the geometry of the buildings. However, the almost exclusive use of square forms for the men's own rooms, or in one instance for the construction of a granary, itself a masculine object, and the use of such forms where traditional building methods are

Bazomyine's room and Azuri's son Kapeon

Bazomyine's room (Lives with Assibi's grandmother)

Adongo's first wife's room

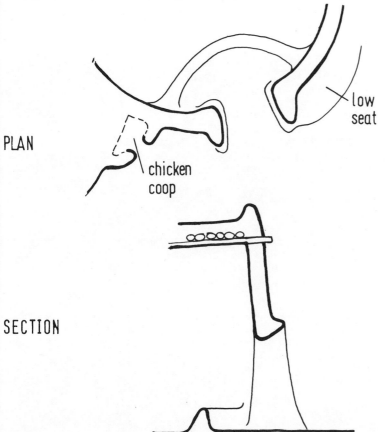

PLAN

low seat

chicken coop

SECTION

PLAN

wall 1'-7" high

seat

SECTION

aluminium porch

timber door

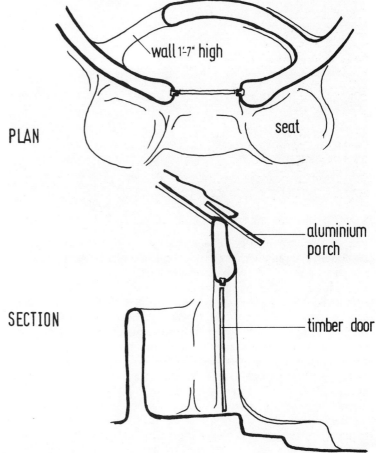

Professional Builders. Babini's Compound

Nabdam kitchen with gourds, clay pots and enamel bowls

Another Nabdam kitchen

Children. Naba's Compound, Nangodi

Sampana's Compound

employed, would suggest that these men associate this with the more prosperous south, and the local administrative buildings closer at hand in Bolgatanga.

The traditional Nabdam door opening into a round house consists of a short, almost semi-circular, tunnel of about 2 feet 4 inches in height through which one has to crawl. Inside there is a low wall over which one then has to climb. This 'lock' effectively keeps out rain, wind and aggressors, man or mammal, while continuing to allow ventilation to take place. Furthermore the form, with its rounded, smooth surfaces, admirably suits the laterite construction, causing no shrinkage cracking. The door openings in Azuri's aluminium house and Sampana's compound of course bear no resemblance to traditional door openings, having timber doors and frames, with sometimes a padlock. Where rectangular openings have been built into round houses there are many variations. Zato's mother's room has no internal wall, while the heavy laterite moulding around the door frame resembles the traditional tunnel-like entrance. Adongo's first wife's room has a large timber door and door frame, the tunnel effect having almost disappeared, while the internal wall is still present but has been cut down in one position to aid entry.

The rectangular openings without the tunnel provide little resistance to the penetration of rain, and small aluminium or reed porches have been built into the thatch over many of the openings. In some cases the rectangular openings were cracking at the corners, due partly to the load on the laterite of hanging a door, and partly due to the uneven distribution of stress, which is not so marked in the rounded openings. Most of the senior women, and none of the men, had traditional door openings into their rooms, which is a measure of the relative impact of external influences according to both sex and age.

Inevitably, it is not only the building-forms that are changing. Assibi, the eldest son of Sugre, is a local teacher and earns a wage. The respect that his intellectual capacities, and wage-earning ability command is illustrated by the fact that the sub-compound that he shares with his father is called by the rest of the compound 'Assibi's House', which is a direct challenge to the age hierarchy in his lineage.

With money becoming available to people like Assibi, and those who have been earning in the south, job specialisation is becoming increasingly common. Professional builders from Bolgatanga were being employed by Babini at Azuri's compound. They were constructing a rectangular building in laterite and thatch. Traditionally, when a man takes a new wife, the general distribution of new buildings is discussed by the family and the *Tendaana*, and marked out on the ground. The buildings are then erected by the men, and rendered and decorated by the women who are to occupy. The wall paintings are bold, and, within limits, excitingly varied from house to house, so that each woman's domain is physically and stylistically delineated. However, Babini's new building did not resemble a Nabdam house in concept or detail. It marks the beginning of the decay of local differentiation of building styles, and more important, curtails the traditional participation in the tailoring of a house. Enamel pots and pans were in use in this compound, along with many small utilitarian consumer products, and the transistor radio is an important enough symbol of status to be carried on ceremonial occasions or for an important photograph.

The impact of change in this area is all the more apparent because of the synthesis of all aspects of Nabdam life. Time has mellowed and refined their farming techniques, their architecture and their social conduct so that all are an essential part of total existence. High infant mortality and the severe endemic diseases are integral parts of a life of subsistence level farming which, although born of poverty, has a measure of equality about it. Hitherto, all men conducted a similar basic existence and were availed of similar basic economic and social opportunities. There had been built up a body of knowledge consisting of traditions, rituals and taboos for dealing with familiar and recurrent situations, and it is evident in the way, for instance, that new building materials are being handled, and the quality of environment that results, that these traditional capabilities are coming under considerable pressure.

With the opening up of roadways the Nabdam are being increasingly exposed to developments in south Ghana and its associated living standards and values. It was even, on occasions, possible to hear 'The Beatles' being played over transistor radios in Azuri's house. The major exports of Ghana, timber and cocoa, are centred in the rain forests. The Nabdam are thus aware of, and yet remote from, these developments. One can simply hope that they are not overwhelmed into discarding the very valuable things that they have without being able to participate in the development of the national economy.

BIBLIOGRAPHY

RATTRAY, R. S., *The Tribes of the Ashanti Hinterland*, Oxford University Press, 1932.
FORTES, M., *The Web of Kinship Amongst the Tallensi*, Oxford University Press, 1949.
FORTES, M., *Dynamics of Clanship Amongst the Tallensi*, Oxford University Press, 1945.
Nangodi Report, 1965. Compiled by students and staff of the Faculty of Architecture, Kumasi University of Science and Technology, Ghana.

HOUSING IN ZARIA

Friedrich Schwerdtfeger

Detail of wall decoration; Emir's palace in Zaria.

INTRODUCTION

Urbanization in Africa is a growing phenomenon and interest in all aspects of urban housing is rapidly increasing. The development of urban centres with its inevitable repercussion on the domestic house-type has a long standing history in the predominantly Moslem region of sub-Saharan Africa.

The object of this article is to discuss the urban settlement pattern in Zaria, a town in Hausaland which forms part of northern Nigeria, and the factors which have contributed to its development.

Hausa domestic architecture can be described as the result of man's struggle to solve his essential needs for shelter in a given society with a specific type of family organisation, a distinctive economy, technology and corpus of social and religious rules. As the centre of most activities of the members of the family that occupy it, the house is an ideal nucleus for systematic social and economic investigation. In this article I will point out some of the historic events which have influenced the present settlement pattern, and then give a brief description of the layout and construction of six compounds drawn from a larger sample which was selected for detailed study within the walled city of Zaria. This will be followed by a discussion on certain features of Hausa family organization and the close relationship between changes in family composition, size and changes in the structure and appearance of these compounds.

Many interesting subjects connected with this topic, such as climatic influences on house design as well as the vital question of building economics, have been omitted from this paper for reasons of space; but I hope to discuss these questions in other publications.

The survey on which this article is based was carried out in Zaria city between May and October 1968.

THE ENVIRONMENTAL SETTING

Climate [1]

Zaria city, lat. 11.07, long. 07.44, with a population of 53,974 in 1952, is situated in the middle of high, rolling savanna plains of Hausaland amidst some striking *kopjes* or *inselbergs* – exfoliation domes that rise abruptly often several hundred feet above the precambrian base.

The climate is dominated by the seasonal shifting of pressure belts, the continental air masses blowing southwards from the north-east from November to March, which is the *harmattan* season, while the equatorial maritime air masses blow northwards from the south-west in May to September to create the rainy season – thus developing monsoon characteristics during the northern Nigerian summer.

However, the local people distinguish four seasons as follows:

Bazara: mid-February to mid-May, the hot dry season of the harmattan;

Damina: mid-May to the end of August, the rainy season;

Kaka: end of August to the end of November, the harvest season; and

Rani: end of November to mid-February, the cold dry season of the *harmattan*.

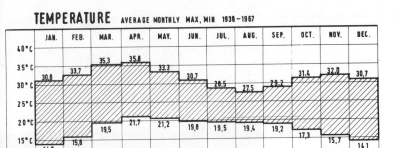

TEMPERATURE AVERAGE MONTHLY MAX, MIN 1936 – 1967

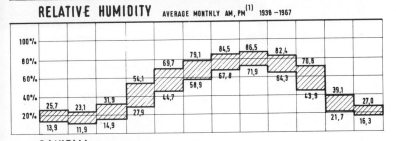

RELATIVE HUMIDITY AVERAGE MONTHLY AM, PM [1] 1936 – 1967

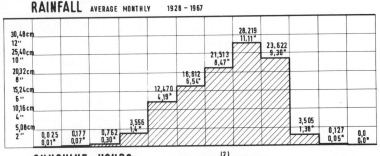

RAINFALL AVERAGE MONTHLY 1928 – 1967

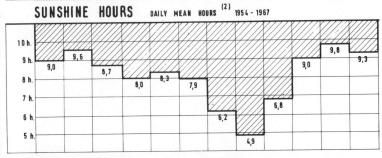

SUNSHINE HOURS DAILY MEAN HOURS [2] 1954 – 1967

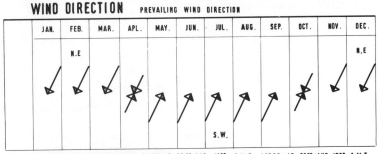

WIND DIRECTION PREVAILING WIND DIRECTION

(1) BEFORE 1953 OBSERVATION TAKEN AT 06°° AND 13°° G.M.T. AFTER AT 09°° AND 15°° G.M.T.
(2) SUNSHINE RECORDS FROM CAMPBELL STOKES RECORDER

The components of climate in Zaria: Temperature, Relative humidity, Rainfall, Sunshine hours, and Wind direction.

Vegetation and Soils

Although Savanna grassland is the climax vegetation over much of Hausaland, the region can be roughly divided into two main zones, with different types of vegetation as follows:

(a) the North Guinea Zone, the subhumid northern part of the middle belt: and
(b) the Sudan Savanna, the southern border of which runs broadly west–east through the northern part of Zaria province.

Human interference with the natural vegetation by cultivation, by burning the grass cover to clear farmland or generate pasture has modified the natural development of the environment to such an extent, particularly around the big Hausa cities,[2] that we can describe the current flora as 'biotically determined sub-climax vegetation'.[3] Vegetation patterns follow closely the gradient of rainfall distribution; as the average annual rainfall dips below 1.143 m, or 45 inches, the high open forests of the North Guinea Zone are progressively replaced by the Sudan or parkland savanna. In the North Guinea Zone, seasonally waterlogged depressions support a fair number of raphia or fan-palms, which being resistant to termites, are in great demand for roof beams. Grasses sometimes 6 feet high, are used as raw material for roofing and mat-weaving. Gallery forests with tree species that have affinities with the South Guinea Zone may also develop alongside streams and well-watered places.

The typical Sudan savanna vegetation is more open and consists mainly of shrubs or low orchard bush, and fine-leaved thorny trees, such as acacias, many of which have Sahilian affinities; but there are also some hardy broad-leaved trees of the North Guinea Zone which decline in numbers further north. Grass-cover in the savanna is more or less continuous but it is usually short and less suitable for roofing material than in the North Guinea Zone. Outside the principal towns, or wherever water is available, we find such economic trees as the shea butter tree, *Acacia albida* and *Tamarindus indica*.

In Northern Hausaland the underlying rocks have been covered by superficial sand deposits that derive from the nearby Sahara. As we move south, these sand deposits lessen, and the soil character changes from a light sandy layer with poor fertility, but easy to work and ideal for cotton and groundnuts, to the heavier type of soil found in the south. The red laterite soil (*jan kasa*) found around Zaria, which often has a high clay content, tends to become waterlogged in the rainy season; but in the dry second half of the harmattan this soil dries out and tends to crack. A well-selected mixture of such soil skilfully prepared makes excellent material for building walls and roofs.

The Human Pattern

The people living in Zaria walled city are generally referred to as Hausa but they fall in fact into two main ethnic groups: the Hausa — who are the indigenous population – and the Fulani, who are divided into three sub-groups: the *Filanin daji*, or bush Fulani, a pastoral nomadic people; the *Agwai*, or semi-settled Fulani, who are only found in rural areas, and the *Filanin gida*, or house Fulani, who are settled mainly in the towns and have formed the ruling class of Zaria emirate since 1807.

THE HISTORICAL BACKGROUND

The origin and early history of the Hausa people is somewhat obscure.[5] It seems probable that during the ninth and tenth centuries A.D. a wave of immigrants from the east came into this area.[6] We have however, some knowledge about the region during the fourteenth and fifteenth centuries from travellers who wrote about their

The position of the big empires in the western Sudan in the fifteenth century and the trade routes across the Sahara.

adventures, e.g. Al Bakri,[7] Ibn Battuta[8] and Leo Africanus,[9] to name only the most important.

The history of Hausaland falls roughly into four periods: the Habe Kingdom, the Fula Empire, the Colonial Period and the period of Independence of Nigeria since 1960.

1. *The rise of the Habe Kingdom, the introduction of Islam and the fall of the Habe dynasties in the early nineteenth century*

Daura Makas Sariki,[10] the legend of Daura, records in the middle of the eleventh century that there was a Habe Kingdom in Daura which was ruled by a queen. A certain traveller named Ba'ijidda, son of Abdullah, King of Baghdad, came to Daura and killed the snake (*sariki*) which was living in the main well of the town. For this he was chosen by the queen as her husband. Their descendants were the first

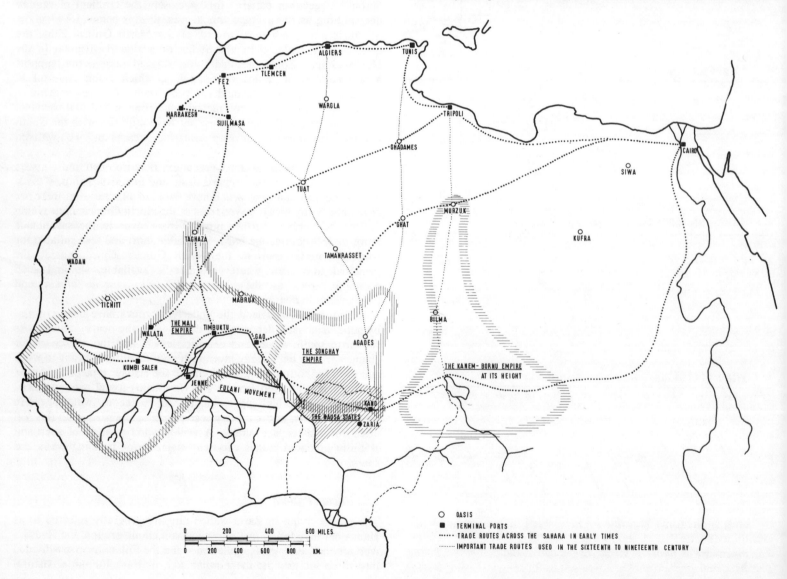

○	OASIS
■	TERMINAL PORTS
┄┄┄	TRADE ROUTES ACROSS THE SAHARA IN EARLY TIMES
┈┈┈	IMPORTANT TRADE ROUTES USED IN THE SIXTEENTH TO NINETEENTH CENTURY

kings of the seven Hausa states (*Hausa bakwai*).[11] One of these states was Zazzau, or Zaria.

A chronicle of the early history of the Hausa Kingdom of Zaria speaks of Amina, daughter of the well-remembered pagan ruler Bakwa Turunku, as a great conqueror, who ruled Zaria from 1492 to 1522, defeating the Jukun and making Zaria independent. It is further reported that Bakwa (Bakwa (f) = Bako (m)) was the last king or queen who ruled in Turunku, a place seventeen miles south of Zaria, and that his (or her) second daughter Zaria, sister of Amina, built the last of the five capitals of Zaria in its present position and gave it her name.

Islam was introduced to Kano, 110 miles north of Zaria from Mali, in the first half of the fourteenth century but only reached Zaria in 1456.[12] The new religion seemed to have spread rapidly, particularly among the wealthy people in the towns of the kingdom, but later occasional pagan rulers, and women who filled important posts in the administration, appear on the list of local chiefs.

The Fulani, first mentioned as Peul or Pullo (sing.), were in the tenth century a small group living in what is now known as Senegal. Over the years they wandered eastwards and in the early sixteenth century they crossed the border of Hausaland. There they were welcomed by the Hausa kings and either settled as *Filanin gida* in towns or continued grazing their cattle as pastoralists.

If we accept the folk tradition, most of the Habe records were destroyed during the Fulani *Jihad*[13] of 1804–10, the Habe kings and their administration were then corrupt, unjust, and imposed high taxation on their subjects to meet their rising war expenses and other commitments. This was the political background against which Uthman Dan Fodio, a Fulani religious leader, began to preach his religious doctrine against the Habe kings of Gobir during the last years of the eighteenth century, thus initiating developments which led in 1804 to a holy war that witnessed the downfall of the Habe dynasties in Hausaland.

Before reviewing the second historical period when Hausaland formed part of the Fulani Empire, it is necessary to mention the trading relations between North Africa and the old Sudan and their effects on the development of the states south of the Sahara from the tenth century onwards.

Trans-Saharan trade expanded rapidly after the Moslem Arabs had conquered the Mediterranean coast of North Africa in the eighth century A.D. A wide network of caravan routes developed and the organised commerce that flowed thereon probably determined the position, wealth and growth of the big Sudanese trading terminals. Initially it seems the trade was mainly an exchange of southern gold for northern salt, but as the traffic expanded, this changed, and an increasing flow of consumer goods from North Africa, Asia and Europe reached the markets in return for gold, slaves, ivory, leather and other Sudanese products. But of far greater importance, and of wide-reaching consequence, was the introduction of a new religion by Arab traders and *marabouts* (holy men). These new religious ideals, with their law and written language, were to have an enormous and continuing influence on the whole of the old Sudan. The first real impact of Islam was naturally felt in the big trading

towns, where scholars and traders from the Maghreb settled down to teach the Holy Koran and the rules of Islam to native chiefs, officials and traders. In the beginning Islam was restricted to these towns and it remained there as a predominant urban religion for many centuries.

As the flourishing trade depended on the safety of its caravan routes, the towns these linked grew rapidly, so that new house types, better suited to cope with the increasing density, and at the same time capable of preserving and possibly improving the security and privacy of the family, were needed.

There is little doubt that the new religion with its strict rules, and the newly built houses of the Maroccan and Arab traders must have influenced local building practices.[14] The seclusion of women, which in the Koran refers directly only to the wives of the Prophet,[15] became an institution of every family with Moslem pretensions, and is still widely practised, with certain exceptions[16] in the Emirates of northern Nigeria. Once the Sudanese kings had become Moslems, the Mukhtassar of Sidi Khalil, better known as Maliki Law, provided the base for the judicial authority and offered legal guidance on religious affairs as well as on matters like marriage and divorce, the rights of women and building regulations.[17]

2. Fulani Empire

After his victory over Makau in *c*. 1807, the last Habe king of Zaria, Malam Musa, was appointed to rule Zaria by his leader, Uthman Dan Fodio, and for the first time in their history, the Hausa states were all united under a single overlord, the Fulani Sultan or Caliph of Sokoto. In a book called *Kitab Al Farq*, which was probably written by Uthman Dan Fodio himself and which certainly reflects his ideas, the foundations for a new system of government were laid down and five points particularly stressed. Uthman proclaimed that 'Power shall not be given to one who seeks it,' and urged 'the need for consultation, doing away with harshness, fair justice and good works'.[18] As a united and peaceful (religious) group, trade as well as art and crafts developed favourably throughout these Fulani provinces, and Kano then became the largest trading centre in the Western Sudan.[19]

A succession of European explorers – Clapperton, Denham and Oudney in 1821,[20] Clapperton and Lander in 1826, and Heinrich Barth in 1851–54[21] – visited most of the Hausa capitals including Sokoto, leaving vivid descriptions of the country, its rulers and the wealth of its people. Under Fulani rule the Moslem religion and religious laws were enforced and strengthened. The conquered land (*wakf*) was distributed among the leading Fulani families for their help in the *jihad* and many slave villages (*rumada*) were founded by them in the emirates. Slave labour was used mainly for agriculture but also to build houses in towns and to carry out the necessary annual repairs.

3. The Colonial Period and Independence

With the advance of British forces from Lokoja under Sir F. D. Lugard, later Lord Lugard, in 1901–2, Zaria came under British rule. Captain Abadie became the first resident in Zaria. The British administration deposed Kwassau, *Sarkin Zassau* in 1902 and replaced him with Aliyu, a grandson of Malam Musa, the Galadima Suleimann acting as regent during the interval.

After the conquest of Sokoto by the British, Zaria Emirate was reduced and its former vassal states Keffi, Nassarawa and Jema'a, were removed as independent chiefdoms. Slavery was abolished and in the following years the foundation of a modern economy with its infrastructure, new laws, educational system and health service was gradually laid down, leading in 1960 to independence.

Zaria township, showing the areas of investigation.

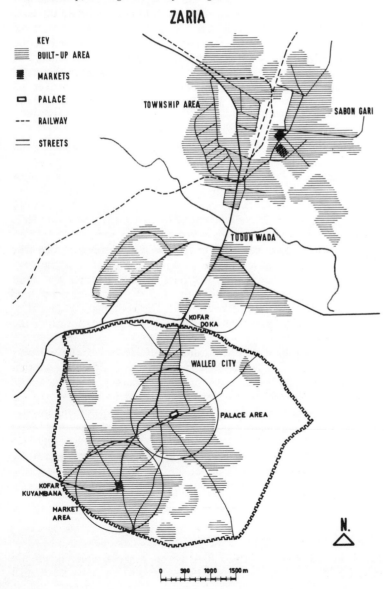

ZARIA

KEY
- ≣ BUILT-UP AREA
- ▮ MARKETS
- ▭ PALACE
- --- RAILWAY
- ═ STREETS

TOWNSHIP AREA

SABON GARI

TUDUN WADA

KOFAR DOKA

WALLED CITY

PALACE AREA

KOFAR KUYAMBANA

MARKET AREA

N.

0 500 1000 1500 m

Zaria is divided into three main parts: Tudun Wada, the Sabon Gari and the walled city.

Tudun Wada is a nineteenth-century settlement which stands just outside the wall near the Doka gate (*Kofar Doka*) of the old town. Hausa traders, mainly from other parts of the north as well as other northern minority groups such as Kanuri and Tiv, being unable to build their houses in the walled city, settled here to make a living in the city markets.

The Sabon Gari (New Town) including the European township area, which has grown up since the railway reached Zaria in 1911 is located on the north side of the river Kubani. Traders and craftsmen from Southern Nigeria have settled in the new town, which developed over the years as a prosperous trading centre exchanging European and Southern Nigerian goods, e.g. Kola nuts, palm oil or fruits for products like cotton, groundnuts, beans, guinea corn, cattle and hides from the north.

The walled city, from within which all the compounds discussed later were chosen, has one main street running roughly from the *Kofar Doka* southwards to the market and thence at approximately right angles westwards through the *Kuyambana* gate towards Kaduna.

The majority of compounds in Zaria walled city, connected by narrow winding footpaths or tracks, cluster around the two most important institutions, common to all traditional Hausa towns, namely the palace and the central mosque which together form the political–religious centre, and the market, the socio-economic centre.

The ruling Fulani families, the religious leaders and the employees of the local administration are concentrated in the palace area. Land for building was first given by the emirs to these families, whose rights of occupation, use and succession continue indefinitely, unless the family dies out, in which case its land returns to the emir. Thus ownership of land in the European sense does not exist, although in the last thirty years the practice of buying and selling land has increased, particularly in the market area, where traders, craftsmen and *mallams* (Koranic teachers) live.

THE COMPOUND (*GIDA*)

The principal layout of present-day compounds in the walled city is surprisingly uniform, and may derive, with little change, from a very early compound. This assumption is based on the fact that throughout its history Zaria has never served as an international trading centre like Kano, Gao or Timbuktu. No, or very few Arab traders settled here in early times; and the influence of the new religion with its associated development may have lagged behind the more important trading terminals to the north.[22] Unlike the Moslem states north of the Sahara, women played an important part in the politico–social life of the town of Zaria, holding high official posts in the Habe kingdom and were still allowed to move freely around the town in the early period of Moslem rule.[23] The segregation of women, which exercises a profound influence on the layout and arrangement of huts in compounds, developed relatively late, in the eighteenth and nineteenth century.

Zaria city within its ancient wall still contains a considerable area of open land used for agriculture. This spaciousness is reflected in the palace area in many of its residential units with their dispersed arrangement of huts. Even around the market area, which has a much higher population density than the palace area, domestic layout does not substantially depart from the general principle of maximum privacy for the women's quarters; but in the market area enclosed open spaces, such as courtyards, are drastically reduced in size. Within the basic principle, a very wide variety of compounds can be found of different sizes and appearances that clearly reflect the wealth and status of their owners.

The compound shown (House number 39) which is situated in the palace area belongs to a *mallam*. The unit is surrounded by a mud wall 3·50 m high. The round entrance hut (*zaure*), numbered as room 1, with a lobby in front, has an internal diameter of 4·40 m. Its round mud wall, supporting the conical thatched roof, is approximately 50 cm thick, with a reddish mud plaster as a finish on both sides. One oval, two round and one square grass mat, as well as several goat skins, are laid out on the floor which has a cement finish. In the *zaure* the compound head (*maigida*) sits often to practise his craft as a tailor or embroiderer, or, as in this case, to teach the Koran. Here

also, he rests and receives his guests and friends. No male stranger is allowed further into the compound and only a very good friend or a trustworthy personality of high rank is entertained in the second entrance hut (*shigifa*), numbered as room 4. The door of the *zaure* which leads to the interior is always covered with a straw mat to prevent male visitors from looking into the first courtyard (*kofar gida*). Here there are normally two or three huts for overnight guests, servants or adolescent sons. Most forecourts also have a pit latrine and a wash place located in one of the corners. If the compound head possesses a horse, it may also be tethered here in an open space.

The second entrance hut (*shigifa*: rooms 4 and 5) is usually divided into a larger room, which is used for meetings and furnished like the *zaure*, and a smaller interior one which is used as a store for mortars, large pots and other heavy kitchen equipment. If the household head entertains guests in the larger room, his wives will often gather silently in the smaller one behind to listen to his conversation.

The interior of the residential unit (*cikin gida*), where only close relatives of the house head — women, girls and boys under the age of puberty — are permitted, contains the women's quarters (numbered on the plan rooms 6–13) and the hut of compound head known as the *turaka* (room numbers 14 and 15). In case the compound head cannot afford a hut of his own, he will sleep with each of his wives in

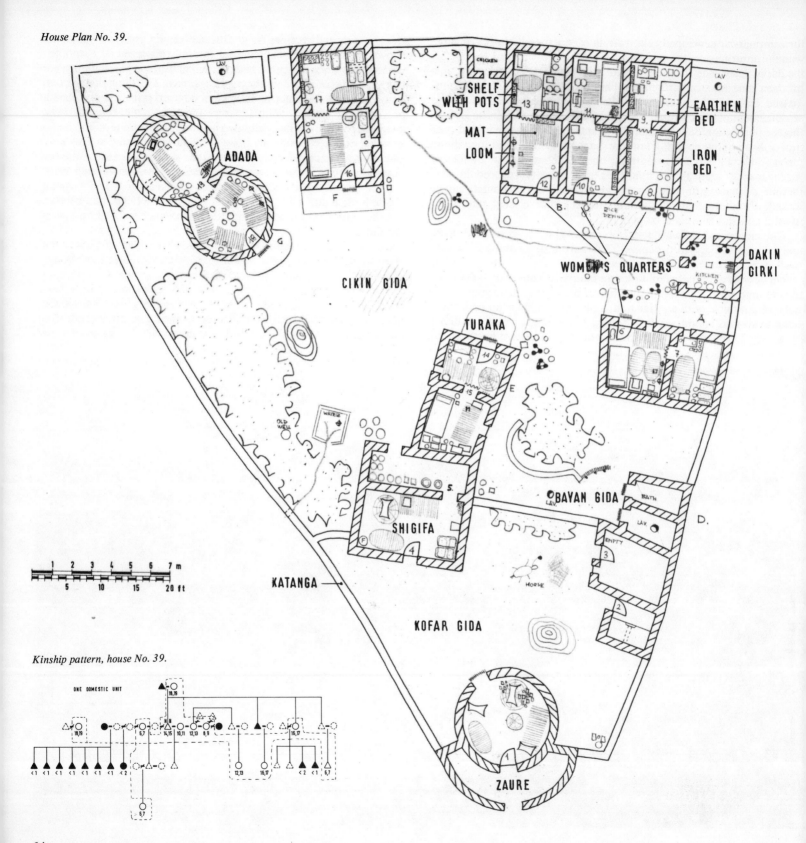

House Plan No. 39.

LAV.

17

ADADA

16

F

G

CHICKEN

SHELF WITH POTS

13

MAT

LOOM

12

11

9

10

8

B

RICE DRYING

LAV.

EARTHEN BED

IRON BED

WOMEN'S QUARTERS

DAKIN GIRKI

KITCHEN

A

6

7

CIKIN GIDA

OLD WELL

WATER

TURAKA

14

15

E

SHIGIFA

5

F

4

BAYAN GIDA

LAV.

BATH

LAV.

EMPTY

3

2

D

KATANGA

KOFAR GIDA

HORSE

1

ZAURE

Scale: 1 2 3 4 5 6 7 m / 5 10 15 20 ft

Kinship pattern, house No. 39.

ONE DOMESTIC UNIT

18,19

18,19

6,7

14,15

10,11

12,13

8,9

16,19

<1 <1 <1 <1 <1 <1 <2

12,13

16,17

<2 <1 6,7

6,7

64

turn in their huts, normally for two days at a time. Otherwise, each wife will join him in the *turaka* in her proper turn. Also located in the *cikin gida* may be the huts of his married son or sons, his brothers' and his divorced sister – as in the present example, rooms 16 and 17 – and his widowed mother (rooms 18 and 19). The dry season cooking-place and the wet season kitchen (*dakin girki*) are located in a central space. Since the women's quarters are segregated, nearly every compound in Zaria city has its own well, and some have piped water. Pit latrines and bathrooms, which are either roofed or surrounded by a wall, stand alongside the main compound wall, often in close proximity to the well, and constitute a serious health problem. Poultry pens and granaries are always located within the *cikin gida*.

The second example (house 78) is chosen from the market area and belongs to a very prosperous trader who has a shop in Zaria city market, as well as one in Sabon Gari.

This compound is located in a very dense built-up area and has an upper floor (*bene*) where the compound head has his rooms. The courtyard floor and courtyard walls are in mud plaster. The square entrance room, measuring $4 \cdot 30 \times 4 \cdot 70$ m, also has a cement floor

which is covered with two huge oval and square grass mats and one or two goat skins. This room is also occasionally used as a store for bags of millet, rice and guinea-corn, commodities in which the owner trades. A second adjoining room, the passage, and the following two small rooms through which every person has to pass before reaching the central courtyard, fulfil the same function as the forecourt and the *shigifa* in the previous example. The women's quarters, rooms 7–10, are characteristically arranged around a common central hall, room 6, which is used by the wives all as a daily working place for food preparation and for weaving, spinning or embroidering caps. The present head inherited the compound from his father in 1964 and lives there with his two wives, one daughter, his half-brother and the latter's wife, and his father's widowed last wife and her grandson.

Our third example (house 68) was chosen from the outskirts of the market area. This compound stands near the town wall and belongs to two brothers and their dependants who are engaged in agriculture and crafts (weaving).

Through the entrance hut, which serves as the working space for the compound head and his brother, the forecourt is reached. The

Kinship pattern, House No. 78.

ONE DOMESTIC UNIT

House Plan No. 78.

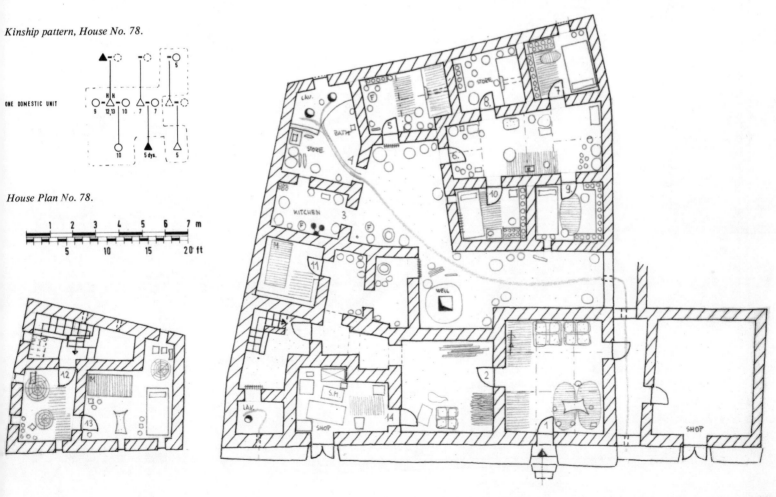

second entrance hut is used as a pen for goats. The *cikin gida* has seven huts with a total of thirteen rooms occupied by three families and two childless couples. All huts are roofed with thatch. the walls are of mud and room floors of rammed earth. Rooms 3 and 4 on the plan were built in 1965 and 1967 respectively to replace a decayed double round hut (*adada*). The ruined double round hut on the other side of the compound, which has no roof on the outer room, formerly belonged to a deceased brother of the present head, and has been allowed to collapse since his death. Of the granaries in the *cikin gida* two belong to the compound head, two to his junior brother, and

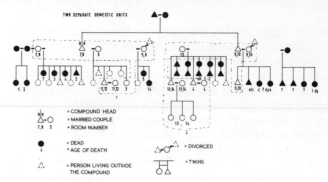

Kinship pattern, House No. 68.

House Plan No. 68.

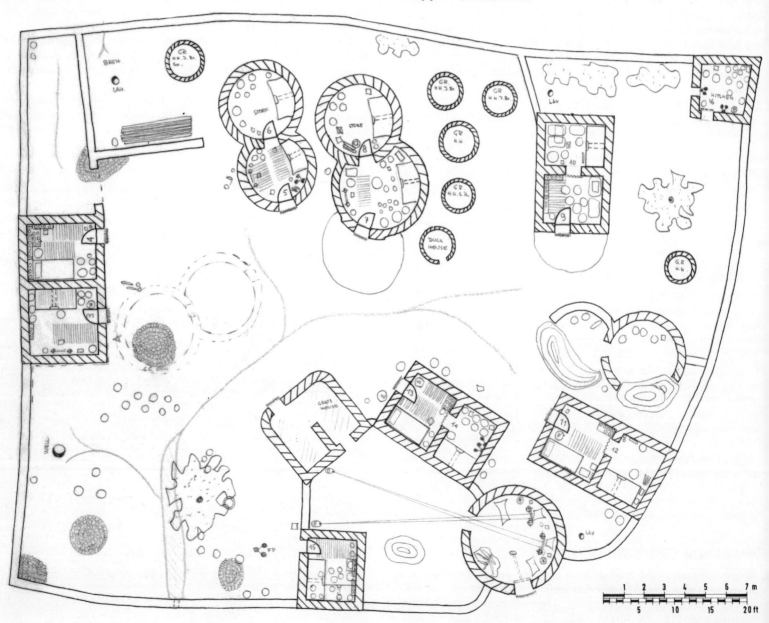

one each to the oldest sons of the compound head and his brother respectively. A common wet season kitchen is situated in the upper right-hand corner on the plan. The whole family group farms and feeds together during the rainy season in a *gandu*[24] under the leadership of the compound head. During this period food is prepared together and cooked by the women in two-day turns, while throughout the dry season each individual family cooks and eats separately from its granaries.

FURNITURE

Furniture, as we understand it, was almost absent from a traditional home at Zaria. People were accustomed to sit and work on grass mats on the beaten earth floors, and the only built-in equipment in a traditional room is the earthen bed which could be heated with embers from underneath. An occasional upright loom, half a dozen clay pots or calabashes, and the very low round wooden stool, which is used by women, complete the traditional furniture of a woman's hut. Basically this has not changed, but the influence of new, mainly western types of furniture is increasingly apparent.

To illustrate the changes that are taking place it is necessary to describe briefly the interiors of a typical women's two-roomed hut such as we would find in the first compound described above (rooms 10 and 11). There the front room is usually furnished with a wooden or iron bed with square or oval mats on the floor, a low stool and frequently a small table or a wooden box. On the wall there may be from one to half a dozen shelves on which decorative metal pots of similar design but differing size are placed, the number ranging from a few to as many as 950 counted in one room. These pots are wedding presents to the woman and their number indicates the status of her family and that of her husband.

A curtain covers the door to the second room which is sometimes used as a store, containing countless boxes, pots, calabashes, bags and baskets, and which usually has an earthen bed for child-birth. Most rooms, but particularly the outer one, are very clean and tidy, the walls are whitewashed, but any window will be narrow and small. Typically the hut will have a cement platform in front which is used as an outside working place for food preparation, cooking and handicrafts, as well as to dry rice and pepper.

The room occupied by the household head (*turaka*) normally contains a wooden or iron bed, one or two chairs, a couple of fair-sized boxes or even a small cupboard where he stores his possessions, and the floor is normally covered with goat skins and a round praying mat. Often a mattress lies beside the bed. Several bags of corn, millet or rice representing the season's food supply may be piled in one of the corners. This room is out of bounds for all members of the household, who may only enter when asked to do so.

CONSTRUCTION AND DECORATION

When the compound head decides to build one or two huts, a sufficient quantity of earth is excavated from the nearest borrow pit and transported to the building site. Here the earth is put in heaps of approximately 80 to 90 cm high, water is added and the mud is trampled until it has the consistency of mortar. This material is then moulded into bricks of traditional type which are shaped like circular cones, about half the size of a rugby football, and then left to dry in the sun for at least two weeks. Meanwhile the foundation of the house is dug about 50 cm deep, to penetrate below the loose top soil. The dried bricks are then laid in courses, each of which is covered with a layer of mud mortar, consisting of mud and horse manure, or short cut grass which is mixed carefully before the mixture is used.

There are basically two types of roof construction used in Zaria city; the thatched roof and the mud roof. The latter falls into two categories; a vaulted roof supported by arches (*baka*) and a flat roof. A corrugated iron roof set on top of a mud roof is increasingly used to ward off the heavy downpours in the rainy season but this is still restricted to the houses of the wealthy.

The frame of a thatched roof is constructed either of bamboo, of raphia palm stems, or, if the roof is small, of guinea corn stalks tied together with bonds of straw and locally woven rope. The thatch is bought in bundles approximately 1 m high, which, if unrolled, would be at least 7·50 m long. These bundles are then wrapped around the frame, each layer being set 10–15 cm above the previous one and fixed to the framework. The roof is then bound by a web of local rope which secures the thatch to the frame against strong winds.

Flat mud roofs are constructed for rooms not bigger than 3 m × 4 m. Poles of deleb palm (*azara*) not exceeding 0·05 × 0·10 × 2·40 m are made by splitting the male palm tree lengthways and set side by side diagonally across the corners at the top of the wall, progressively inwards. The remaining central parts are filled in as shown in the picture. A *zana* mat is then spread over the sticks and covered first with a 5-cm layer of mud mortar, then by another layer approximately 10 to 15 cm thick and finally with a layer of waterproof plaster.

Brick manufacturing.

Underside of a conical thatched roof construction.

Underside of flat mud roof construction.

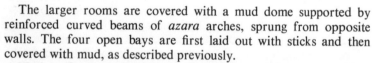

The construction of a mud wall, lower part already plastered.

The larger rooms are covered with a mud dome supported by reinforced curved beams of *azara* arches, sprung from opposite walls. The four open bays are first laid out with sticks and then covered with mud, as described previously.

Mud roofs are drained by spouts which were formerly made of wood, but are now made from old petrol tins. These spouts project outwards sufficiently to prevent the splashing rainwater from damaging the wall.

While the walls of the building are finished by rendering the inside and outside with a mud or cement plaster, the floor may either consist of rammed earth (*debe*) or will have a cement finish.

The top layer of the external mud plaster on walls and roofs is mixed with *katsi*, a binding substance produced by the dyeing trade, or with *makuba* which is made from the fruit pod of the locust bean tree. Either plaster will keep the roof and walls reasonably waterproof for at least one year.[25]

The structures described above require constant maintenance which is expensive over the years. Inadequate maintenance results in rapid deterioration of the building, which soon becomes unsafe for habitation.

One of the most striking features of Hausa architecture is the external decoration of buildings, which usually surrounds doors but which may cover whole building walls that front upon the street. This striking feature of the local architecture naturally attracts the attention of every visitor and stimulates speculation about its origin and meaning.[26]

68

Underside of vaulted mud roof construction, showing ribs.

Section of a vaulted mud roof.

Entrance to compound, decorative wall pattern cut into cement plaster.

Three main types of such decoration are found in Zaria city. The first is made by modelling the fresh mud plaster manually into arabesque features, as shown in the picture above; the second by cutting ornaments into the wet cement or mud plaster and the third by the painting on a plain white wall.

It is widely believed that only the front elevation facing the street is decorated, but some older and very fine examples of the first-mentioned decorative style can be found around doors within some of the two-roomed huts inside the *cikin gida*. Decorative art as shown above is therefore not only a public demonstration of wealth and social prestige but seems also to be appreciated for its own sake as an inspiring source of private pleasure. Finally along the parapets of buildings stand horns of mud (*zanko*) like rabbits' ears. Though often misinterpreted as phallic symbols, these projections undoubtedly give the massive mud construction a lighter and more picturesque appearance.

HOUSES AND HOUSEHOLDS

The Domestic Grouping

A brief description of the domestic grouping is necessary to demonstrate the relationship between the changes in the family composition and size, and in the development of the compound as a residential unit.

The majority of co-residential units are extended family groups

Interior wall decoration and display of pots.

Detail of interior wall decoration.

A compound wall painted by the household head.

based on agnatic kinship. These family groups can be divided into three main categories: the nuclear family, with or without additional kin such as the compound head's widowed mother or other divorced or single close relatives and composite units of two types, the compound head's family, his married sons and their descendants and, collateral agnates and their dependants. The two latter types are usually divided into a number of households, each forming a separate unit of domestic economy and occupying a section of the *cikin gida* known as *sassa*. These individual family units (*iyalai*) are responsible for their own food, clothing and maintenance of their hut or huts.

Distribution of wives per man is shown in the following table based on 77 compounds:

Unmarried male over 18 years of age	19	= 9·05%
Adult male with one wife	112	= 52·80%
Adult male with two wives	54	= 25·70%
Adult male with three wives	18	= 8·60%
Adult male with four wives	8	= 3·85%
Total adult male	211	= 100·00%
Total wives	306	
Average wives per man	1·45	

If an extended family depends on agriculture as a means of livelihood, it may form a single work-unit known as a *gandu* which thus consists of the adult male kin and their families, e.g. married brothers and/or a man and his married or unmarried sons. Individual families within a *gandu* farm and cook together in the rainy season, their common meals being prepared in turn by each of the members' wives. In the dry season each individual family-head (*mai-iyalai*) may pursue another occupation, e.g. weaving, rope or mat making, embroidery, trading or teaching the Koran; and at this time each family operates a separate domestic economy.

Adoption (*tallafi*) is widely practised but restricted to children from the wider kinship group; women usually adopt girls and men, boys. However, a distinction must be made between adopted children (*tallafi*), and stepchildren (*agolai*), who, under Moslem law, cannot be retained when their father demands them. Clientage is practised widely in towns and villages. Under this institution a boy is placed under the care of a well-known man, who looks after his education and later provides him with a wife, in return for faithful service.

The creation of a new compound and its possible causes must now be briefly discussed. The most common reasons for the subdivisions of compounds are the rapid increase in the populations of the families within them due to recent reductions in infant mortality,[27] or to the arrival of collateral kinsmen, and domestic separation after the compound head's death. Households faced with overcrowding must decide whether to extend their compound, or to split and build a new one elsewhere for some of their members. In such situations full brothers, having closer ties, are less likely to separate than are groups of half brothers or parallel cousins.[28] Combinations of half brothers and cousins are always likely to subdivide and set up a new

residential unit. Thus fraternal extended families dissolve at each generation, for fission in families is partly socio-economic. Many young men, with a western type of education and relatively high income, desire to leave their father's compound after marriage, in order to build their houses elsewhere where each will live alone with his wife or wives, their children, and perhaps with his widowed or divorced mother.

The Changes in House Design and the New Design Pattern

It is a common practice that every compound head, after he takes over the responsibility following his father's death, will rebuild part or more often the whole of his compound to meet his family needs, except for the surrounding wall and sometimes the *zaure*.

A Hausa custom which harks back to pre-Moslem times, though it is no longer universal, is for a dead person to be buried under the floor of his hut, which is then abandoned and left to collapse. After the roof and parts of the walls have broken down, the roofing poles of deleb palm are removed and used as fire wood or, if in good condition, for new construction. The walls disintegrate quickly, forming a small mound which marks the site of the former hut for several years; but when a new hut is necessary this mound of earth may be used to make bricks for the new building.

This continuous process of destruction and rebuilding of the compound is a direct response to continuous changes in the composition of the family that occupies it. When an oldest son first marries between the age of fifteen and twenty-four, his father will either build a new compound elsewhere for him, or more commonly, he will build him a new hut, preferably with two rooms within his own compound. By the time this son marries a second wife, he will himself have some kind of regular income and be able to build a hut for her. He will also pay now the annual maintenance costs of his wives' huts and may try to construct another for himself, or if he already has a hut of his own, to improve it: for example, with cement plaster on the walls, a cement floor or a corrugated iron roof. As the years go by and the young man matures, he takes over more responsibility for the compound's upkeep, and when his father retires from active work, he will support the family. After the old man's death, when the first son is often between 40–54 years old, he automatically becomes the compound head (*maigida*). He now has full responsibility for the entire family which may already include several partially independent households. If the new household head can afford it, a period of intense building activity begins. He constructs new buildings for himself, for his wives and their children, as well as for his other dependents as his father's (*turaka*) falls in ruins. After this several important improvements are undertaken, such as cementing the house and fixing corrugated iron roofs. The compound head finances this construction mainly from his own savings, but if this is not enough, family members, good friends, and more recently, small private savings societies, may often provide part of the money required. Private loans for construction will either be made openly without interest as Islam ordains, or secretly at very high interest rates to cover the risk involved, as such money cannot be re-claimed in Moslem courts.[29] Alternatively, the household head may sell or

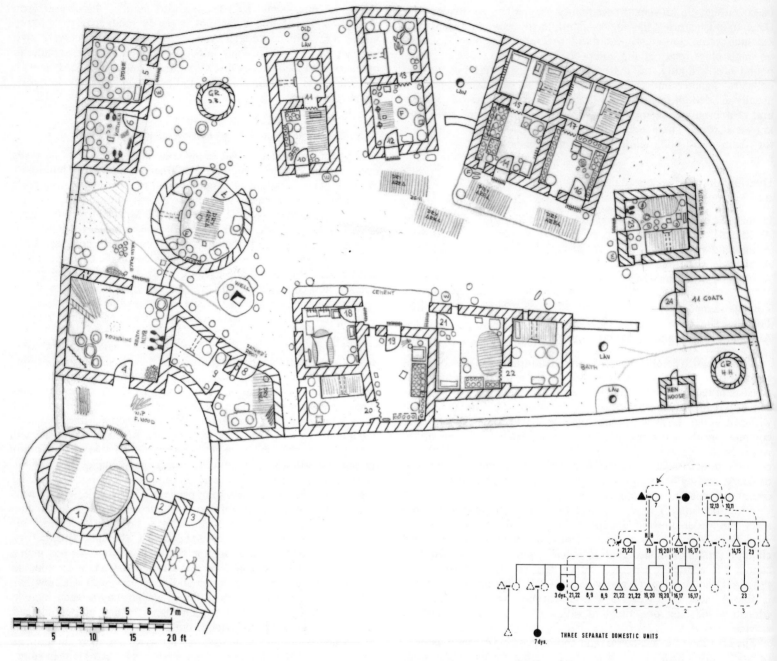

House Plan No. 71.

Kinship pattern, House No. 71.

THREE SEPARATE DOMESTIC UNITS

pledge (*jingina*) one of his farms. With the forthcoming marriage of the eldest son, the compound head will also provide new accommodation for him; and so the cyclic process of construction and growth will start again.

The fourth example (house 71) was chosen to demonstrate the close relationship between the changes in family composition and size and the changes in the layout and construction of the compound

resulting from the need for new huts to house the growing family. The house is situated in the market area and for at least three generations has belonged to a family of wealthy butchers. M. G. Smith in his book on the economy of the Hausa communities of Zaria points out that this profession ranks near the bottom of the social scale in Zaria; traditionally it was only practised by Hausa proper.[30]

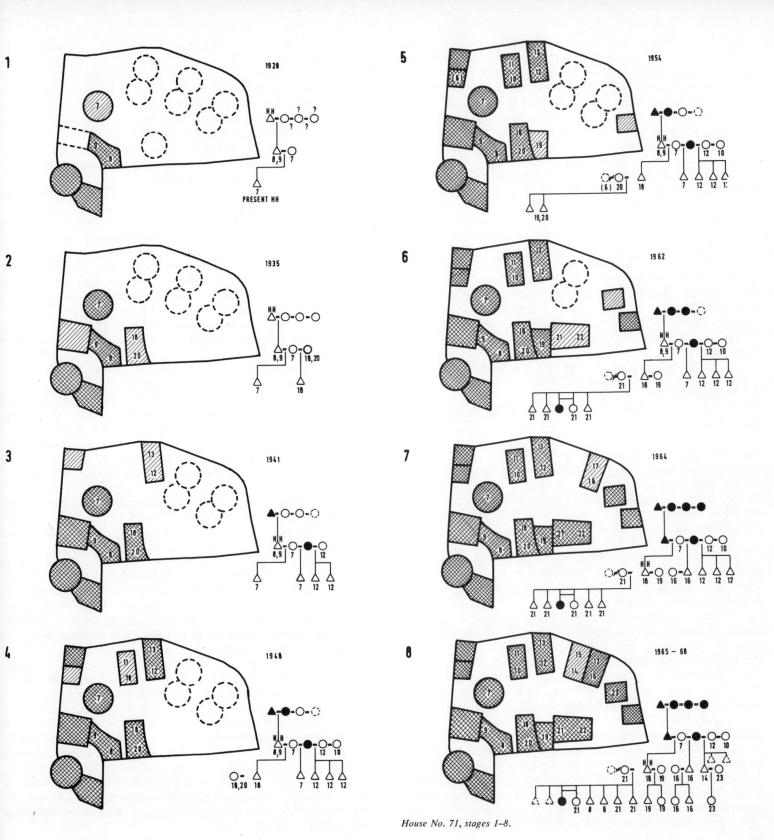

House No. 71, stages 1–8.

According to the present compound head, his grandfather re-built the compound around 1900 shortly before the British occupation. The grandfather occupied three double round huts along side the main wall, the exact positions of which are no longer known. There was also some dispute about the number of his wives and children. Only the surrounding wall and the entrance hut with its two adjoining rooms still survives, it is believed, from this early period.

1. None the less, from the data collected it was possible to draw a plan of the compound, which is probably incomplete, as it was when the father of the present compound head married his first wife. Rooms 8 and 9 were either built at that time or given then to the newly wed couple, and shortly afterwards when she became pregnant, a round hut, room number 7, was constructed for the young wife. Her first child – the present compound head – was born in 1928 and grew up there in his mother's hut.

2. In 1935 when the father of the present compound head married his second wife, two more rooms, 18 and 19, which are now used by the present compound head and his third wife, were built. After the second wife had given birth to a boy, who is now married and occupies the rooms numbered 16 and 17, she died. However, at about this time a new and bigger second entrance hut (*shigifa*) was constructed (room 4).

3. After the death of his second wife, the father of the present compound head married a third wife who gave birth to two boys in 1939 and 1941. A new, square, two-roomed hut containing rooms 12 and 13 was built for her. A storeroom was also finished during this period.

4. In 1948–49 the oldest son, the present compound head, and his father married their first and last wives respectively. One hut with two rooms numbered 10 and 11 was built for the father's fourth wife. At the same time, the young couple moved into the recently renovated rooms 18 and 20 which the father of the groom's deceased second wife had formerly occupied. A new room, which now serves as a kitchen, was also built that year.

5. After the son's wife had given birth to two boys, room number 19 was added. The son's second wife, whom he married in 1956, had no children and was divorced after eighteen months. I failed to learn where she lived, but it is possible that she occupied room number 6. A goat hut was also built at this time.

6. Before the son married his third wife in 1962, a hut containing rooms 21 and 22 was built and his first wife, who now had four children, moved there, leaving her old rooms for the new wife. A wet season kitchen was also built in that year.

7. With the death of his father in 1963, the oldest son became house head and assumed responsibilities for his mother, his father's two junior wives and his two younger half brothers. During the last years of his father's life, from 1960 to 1963, the following improvements on the house were carried out: rooms numbered 18 to 20 were re-roofed with mud instead of thatch, the old mud plaster was removed and replaced by cement plaster and all floors were cemented. In 1964 the oldest of his half brothers married and the last of the old two-roomed round huts was demolished to make way for a new rectangular hut with two rooms numbered 16 and 17.

8. One year later, the younger of the household head's two resident half-brothers married and a hut with two rooms numbered 14 and 15 was erected adjoining the latest building. Room 23, the compound head's kitchen, which has an earthen bed, was used at the time of the interview by his youngest brother's wife for lying-in, after delivering a baby three weeks earlier. During the post-partum lie-in, which lasts for six weeks, the earthen bed is constantly heated, and the young mother takes a hot bath twice daily. For the following six weeks she has then only one bath per day. Water for these daily baths was heated in a drum in the second entrance hut (*shigifa*). The bathing took place behind room number 22.

Until the Second World War, the traditional pattern of demolishing and rebuilding the residential unit, which reflected such family developments, had been followed for hundreds of years without any great changes in building methods, materials and compound layout. But in the last thirty years general changes have taken place. Perhaps the most obvious is the virtual disappearance of the traditional round thatched hut which is now disesteemed as old fashioned, and its replacement by a larger square building with bigger windows and a flat or vaulted mud roof.

The following two examples, still constructed in mud, will illustrate how recent changes have affected the layout and appearance of the compound.

The house plan of compound 77 shows a residential unit of substantial age, situated in the market area and inhabited by a butcher and his family. The missing forecourt (*kofar gida*) is noteworthy and characteristic of the low social status of the butcher's profession. The compound head lives with his wife, who is forty-five years of age, in *quren jahilai* (the marriage of the ignorant) and allows her to move freely around in public. In such circumstances the forecourt, as an intermediate zone between the outside world and the *cikin gida*, is not required.

All four double round huts in this compound were built by the father of the present compound head around the turn of the century. With the exception of the entrance hut (*zaure*) all its square rooms were built in the last eight years and are occupied by the younger generation.

Rooms 9 and 10 were formerly occupied by the compound head's deceased brother and his wife. Their graves can be seen behind the hut, which now is in a very bad state of repair. Only room 9 is now used as a bedroom by three of the dead brother's younger children. The earthen bed in room number 10 has already partly collapsed.

The second residential unit, number 30 in my sample, is located in the palace area and belongs to an employee of the local (Emirate) administration, who built the house between 1961 and 1967 on an open piece of land. It is a fine example of the contemporary house design. The rooms are well organised and of fair size, with vaulted mud roofs and corrugated iron sheets above. Walls and floors are cemented and the former are also whitewashed. Most rooms have at least one window about 45 × 45 cm with a wooden shutter. The well and the two pit-latrines are placed far apart. A number of trees have been planted in both courtyards to provide shade. The family is small, typical of a young well-educated household head with a relatively high income, who could afford to leave his father's house and build his own residential unit.

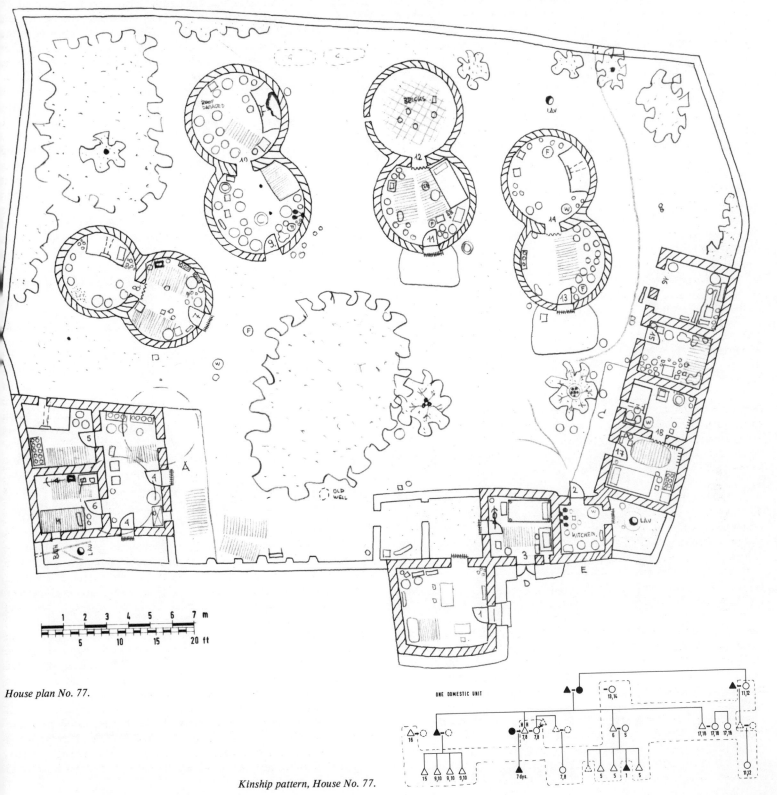

House plan No. 77.

Kinship pattern, House No. 77.

ONE DOMESTIC UNIT

75

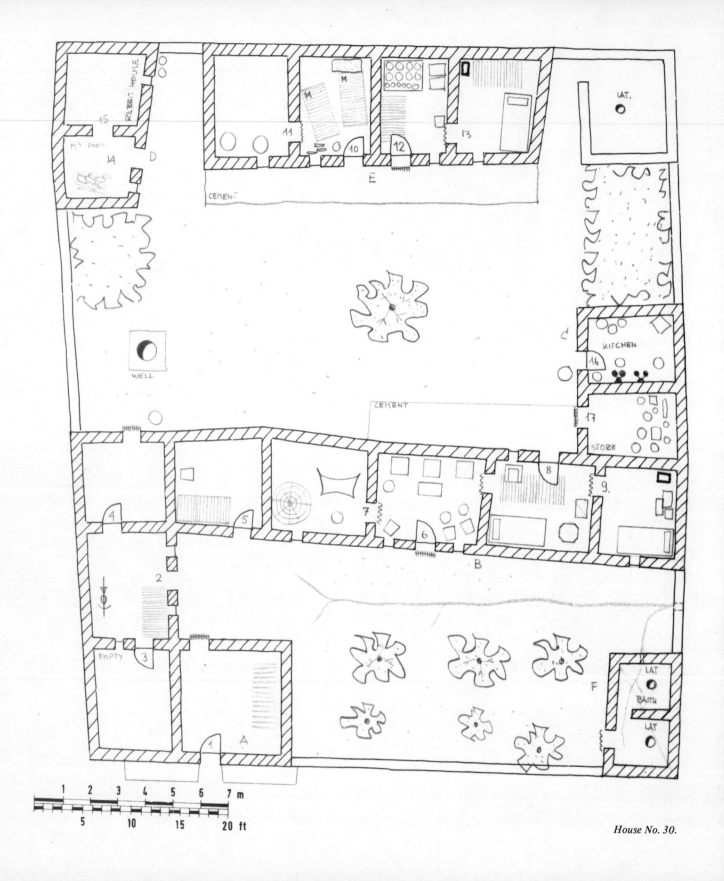

House No. 30.

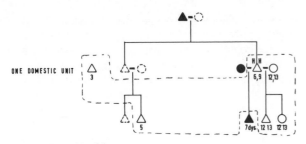

ONE DOMESTIC UNIT

Kinship pattern, House No. 30.

ACTIVITY WITHIN THE COMPOUND

A note on human activities in some of the homes discussed above will close the description of these six compounds of Zaria walled city.

Within residential units the dsitributions of tasks and work places are predetermined by the social roles which Hausa culture ascribes to the sexes. Except for older women or those who live in *auren jahilai*, the activities of married women are largely confined to the *cikin gida*. These activities can be classified under four heads as follows:

(*a*) Preparation and cooking of food for the family. This is carried out by co-wives in rotation in polygynous families.

(*b*) Preparation and/or cooking of food for sale by young girls who hawk the food through the city market, wards and streets.

(*c*) Spinning, weaving country cloths called *gwadaua* (s. *gwado*) on the woman's vertical loom, or making caps which may be sold by the household head or through commission agents on the city market.

(*d*) Petty trading with farm products, e.g. groundnut oil, cassava or textiles, which are either sold by young girls on the city market, or to older women who visit the residential unit.

The men's work place at home is usually the entrance hut (*zaure*). There the compound head can observe and greet passers-by or entertain his friends while working. For example, in one of our sample compounds number 68, the compound head and his brother both work in the *zaure* eaving on the narrow looms reserved for men. The thread is fixed to an old grindstone, called *kunkuru* (the tortoise), which is placed at the far end of the *kofar gida* and drawn steadily towards the loom as the weaving proceeds. The average daily output of a weaver during the dry season is one and half lengths of cloth, 12–15 cm wide. The three wives of the compound head also weave a broadcloth in their own rooms (numbers 3, 5 and 7), on the large vertical looms reserved for women, and each produces two to three cloths per month on average. The *zaure* may also be used for religious instruction and discussion. In a malam's home, it houses the school in which to teach the Koran to approximately ten students, some of whom would sleep there at night.

Fulani housewife washing rice.

Men working at the narrow looms in the zaure.

In like fashion, the butcher in house number 77 uses his *zaure* as a petty shop retailing some uncooked meat and roasting other portions in front of the *zaure* for sale to passers-by or in the city market. Shops can also be found in those compounds having household heads or adult male residents engaged in selling provisions for a livelihood even though most of their sales are transacted in the city market.

In conclusion, five main factors have helped to give Hausa residential units their present form. These are: (1) The law and rules of Islam as practised locally; (2) The need for security, particularly during the pre-colonial period; (3) The skills and building materials available to the community; (4) The continually changing requirements of Hausa families at each new generation for domestic space, building and the like; and (5) The custom, which was later abandoned, of burying a person in his own hut which was then allowed to collapse.

These factors have produced a highly distinctive and standardised house type with a clearly defined centre, the *cikin gida*.

Unlike many African towns, the population of Zaria city has grown rather slowly during this century, thereby preserving the old structure of the community and city more or less intact. Two reasons for this restrained rate of population growth are the various restrictions placed on immigrants who wish to settle in the old city and the still high rate of infant mortality. But there are indications that this period may now be coming to an end and that the coming decades will see a rapidly growing population. The economic and technical advances of the second half of the twentieth century with its new ideas, new building methods and materials should surely have increasing effect on Hausa domestic architecture.

The greatest asset of the present building practice is undoubtedly the flexibility of the compound which reflects clearly any change in the family structure and size Any further development has to take into account the changing needs of the developing family groups, the most effective and economic utilisation of new materials and local resources, and the need to increase educational opportunities at all levels of Hausa society.

A Hausa compound.

NOTES AND BIBLIOGRAPHY

[1] Climatic data were recorded at the Agricultural Research Station, Samaru, Ahmadu Bello University, Zaria. The wind records are from Kano airport.

[2] MORTIMORE, M. J., and WILSON, J., *Land and People in the Kano Close-Settled Zone.* A report to the Greater Kano Planning Authority Department of Geography, Paper No. 1, March 1965. A.B.U. Zaria.

[3] BUCHANAN, K. M., and PUGH, J. C., *Land and People in Nigeria*, University of London Press Ltd., 1966, p. 33.

[4] KEAY, R. W. J., *An Outline of Nigerian Vegetation*, Lagos, 1949.

[5] (i) ORR, Sir C. W., 'The Hausa Race', *Journal of the Royal African Society*, Vols. VII and VIII, 1907, pp. 278–84, 272–8.

(ii) BARTH, H., *Travel in Central Africa*, Vol. 1, London, 1890, p. 274.

(iii) LUGARD, Lady, *A Tropical Dependancy*, London, 1905, p. 146.

[6] SMITH, M. G., 'The Beginnings of Hausa Society, A.D. 100–1500', in VANSINA, J. and others (eds.), *The Historian in Tropical Africa.*

[7] AL BAKRI, *Description de L'Afrique Septentrionale.* Trans. by De Slane, Algiers, 1913.

[8] IBN BATTUTA, *Travel in Asia and Africa 1325–1354*, trans. by GIBB, H. A. R., London, 1929.

[9] AFRICANUS, LEO, *The History and Description of Africa*, trans. by PORY, J., London, 1896.

[10] ARNETT, E. J., 'A Hausa Chronicle', *Journal of the Royal African Society*, Vol. IX, 1909–10, pp. 161–7.

[11] DAURA, KATSINA, GOBIR, KANO, ZARIA, RANO, BIRAM.

[12] ARNETT, E. J., op. cit., p. 163. It is interesting to note that according to tradition the king of Songhay, Dia Kossoi, became a Moslem in 1010, and the king of Bornu, Ibn'Abd Al Jelil, in A.D. 1086.

[13] Holy war against the Hausa kings.

[14] KIRK-GREENE, A. H. M., *Barth's Travel in Nigeria*, Oxford University Press, 1962, p. 113. '. . . the houses of Kano are very inferior to those of Agades and Timbuktu, which are built almost on the same principle as the dwellings of the ancient Greeks and Romans'.

[15] *The Holy Quran.* Trans. by MAULANA MUHAMMAD ALI-SURAH AL-AHZAB, Part XXII, Lahore, 1963, p. 808.

Verse 32. 'O wives of the Prophet, you are not like any other women. If you would keep your duty, be not soft in speech, lest he in whose heart is a disease yearn; and speak a word of goodness.'

Verse 33. 'And stay in your house and display not your beauty like the displaying of the ignorance of yore; and keep up prayer, and pay the poor-rate and obey Allah and His Messenger. Allah only desires to take away uncleanness from you, O people of the household, and to purify you a (thorough) purifying.'

[16] SMITH, M. G., *The Economy of the Hausa Communities of Zaria.* Colonial Research Study No. 16, H.M.S.O., London, 1955, p. 50.

'Hausa classify their various modes of marriage in the following ways: The "religious" classification distinguishes *auren kulle* = purdah-type marriage with complete seclusion of the wife; *auren tsare* = partial seclusion of the wife, and *auren jahilai* = "marriage of the ignorant", with no seclusion of the wife.'

[17] RUXTON, F. H., *Maliki Law.* Summary of Mukhtasar of Sidi Khalil, London, 1916, pp. 197–8. Building Regulation §§ 650, 653, 654, 655, 657, 658, 660, 662.

[18] DAVIDSON, B., *et al. History of West Africa.* London, 1965, p. 253.

[19] MABOGUNJE, A. L., *Urbanisation in Nigeria.* University of London Press, 1968, p. 57, Figure 4.

[20] DENHAM, D., CLAPPERTON, H. and OUDNEY, N., *Narrative of Travels and Discoveries in Northern and Central Africa in the Years 1822–1824.*

[21] BARTH, H., op. cit., Vol. 1.

[22] ROBINSON, C. H., *Nigeria our Latest Protectorate*, London, 1900, p. 142. '. . . a small colony of Arab merchants some fifty (are) found in Kano. Their houses are distinguished from those of the other inhabitants of the city by the fact that they are built with two storeys.'

[23] IBN BATTUTA, op. cit., p. 324.

'Yet their women show no bashfullness before men and do not veil themselves, though they are assiduous in attending the prayer' (at Iwalatan, Mali Empire, 1352).

[24] GANDU. A unit of domestic economy based on close kinship of two or more adult males living in a common residential unit. During the rainy season the group work together on the common land to produce the necessary grain. They also eat together during this time.

[25] DALDY, A. F., *Temporary Buildings in Northern Nigeria*, Public Works Department, Nigeria, Lagos, 1945, pp. 20, 21.

[26] KIRK-GREENE, A. H. M., 'Decorated Houses in Zaria', in *Nigeria Magazine*, No. 68, 1961, pp. 53–78. Kirk-Greene suggests that the design adorning leather cases of the Koran brought back from Mecca by pilgrims, may have been used as examples.

CROWDER, M., 'The decorative architecture of Northern Nigeria: Indigenous culture expressed in Hausa Craftmanship', in *African World*, London, February 1956, pp. 9–10.

[27] SMITH, M. G., op. cit., p. 174.

'The combined infant mortality rates of these samples (G and Z) is 460 per 1,000 live births (in 1949–50). On this data, 48·1 per cent of infant deaths occur in the 1st year of life, and 76·3 per cent in the first 3 years.'

According to my sample in Zaria walled city the infant mortality has been reduced to 387 per 1,000 live births in 1968.

[28] Ibid., p. 32.

[29] THE HOLY QURAN, op. cit., Section 38, 'The Cow', p. 120. Verse 275 'And Allah has allowed trading and forbidden usury.' Also footnote 365, p. 120.

RUXTON, F. H., op. cit., *Maliki Law*, Ch. XXVI, p. 172, Bailment (*commodatum*) or gratuitous loans for use. 'Loan involving interest is prohibited . . .'

[30] SMITH, M. G., op. cit., p. 16.

ACKNOWLEDGEMENTS

I would like to thank Alhaji Muhammadu Aminu, C.M.G., C.F.R., the Emir of Zaria, for his interest and generous help during our visit to Zaria. Without the Emir's keen interest and support this survey could not have succeeded.

I wish to express my thanks to the German Academic Exchange Service Bad Godesberg, for the generous financial help I received for this research project.

I would also like to thank Mr. D. M. Stewart whose kind services never failed throughout my survey in Africa. I am also indebted to the many citizens of Zaria who welcomed us into their homes and devoted much valuable time to answering our questions with courtesy and good humour.

Finally I would like to thank Professor M. G. Smith of University College, London, for his helpful guidance in the preparation of this article.

ZANJ, THE EAST AFRICAN COAST

Ronald Lewcock

'... the very last market-town of the continent is called Rhapta which has its name from sewed boats; there is ivory in great quantity, and tortoise shell. Some ancient right subjects it to the state that is the first in Arabia. The people of Muza now hold it and send thither many large ships, with Arab captains and agents. These are familiar with the inhabitants, and both dwell and intermarry with them and speak their language.'

The Periplus of the Erythraean Sea
Alexandria, *c.* A.D. 60

The civilisation of the East African coast reaches back into remote antiquity. Visitors to the area were helped by the fortunate direction of the monsoon winds, blowing ships from India and Arabia towards Africa during half of the year, and then reversing to blow them back again. Rhapta, in the quotation above, is thought to have been on the African mainland opposite Zanzibar. From India was imported, according to the *Periplus*, grain, honey and cloth. The goods exported were gold, ivory, rhinoceros horn (which was thought to have magic properties), tortoise shell and palm oil. Trade in these goods was to keep the East African people in contact with the major civilisations of the Indian Ocean until the present day.

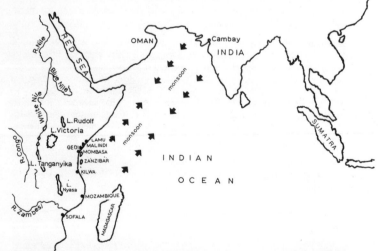

Map of the Indian Ocean showing the settlements on the East African coast and the seasonal monsoons.

In the centuries following the writing of the *Periplus* two new factors of far-reaching importance affected the coastal settlements. The first was the spread of dark-skinned people, probably Bantu-speaking, into the region from the west and south. They brought with them a knowledge of iron-working, which led to the discovery of rich deposits of iron-ore near the coast, and they forced the coastal inhabitants into defensive sites on islands or peninsulas. Further, when they could be captured and sold as slaves these raw Africans became a valuable addition to the Indian Ocean trade, appearing in early records as far afield as China and Byzantium. Intermarriage seems gradually to have introduced a large element of Bantu blood into the Swahili people (Arabic, meaning 'the coast') of the trading ports, and their language became basically an African language in grammar and much of its vocabulary, although leading families knew Arabic as well.

The second important factor affecting the region was the gradual spread of Indonesian influence, leading to the introduction of bananas and yams into Africa, which are believed to have greatly eased life on the tropical coast. Eventually Madagascar and possibly part of the African mainland were settled by Indonesians. This was followed by a period of four centuries, from the eighth to the twelfth centuries A.D., when the Hinduised kingdom of Sri Vijaya in Sumatra dominated the trade of most of the Indian ocean.

It is not known when the Chinese first reached the shores of Africa, although there are tantalisingly oblique references in records of the Early Han Dynasty (202 B.C. to 9 B.C.). By the time of the Tang dynasty (seventh to tenth centuries A.D.), when Arab dhows were regularly sailing to Canton, some Chinese expeditions were certainly making the voyage in the other direction, and mention is even made of the port they reached, named Malin (Malindi). A few coins of the Tang dynasty have been found in excavations in Zanzibar, and a large number from the Sung dynasty (tenth to thirteenth centuries).

By A.D. 900 the East African island ports and mainland settlements were growing into wealthy towns, and many refugees from the religious disputes of Arabia and the Persian gulf had settled there, according to local chronicles. The coast of Zanj (*Zanj* = black in Persian) was visited by Al Mas'udi in A.D. 916: 'The sailors of Oman go on the sea of the Zanj as far as ... Sofala ... The merchants of Shiraf are also in the habit of sailing on this sea. [Ivory and other goods from the country of the Zanj go] generally to Oman, and from there are sent to China and India . . . In China the kings and their military and civilian officers use carrying chairs of ivory. . . . Ivory is much prized in India; there it is made into handles for . . . daggers. . . . But the biggest use of ivory is in the manufacture of chessmen and other gaming pieces . . .'

Al Idrisi (c. 1154) writes of 'a great number of iron mines in the mountains of Sofala. The people of the Zanedj Islands and other neighbouring islands come here for iron, which they carry to the continent and islands of India, where they sell it at a good price, for it is a material of great trade and consumption in India . . .'

The importance of Indian influence is borne out by a number of Hindustani words in Swahili, such as *Jahazi* the deep-sea dhow. That these ships often traded directly between India and Zanj is reflected in several references in the chronicles; setting out with the prevailing monsoon they often made the passage of two thousand miles in three to four weeks, generally steering for the powerful state of Cambay, or (as Vasco da Gama's Malindi pilot did) making a landfall at one of the great trading ports farther south, Calicut or Cochin. In East Africa, Indians probably commanded a good deal of the economic life, for which they, unlike the Arabs, had long shown ability. But the expansion of Islam and entrenched Arab influence ensured strong links with Arabia. Neither Indian nor Arab explored the great continent inland from the coast. Their trade might necessitate sending caravans into the interior, but except in the interests of commerce, they kept to the port towns. United by the common interests of trade, with the same culture and the same language, the people of the Zanj coast experienced a quite remarkable prosperity from the twelfth century until the arrival of the Portuguese at the end of the fifteenth century – as is testified by the luxury of their buildings and possessions.

SETTLEMENT PATTERN

By the middle of the thirteenth century all the seacoast was becoming well-peopled with villages and ports of the Swahili, a mixture by this time of Arab, African, Persian, Indian and possibly Indonesian elements, in which African predominated. Although the growth of prosperity was remarkable, the main impetus of this thirteenth-century revival seems to have been religious and cultural. This was the century of the spread of Islam from one end to the other of the Indian Ocean. The bulk of the trade of the ocean passed into Muslim hands, Islam penetrated into Cambay and Indonesia, and the civilisation of the African coast acquired a new stability.

The growth of new Swahili urban political organisations was paralleled by the establishment of new ports and villages, centred in most cases on the nucleus of a mosque, adjoining which was usually an open area reserved for graves. Around this the stone or rough timber houses were grouped, often in an apparently unplanned open arrangement at first, with small areas of systematic planning perhaps added later – as in the southern area of Songo Mnara, fifteenth century. The towns were seldom elaborately walled, although Songo Mnara had a semi-continuous protection made up of projections of house walls on the south and east, and a low rough wall along the north shore.

Houses opened to a courtyard on the north side, with, in the case of larger dwellings, a further suite of rooms opening to a courtyard on the south side. As the town expanded and the original graveyard became filled, further mosques might be built, and open spaces between houses became graveyards, creating a seemingly important juxtaposition of home and grave which may suggest the infiltration of some aspects of African ancestor worship into coastal Islamic practice. (Except in the case of royal personages and saints, tombs in Arabia and Mesopotamia were built in specially sanctified areas on the fringes of towns.)

The pillar tomb of the fourteenth and fifteenth centuries seems an architectural feature peculiar to East Africa. The tall pillars usually rise from one end of a low panelled tomb with cut stone margins, which duplicates in miniature the panelling and sometimes the treatment of openings of the mosques and houses. The pillars vary in size and type, and some appear to be phallic. Similar phallic tombs survive in Syria from ancient times, but it is possible that this type in Africa is a survival of the pre-Muslim funerary practice of the coast, linked to the phallic monuments of stone or wood still to be found in the southern Ethiopian highlands and parts of Madagascar. An alternative possibility is that the form of the pillars represents the translation into masonry of a tradition of mounting a turban or head-dress on a wooden pole over each grave. Smaller pillars, sometimes of similar form, are found on eighteenth- and nineteenth-century coastal graves.

Among the luxury goods imported into Zanj were precious pottery and porcelain from China and stoneware from Siam. Remarkable quantities of fragments of these precious green, celadon or blue and white Ming bowls and dishes are found in East Africa, and give a clear idea of the high standard of living their purchasers must have enjoyed. The rarest dishes were set into the walls of fine houses, into the vaults and domes of the mosques, and into the panelled sides and pillars of tombs, where some survive intact to this day, providing bright splashes of colour against the drab coral stone.

Many of the towns were protected from the mainlanders by their situation on islands, but whether on islands or the mainland they were generally built against the seashore facing the anchorage, or sometimes hidden behind mangrove swamps. They depended always for their wealth on the trade that came to them by sea.

Population size is not easily estimated, especially since the poorer people lived in flimsy dwellings of which no trace survives. But it is clear that while the larger towns numbered thousands of people, there were many smaller settlements with a few hundred inhabitants.

Each independent town was reported to have kept a Great Drum or an Ivory Horn, a symbol of the power of the state, which was kept guarded as a ritual object, a custom that seems to relate back to African traditions.

URBANISED PATTERN – GEDI

'. . . well-walled with stone and mortar, inasmuch as they are often at war with the heathen of the mainland . . . well laid out in streets . . . [with] many fair stone and mortar houses of many storeys with great

81

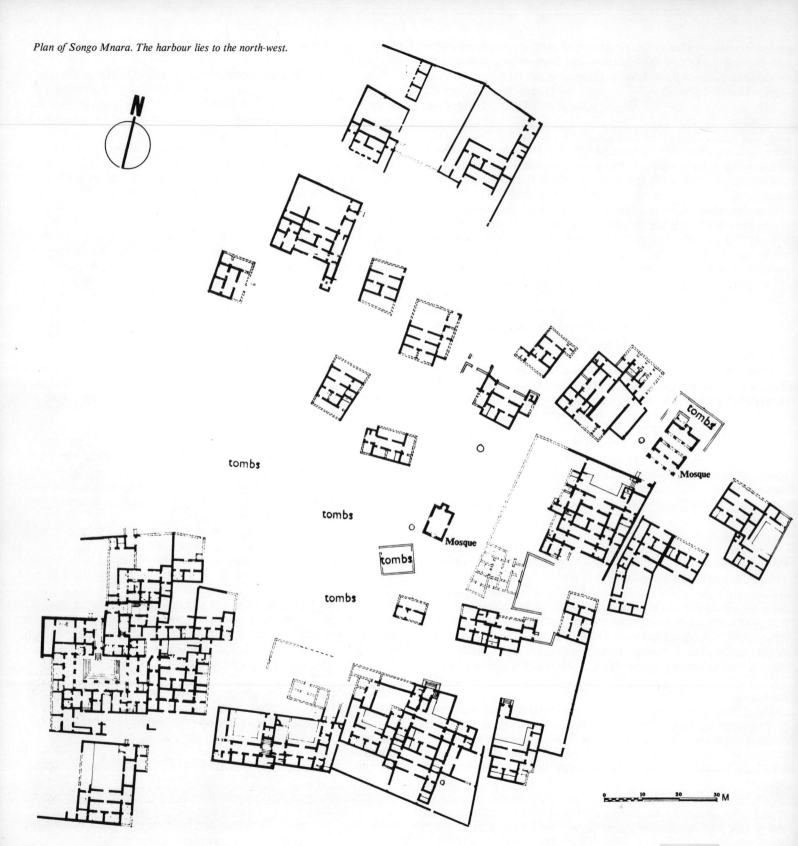

Plan of Songo Mnara. The harbour lies to the north-west.

N

tombs

tombs

tombs

tombs

tombs

Mosque

Mosque

0   10   20   30 M

plenty of windows and flat roofs, after [the Portuguese] fashion. The folk are both black and white. Around are streams and orchards and fruit-gardens with many channels of sweet water.'

Duarte Barbosa, *c.* 1500
Description of Malindi, Pate and Kilwa

Gedi was a rare example of a mainland town set back from the shore; it was four miles from the sea near Malindi. Otherwise it was typical of a number of such towns up and down the coast of East Africa.

The site of Gedi was probably not occupied until the late thirteenth century; it reached the height of its prosperity in the mid-fifteenth century and was abandoned in the early seventeenth century, apparently after the incursions of the Galla, a fierce African tribe. Although only part of the town has been excavated, and even there some evidence is lacking, the main features of the plan can be established. The town at its greatest extent covered about forty-five acres, surrounded by a wall about nine feet high with three or more gates. It is probable that only part of the area thus enclosed was ever built up, and the poorer houses must have had rough timber or mud walls with roofs of palm-leaf or grass thatch. Later, another wall was built enclosing a smaller area, and it is surmised that this was done after a partial abandonment of the town in the late sixteenth century.

Although both walls follow somewhat erratic patterns, it appears from the layout of the largest concentration of houses adjoining the Palace and the Great Mosque in the north-west corner of the town that there was originally a rough rectangular grid of narrow streets oriented approximately north–south and east–west. An open space in front of the palace took up two blocks of this grid and was approached down a street which led directly from the North Gate. Later rebuilding of some of the houses has encroached on the street pattern, in one case closing a street completely. The houses look out to courtyards on the east and north sides, with occasionally a domestic court on the south. The town walls in this corner of the town are parallel to the street grid.

The typical house plan, illustrated here by houses on the east side of the town, shows a spatial progression from the narrow street through a large-scale doorway into a private courtyard and thence into covered space which became increasingly private and small in scale as one penetrated in depth. Doorways were generally formally designed, with a wide pointed arch set in a recessed rectangular field. They were frequently flanked by small rectangular niches for lamps.

The houses were initially single-storeyed – upper floors were usually later additions of the fifteenth and sixteenth centuries. Even the flat roofs do not appear to have been used, as no masonry steps lead up to them – although there may have been timber ladders. The shape of rooms was usually defined by the limited span of the mangrove beams supporting the roof (less than three metres). The system of planning therefore resolved itself into building up accommodation by placing long narrow units parallel to each other.

GEDI – CLUSTER OF HOUSES

This cluster of houses, the largest excavated so far in Gedi, adjoined the palace and the palace square. It included the oldest unaltered

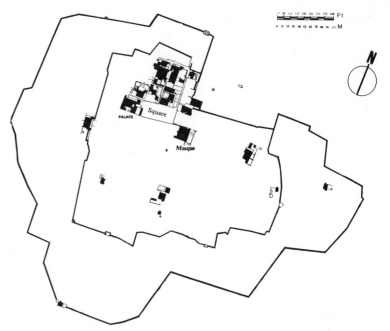

Town plan of Gedi.

Tombs at Kaole, on the mainland opposite Zanzibar.

house, shown on page 86, in plan, which was built at the end of the fourteenth century, and a number of other old houses which were altered or rebuilt in the following centuries. Gedi was essentially a country town, which may explain why so many of the houses were single-storeyed, unlike those in Malindi, Pate and Kilwa described in the quotation from Duarte Barbosa on an earlier page.

The early type of plan was characterised by a long narrow court with the main room fronting on one long side, and the private quarters behind it, consisting of a long room with three small rooms opening off it (bedroom, kitchen and store). The lavatory was to be found off one end of the main front room. Later this plan was changed by dividing the private middle room into two, thus making a house of one long room and two private suites, presumably for the owner's two wives. The further addition of a domestic court facilitated cooking, and the final improvement sometimes was the enlargement of the front courtyard to a wide rectangle suitable for a commercial use. Such a house in one of the larger coastal towns would have been at least double-storeyed, the upper floors with

General view of Gedi.

Typical doorway in Gedi.

Houses in Gedi on the east side of the town.

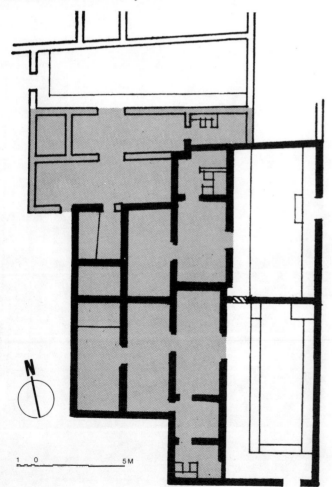

windows and doors overlooking the courtyard, probably quite like the example from the Persian Gulf illustrated here. The front court usually had a sunken centre, with a raised walkway around three sides which was high enough to provide a seat in the open air. Wells and even latrines were sometimes shared between two houses.

Only the richer citizens lived in stone houses, although we can trace a big increase of domestic buildings in stone in the century before the Portuguese arrived. The stone used was coral ragstone, common on the coast, and in the case of Gedi found on the site. It was cemented and plastered with white lime made by burning the coral. The walls supported ceilings of rough planks or tiles carried on mangrove poles, with a thick layer of lime concrete on top to provide waterproofing and insulation against the heat. In the best work the ceilings were made of squared and jointed woods from the African interior. Mouldings and decorations around doorways, windows and niches were frequently executed in finely cut and dressed coral stone. Floors were of coral and lime concrete. The

Courtyard elevation of a double-storeyed house in Iran, on the Persian Gulf.

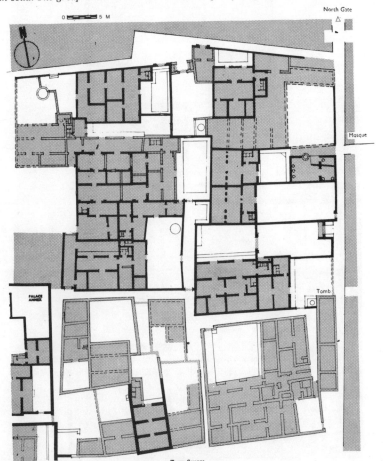

Gedi. Cluster of houses near the town centre, in plan. The earlier houses are shown in solid. The group in the south-west corner are partly conjectural.

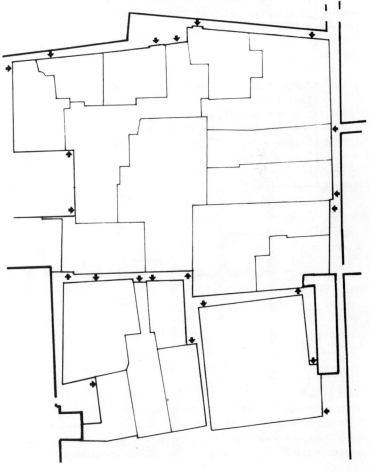

Gedi. Cluster of houses. Diagram identifying eighteen different houses, showing the cluster, the street pattern and the entrances to the properties.

characteristic pointed arch, with the apex formed by two large shaped stones with a joint between, is related to the Indian ogee arch discussed on a later page, and is evidence of the extent of Indian influence in the region.

GEDI – THE PALACE COMPLEX

The palace was entered from the public square through a fine portal with flanking seats which was approached up several steps. Passing through the doorway one reached the sunken reception court, where one waited one's turn to be led to the audience court beyond. This court had raised seats around all four sides of its lowered centre. The ruler's quarters, facing on to the audience court, were no larger than those of the better houses; the plan followed the early plan of a typical house, with the long private room later divided to provide a pair of suites. One of the back rooms was a chamber without a door, entered by a small trap door high up in the wall, which formed a strong room for storing valuables.

Three further suites of rooms related to courtyards surrounded the ruler's quarters, and interconnected with it through the private back rooms. These presumably provided accommodation for attendants and the ruler's family. Yet another court served as a laundry. A later addition to the palace was its annex across a narrow street, which had the unique plan of four suites, each composed of outer room, inner room and lavatory, and four open courts. The street between the annex and the palace served as a secondary public access to the audience court (entered directly through a side door) and contained a group of tombs, including a hexagonal pillar tomb.

The audience quarters of the palace were richly embellished. The façade on to the courtyard and the interior of the front room had richly modulated wall surfaces, with long horizontal niches which served as shelves, recesses in the door frames for lamps, and door surrounds stepped elegantly inwards to thin frames. Carpets hung from rows of pegs set in holes specially provided in the walls, and curtains hung in the doorways.

Although little remains of the external façades of the palaces and houses of Gedi, it is possible to reconstruct what they were like by referring to the miniature façades of the pillar tombs which reproduce the current architectural vocabulary of the larger buildings. In the sculptured base of the great pillar tomb at Malindi, near Gedi, and in the Gedi tombs themselves, dressed stone mouldings outline the rectangular fields of doors and windows, and culminate in horizontal cornices containing a single row of large square coffers set in their centres with precious porcelain bowls. Each vertical pilaster contained a lamp recess a little larger than the coffers above, and the resulting play of textured form across the façades accords with the later Portuguese description of the coastal houses as being panelled and plastered with various patterns (Hans Maur). A ruined house in Lamu illustrated here probably represents a descendant of this architectural system, though elaborated and overdecorated, into the early nineteenth century. In its original form it was a most sophisticated style, derived from Persia via India and Oman rather than from southern Arabia.

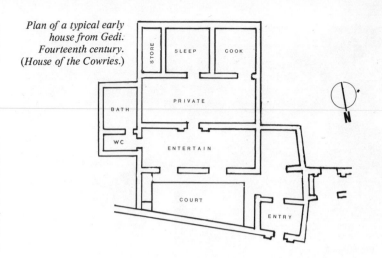

Plan of a typical early house from Gedi. Fourteenth century. (House of the Cowries.)

Gedi. Plan of the palace and its annex.

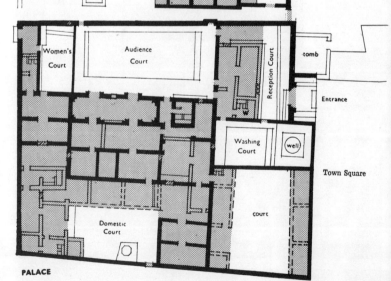

86

Gedi. Typical doorway.

Front of a ruined house at Lamu. Probably late eighteenth or early nineteenth centuries.

Gedi. The outer and inner walls of the main Audience Room seen from the Audience Court.

Mihrab of a mosque at Kaole, on the mainland opposite Zanzibar.

Detail of a thatched roof, double thatched on one side. Moçambique.

Tomb at Kaole. Probably fifteenth century.

Porch and entrance to a modern thatched house at Kaole.

THATCHED BUILDINGS

In all the coastal settlements a large proportion of the population probably lived in wooden or mud-walled structures of indigenous African construction under grass or *makuti* (palm-leaf) roofs. These are seen represented in the early Portuguese drawings of the towns, and doubtless inspired some forms of tomb, like the one shown here, which represents a miniature building in its elevations and roof. The modern descendants of this type of house have lost the pointed-arch doorways, but in construction and plan are very similar. The *makuti* is frequently put in the form of a double-roof on the exposed side of the house, to increase its life and its weather-proofing and insulating qualities.

According to tradition, Zanzibar has preserved close ties with the Persian Gulf, particularly with Oman, since early times. This seems to be borne out by the distinctive form of the sixteenth-century houses at Mvuleni, on the north-west coast of the island. Comparison of the plan of one of these houses with those of old houses in the Persian Gulf, like that illustrated below, reveals a close similarity. These are 'double-houses', resembling those late houses of the same type we have observed at Songo Mnara and Gedi; but here the front room has become a veranda with square piers supporting an upper storey or heavy roof. The sides of the plan are braced by flanking walls at right-angles which appear to be buttresses, but in reality serve to carry terraces and roofs to provide shade on the external walls during the heat of the day.

Plan of the 'House by the Shore'. Mvuleni, Zanzibar.

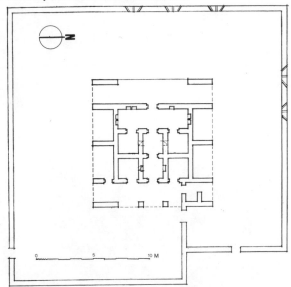

House in Bandar Abbas, Iran, Persian Gulf.

'Kilwa is one of the most beautiful and well-constructed towns in the world. The whole of it is elegantly built'.

Ibn Battuta. A.D. 1331.

The Kilwa sultans began to mint their own copper coinage during the thirteenth century, the earliest mint to be established anywhere in Africa south of the Sahara. Kilwa lived on the Rhodesian trade, with governors in the gold-port of Sofala, and grew rich on the large duties taxed on seaborne traffic in both directions.

The great palace of Husuni Kubwa is attributed to al-Malik al-Mansur al-Hasan b. Sulaiman, one of whose inscriptions has been found there, which dates it to about A.D. 1245. With well over a hundred rooms, courtyards, terraces, ornamental swimming-pool, vaults and domes of varied shapes, and carved decoration, this was the most magnificent piece of Islamic architecture in Africa south of the Sahara. It was situated on a high sandstone headland with fine vistas over the entrance to the harbour of Kilwa to the north and the town to the west. The layout of the building follows closely the shape of the headland.

The northern end, a narrow rectangle on the headland itself, housed the private quarters of the sultan. This had in the centre a courtyard bounded by two suites of rooms of the same size and arrangement as the large single-storeyed domestic units we have already seen in Songo Mnara and Gedi, although here much earlier in date. These quarters were elaborately decorated; the most northerly rooms, probably bedrooms, were vaulted. Beyond them there was apparently a private viewing terrace at the end of the headland. At the other end of the private court (P) the domestic unit was of the double type, so that the other side of it related to a domestic court (D). A stairway cut in the cliffs led up the end of the headland and around the side of the palace to an entrance point on the west. This in turn connected with a corridor, between the sultan's quarters and the ornamental pool, which formed the main axis for circulation of the whole complex, passing through the Audience Pavilion and the ante-chambers beyond to merge on the central axis of the great forecourt (F). A second approach to the palace from the beach and the town passed under the open terraces on the west side into the anterooms of the deeply sunken Audience Court (A). Here the public were received in audience by the Sultan, seated on a divan in a pavilion at the head of a high flight of steps. This Audience Pavilion, set between two courts, and open on both sides so as to catch the slightest breeze, commanded a magnificent vista across the open terraces to the anchorage of Kilwa. A third approach to the palace brought merchants to the southern end of the complex, where the sultan's factor apparently received them in state to conclude business.

The great forecourt (F), surrounded by a vast area of suites of storage rooms, demonstrates the trading base of the sultan's wealth. It bears some resemblance to a Persian or Mesopotamian *serai*, with *iwans*, or recessed porches, in the centre of its four sides.

Above the north-west corner of the forecourt storerooms was an additional floor of richly decorated reception rooms. Although the rooms were narrow, and can have given little impression of space, they were imaginatively roofed with a variety of concrete vaults and domes. That on the corner was the largest and finest, a conical, fluted dome, with a boldly ribbed surface. Its finial was nearly a hundred feet above the sea, the highest point for miles around.

The great fortress-like enclosure on the neighbouring headland is known as Husuni Ndogo. It is possible that it was a fortified barracks for troops (the title of the builder, al-Malik al-Mansur, means 'the conquering king'). There is some evidence that part of it may have been a mosque.

Kilwa. Plan of Husuni Kubwa and Husuni Nnogo.

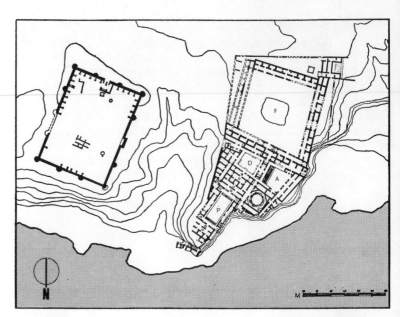

Kilwa. Detail of the conjectural restoration of Husuni Kubwa based partly on the restoration of P. S. Garlake. H. N. Chittick, who excavated the site, doubts the existence of the direct entrance into the Audience court (dotted arrow); the cliffs and the palace at this point have subsided, so accurate restoration is impossible.

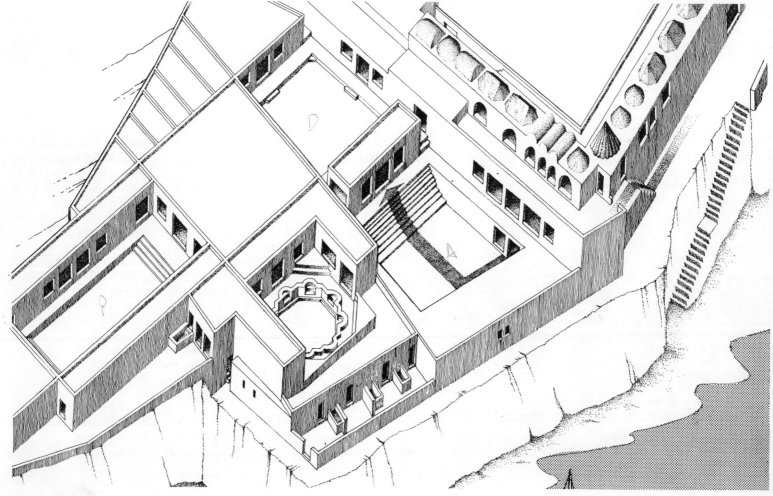

DOORS

'The doors are of wood, well carved, with excellent joinery'.
Duarte Barbosa, *c.* A.D. 1500.
Descriptions of Kilwa and Mombasa.

Two basic types of ornamental door are found today in the old towns of the coast. The first is Indian in origin. The examples surviving in Mombasa and Moçambique (one is shown on the left, in general view and detail) seem very old, and are flanked by Indian sculptured bands and high niches for lamps, and crowned with fine carved cornices. The small sub-doors follow the typical Indian west-coast pattern. All the elements, including the wooden doors, may have been imported, probably from Cochin.

The second type of door is common throughout the length of East Africa. It originates in the Persian Gulf, but far exceeds the Gulf examples in scale and richness. Similar doors with projecting brass bosses spread through Afghanistan to the Punjab in India in the first half of the twelfth century (P. Brown). Characteristic of these doors are the elaborately carved central cover-pieces. The doors and these centre-pieces are studded with long, pointed, brass bosses; the wooden frames, though intricately carved, are restrained in comparison. Richly decorated brass locks, with clasps hanging on three or four parallel chains, secure the doors. The carving of the doors and their frames is a craft retaining great prestige along the coast, where the construction of a new Swahili house begins with these entrance doors.

Detail of a door in Moçambique.

Zanzibar. Detail of bossed door and carved centre-piece. Showing the fish motif of the bottom of the door frame on the right and the elaborate clasp for locking.

Zanzibar. Bossed doors and carved door frame.

ZANZIBAR

Zanzibar has the oldest surviving building in the whole of Zanj, to judge by an inscription in the mosque of Kizimkazi which bears the date 500 A.H. (A.D. 1107). From the seventeenth century date Persian baths like those shown were once attached to the palace of Mwenyi Mkuu at Dunga.

The great houses of the trading port, built on an islet cut off from the main body of the island by a narrow lagoon, are not thought to be much older than the early nineteenth century. Three, four and sometimes five storeys high, painted white, ochre or blue, they crowd along the twisting narrow streets of the old city, their magnificent brass-studded doors shining with polish and oil in the bright sunlight; some of the finer houses have doors set back in arched portals. Inside, the spacious halls of the ground floor were the abode of the servants and slaves, who slept on stone shelves around the walls. From a central courtyard, with clear water splashing in a raised pool, the wide staircase led up to the main living quarters on the first floor, which had the typical long narrow rooms of the coastal plan. Open terraces on the flat concrete roofs were reached up wooden staircases, and often low arched openings were pierced below the balustradings so that women could look out while preserving their privacy – a pattern which was used five hundred years earlier on the thirteenth century terraces of Husuni Kubwa.

Zanzibar. Two views of a typical house in the old town.

Zanzibar. Crenellated ballustrading with viewing openings below on the roof terrace of a mosque.

Zanzibar. Courtyard of a house in the old town, with a circular pool and fountain in the centre.

MOSQUES

The largest mosque on the coast was the Friday Mosque at Kilwa, shown on page 94 in section plan and a view from the west. The northern section was built in the twelfth century, and had a flat concrete roof over wooden rafters supported on polygonal pillars of wood. The great southern enlargement was added in the thirteenth century. This was re-roofed with barrel vaults and domes over alternate bays in the period 1420–40. Kilwa was abandoned after the last sultan was deported to Muscat by Sa'id bin Sultan of Zanzibar in c. 1843.

The other mosques in Zanj were not as large or elaborate as this, but as they are the oldest buildings surviving in use they illustrate clearly the character of coastal architecture. Limited by the narrow span of the timber or vaulted roofs, they nevertheless follow the rare pattern of providing a large covered space for worship instead of the more common Islamic solution of a series of shallow pavilions around a square open court. This type of mosque links the coastal architecture once more to India, especially when built with 'Tudor' arches raised on heavy piers, as in the mosques of Zanzibar. Very similar mosques were built in the early period of Islamic expansion in India, and particularly by Firuz Shah (1351–88). It is interesting to note that the most characteristic of all the stylistic features of the architecture of Zanj, ogival and nicked arches, as well as corbelled

Zanzibar. Interior of the Persian baths at Mtoni palace, c. 1820.

Zanzibar. Domed turret to the small el-Hadith Mosque.

vaults and domes, are all characteristic of western India. In particular, the curious association of the ogival shape with the corbelled arch (that is, without a central voussoir, and hence not a true arch) occurs nowhere else in Islam except India, where it is traceable back to the seventh century A.D.

The Zanzibar mosques give only a pale impression of the original style of the coast. Along with the refinement and sophistication of Persia and India there went, in the earlier centuries, a directness and simplicity of form which suited the strong sunlight and clear air of the Zanj seaboard. The result was the creation of a fine architecture with a character which was uniquely East African.

Kilwa. Section plan and general view from the west of the Friday Mosque.

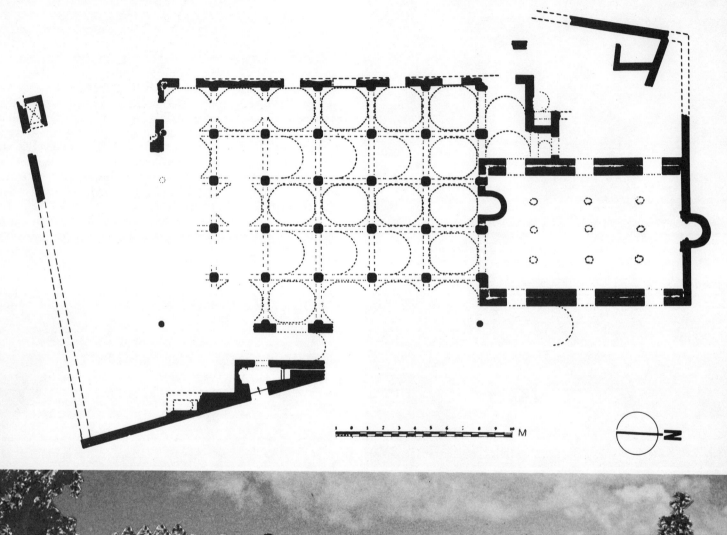

Zanzibar. Interior of the small Friday Mosque. Views in two directions.

Zanzibar. Interior of the great Friday Mosque.

BIBLIOGRAPHY

BROWN, PERCY, *Indian Architecture (Islamic Period)*, Bombay, D.B. Taraporevala Sons, 1956, pp. 6, 11, 22–5.

CHITTICK, H. N., 'Notes on Kilwa', in *Tanganyika Notes and Records*, Dar es Salaam, 1959, No. 53, p. 179.

'Kilwa and the Arab Settlement of the East African Coast', in *Journal of African History*, Cambridge, IV, 2, 1963.

Guide to the Ruins of Kilwa, with some notes on other antiquities in the region. Dar es Salaam, Ministry of Community Development and Culture, 1965.

COUSENS, H., *Architectural Antiquities in Western India*, London, India Soc., 1926.

DAVIDSON, BASIL, *The African Past*, London, Longmans, Green & Co., 1964.

GARLAKE, P. S., *Early Islamic Architecture of the East African Coast*, Nairobi and London, Oxford University Press, for British Institute of History and Archaeology in East Africa, 1966.

GRENVILLE, G. S. P. FREEMAN-, *Mediaeval History of the Coast of Tanganyika*, Oxford University Press, 1962.

The East African Coast. Select Documents, Oxford, 1962.

KIRKMAN, J. S., *The Arab City of Gedi. Excavations at the Great Mosque*, Oxford, 1954.

Gedi – The Palace, Hague, 1963.

MATHEW, G., 'Songo Mnara', in *Tanganyika Notes and Records*, Dar es Salaam, 1959, No. 53, p. 155.

ACKNOWLEDGEMENTS

The British Institute of History and Archaeology in East Africa for drawings on which were based many of the figures.

Elspeth Huxley and the publishers Chatto and Windus for permission to reproduce from *The Sorcerer's Apprentice*.

Mr. P. S. Garlake for drawings he made for the British Institute cited above on which were based many of the plans.

Mr. James Kirkman for drawings on which were based the restorations of Gedi.

INDLU: THE DOMED DWELLING OF THE ZULU

Barrie Biermann

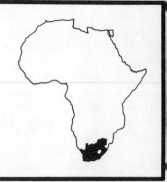

Map of South Africa, showing indigenous building types.

Every age is, in respect of some historical institution that has out-lived its time, an age of transition, and scholars are constantly called on to record and assess aspects of experience that are about to vanish without trace. That time has now come for the traditional form of dwelling of South Africa's indigenous peoples. Since those years when the migrations from the north and south first disturbed the pattern of the oldest recorded cultures in South Africa, there has been a change, progressively accelerated, in their ways of building. This change took place for the most part along the advancing frontier of the white man's culture, and can be traced as a chronological process affecting the various tribes in the order in which that frontier

passed by them. The Strandlopers, the Bushmen, the Hottentots, the Transkei tribes and finally the Natal tribes have in turn, where they survived as identifiable entities, modified their traditional methods of building. There is some record of those that have already disappeared in the accounts of travellers and missionaries over the past four hundred and fifty years, but the present time, when the process is nearing completion, affords the last opportunity to collect material for the record at first hand.

Apart from these external considerations, the intrinsic merits of the subject recommend a new evaluation. Even a sympathetic obser-ver like Bryant, the leading authority on the Zulu people, echoes the attitude of his time in dismissing 'so rubbishy a structure as the Zulu grass-hut'. He is impressed with the material standards of performance, as well he might be: 'the untutored Zulu has succeeded in evolving one of the cosiest, safest and best ventilated types of habitations ever conceived by primitive man'; but in assessing its architectural qualities purely by Victorian standards of durability and concepts of hygiene, he overlooks the more imponderable implications of the superlatives in his description.

Assessed by contemporary standards of excellence in architecture, considered as absolutes and not relative to any preconceptions, the Zulu hut stands in the forefront of architectural designs. Unless mere lip service is paid to the ideals of functional efficiency, constructional economy and exploitation of the nature of the material, the Zulu hut has achieved more in its own right than the latest advances of contemporary architecture. Any human endeavour, no matter how humble, that has attained perfection in its own field, is a rare enough phenomenon to merit due acclaim.

There is, besides the chronological sequence, a fitting sense of climax to the study of the dwellings of the last Nguni tribes to enter South Africa. The frontier of change passed over our indigenous structures not only in space and time, but in order of their evolution from the simplest to the most highly developed. There are also indications that when the tide of change is about to overtake the last survivors, these crowning examples of the Nguni building tradition have made one final evolutionary spurt to present, at the end, their finest aspect.

Another absolute standard in architecture, more difficult to define, most subject to the vagaries of fashion, by which the Zulu hut can claim to excel, is that of intrinsic beauty. Although beauty for its own sake is not an ideal nor even a preoccupation of our present culture, it has claims which, if only for the completeness of the record, cannot be ignored. More compelling than any of these considerations taken individually is, from the human point of view, their total implication. We accord unbounded admiration to the Greeks for achieving perfection in their architecture, although we ourselves do not build Greek temples; might we not extend the same consideration to the perfection of Zulu building?

There is one item of difference which lends further point to this study. The Zulus have not passed into history, and their building tradition is still alive.

THE CIRCLE AS DESIGN THEME

What most distinguishes the Zulu dwelling from other domical structures in South Africa, in particular those which are now extinct, is its advanced stage of development. The Hottentot peoples, displaced by the Nguni invasion, built shelters remarkable enough in their own right – prefabricated and portable, eminently suited to the nomadic habits of the builders. These itinerant domes were in fact tents, and the temporary settlements in which they were sited at random, no more than encampments (left). A stronger sense of hierarchy had developed among the Zulu, which found expression in their relatively permanent settlements.

Among these the Royal Kraal called for structures of unusual scale, making demands which went beyond their technological capabilities (page 97). However, since most ceremonial functions involving large numbers of people were conducted in the open, the need for clear spans over large interiors was not urgently felt.

Their organisational and aesthetic resources were directed more towards planning and ordering the environment, in the arrangement of the various units to accommodate domestic and ritual activities; and in this they excelled.

With the same capacity for elaborate logic that made their language pre-eminent among the many others of the South African Bantu, the Zulu formalised the homely universals of family circle, circle of friends, circle of admirers, circus – all the applications of the concept 'round' which in English survives merely in the idiom pertaining to sport, drinking, applause or daily routine. What is indeed ubiquitous and therefore accepted unconsciously, the Zulu sense of organisation makes deliberate and manifest, so that the observer in the Zulu homestead discovers with new-found delight the latent consonance and harmony of common objects in the casual juxtaposition of baskets and bowls, pots, posts, pits, sheaves of grass and cakes of dung. When the larger context asserts the principle so compellingly, the eye never tires of seeing the echoes, even in the detail of the beadwork and the texture of the thatch.

It is necessary to dwell somewhat on these implications, since the aesthetic content of a design based on a simple theme and variations can not easily be expressed in words nor convincingly illustrated any more than a symphony can be adequately explained in default of the experience of hearing it. Perhaps the most persuasive demonstration of the generic powers of an elementary geometrical principle consistently applied as a design theme, are the royal Zulu cities.

AUTOCRACY AND GEOMETRICAL CITY PLANS

The sudden emergence among the Zulu people of dense settlements built to a master plan of geometrical clarity and precision, affords yet another insight into the vexed problem of the origin of cities. Only over the last decade has archaeological work in the Middle East

begun to yield evidence in conflict with the traditional conception of the growth of cities by a process of slow evolution by way of villages towns and trading centres based on the surpluses of settled and intensive agriculture. Yet the same evidence has long been available to anthropology. That sudden mutations can occur spontaneously and unpredictably, leading to revolutionary changes in sudden bursts of energy, is accepted in the physical and biological sciences: on the African continent three well-documented examples point to the operation of similar processes in human affairs.

The emergence of monumental Egyptian architecture at Saqqara within a single generation, is on first consideration the most impressive of these. At Zimbabwe the creation of a monumental Bantu architecture on an even larger scale – seen in relation to the resources of its region – must, however, be considered the more remarkable. Both these examples are remote in time and lack contemporary records. In the case of the Zulu city we have first-hand accounts from observers who witnessed the event a mere century and a half ago.

The prelude to the foundation of settlements larger than those built hitherto, was the growth of population among a nomadic pastoral people settled for a century in the confined area of Natal. Friction between neighbouring clans, which had always found a traditional outlet in battles of the Homeric type, involving more speeches than corpses, grew bloodier as the pressure mounted. When, in 1817 Dingiswayo, king of the Mtetwa, had been entrapped and murdered while engaged in an audacious border raid, the vacant paramountcy was contended for by a multitude of tributary chieftians.

'Among all these clans,' Bryant writes in his *History*, 'that of the Zulus led by the youthful Shaka, was by far the most ambitious and aggressive. ... Shaka had conceived the then quite novel idea of utterly demolishing his rivals as separate tribal entities by incorporating all their manhood into his own clan or following, which brilliant manoeuvre immediately reduced his possible foes for all time by one and at the same time doubled the number of his own army. With this augmentation of strength, Shaka's ambitions grew apace ... if from the centre we describe a circle stretching twenty miles in every direction, we shall encompass the extent of country which Shaka operated in, conquered and annexed in this his first Natal campaign, probably about the year 1817.'

At the centre a royal kraal was built commensurate in size with the hinterland it preyed on. Once under way, the process continued with its own momentum, cities growing in scale and number as the waves of devastation spread ever wider. Unproductive in themselves, the predatory cities maintained themselves by pillage and genocide until within two decades their reign of terror had depopulated a vast tract of the sub-continent.

The instrument of terror was the Zulu *impi*, a regiment organised to attack in the form of a hemicycle, a crescent directed against the enemy like the curved horns of the Zulu bull, but in the act of annihilation closing the open arc into a circle of destruction. The city from which the *impi* set forth was as regimented and disciplined as its operation in battle. J. R. Mackenzie relates of the successor to Shaka's murderer Dingane: 'The king's kraals are of enormous dimensions, and are several in number. Panda, for example, has one kraal, the central enclosure of which is nearly a mile in diameter. This enclosure is supposed to be filled with the monarch's cows, and is consequently called by the name of *isiBaya*. Practically, however, the cattle are kept in smaller enclosures arranged along the sides of the *isiBaya*, where they can be watched by those who have the charge of them, and whose huts are placed conveniently for that purpose. The vast central enclosure is used almost exclusively as a parade ground, where the king can review his troops, and where they are taught to go through the simple manoeuvres of Kaffir warfare. Here, also, he may be seen in council, the *isiBaya* being able to accommodate an unlimited number of suitors.

'Around the *isiBaya* are arranged the huts of the warriors and their families, and are placed in four or even five-fold ranks; so that the kraal almost rises to the dignity of a town, having several thousand inhabitants, and presenting a singularly imposing appearance when viewed at a distance (below).

'At the upper portion of the kraal, and at the further end from the principal entrance, are the huts specially erected for the king, surrounded by the other huts containing his harem. The whole of this part of the kraal is separated from the remainder by lofty and strong fences, and its doors are kept by sentinels . . . at that time Panda had thirteen of these great military kraals, and he had just completed a fourteenth. He takes up his residence in these kraals successively, and finds in each everything he can possibly want – each being, indeed, almost identical in every respect with all the others. As a

general rule, each of these military kraals forms the residence of a single regiment; while the king has many others which are devoted to more peaceful objects.'

Such was the system, institutionalised a bare generation after Shaka had initiated it. In his book *The Zulu Aftermath*, J. D. Omer-Cooper states that 'the reorganisation of society on military lines was accompanied by a new ethos. The informality, hospitality and naïve curiosity which meant that the visitor to a Bantu village was immediately surrounded by a mob of men, women and children, staring, asking questions and openly begging for gifts, was replaced by a more reserved attitude. A pride amounting almost to arrogance and an indifference to human life were accompanied by a sense of discipline, order and cleanliness . . . at the same time political loyalty was enhanced to a high degree, and came to be regarded as an absolute value.'

Since the form of the city was an ingenious adaptation of the isolated homestead, without any further technological innovations to meet the strain placed on primitive services and sanitation by a dense population, strict civic discipline was essential for it to function at all. There is no reliable record of the absolute numbers involved. At one of Shaka's foundations, Gibixhegu (a name meaning 'finish off the old men' – symptomatic of the new dispensation), there were one thousand, four hundred huts strung around a circumference of three miles. The rate of occupancy per hut was variable: some may have been dwelling units, but most served as barrack-room dormitories.

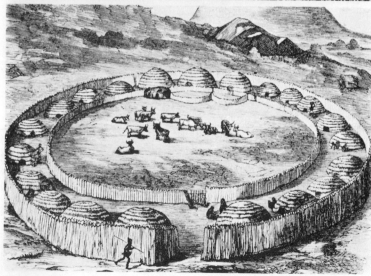

THE LEGACY OF INSECURITY

The individual unit had always been flexible as regards usage. The same constructional principles applied to miniaturised items serving as grain stores, as to the large royal palace, save that in the latter it extravagant span required a cluster of intermediate supports. The standard unit tended to exploit the maximum free span of the sapling framework carrying its final load of heavy thatch. There was also the requirement of portability, since custom decreed that when an inhabitant died, the unit assigned to him be burnt or abandoned, the others being moved bodily, or the thatch stripped and framework removed to a new site some short distance away. As a whole the nomadic tradition militated against the idea of ground ownership and permanent sites, while intermittent warfare entailing the razing of homesteads put a premium on structures that could easily be replaced.

The form of the homestead was dictated by the requirement of protecting the wealth of its owner: his cattle. The cattle kraal – *isiBaya* – occupied the centre, and indeed generated the layout. Its protective stockade utilised the heaviest available timber. In olden times protection was extended to the homestead as a whole by a second stockade, concentric with the *isiBaya*. The dwelling units occupied the space between. Their security was limited to safety from animal predators; they were defenceless against the onslaught of the *impi* and the firebrand. A rigid hierarchical pattern determined the order of the units around their circle.

'In the good old days when wives were cheap and many, a high-class Kaffir kraal was organised in two distinct sides or branches. There was the *ekuNene* (or right-hand side) whose huts ran up on the right side from near the kraal entrance till they reached and included the *iNdlunkulu* (or Great hut) occupying exactly the central position at the top of the kraal (under the dominion of the Great Wife and her son); and there was the *iKohlo* (or left-hand) branch, whose huts formed the opposite side of the circle' (Bryant).

The latter represented the interests of the lesser wives. The whole layout embodied a social pattern devised to eliminate friction, assign every member of the family his rightful place and ensure an orderly succession when the patriarch died. A recognition of the elemental conflicts engendered by the mother's ambitions for her sons, the sons' premature designs on their father's authority and the jealousies latent in a polygamous household, informed the geometry of the Zulu homestead.

HOUSE-BUILDING AS HOME-CRAFT

In domestic affairs the woman was paramount. The nominal head of the household had no dwelling he could call his own: he merely visited one wife after another. The women built the shelters – sometimes with assistance from the menfolk on the framework of larger units – and they maintained the ageless tradition of weaving and plaiting the grass covering.

Construction of the typical sleeping unit of some 5 m span proceeded as follows: in the foundation trench, 165 mm deep, commenc-

ing across the circle from the site of the eventual doorway, saplings are planted close together in a double row, inclined in opposite directions laterally so that they crisscross; at about 1 m above ground level, their tops are bent over and lashed together to form a series of interlacing arches in the plane of the wall. At this stage the doorway is established by arching a plaited bundle over the opening and filling that section of the trench as a threshold. A series of arched saplings concentric with the doorway serve to integrate it into the general wall structure, which is now inclined inwards until the crests of the arches touch and are lashed together at the apex of the resultant dome. Although there has been no actual weaving or plaiting of the saplings, the total framework has the dense texture and resilience of basketwork, acts as a homogenous structural unit and resists the thrust of the marauder's broad-bladed assegai.

The doorway is sealed with a loose panel of wicker-work, secured against the inside face of the jambs by means of an external cross-beam threaded through looped thongs attached to the panel.

The dome may be self-supporting or require props, depending on the inherent stiffness of the saplings, the weight of the super-incumbent thatch and the free span. Props occur in pairs and multiples of pairs, carry simple cross-beams and take a final finish

of woven grass among the well-to-do, or of beadwork among royalty.

Externally the thatch is kept in place by means of grass ropes, or withies, which are simply deeply embedded in the thatch at both ends. Most elaborate and durable is the rope grid composed of longitudes radiating from a ring around the apex, with latitudes knotted to them at regular intervals to form a network. In the colder highlands the thatch is often supplemented with grass mats, laid in overlapping layers terminating in a final mat at the crest which runs from the lintel of the doorway over the apex to the back.

Where the construction allows the thatch to be gathered in a finial, great care is lavished on its finish and decoration, both to ensure waterproofing at a crucial point where the thatch lies horizontally, and because the finial houses the *abaFana*, ritual thundersticks invoked as protection against the lightning.

Final thatching is carried out in the last decades of the occupant's lifetime. The decoration now attains a baroque exuberance. Bands of criss-cross ornament, reminiscent of bead-work patterns, alternate with the swags and festoons more appropriate to the medium of plaited grass.

For a short period around the middle of this century, when fifty years of peace and prosperity had held the balance against the constant threat of over-population, the architecture ripened into unprecedented effulgence. In the Drakensberg mountain region, surrounds to the doorways burgeoned into lace-like porticos (above), a development so novel that the Zulu language, which is seldom at a loss for words, had not yet evolved terms to describe it.

In the event, this and other evolutionary trends have been both unbaptised and still-born. The relentless pressure of grazing, ploughing and building on the lush grasslands which yielded the thatching material, has begun to take its toll. The beehive dome of the Nguni peoples in Zululand is now in its last generation.

CHANGING PATTERNS

The devastating wars of the last century, culminating in the Zulu Rebellion in the first decade of the twentieth, impressed on all the Nguni peoples that the great migration was over, and that the pattern of settlement would not be determined by any one tribe. The cities of Shaka and his successors would not be rebuilt. Instead, the descendants of the Zulu warriors, and hunters and herdsmen, have turned progressively to agriculture. As regards the homestead, the change was marked by the dwindling importance of the *isiBaya*. Cattle were no longer a viable index of wealth, and the goats that replaced them require smaller enclosures; while the polygamy maintained by a cattle economy yielded to the system of a single wife. Around the diminished *isiBaya*, there would be at most three sleeping units: the wife's, the girls' and the boys'.

As the diet changed from fresh meat and curdled milk to maize, so the storage units acquired greater importance, and as the cultivated fields encroached on the grazing, the traditional building material grew scarcer. It was now reserved for roofing only — mudbrick walls rose ever higher to eke out the meagre supply of thatch. The availability of heavy timber from the wattle plantations around Zululand encouraged the building of conical roofs based on the principle of rafters and battens. Adoption of the white man's customs, in particular the use of vehicles and furniture, called for rectangular interiors.

Increasingly the changing pattern of the daily round called for an architectural expression differing from the traditional. It is too early to make a final assessment of the Zulu response to this new challenge: its conformation depends on too many variables, of which the predominance of any one could stamp a unique character on the trend of development. There are, however, certain pointers.

The Zulu capacity for organisation emerges time and again over a wide range of localities in the welter of new forms and unfamiliar materials with which the unsophisticated builders are confronted. Their innate discipline and ancestral pride is still manifest in scrupulously kept homesteads, no matter how unconventional their form. Together these qualities make for environments richer and more varied in visual delights than the traditional, gaining in amplitude while sacrificing the overpoweringly single-minded unity of the old dispensation. Where their neighbours have yielded all too readily to the seduction of painted wall surfaces with the new techniques now made available to them, the Zulu, with admirable restraint, rely on the textural effects inherent in the natural material. Their transitional architecture thereby retains the classical qualities which in the past distinguished their traditional buildings from those of their contemporaries in Southern Africa.

The *indlu*, or dwelling unit, is termed *ukwakha umduzo* (stitched work) to distinguish it from other types of covering: *ukwakha umdeko* (stepped thatch) and *indlu esikutulo* (jointed house), which has a covering mat and no finial. In the finial (*isicholo*) are placed the *abafana*, literally 'the children', since these ritual thundersticks may be handled only by youngsters who have not undergone initiation. The supporting framework is made up of a post (*insika*) and lintel (*umjanjato*) carrying the roof beam (*umshayo*). Slung between the posts is the clothesline (*umgibe*), more often found at the rear of the unit (*umsamo*), a storage area screened or defined by the *iguma*. In the centre is the hearth (*iziko*) and its structure (*umbundu*), while

between it and the doorway (*umnyango*) is a zon[e] ...ngu *lungulu*. The remainder of the interior is zoned on ...er (*isilili sesinina*) and on the right for men (*isilili san*... ...a ior is sealed off by a wicker door (*isicabha*) hel[d] ... cross-piece (*ibhaxa*). The fringe of thatch around ... perimeter is termed the *umshaba*. The thatch itself ... down by the net of the ropework (*umtwazi*) and car[ried] ... work of arched withies (*izintungo*). This nomenclatu[re] ... for the most part by the *Zulu Dictionary* of Doke ... some terms are regional, and many are becoming ... example, *umtwazi*, the grass rope ('which we make fro[m]... is yielding place to *intambo*, rope or string ('which we ... shop').

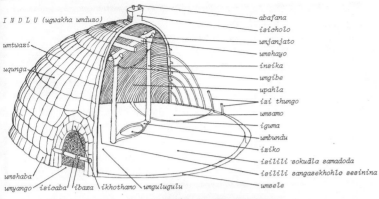

_I N D L U_ (_ugwakha unduzo_)

umtwazi

uqunga

umshaba
umyango isicaba ibaxa ikhothamo umgulugulu

abafana
isicholo
umjanjato
umshayo
insika
umgibe
upahla
izi thungo
umsamo
iguma
umbundu
iziko
isilili sokudla samadoda
isilili sangasekhohlo sesinina
umsele

BIBLIOGRAPHY

BRYANT, A. T., _A History of the Zulu and Neighbouring Tribes_, Cape Town, C. Struik, 1964, p. 48.
OMER-COOPER, J. D., _The Zulu Aftermath_, London, Longmans, 1966, p. 37.

ACKNOWLEDGEMENT

MALCOLM, D. McK. late Head of the Department of Zulu, University of Natal, Durban: guide and interpreter for the Documentary Survey of Zulu Building, 1957.

SOME TRADITIONAL TYPES OF HOUSING IN ETHIOPIA

Naigzy Gebremedhin

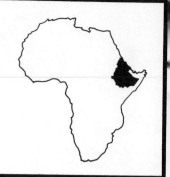

THE NATURAL SETTING

Ethiopia has been called the citadel of Africa. It is a mountainous country; various peoples, speaking many languages, form the present nation of 25 million. It has an ancient culture and a recorded history dating back several thousand years.

Altitude is the most important factor regulating the tempo of life in Ethiopia: the fauna and the flora of the country vary essentially according to altitude. The types of agriculture, indeed even of personality traits, are said to depend on their specific location. Ethiopians believe that the highlanders are slow and even-tempered and that the lowlanders are easily angered. There are three traditional classifications of altitude: *dega* or highland, *weina-dega* or middle altitude and *kolla* or lowland.

The mountains offer three advantages in so far as human settlements are concerned. First, mountains provide protection to villages and large settlements and all `important Ethiopian towns are located in areas difficult to reach. Secondly, although most of highland Ethiopia is situated within the tropics, it enjoys a softness of climate, rather like the summer climate of Switzerland. The altitude is chiefly responsible for this. Thirdly, altitude provides a remarkably healthful environment. Above the middle levels, *weina-dega*, the tsetse fly cannot survive, and as a result cattle and draught animals are found in abundance. As we shall see later, cow dung constitutes an important element in the construction of housing, and even cattle horns are used, as hooks for hanging a variety of utensils. The anopheles mosquito does not breed above 1,900 m; hence malaria does not exist above this level. The same is true of yellow fever and cholera above 1,500 m.

ETHNIC GROUPS AND HOUSING TYPES

Ethiopia has a remarkable variety of peoples. A simple grouping, while it does not provide a clear picture of every tribal group, nevertheless affords an opportunity for presenting an overview. Ethiopians may be grouped into three major ethnic groupings. These three groupings and their distribution over the country is shown in the following map. The groups are: (1) Semitised Cushitic Group.[1] (2) Cushitic group. (3) Nilotic group. The Tigré Chief's House and the Tigré farmer's house are samples of the house-types produced by the first ethnic group, i.e. Semitised Cushitic group. In this context, the Gurage people and the Gurage house-type described here are an exception. The Gurage people are regarded as Semitised Cushites, though their house-type is in substance no different from the typical house-type of the great majority of Cushitic tribes. The Shoa Gala house is a sample of the type built by the most important sub-group of the Cushitic group. As can be seen from the map, this group is distributed throughout the whole of Ethiopia.

Map of Ethiopia showing distribution of ethnic groups.

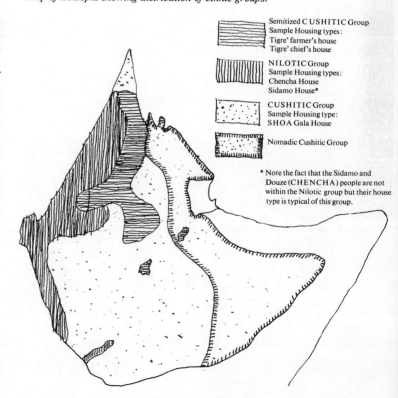

Semitized CUSHITIC Group
Sample Housing types:
Tigre' farmer's house
Tigre' chief's house

NILOTIC Group
Sample Housing types:
Chencha House
Sidamo House*

CUSHITIC Group
Sample Housing type:
SHOA Gala House

Nomadic Cushitic Group

* Note the fact that the Sidamo and Douze (CHENCHA) people are not within the Nilotic group but their house type is typical of this group.

Chencha and Sidamo bamboo houses are built by people whose tribal affinity is closer to the Cushitic group than to the Nilotic group. However, since there is a close similarity between these type-houses and the house-types built by Nilotic peoples, the Sidamo house and the Chencha houses will be taken as representative samples of the type of houses built by the Nilotic group.

SEMITISED CUSHITICS AND THEIR HOUSE-TYPES

This group occupies what is classically known as the historical part of Ethiopia. They are proponents of early Ethiopian Christian culture. The influence of their culture is felt throughout Ethiopia. The most important sub-group is the Amharic-speaking group which is found throughout the provinces of Gojam, Begemeder and Shoa. These people occupy the salubrious highlands practising sedentary farming. They raise a variety of crops and keep different kinds of domestic animals and their agricultural practice is generally of a very high standard. The tribal structure varies a great deal according to the sub-groups.

THE CUSHITIC GROUP

This group is the largest ethnic group of the country. Ullendorff writes, 'The peoples of Cushitic speech in Ethiopia occupy not only

Map of Ethiopia showing distribution of housing types discussed in the study.

I Tigre' farmer's house
II Tigre' chief's house
III Shoa Gala house
IV Gurage house
V Chencha house
VI Sidamo house

Above 6,000 feet

the vast area of the eastern, southern and western plains and mountain slopes, but they also constitute the substrata upon which the Semitic-speaking emigrants have been laid.'[2]

Numerous sub-groups exist. The largest sub-group, the Gala, is believed to be composed of no less than two hundred smaller groups. The language of this group, *Galigna*, is spoken almost as widely as is Amharic. Ullendorff writes: 'Their original habitat was probably in the corner of the horn of Africa, but continual Somali pressure drove them west and south-west. It was only in the fifteenth and sixteenth centuries that they began to penetrate into the Abyssinian highlands, and once they had ascended the fertile plateau, they abandoned their way of life as nomadic herdsmen and became sedentary cultivators.'[3]

As the accompanying map shows, the Cushitic people who occupy a large portion of eastern Ethiopia are still nomadic herdsmen. Among these both Gala and other tribal sub-groups are found. The house-type produced by nomadic herdsmen has much in common with the house-type produced by the Nilotic groups (see below). A major distinction should be noted, however, which concerns the use of materials. Whereas the typical house produced by the Nilotic group uses materials collected from the immediate vicinity, nomadic herdsmen have tended to use more permanent materials, such as woven mats and skins of animals, and even their wicker-work tends to be well prepared and of a permanent nature. These materials are light so that they can be easily transported from place to place, as the nomadic herdsmen move in search of grass and water for their animals.

NILOTIC GROUP

This group is the smallest of the ethnic groups, and occupies the western border. The type of house they build is similar to the Chencha house and the Sidamo house described farther on in this report. The people who belong to this group live in the remote lowlands near river banks and on the shores of the large lakes of Ethiopia. Among the sub-groups may be mentioned the Baria and Kunama tribes in the north, the small Nilotic tribes along the Ethiopian-Sudanese border such as the Mekan, Mao, Gunza, etc. These people have traditionally made their living by hunting, trapping and fishing. The Weito for example, who live along the banks of the Nile are despised by the highlanders because they hunt the hippopotamus. Nowadays, many of these sub-groups have learnt to till the land and cultivate crops.

THE HISTORICAL SETTING

Ethiopia's long historical heritage and architectural achievements provide a useful reference point for the analysis and understanding of traditional housing types. Often one can easily trace some traditional housing details to past Ethiopian architectural practice. The buildings of the ancient kingdom of Axum are well known; Axumites erected truly imposing structures. One of the stelae which now lies broken in pieces appears to be the highest monolithic block ever built by ancient man. 'Decorations of the largest stelae at Axum symbolise building structures. One cannot assume that the Axumites in reality constructed eight- or ten-storey buildings even if the ruins indicate this.'[4] The plan of a palace recently excavated at Axum may be favourably compared with the layout plan of a *hudmo*, or farmer's house of the Eritrean type.

It was not until the middle of the seventeenth century that Ethiopians learned how to make lime mortar, nor is it surprising that it took so long. The sedimentary rocks of the central highlands have a deep cover of lava so that limestone does not show in many areas. The art of making strong mortar opened up the possibility of constructing arches and vaults, and gave rise to the tendency towards the use of monumental dimensions. Lindahl suggests that the break with Ethiopian tradition in this respect affected the change in height of rooms and the size of window openings.[5]

Plan of a hudmo, *rectangular farmer's house, Eritrean type. This house is shared by several households. (Adapted from Danielli, Marinelli,* Villagi e Tipi di Abitazioni, *p. 417.) (right)*

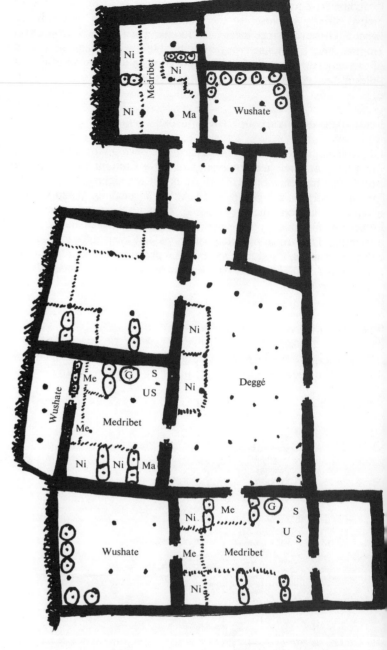

Plan of a palace recently excavated at Axum. (below)

Medribet = Main living room
Wushate = Kitchen storage
Ma = Methan, grinding stone
Me = Medeb, built-in seating bench
S = Seregela, built-in kitchen shelf
U = Uton, stove

G = Gubutish, fumigating device
○ = Kofo, grain storage
● = Supporting pillars
Deggé = Courtyard
Ni = Ni'ed, built-in bed

108

COMMON CHARACTERISTICS

Most Ethiopian traditional houses represent a very refined product. House-types in the northern region exhibit a remarkable continuity of characteristics, possibly as a result of continued improvement of the building process, which must be regarded in the context of an economy that has not changed for a long time. In this respect, it is useful to compare two illustrations. The first represents a model of a house believed to be about fifteen hundred years old. This clay model was found near Axum in 1959. It is about 25 cm long. The second figure shows the elevation of a Tigré farmer's house as it is built today. The similarity between the two plans is striking. Ethiopian traditional house-types are also characterised by their simplicity. Decorations are rare and the internal arrangement of the houses is marked by a stark austerity, though the Tigré chief's house is an exception. On the whole, it appears that great pains are taken to avoid flamboyance of style. Materials are used in the simplest and most obvious ways, and the use of wood and stone *au naturel* is preferred.

Elevations, sections and plan of clay model house found near Axum.

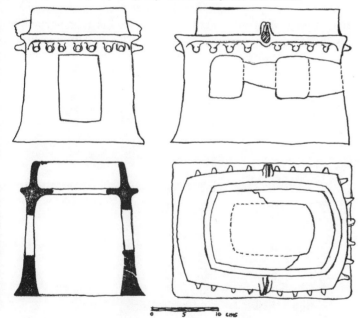

Section and Elevation of a Tigré farmer's house.

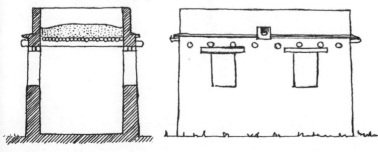

In nearly all traditional Ethiopian houses, irrespective of the tribal and religious affiliations of the people who build them, the central area is reserved for important people and/or for specially important occasions. This practice is less frequent in the case of rectangular houses, probably because partitioning in rectangular houses is relatively easy. The designation of the central space in the house as the place of honour is not only of Christian origin. Danielli, Marienelli and Cipriani suggest that this practice exists also in Moslem communities,[7] but the similarity between the designation of space in a Christian church and that of an ordinary residential house is worth mentioning.

In traditional circular Ethiopian churches, the three concentric parts have the following functions: (1) *quené mahlét*, i.e. the place where hymns are sung and where the *däbtära* or cantors stand. To this part the community at large has ready access. It corresponds to the outer part of the Tabernacle, or of Solomon's Temple. The next chamber (2) is the *queddest* or *enda ta'amer* 'place of miracles', which is generally reserved for priests, but to which laymen have access for the administration of communion. This is equivalent to the middle part of the Tabernacle, or of Solomon's Temple. The innermost part (3) is the *mäqdäs* or *qeddusä qeddusan*, where the *tabot* rests and to which only senior priests and the king are admitted. 'This corresponds to the Holy of the Holies of the Tabernacle and the Temple. This room is carefully guarded, and by its subdued light or virtual darkness the air of awe and mystery is greatly accentuated.'[8]

In the traditional Tigré house, the four central pillars define the space, which, as in church nomenclature, is called the *mäqdäs*, the *sancta sanctorum*. In some cases, women are admitted to the area outside the pillars only.

TYPOLOGY OF HOUSES

Cipriani subdivides Ethiopian house-types according to the characteristics of the supporting frameworks. He recognises three fundamental types: (1) rigid elements; (2) flexible elements 'planted' to the ground at one end; (3) flexible elements 'planted' at both ends. This classification does not apply to rectangular houses.[9]

Typology of houses, adapted from L. Cipriani, p. 47.

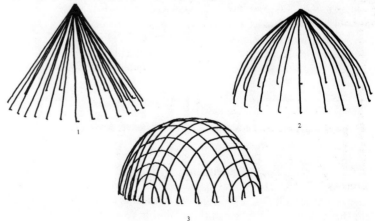

Ethiopian house-types may also be classified according to the building process used. Three main processes are: (1) Piling, i.e. the process used in connection with elements such as blocks, burnt bricks or stones; (2) Twining or tying, i.e. the process by which building elements are tied together by rope, plant twigs or other suitable tying material; (3) Weaving: bamboo and grass are two excellent examples of materials that can be woven to produce houses.

Graph showing differentiation of structure and materials used in relation to economy.

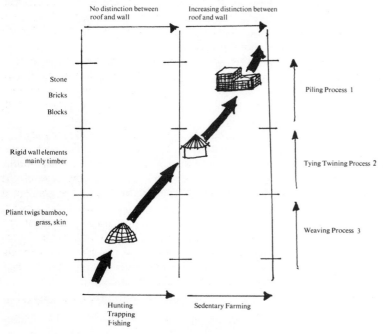

The six house-types which will be described below may be classified as follows:

PROCESS	PROTOTYPE	SHAPE AND FORM	WINDOW OPENING
1	Tigré chief's house	Round conical roof	Yes
1	Tigré farmer's house	Rectangular flat roof	Yes
2	Shoa gala house	Round conical roof	No
2	Gurage house	Round conical roof	No
3	Chencha house	Paraspherical	No
3	Sidamo house	Paraspherical	No

Some important characteristics of these house-types are:

(1) Houses produced by processes 2 and 3 are usually without corners. They have either a cylindrical wall and a conical roof or are roughly hemi-spherical. The reason for this may be explained as follows. Tying and weaving lend themselves admirably to the production of plane surfaces that have no abrupt change.

(2) One also notes that house-types produced by processes 2 and 3 generally have no window opening. This also appears obvious. Surfaces produced by the *tying* or *weaving* process do not accommodate openings easily and naturally. In practice, openings are made by literally cutting a hole in a finished surface. This exercise is both wasteful and awkward. In the case of a house built by the piling process on the other hand, an opening can be fairly easily accommodated. Ethiopian stone house-types are likely to have many more openings than other house-types.

(3) The roof and wall of house-types produced by process 3 are not distinctly differentiated.

(4) Producing house-types by process 1 is slow and expensive, since the weight of the house is very great. It also requires some additional thought in arranging for an adequate and safe foundation. House-types produced by processes 2 and 3, however, are quickly put up, and their weight is very light. Not much thought need be given to the foundation of such houses.

At present, it is not clear which process is the most advanced, although Cipriani suggests that as the mode of life changes from hunting to sedentary farming the house-type changes from a spherical shape to a differentiation between the wall and the roof. He thereby implies that the construction of a wall is an important milestone in the development of housing. Clearly, each area in Ethiopia

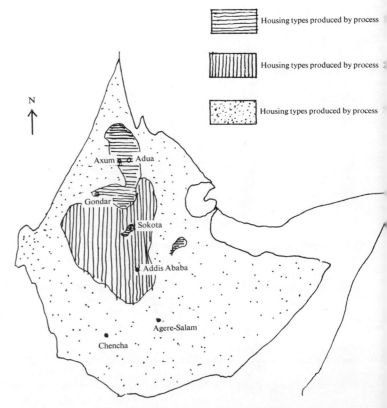

110

has developed and refined the process presently in use because the materials used are found in abundance in the immediate vicinity. In Tigré an excellent quality stone for masonry work is found in great abundance, and masonry work appears to be of a very high standard there. In the south and the southwestern parts of the country, bamboo and various other building materials of a vegetable character are commonly found, and tying and weaving are therefore used for building houses. In some areas of Ethiopia there is a thorough mixture of styles and building methods. These areas are endowed with materials suited for the production of housing by all the three processes.

HOUSE-TYPES

TIGRÉ FARMER'S HOUSE (Hudmo)[10]

The area where such houses are to be found includes the present provinces of Tigré and Eritrea (see map).

Three important public activities are included in the land-use plan of a typical village.

(1) A church and a graveyard attached to it.

(2) An open-air meeting place (*baito*).

(3) A place for the accumulation and burning of village waste products.

(Guaduf)

Apparently the villages have a fairly well-articulated logistic plan for waste disposal, based on the voluntarily donated service of the head of the family.

Houses in this area are built very close to one another, and in

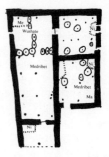

A two-family hudmo *house Eritrean type. Note that one of the families has only one room and the other has three. (Adapted from Danielli and Marinelli, p. 397.)*

some cases units are constructed so as to share a party wall. The village layout in Eritrea and Tigré is in sharp contrast to that in the southern part of Ethiopia. The pattern in the other area is to have a rather dispersed type of settlement.

In general it is possible to detect two types of Tigré farm houses. The Eritrean type is built into the steep side of a hill or mountain. The casual observer has great difficulty in detecting these houses, particularly from a distance, since they tend to blend completely with the surroundings.

The other variety, which is found around the Adi-Grat area, is readily visible even from a distance. Both types have flat roofs composed of compacted earth resting on a system of round timber beams. These houses have very well-defined partitions. In the case of the Eritrean type, a string of grain-stores (*kofo*) built in a connected system serves as a partition. In other cases, a stone masonry partition is provided, distinguishing and setting aside certain areas of the house for specific use. Basically, there are two indispensable rooms in such houses; the *medri biet*, an all-purpose living and sleeping room, and *wushate* an area for storage and cooking. The farmer would add to this plan according to circumstances.

Elevations and plan of Tigré house, Adigrat type. The partly covered courtyard shelters the cattle.   *Sections through Tigré farmer's house, Adigrat type.*

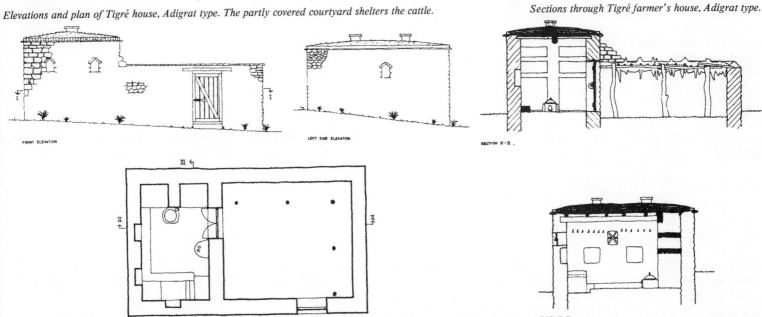

FRONT ELEVATION   LEFT SIDE ELEVATION   SECTION II-II.

SECTION I-I   SECTION III-III

Construction Method

The stone masonry for these houses follows the old Axum tradition, i.e. large well-dressed stones at the corners and small stones elsewhere. Nowadays the stones are joined together with *chika mortar*. *Chika* is basically any kind of earth – though clay is preferred – that is thoroughly mixed with water. It is usually reinforced with straw before it is applied. Occasionally one sees an excellent example of the system of masonry construction which is called 'monkey head'. This same construction method was copied in the ancient monolithic structures of Axum, as well as in the monolithic churches of Lalibella dating from the eleventh century.

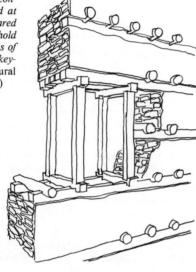

'Monkey head' system of masonry construction. The walls are strengthened at narrow intervals with long, squared timbers. Short, round cross-pieces hold these in place. The protruding sections of the cross-pieces are termed the 'monkey-heads'. (Adapted from Architectural History of Ethiopia in Pictures, *p. 18.)*

The pillars supporting the roof are placed throughout the house without much regard to symmetry. It appears that their spacing is more a function of the length and size of the beams used in supporting the roof than of anything else. The collection of stones for a house is a long and painful process usually lasting more than three years. Building time for a medium-size house is reported to be about four to six months, provided work is carried out steadily on the project.

Internal Arrangements

The farmer's house is remarkably rich in the variety of built-in furniture provided. The word 'furniture' is used in a broad sense, since the things to be described below are indistinguishable in some respects from the structural elements of the wall and floor. Three kinds of built-in facilities are usually provided. One is a raised platform that serves as a sitting bench, *medeb*, which runs along walls. Another is a slightly higher platform built adjacent to the wall and meant to serve as a bed, *niidi*. A variation of this kind of bed called *ni'edi merauti* literally, a bed for married couples, is given an extra measure of privacy in one of two ways: either it is built up to a height of five feet, or a small stone fence is built around it, complete with a

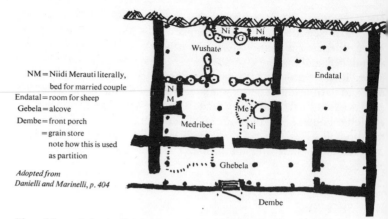

NM = Niidi Merauti literally,
    bed for married couple
Endatal = room for sheep
Gebela = alcove
Dembe = front porch
    = grain store
    note how this is used
    as partition

Adopted from
Danielli and Marinelli, p. 404

Plan of farmer's house, Eritrean type, built into the steep side of a mountain.

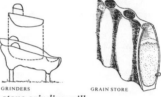

Grain store and methan, *stone grinding mill.*

little gate usually made of bamboo. Various recesses in the wall are created to serve as shelves. In the *wushate*, a special shelf is provided for storing various utensils.

Other noteworthy built-in equipment is indicated on the plans. The most important items are the *uton*, a furnace for baking *enjera*, the staple bread of Ethiopians. (Note that this is different from the ordinary fireplace.) Another important piece of built-in equipment is the stone-grinding mill, *methan* (see sketch). A third item worth mentioning is the *gubutish*, a special fumigating device that women use for hygienic and health purposes. The device consists of a fireplace with a clay pot that funnels smoke to any desired position.

TIGRÉ CHIEF'S HOUSE

Occurrence

Two-storey round houses made of stone are found in the Axum and Adua areas of Tigré province. Variations of two-storey round houses are also seen in and around Gondar, and around the Sokota area of Wollow province (see map). We will describe the type usually seen around Adua and Axum.

This kind of house can only be afforded by the well-to-do. The amount of material it requires and the specialised details that it incorporates represent a major outlay of resources which only a few persons in the community can afford. These houses have been used as residences for governors, high priests and soldiers. Modest two-storey houses have also been built by farmers particularly in the Sokota area, apparently to circumvent the lack of large plots in the important villages.

The house-types around Axum and Adua have borrowed much

from the practices of ancient Axumite architecture. Their form and plan layout have changed very little over the years, to judge from a study of houses and architecture carried out by a German scientific expedition some time before the turn of the century. The similarity of this plan with the ones displayed alongside is striking. Such houses must have existed in great abundance as long as forest supplies lasted in the area. In the Tigré province the last houses of this type were probably built at the turn of the century.

Much of the timber supplied in the construction of these houses is

Plan of Axumite house.

wasted in the process of carving out required shapes for windows, doors, lintels, floors and ceilings.

Construction Method

The foundation trenches are dug with generous dimensions, usually 1 m in width. For the foundation, blackstone (basalt) is used since it supposedly does not absorb water. An excellent quality of basalt is found throughout the northern provinces of Ethiopia. Furthermore, this stone has the tendency to cleave into flat pieces, making it relatively easy to cut and handle. The mortar used is *chika*, which has been described above. For the main wall, a softer, greyish rock – trachyte – or sandstone, is used.

The woodwork for this house is indicative of the level which Axumite building practices had attained. Impressive pieces can be produced by the use of such simple tools as the axe and adze. However, it is a very slow, trial-and-error kind of process. All joinery elements are cut from tree trunks. The elements are made to fit by successive adjustments. The pieces are assembled together and dismantled until the right fit is obtained.

At every floor level, a shelf is created by using flat pieces of stone. The function of this shelf is to stop rain from washing down the wall and damaging the *chika* mortar.

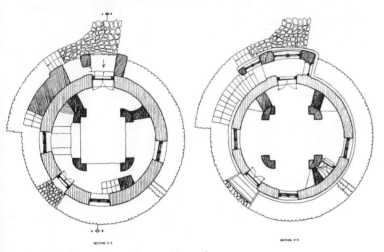

Tigré Chief's house. First and second floor plans.

Tigré Chief's house. Elevation and section.

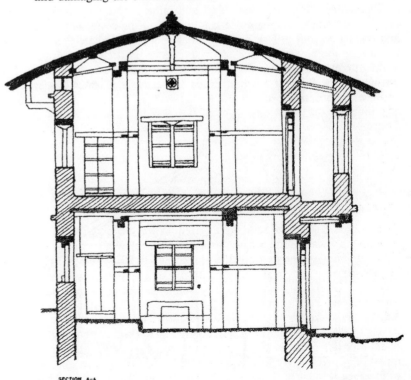

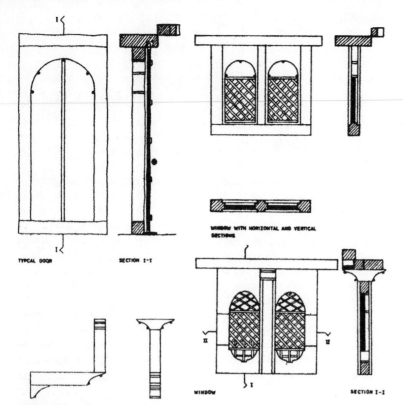

SHOA-GALA HOUSE

It is estimated that well over three-quarters of all Ethiopian houses have the basic form of a cylindrical wall and a conical roof. The Gala house is a good example of this type. The Gala people are the most numerous tribal group of Ethiopia, and their language is spoken throughout the country, except in the north and north-west. The Gala house described below is found close to Addis Ababa, in the Managashea area.

This is an area rich in forests of eucalyptus and junipers, and it is also an area where suitable grasses for thatching grow. The plan shown is a simple one without distinct partitions. Particular note should be taken of the structural system which carries the roof. This system known as *kebaas*, makes it possible to have a larger house than would normally be the case with a central supporting pole. Another way of expanding the area of the house is by using concentric walls. This type of house is found in great numbers in the western part of Woolloga province.

Construction Method

The basic construction consists of a framework of split eucalyptus poles set in the ground (*kwami*). Horizontal, and sometimes diagonal, braces are then tied to the vertical pieces (*mager*), thus creating a very sturdy wall. The wall is then plastered on both sides with *chika*, a versatile material. We have noted its use as a mortar and as a finishing material (plaster).

Thus far building is done by the owner alone, but when the time comes to install the structural members that will carry the roof (*kebaas*), the closest neighbours are called in to assist, and in a matter of hours the poles and the central carrying beams are fastened in place. Co-operative building of this kind is common among the Gala.

Thatching requires the advice and occasional supervision of an expert. Rains in these parts are heavy, and the roof must therefore

The ceiling at the first-floor level is a rather impressive work of art. The attempt is to create one large cupola at the centre bordered and resting on four pillars, and two smaller ones immediately to the north and south. The surface of these cupolas is decorated with a multicoloured design. Just below the ceiling, facing east, is a tiny opening in the form of a cross, called *kesate berhan*, which lets in the first light of the morning.

Gala House – section and elevation.

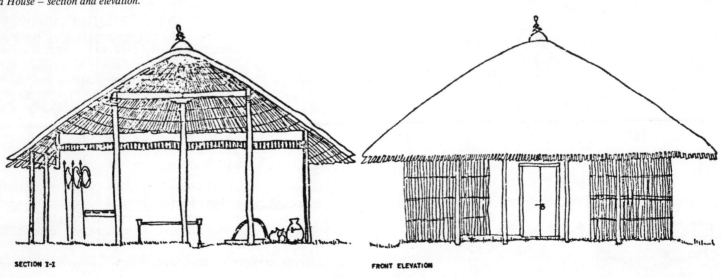

SECTION I-I

FRONT ELEVATION

be tightly built. The best grass for this purpose is called *semblet*; it is found in great abundance, especially around the Managashea area. Thatching is usually carried out from the edge of the roof to the apex. Bundles of the grass are neatly tied together and thrown up to the person working on the roof. A rope made of the same material (*tusha*) is used to tie the grass to the roof framework. At the apex of the roof, the grass is neatly tied together, and a clay pot (*gullelat*) is placed on top. The pot comes in various shapes and can be extremely decorative. A house with the carefully made *gullelat* is greatly admired and can in fact be good cause for boasting by its owner. There is a recent, unexplained habit of placing an inverted bottle through a tiny hole at the very top of the *gullelat*.

The internal arrangement of a Gala house is very simple indeed. To the left of the main entrance is the area reserved for calves. At the centre there is a fireplace made of three clay bricks. A bed made of wooden legs and leather strapping is kept close to the centre of the room, adjacent to a low-partition wall. It should be noted that Ethiopians differentiate between a built-in bed (*ne'idi*) in the north and a movable four-legged bed (*angereb*). The term *angereb* appears to be of Arabic origin. Along the wall one finds several earthen clay pots of different sizes. A built-in grindstone is always included in the basic plan.

As a rule, nails are not used for fixing the door to its hinges, which work on the ball-and-socket system. Nowadays, because of the scarcity of large planks, smaller planks are joined together to form the door leaves. There are no other openings except for the door. At the very top of the wall, a section of about 20 cm is left unplastered so that smoke can finds its way out through the cracks and crevices of the vertical members.

Vessels.

TELLA   POTS FOR WATER   TELLA

Plan of Gala house showing Kebaas *system using concentric walls to expand the house.*

Gala House – plan.

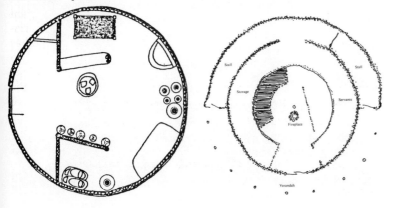

THE GURAGE HOUSE

Occurrence

The Gurage house type prevails throughout four sub-provinces of Central Ethiopia, where the majority of the Gurage people live. Some regions in the surrounding provinces, notably Arusai and Sidamo are inhabited by the Gurage so that here too a facsimile of the Gurage house can be seen. It is estimated that about 6 million people belong to this group and that there are 100,000 Gurage houses of the type described below.

The Gurage People

The Gurage have been described as '. . . a Semitic island in an otherwise completely Gushitic environment'. Ullendorff suggests that 'the basic Gurage stock appears to be of Sidamo origin upon which various layers of military expeditions from the north were imposed, resulting in that curious mixture of Semitic and Gushitic traits, in appearance as well as language.'[11]

The Gurage are an industrious people, but large numbers of them have had to migrate to Addis Ababa in search of employment, since their land is small and is becoming overcrowded. All Gurage houses look remarkably alike; furthermore, in the construction of the house, details are treated with a uniformity that is unique among Ethiopian traditional house-types. The Gurage house is a good example of the well-developed house with cylindrical walls and conical roofs. This fact is all the more surprising when one recalls that the Gurage people are composed of diverse religious and linguistic sub-groups.

Village Setting

The Gurage cultivate enset. A typical village has rows of this plant, popularly known as 'false banana' around each house. Enset provides a livelihood as well as a secondary building material for the house. Ideally there is more than one hut per family and sometimes there are as many as three. Where there is more than one hut, each unit is used for a distinct purpose. The *xarar* unit is for sleeping, the *gwea* is for cooking and keeping cattle and the *zagar* serves as a kind of everyday living room. As often as not, families can afford to build only one large, all-purpose unit. As in the case of the northern highland villages, Gurage villagers reserve an area, usually around a large tree, where meetings are held.

Method of Construction

The ground on which the house will stand is levelled and compacted, if necessary. A peg is then driven approximately in the centre of the levelled ground. A rope is tied to the peg, and sharp stick (or handsaw) is tied to the free end. The rope is kept tight, as a circle is drawn on the ground.

As a rule, the house radius varies between 3 and 4 m, measured from toe to toe. One group of workers starts on the roof and another group works on the wall frame.

House construction is essentially a co-operative endeavour. Neighbours help each other willingly, but certain details require the attention of master craftsmen. These include the door frame, the central supporting pole and the various struts supporting the roof. Thatching also calls for special skills. The roof frame is partially assembled on the ground and then lifted into position for completion. As the roof frame elements are tied to the wall, the whole surface assumes a slightly convex shape. The addition of the struts further accentuates this shape.

The predominating materials for the roof frame are split wood, either red eucalyptus or *tid* (juniperus procera) and bamboo tied with rope made from the *enset* plant (*kacha* in Amharic).

As a rule, the number of *wakas* (struts) placed from a point on the pole to the roof, is in direct proportion to the radial distance of the house, measured in feet; thus a house with a radius of ten feet would require ten *wakas*. This rule does not always necessarily apply, but it brings to mind the point made by an authority on Ethiopian architecture that Ethiopian building practice applies simple and straightforward rules whenever proportioning is concerned.[12]

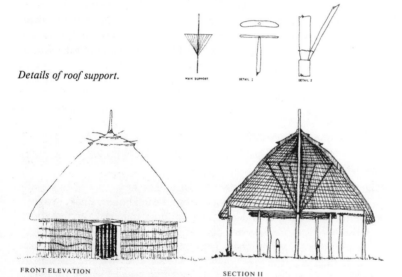

Details of roof support.

MAIN SUPPORT   DETAIL 1   DETAIL 2

FRONT ELEVATION   SECTION II

Elevation and section of Gurage house.

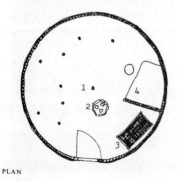

PLAN

Plan of Gurage house showing: (1) Central supporting pole; (2) Fireplace; (3) Movable bed, angereb; *(4) Kot, platform for storage.*

The wall frame is made from roughly split wood, normally *tid*, but nowadays when *tid* is hard to find, whatever is available is used. The individual pieces are tied together with *enset* rope. If *chika* plaster is used, its function is to fill in any unavoidable openings that may remain between the split-wood members of the wall frame. Generally, very little *chika* plaster is used in Gurage houses, and then only on the inside surface.

The horizontal rings of the wall framework are made from split bamboo, *gerkaha*. These are usually placed at intervals of no more than 30 cm. The height of the wall ranges between 2 and 2·5 m.

Thatching begins at the bottom and gradually works up to the top in a spiral pattern. Sometimes an additional layer is added so as to thicken the thatching and ensure that there will be no leaking.

The slope of the roof frame of a Gurage house is very steep, and a thatcher must take precautions not to slip and fall. A rope extending from the central supporting pole and securely tied around the waist of the worker eliminates the possibility of accidents.

Other details[13]

There are no windows and no other openings except for the door. Gurage houses are apparently very poorly ventilated. Smoke must find its way out through the roof.

The fireplace is made of cut stone, roughly circular in shape, and is normally placed between the door and the pillar. On one side of the room elevated storage places are constructed from wooden pillars and bamboo platforms (*kot*). Underneath this platform, posts are fixed to the ground and around them cattle are tied. The door frame is normally made of *wanza* but when this is not available any other timber is used.

The door itself is woven of split bamboo. The width of the door is reportedly proportioned so as to equal the circumference of a man's head. In the author's experience, however, door width invariably exceeds this circumference.

CHENCHA AND SIDAMO BAMBOO HOUSES

Two types of houses are representative of the 'woven' type. Cipriani calls these 'bee-hive frame' houses. They are typical of several variations of hemispherical houses found in many parts of Ethiopia. It has been suggested that such houses are the natural abodes of people who make their living by hunting and trapping. For example he mentions the Wobani, who live between the rivers Wabi Shebele and Juba the Manago of Kafa; the Weito, hunters of the hippopotamus, who live along the banks of the Nile, in the vicinity of the first cataract; the people who live around Hamar Koki, on the shores of lake Stephanie; the inhabitants of western Eritrean lowlands, including the Baria and the Kunama.

Cipriani has very aptly said that these houses are built from 'materials of fortune'.[14] Whatever material is available is readily used for the speedy construction of the house.

Observation of the development of Ethiopian house types indicated that the process of change from hunting to the sedentary farming mode of life parallels the change that takes place in the house type, from an essentially hemi-spherical form to the functional distinction between roof and wall. In the case of the Sidamo and Chencha bamboo houses, this development apparently did not take place. The basic hemi-spherical shape of the house has been maintained and gradually refined. Both samples represent, under the circumstances, an optimum solution to the problem of shelter.

THE CHENCHA HOUSE

Occurrence

The Chencha house is found in a small relatively high area west of lake Margarita, south of the city of Boroda. Chencha and its surroundings are the home of the Dorze tribe, an industrious people renowned for their skill in weaving. The Chencha house is more oval than hemi-spherical in shape. The height of the hut sometimes exceeds 8 m, and is usually not less than 6 m. Apparently there is a good reason for making it as high as it is. As soon as the portion which is directly in contact with the soil begins to rot, as indeed it does, the whole house is sunk to an appropriate extent allowing the fresh portion of the wall to come in contact with the earth. This is done as often as necessary until the hut becomes too low for normal human activities to take place inside it. As a rule the

height of the house is reportedly reduced by about 20 cm every four years.

After this planned obsolescence has taken its course, a new house is built. Prior to this, the collection of bamboo and leaves to cover the house will have been gradually completed.

Method of Construction

A circle is drawn on levelled ground outlining the outer sections of the wall. On this circle split bamboo pieces are driven into the ground, approximately 10 cm apart. A series of horizontal rings is then interlocked between the vertical pieces, from the bottom to the top. The diameter of the series of horizontal rings of bamboo is gradually reduced until it almost closes at the top of the hut. When the hut reaches a height beyond which it is not possible to work, scaffolding is built, on which the workmen stand to continue the weaving process. When the main framework is completed, a portion is added around the house. This portion starts from the floor, continues on both sides of the door openings and gradually tapers off at the top, giving the impression of gigantic nose appended to the hut. The area created by this nose serves as a kind of entrance hall to the main enclosure. Once the bamboo framework is completed, layers of leaves are placed outside the framework of the hut. The leaves used for this purpose are those of the bamboo shoot, which in Dorze are known as *honchie*. The leaves are bought in bundles; they are scarce and therefore cost more money than the bamboo itself.

Chencha house. Construction of the wicker walls, typical of Process 3, weaving or pleating.

Chencha house, under construction.

117

Interior arrangement

The plan layout of the Chencha House has two distinct areas separated by a bamboo partition approximately 2 m high. The back portion of the hut appears to serve as a kind of store, whereas all other activities are carried out in the front area. A small fireplace consisting essentially of three stones is located almost in the middle of the room. Half way along the wall there are tiny openings that serve mainly for letting smoke out. The house is completely water-tight and has no opening except for the door. The door height appears to be dimensioned so that it is less than the height of a man for one has to stoop rather low to enter into the hut. There is no central supporting pole, nor does there seem to be any need of it. In addition to the usual earthen utensils found in nearly all Ethiopian huts, there is a bed made of four wooden legs and a row of bamboo stringers. The average diameter of huts is about 7–8 m. This space provides accommodation for the family as well as for their cattle. As in the case of the Sidamo house, it appears that more space is allocated to calves and cattle than to the family.

Chencha house, showing the fastening of the honchie *bamboo leaf layer.*

Chencha house showing completed woven dome and addition of the 'nose' porch which serves as an entrance hall to the house.

The completed Chencha house.

THE SIDAMO BAMBOO HOUSE

This type of house is located in a small area around the town of Agereselam, on the high plateau east of lake Margarita. The area where these houses are found corresponds very closely to the area where bamboo grows. The Sidamo people who build this type of house are closely related to the Dorze, who house-type was examined above. Both the Dorze and Sidamo people are part of the larger linguistic group of sedentary farmers and cattle keepers.[15]

The characteristics of this house are similar to the Chencha house which has just been described, but there are however, two important differences concerning construction detail. The Sidamo bamboo house has a central supporting pole whereas the Chencha one does not. Secondly, the honchie leaves that are designed to make the house waterproof are in this case placed in between two layers of bamboo, wicker-work. This 'sandwich' construction is shown in detail in the sketch.

TRADITIONAL HOUSES IN THE CONTEXT OF NATIONAL RE-HOUSING PROGRAMMES

As the housing needs of the urban masses become more pressing in the country, it might be advisable to examine the traditional housing system for possible solutions. Let us consider some issues that arise with regard to the role of traditional housing institutions in the context of innovation.

Traditional house-types are the result of the co-operative endeavour of unskilled or semi-skilled builders who use traditional materials. In urban environment, where the standard of house required is in any case imperatively higher, house building *needs* to involve the systematic co-operation of a number of specialists who use a variety of manufactured building materials. The difference between these processes may be illustrated by the way in which two roofing materials are featured in the production of housing.

In traditional houses, thatch is used extensively. It is such a flex-ible material that it can tolerate wide margins of error in both planning and execution. Manufactured materials, on the other hand, require accuracy. In contrast, corrugated iron sheets must rest on purlins spaced at specified distances. A crude patchwork of repairs cannot always undo mistakes of construction. Nails fastening the iron sheets to the purlins cannot be driven just anywhere. A hole in the gulley means a leaky roof.

Traditional building materials lend themselves to being handled by almost everyone. There are no tolerances to observe, and elements can always be put in place, at best by a trial-and-error method, and at worst by force. Hardly any damage can occur.

The duplication of this process in the current housing effort is not entirely applicable, nor is it practical. For one thing, the present qualitative demand for housing is not only greater, it is different. Nowadays the urban house, or for that matter the traditional house, is required to provide services generally unknown in the traditional Ethiopian setting: a child brings homework from school and needs light to work by.

In this respect all Ethiopian houses are deficient, particularly those built by the weaving process. The Sidamo house is a typical example. In its present form, fitting it with a window opening is not a straightforward proposition, particularly if protection against rain is required. Of course, it is possible to reach a technical solution to the problem.

Sidamo bamboo house. Plan.

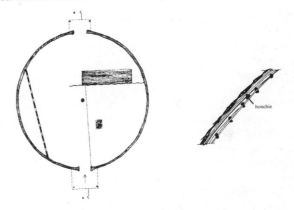

Sidamo bamboo house. Section.

Sidamo bamboo house. Elevation.

119

Sidamo Bamboo house. Splitting bamboo for use in construction.

Sidamo bamboo house under construction. Beyond the lower woven wall the upper section of the house is being assembled.

Sidamo bamboo house. Apex of the roof frame showing method of fixing to the centre pole and rings of lashed bamboo.

An example from a student solution is given in plan and section on page 123. In the final analysis, such a solution tends to be contrived and is feasible only because 'large dark enclosures' were replaced by 'smaller light enclosures'. The students who propose this solution imply that it is a stop-gap at best. There may be some truth in this.

This example seems to suggest that traditional house-types do not always lend themselves to partial or intermediate improvement. Indeed, innovation may only make them unworkable. For example, the smoke from open fires (especially the ones fuelled by cow dung) is believed to provide the thatch with increased protection from rotting. If open fires are to be abolished (and well they might since small children often fall into them), it must be remembered that the thatching may rot more quickly.

It has been suggested that the mere reduction of persons per sleeping room in tropical housing without a corresponding improvement of the thermal qualities of wall results in the excessive lowering of temperature. This argument might be valid in the case of traditional Ethiopian houses occupied by both animals and human beings. Segregation of the two may result in such a loss of latent heat that the temperature inside huts (at least in the highland areas of Ethiopia) will fall to uncomfortable levels.

House building is traditionally an exercise in improvisation carried out within the framework of a few basic facts which have long been committed to memory. Complicated as it appears, a model of the Tigré Chief's house (see page 113) was recently duplicated in Addis Ababa by two traditional builders. It was built out of memory without the aid of plans or drawings. The builders were asked how it was possible to carry out a project of this nature without the assistance of plans and drawings. They are credited with the following response, 'plans are only for those who don't know what they are doing'.

120

Sidamo bamboo house. Assembling the roof frame.

Sidamo bamboo house. Dome nearing completion with final cladding stalks being added. With seven men standing on the dome there is no evidence of sagging.

Completed Sidamo bamboo house, showing porch.

There is some indication that traditional skills are dying out. A survey in an area of Addis Ababa shows that only 8% of the adult population stated that they had had any experience in the construction of Chika houses.[16] Furthermore traditional skills are not being replaced fast enough by modern skills. According to the above survey, less than half of 1% of the adult population stated they had building experience using permanent materials.

'MATERIALS OF FORTUNE'

Traditional housing utilises material which is collected from the land. Nearly always such materials are free for the taking: Cipriani's 'materials of fortune'. If one excludes labour no exact monetised value could be assigned to them. The semblet used for thatching the roof of the Gurage house is acquired fairly easily in the area around Woliso-Wolkite, 50 km south-west of Addis Ababa. When a model of this type of house was built in the compound of the Ethio-Swedish Institute at Addis Ababa, the expenses of bringing semblet from this area to Addis Ababa were so great that had the hut been roofed with iron sheets, it would have cost only half as much.

The neat process of obsolescence built in the Chencha house has already been mentioned. But what does it tell us about the relationship between tradition and innovation? It is of little value to develop a technique for, say, making bamboo rot- and insect-proof, if it is going to cost considerably more than periodic replacement.

It is necessary to be objective in determining what kind of 'traditional approaches' are likely to be worthwhile and deserve propagation. On the whole, there should be no qualms about rejecting such traditions if they prove to be inadequate and inappropriate in the context of a changing mode of life. The Chencha house is one example. It will probably not manage to endure even in Chencha. It is good only as long as bamboo costs almost nothing.

Many western advisers to Ethiopia have pointed out the importance of preserving traditional methods of construction. However, it is not clear as to whether this is, as David Buxton suggests, 'The visitors' perverse preference for the colour, texture and association of thatch . . . and the inadvertent 'pursuit' of thatch and the rejection of corrugated iron.'[17]

Another writer decries the tragedy that may befall the country if traditional buildings disappear.[18] In point of fact, these arguments may already be academic. The crucial issue is the need to fill the vacuum created by the disappearance of traditional knowhow.

Efforts from outside to improve local traditional techniques are, on the whole, destined to fail. It is important to understand that when traditional practices break down, it is usually because craftsmanship is dying out and/or suitable materials are becoming scarce. It has already been suggested that the upgrading of inferior materials by such means as chemical treatment of grasses is unlikely to be economic.

These remarks suggest that in areas like Addis Ababa better housing for all income groups will depend more on the introduction of sound financial, management and training practices than on anything

Present layout of a typical house in the Sidamo area. Plan.

Present layout of typical Sidamo house, section.

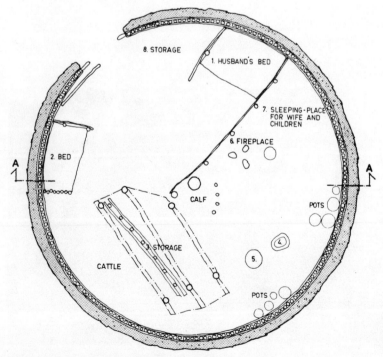

PLAN

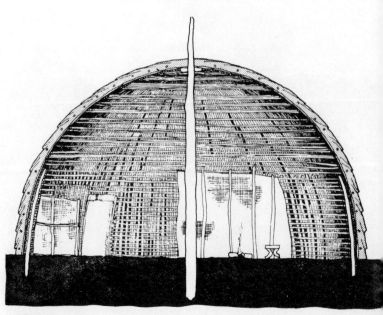

SECTION A-A

else. Although under certain circumstances there is a place for families building their own homes, public initiative might be made to concentrate on providing quality education for professional house-builders.

Obviously, it is foolish to argue for the wholesale abolition of the so-called traditional approach in housing. On the contrary, it should and must be allowed to run its course. A warning against burdening it with cumbersome and what often appear to be inappropriate innovations may be in order.

Fifty-seven per cent of the migrants to Addis Ababa came to town in search of employment. Several thousand families in the middle-income range can afford to buy housing that the present private market is able to produce. However, only a fraction of these families are able to do so because a homebuilding industry worth the name does not exist. Here is an excellent opportunity to kill two birds with one stone; creation of employment and encouragement of a building industry.

NOTES AND BIBLIOGRAPHY

[1] This sub-division into ethnic groups follows the suggestions of Ullendorf. See *The Ethiopians*, p. 33. He suggests that of all factors language affinity is the most significant in deciding the ethnic groups of Ethiopia. With reference to the Semitised Cushitic Groups the generally accepted theory is that strong elements of Semetic immigrants, mostly Arab, settles along the Red Sea Coast and gradually implanted their culture on Cushitic strata of the interior.

[2] ULLENDORFF, EDWARD, *The Ethiopians*, Oxford University Press, 1961, p. 39.

[3] Ibid., p. 41.

[4] LINDAHL, BERNHARD, *Architectural History of Ethiopia in Pictures*, Mimeographed, 1970, College of Architecture, p. 17.

[5] LINDAHL, BERNHARD, *Architecture and Art During the Gondar Period*, Mimeographed, 1969, College of Architecture, p. 5.

[6] LINDAHL, *History*, p. 9.

[7] DANIELLI and MARINELLI, *Villagi e Tipi di Abitazioni*, Resultati Scientifici. Roma, 1939. See section on round houses.

[8] ULLENDORF, EDWARD, *Ethiopians and the Bible*, London, 1968, p. 88.

[9] CIPRIANI, LIDO, *La Abitazioni Indegeni del A.O.I.*, Milano, 1938, see pp. 47–50. See also sections related to diagram on p. 122.

[10] *Hudmo* appears to be the term used by both Tigreans and Eritreans, and is generally applied to a rectangular house with a flat roof. A house with a cylindrical wall and conical roof is generally known as *agdo*. The term *tukul*, also popularly used, appears to have Arabic origin. See Danielli, p. 400.

[11] ULLENDORF, EDWARD, *The Ethiopians*, p. 38.

[12] LINDAHL, BERNHARD, *History*.

[13] See also the studies of Gurage housing in SHACK, WILLIAM, *The Gurages*, Oxford University Press, 1968, and LEBEL, PHILIP, 'On Gurage Architecture', *Journal of Ethiopian Studies*, Vol. 111 (1969), No. 1.

[14] CIPRIANI, LIDO, p. 48.

[15] In the sense that both the Dorze and Sidamo people who build these houses *are* sedentary farmers, though their house-type is typical of the hunting and trapping groups.

[16] Survey of Housing Conditions. 'Tekle-Haimanot Area of Addis Ababa', ESIBT, 1961.

[17] BUXTON, D. R., *Travels in Ethiopia*, London, 1949.

[18] Economic Commission for Africa, Seminar on Urbanization. Document SEM/URB/AF/27, April 1962.

Improved house proposed by students from University of Lund, Department of Architecture, Sweden.

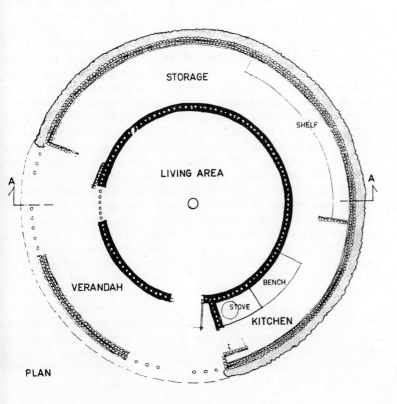

PLAN

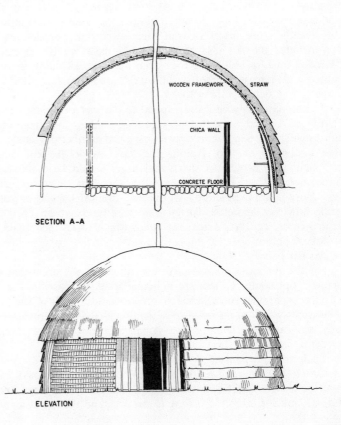

SECTION A-A

ELEVATION

TENTS OF THE TEKNA, SOUTHWEST MOROCCO

Peter Alford Andrews

INTRODUCTION

The Tekna are a confederation of tribes dominating the extreme south-west of Morocco. Their neighbours to the north, and in fact the northerly tribes of the Tekna themselves, are settled, but fully nomadic tribes from the south come into Tekna territory regularly to trade, and in some circumstances to graze their animals. The Tekna resemble them in many respects of material culture and speech, and buy many of their finest artefacts from them. But the Tekna are nomadic to only a limited extent: the degree varies. Some of the more sedentary of them, like the Lansās, rarely move more than a score of kilometres from their villages inland. Others, like the Ait Lahsen, migrate up and down the coastal strip, where the pasture is richer and more reliable, for an hundred kilometres. Others still venture far out into the more desert areas in Algeria and the Spanish Sahara, as for instance the Ait Ūsa roam over the great stony slope of the Hamada du Dra. All these tribesmen may live all the year in their tents or they may return to a house for a season, according to the number and needs of their flocks.

The animals they herd correspond to the way of life they lead. A family of Ait Lahsen with moderate means might own from four to ten camels, fifty to a hundred sheep, an equal number of goats, a mule and a donkey or two. Among the Ait Ūsa on the Hamada the proportion of camels to sheep and goats would be much higher, about one to four. The Lansās, on the other hand, own few camels, and more goats than sheep. All the tent-dwellers depend on camel's milk, however, as well as barley and, more rarely, meat. Their grain is grown on local fields near the *oueds* which water them from time to time. There is a settled population in every tribe: half, for instance, of the Ait Lahsen.

All the nomadic Tekna speak Hasāniya, the Moorish dialect of Arabic, but some of them are bilingual speaking Tašelhīt, the local variety of Berber speech, which predominates north of the Noun. The tribespeople are a mixture of Arab and Berber elements which can no longer be clearly distinguished; there are also Negroid Haratin, formerly a slave caste.

Their social organisation is very complicated. For the present it is enough to say that they are divided into two main *leffs*, the Ait Ejjmel and the more numerous Ait 'Atman. Of the tribes discussed, the Ait Lahsen and the Izargiyīn belong to the first, and the Ait Ūsa and the Lansās to the second. Moroccan influence has been slight in the past; the Hassānia, who dominated the Moors in the south for centuries, were descendants of the Ma'qil, Hilalian Arab invaders originally from the Yemen who reached the Ocean in about 1220. Most of the Tekna became independent in about 1765, and a little later they formed a separate state known as Oued Noun. This is still the heart of their territory, and it has always been an important point of contact between Saharan and coastal peoples. One trading centre after another has grown up there: the present one is Goulimime. The population can hardly be analysed tribally from the last census; in 1942 there were some 44,500 Tekna in Morocco, of whom one third were Ait Ūsa and Ait Lahsen. They then had 200,000 goats, 100,000 sheep and 30,000 camels.[1]

The country is hot, dry and meagre. There are occasional oases which surprise one by their luxuriance, such as Assa with its groves of date palms crowded between canals. A few villages have small stands of palms and gardens of fruit trees. But the greatest part is semi-desert, a transition from the Atlas to the Sahara. In the Ait Lahsen country it is sandy; elsewhere the sand is strewn with stones, and the Bani is rocky. There is hardly a skyline that is not broken by one of the ranges of bare, dry hills in the distance. The pasture is very sparse, but almost continuous. There are always at least three different types of scrub scattered about, and in some areas one cannot take more than three paces without encountering a desert thorn bush or a straggling yellow bunch of shoots or a parched green shrub with minute leaves. Sometimes there are wide areas of cactus clumps too. Trees are rare: occasionally one may be seen standing quite alone with a peculiar flat, compressed parasol of branches. Still more rarely, and usually near the coast, one comes across patches of bright green grass growing thickly and richly where rain has fallen, even on sand and in midsummer. There is no running water to be seen outside the villages, except when rains suddenly fill the river beds for a day or so. The herdsmen depend entirely on wells.

The north-east trade winds dominate the region, and sea breezes can bring the coolness of the Canaries current as far as 80 km inland, on summer mornings. The sky near the coast is often overcast or hazy until noon, even in July. Nevertheless, summer temperatures are high, rising to 40°–45°C in the afternoon at about 20% relative humidity. The temperature may then fall at night to 20°C.

Near the coast the humidity can be very high at night. A hot and extremely unpleasant wind occasionally blows relentlessly from the Sahara for several days on end. Rainfall is slight, sporadic and unreliable.

METHOD

The fieldwork on which this study is based was done during a detailed investigation of all the Moroccan tent types in 1968. This was generously sponsored by the Social Science Research Council. I was later helped by the R.I.B.A. when writing up the material of which this is a part. I am particularly indebted to the Moroccan government for their help in providing a guide for most of the fortnight I was working in the area.

The nomads I visited belonged to the following tribes:

Ait Ūsa	Ait Idder and others including the Moqaddem at Assa
Ait Lahsen	Oulad Bel Lehwilat and Ait Bū-Meggūt
Lansās	Oulad Bu 'Ašra

I studied eighteen of their tents in detail, and visited scores of others during June and July. I am grateful to all my anonymous helpers and hosts, without whom this could not have been written.

I have omitted any discussion of weaving techniques or of language from this article for lack of space: in consequence for this reason I have avoided using Arabic words completely.

I have drawn heavily on Vincent Monteil's *Notes* for the map, have followed his transcriptions of tribal names and have relied heavily on his writings for confirmation of my material. Nevertheless, I have shown place names as they are shown on the Michelin map of Morocco. Lastly, I have followed the examples of Mlle du Puigaudeau and Julio Caro Baroja in setting out certain drawings.

Map of south-west Morocco showing tent-dwelling tribes of the Tekna.
Tribe names in upper case, place names in lower case. Uplands shaded.

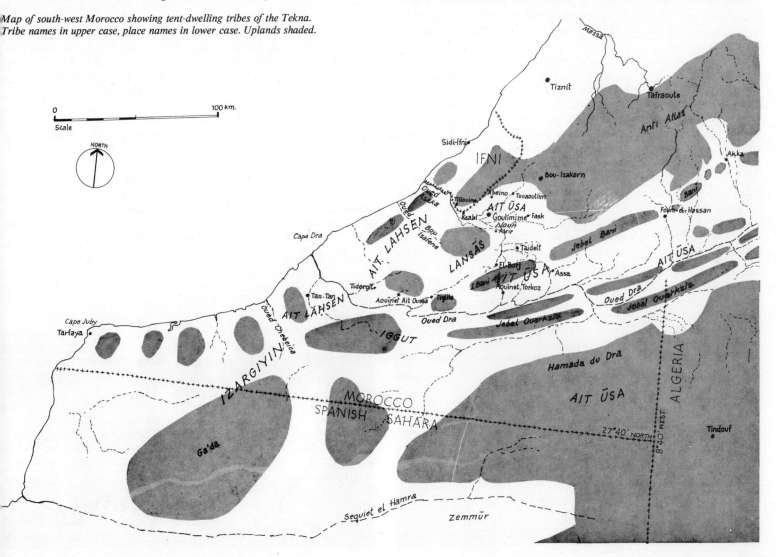

The peaked silhouettes of a line of tents can be recognised from some distance, dark incidents against the dull brown of a valley floor and almost lost in scale against the cushions of mean vegetation in the foreground; or they may be discovered as a formal array on the open horizon of white sand in the south, drenched occasionally in the shadow of passing clouds, and fallible under the harshness of sunlight. Nearer, the shape emerges as an unexpected streamline. The roof is the whole form, and it tilts in each sweep of the surface. The single peak rakes backwards away from the low, shaded mouth where the entrance side is lifted by two short props, and heaves the *velum* up in a gentle curve, to fall away in a much steeper slope behind. The two rear corners are pinned to the ground, and on either side the cloth sweeps down in a constantly broadening parabola spread by the guy ropes. The front is flattened and taut like an awning between the props, sloping away a little outside them to leave the sides open. The triangle of space between the edge and the ground may otherwise be filled with a tattered cotton wall, though the mouth is left empty.

Inside, the floor is clear, and bright with the fresh yellow of esparto matting. Two tapered poles, the sole structure of the tent, straddle the mats and meet under the peak. The one at the front is quite clear of the roof except at the very top, and its foot rests just inside the entrance; the rear one supports the roof for at least half its length, losing its lower end in the loose folds of cloth which form the tail skirts. The indeterminate bundles and boxes of the household are stacked on or under racks which are crowded under each of the low sides; but all the clutter of fire and kitchen pots lies outside, sheltering under the curve of thorn hedges built out as a forecourt from either corner.

The same kind of tent is used throughout the Noun and the southwest as far south as the Zemmour by the Tekna, whether they are full nomads or small herdsmen, and by the Ait Ba-'Amran, the Ait-Umrībet

and the Rguibat. It is very like the Moorish tent farther south; it is furnished in much the same way and it is even subject to the same variations. Nevertheless there are enough consistent differences to mark it out as a separate type. Compared to tents in central Morocco it is small, and simple, and it varies surprisingly little in size. It is also rather low, except for the area under the peak: a reflection perhaps of the inertia which the heat imposes on the tribesmen much of the time. This lack of headroom has forced its effect on the local culture in one odd respect: the women dance on their knees. It is also characteristic of nomad life that the name of this dance, the *Guedra*, is taken from a large earthenware cooking pot, which is put to double use as a drum after a piece of skin has been stretched over the neck. No one can afford to carry superfluous equipment about the desert.

THE VELUM

The roof is the tent. The structure reckoned apart, all the other elements, and there are not many of them, are much less important. At first glance it seems that it must be rectangular if laid out flat, and made up from parallel strips of coffee-coloured cloth, each with a paler stripe down the edge, all running in the direction of the length.

The material from which this *velum* is made is the animal hair to hand, which varies according to the district, though the larger part is always goat hair. If wool or camel hair are used, they are washed, but the goat hair remains unwashed, in black locks about 10 cm long. The mixture is carded, spun, twined anti-clockwise, stretched between two pegs with a tourniquet, and laid up into hanks. The warp and weft yarns are similar, though the weft is in some cases half as thick again as the warp. The threads are laid out on a ground loom, in which the heddle is supported simply on two stones, and woven into cloths of an even and fairly standard width.

The number of cloths, and their length, determine the size of the

Rear view.

Forecourt with water trestle in foreground.

tent. Once they have been woven cloths are rarely cut — trimming would be a waste of precious resources — so the loom is set up at the length decided for the tent. Though all the cloths are woven in the same way, in a warp-covered, ribbed plain weave, two distinct ranges of width are made, which are called by different names in the vernacular. One width, for the main body of the roof, is between 40 cm and 70 cm at the extreme, though more usually from 45 cm to 65 cm. The other, which is used for the front and rear edges of the roof, is from 20 cm to 35 cm, and more usually from 20 cm to 25 cm. The cloths are finished with a weft wrapping to prevent their unravelling at the ends, and they are sewn together selvedge to selvedge in a raised seam which appears on the outside of the *velum*. Most tents are made up of seven or eight of the broader cloths together, as the middle, and a narrower cloth at either side as the lip. All the seams are sewn in the same tent stitch, using a whitish or fawn woollen yarn which is twined in the same way as the cloth yarns.

The short sides of the tent are finished with a bolt rope. Though commercial rope is sometimes used nowadays, the traditional material was a woollen rope wrapped in scraps of cotton cloth. The ends of the tent cloths are turned over it and sewn back to the *velum* underneath with a line of running stitches, each about 2 cm long and 2 cm in from the edge. A stitch is taken around the rope-filled edge after every two running stitches to hold all firmly together, and both rope and stitching continue uninterrupted across the seams from one corner to the other, where they stop short. There is no bolt rope along the front and rear edges, where the selvedge of the lip cloth finishes the *velum*.

A tent made up from eight middle cloths is likely to measure some 8 m along the front. However, the bolt ropes are sewn in on a slight bias down the sides, so that the *velum* is trapezoidal in plan, and measures about a metre less along the back.[2]

If an individual cloth should fall short of the general length, which may well happen if the owner is poor and is obliged to skimp with materials, or if his wife miscalculates a little in her weaving, it is

Front quarter view.

made up to the bolt rope in a standard technique. A cloth newly taken off the loom is left with tails of unused warp threads at the finishing end of the weave, since the shed between the upper and lower layers of warps cannot be opened adequately close to the lease rods. Normally the extra warp yarns are cut off and used for sewing and other odd jobs, but in this case they are left on the cloth. They are grouped into tails of sixteen or so yarns, and the weave is stopped with a weft wrapping. Each tail is divided into two parts, and each part is twisted together with a part from a neighbouring tail into a clockwise tassel. These tassels are then used to span the gap to the bolt rope — usually 15 cm or so — and they are wrapped over it, to be caught by a yarn running along it in a chain of half hitches. The warp tails are tucked once more under this yarn and cut. This leaves a grille-like arrangement of warp twists at 3 cm centres. Sometimes these gaps are made up with odd remnants of either broad or narrow cloths stitched together, and the warp twists are omitted.

Though the lip cloths are usually single on either edge of the tent, they are sometimes doubled, especially at the rear. The corner fastenings (q.v.) are then attached to the outermost of the two. A tail cloth is occasionally sewn on to the rear lip with the usual raised seam, outside the corner fastenings. It may be made from an old and worn tent cloth, either broad or narrow, or sacking up to 90 cm broad.

Because the tent is peaked from the meeting of the two poles, the otherwise flat *velum* is marked to show where the peak is to occur. This is always midway between the two sides, but it tends to lie nearer the rear edge than the front. In all the Ait Ūsa tents I examined, the peak was placed within the width of the cloth immediately behind the central seam, as the number of middle cloths was even. The Lansās, on the other hand, always placed it on a seam, leaving either an equal number of cloths before and behind it or, if the number of cloths was uneven, one more cloth in front. The Ait Lahsen also placed it on a seam with the same variations, and so do the Rguibat, who almost always use the unequal arrangement. As an exception, however, a small Rguibat tent that I bought follows the plan typical of the Ait Ūsa. The peak is marked by a little crest of white woollen yarn stitched in the *velum* to form a semicircular loop 5 cm across on the outside. This is stiffened with closely laid turns of the same yarn. It is usually, but not always, sewn across the warp threads.

The peak is also embroidered with parallel lines of white stitching on the outside which almost certainly have a prophylactic meaning. Though there are small variations in the pattern, I was assured that they are not signs by which the tribes can be recognised in the Noun. On either side of the crest loop three white patches are made in a row over the same wefts: each patch is of about six stitches lying close together, 5 cm long, and the patches are 10 cm or more apart. Doubled yarns of the same wool are run in stitches 10 cm long under each edge of each row of patches, and prolonged beyond them in the direction of the wefts, making two double lines of white up to 45 cm apart, and each about 100 cm long. The ends of the lines are stopped and small triangular decorations are made on the ends and on the outside of the patches, all in white. The Rguibat, like some of their Moorish neighbours, use single lines of stitching, in alternating long

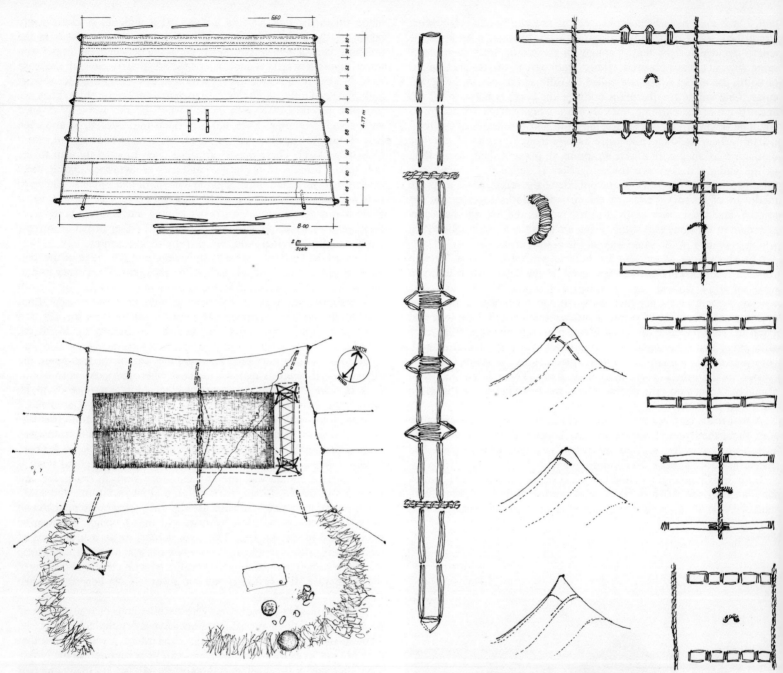

A typical Tekna tent, of the Lansãs, Oulad Bu ʾAʿsra, in the area of Taidelt.
Top: *plan of* velum *spread flat, with poles and props.*
Bottom: *plan of tent as erected. The two mats are shaded, with the womens' side on the right, showing the line of a cotton screen, and the shelving. The fireplace and oven pit are in the forecourt to the right, and the object on the left is a water skin on its trestle. Brushwood is shown hatched. Canopy in tent is shown dotted. In both plans the front of the tent is to the bottom.*

Details of crest ornament on velum *for different tribes.*
Left: *Ait Ūsa: one side only, with peak tag shown top centre.*
Right: *from top to bottom: Ait Ūsa, Lansãs, Lansãs, Ait Lahsen oulad Bel Lehwilat, specimen from Tan Tan (Izargiyin?). All to same scale.*
Middle perspectives: *from top to bottom: Ait Ūsa, Ait Lahsen, Rguibat (for comparison, not Tekna).*

titches and groups of points, to build up a square around the peak, with the lines overrunning the corners in the direction of the warp. This is sometimes done in dark thread.

Cloth yarns are never dyed at any stage of the weaving, but the natural colour of the animal fibres is exploited to decorate the tent. Though the *velum* is mainly coffee coloured, the paler stripe which runs down the edge of each cloth is very noticeable at close quarters. The change of colour is really from one shade of brown to another, though at times the paler part is almost cream. The shade is affected by the age of the cloth, as it is bleached somewhat by the sun. The central cloths tend to be much darker — a black coffee in fact — because of the habit of replacing these cloths with new ones. The type of stripe varies from tribe to tribe. The Ait Ūsa use a characteristically narrow one 3 or 4 cm broad, which usually appears on the rear edge of each cloth. There may be plain cloths too, while the narrower lip cloths may be given a stripe down the middle, or one on both edges. Small variations occur: lip cloths are sometimes woven in three shades, and on the main cloths the stripe is occasionally contained by a dark and narrow selvedge, or the stripe may be only 1 or 2 cm wide, so that it is hardly visible.

In Lansās tents the stripe is wider, from 3 to 15 cm, mostly from 6 to 10 cm. The stripes are arranged to appear on the selvedges towards the front and rear, parting from the peak seam which is left unstriped. The same variations occur, and the lip cloths may carry five or six stripes each in patterns of the three shades.

The Ait Lahsen use very broad stripes, from 8 to 40 cm, which are easily recognised. In most cases the stripe is placed to front and rear, as with the Lansās, but there are also tents in which it appears on the rear edge of all the cloths. The lip cloths may be striped in two or four alternating bands or they may be plain. There is greater use of three shades than among the other tribes, especially in the middle

Detail of tent cloth showing stripe and overstitching at seam.

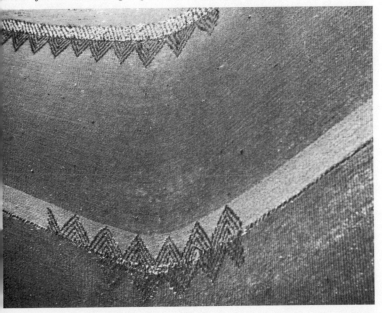

cloths, though these may also appear plain dark or plain cream. Where multiple stripes occur they may be very narrow, perhaps 2 cm. Dark stripes set off the light ones next to them. The use of the three colours is most marked to the south-west, among the Izargiyin and their neighbours in the Spanish Sahara. They also use the broad stripe.[3]

Another element of decoration is introduced by dark overstitching on the *velum*. This is worked in the usual black twine in lines of running stitches each 1 cm or so long across the warp at intervals of 1 cm. The stitches are staggered in each line to form a diagonal pattern, or a series of chevrons one inside the other. The patterns are sometimes said to have the supposed power of protecting the tent,[4] but I was told by Lansās and Ait Ūsa that they are simply for strengthening the tent cloth where it was likely to give way. Although the overstitching is very common I never saw any evidence of such weakness, but the chevrons are often near a seam where the stitching might tend to pull the warp threads apart. The extent of such darning varies a great deal: the chevrons may be from 15 to 40 cm wide and from 5 to 10 cm deep, or even more.

Lansās tents are sometimes decorated with single lines of stem stitch in white twine which run across the cloths near their ends.

The ends of the cloths are either trimmed or left to dangle below the bolt rope, where they form triangular flaps because the sides of the *velum* are cut on a bias. They then hang for the most part inside the side cloths.

Surprisingly little sunlight is to be seen from the interior, for the weave is dense. It is as a shade against sun and glare, a screen against wind, dust and unwanted glances, that it is important, and in its meagre way as an insulator against winter cold. Since air does filter through the roof, an extra lining of cotton cloth is hung inside for the winter, as a canopy with sides that reach to the ground, and this is kept sometimes in summer too. The oiliness of the unwashed goat hair is known to prevent water from penetrating the cloth, but rain showers are so rare that I have had no opportunity to judge its effect. However, the majority of tents are so dried and bleached by the sun that I should guess that whatever waterproofing properties they have at first pass away quite rapidly. The thread counts are fairly constant: between 13 and 20 wefts per decimetre, and most usually 16, as against 62–76 warps, usually 68–70, with an exceptionally low count of 50 in one case.

Since the majority of their herds are goats the Lansās use goat hair alone. The cloths are therefore blackish at first, fading to a dark coffee colour. Paler stripes along the edges are simply of paler goat hair. This is apparently the best material, but camel hair may be used, particularly if there is not enough goat hair for the whole weave. It is then carded with the goat hair into a mixture of which goat hair is the main element — especially so for the warp threads which must be strong enough to withstand all the tension on the *velum*. Camel hair can never be used by itself, for the fibres are short and weak: it is rather a despised material. The weft threads, which are a stuffing rather than a means of strength, may contain a stronger admixture of camel hair. It is not unusual to find cloth in which the warp is pure goat hair except for the stripe, which contains camel, while the weft is of the weaker mixture.

Side view of tent. Lansãs.

The Ait Ūsa also use goat hair for the warp and a mixture of goat and camel hair for the weft, but the pale stripes are made by warps of a mixture of goat hair and wool. On the other hand the Ait Lahsen, even though they keep equal numbers of sheep and goats, use very little wool. Both weft and warp are of pure goat hair except for the stripe, which contains a large proportion of camel hair in the warp.

The weft mixture is usually greyish in colour, though after it has been woven and exposed it soon becomes the same brown as the warp. Both warp and weft threads are made up from yarns spun clockwise which are then paired and spun again on a hooked spindle into an anti-clockwise twine. The white woollen thread for the crest is spun in the same way, as is the yarn for the seam stitching and fastenings. The beckets (q.v.) are sometimes attached with a goat hair twine, sometimes with a wool and camel hair mixture.

The whole work of preparing and weaving the wool is done by the mistress of the tent, who works alone for much of the time. It is the women too who sew the cloths together, but they make a party out of the occasion, with fifteen to twenty working together. Despite all this, the tent remains the husband's property.

THE FASTENINGS

However large or small the tent, it is always provided with fastenings for four guy ropes on each of the short sides. These beckets are carved out of forked or bent branches to form a broad V, with notches or shoulders near the tips of the horns. They are lashed by these shoulders to the edge of the *velum*, one at each corner at the ends of the lip cloths, and two at intermediate points near the centre of each side. The lashings are of goat-hair twine passed through the *velum* with a needle, around the shoulders, over the bolt-rope and through the *velum* again for half a dozen turns, so as to hold the bolt-rope and becket tightly together. They are finished off with a seizing of several turns of the end around the standing part. Each horn of the becket is lashed separately.

The size of these V beckets varies not only with the size of the tent but according to their position along its edge. In general the smallest are those at the corners of the *velum*, and particularly those at the rear corners. These measure from 12 to 16 cm across the horns in an ordinary tent and about 10 cm deep, while those at the front corners may be the same size or a few centimetres larger. They are both about 2 cm thick. Both of the central pairs of beckets are larger than either of these, and the pair nearer the front is usually the largest, being between 18 and 28 cm wide and from 11 to 15 cm deep. The hinder pair is from 16 to 25 cm wide and from 8 to 14 cm deep. The thickness of both pairs lies between 2·5 and 3 cm. Since the beckets are carved from whatever timber is available, there is naturally some variation from such norms, and further variation is caused by haphazard replacement of broken or lost pieces.

The exact position of the central pair of beckets depends on the placing of the peak. Where the peak lies on a seam, the beckets are fastened to the two cloths on either side of the seam. They may be placed on the corner of the cloth, close to the next seam along to the front or the rear, or they may just as often be astride the seams. Where, on the other hand, the peak lies in the middle of a cloth, the beckets are sewn to the two cloths adjoining the central one. The rear pair of beckets then appears on the forward corners of their cloth, while the front pair may apparently be fastened at any point on the width of theirs. The pairs of beckets are always in corresponding positions on each side of the tent. I have seen two cases in Ait Oussa tents where a rear corner has been bevelled, and the becket fixed at a diagonal as in some Mauretanian tents, but this seems not to be typical.

The effect of the central pairs of beckets is to stretch the *velum* downwards and outwards on either side of the peak, once the tent has been erected, so that the junction of the poles cannot slip under the cloth. They are placed just far enough apart to allow the *velum* to stretch a little at this point. The hind corners are fastened close to the

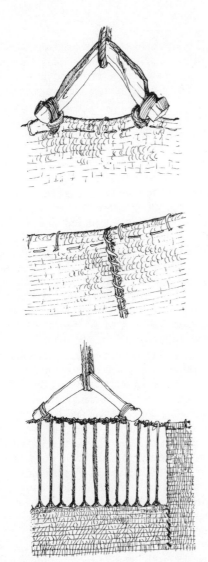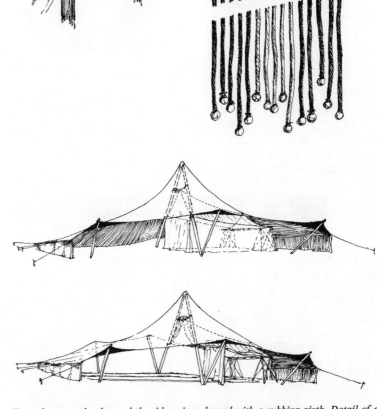

Top: *fixing of becket to bolt rope and* velum.
Left: *standing seam between cloths, and stitching of cloth to bolt rope.*
Centre: *Overstitching on velum.*
Bottom: *method of making up cloth which falls short of bolt rope, with becket. Aït Üsa.*

Top: *the crossed poles and the ridge piece draped with a rubbing girth. Detail of a rubbing girth and its fringe: Lansâs, Oulad Bu 'A̱sra, near Taidelt.*
Centre: *front view of tent showing canopy as at night.*
Bottom: *the same, as for daytime use. The tent is the same as that shown in plan on p. 123. Lansâs.*

ground quite near the rearmost of these pairs, holding the back of the tent taut. The front corner beckets are at a wider interval from the central ones, leaving the fore-part of the tent free to develop its awning-like spread, from the thrust of the props against the tension of the corner guys.

Both props bear against lifting rings which are fastened to the front lip of the velum between 60 cm and 1 m in from each corner. Each of the metal rings is sewn into the end of a tag-girth, a piece of specially woven webbing, and this in turn is sewn for part of its length to the underside of the *velum*. There are three forms of ring in current use, all made from wrought iron. The first is a simple ring about 5 cm in diameter. Then there is a triangle whose sides also measure 5 cm. The most common arrangement is more complicated, and rather like a shackle: the body is of flat section iron up to 1 cm wide by 0·15 cm thick, bent into a U, 5 or 6 cm wide, the tips of the arms being bent back to form loops, so that the U is from 6 to 8 cm long. An iron pin is passed through the loops, which are beaten tight on to it, and it is to this pin that the tag-girth is sewn.

Fastenings are also provided for the inner canopy which is sometimes hung inside the tent. These are simply long tails of goat hair twine stitched through the *velum* on the line of the peak, half way between the peak and one or both short sides of the tent. They can sometimes be seen hanging down even when no canopy is in evidence, though it seems that they are often put in and removed as required.

131

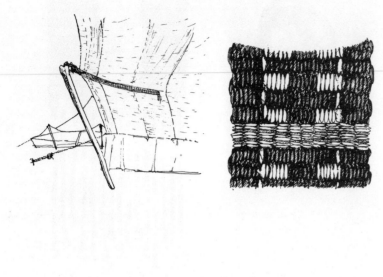

The strips of webbing used by the Tekna appear to be vestiges of much longer girths which play a more important part in the tents of tribes elsewhere in Morocco and the Arab world.

The tag-girths are often ragged or makeshift, yet good examples play a decorative part in the construction of the tent. They are woven on a ground loom in the same way as the cloths, only 5 to 8 cm wide and from 50 to 100 cm long. Two groups of white woollen warp threads alternating with the dark goat-hair yarn which forms the rest of the warp, give rise to two stripes of repeated short white lines, like the rungs of a ladder, along the length of the material. Each stripe is about 1 cm wide, and it is often trimmed by a continuous white line running along either the outside edge of the 'rungs' or both edges. The two stripes are placed so as to divide the width of the girth into three equal dark bands. One end of each girth is finished with a fringe of some six tassels made by twisting groups of the warp threads together clockwise, and cut to a length of 5 to 10 cm. The weft is finished with a double line of weft wrapping in wool. I have seen this done with white wool among the Ait Usa, but the Lansãs elaborate it using about eight lines of coloured yarn as a transverse stripe, which is repeated once in the middle of the girth and again near the other end. In a typical example the stripe was built up from double lines of scarlet wool on either side, and a double line of lemon yellow in the middle, with single lines of lilac on one side and sage green on the other between the yellow and the red.

The weave of these girths is quite fine, with about 100 warp threads per decimetre, and between 12 and 39 weft shots. The unfinished end is turned back over the lifting ring, and the girth is sewn beneath the *velum* for part of its length, the free end with its tassels being allowed to hang down inside the tent. The manner in which the girth is stitched varies. The lifting ring is in any case spaced out from the front edge of the lip cloth by 1 to 8 cm. In the elaborate Lansãs girths described above, almost the whole length was sewn in a broad herringbone stitch of white woollen thread crossing from one side to the other. This appears only as a double line of white points on the upper side of the *velum*. The Ait Ūsa sew on the first 5 cm or so to the lip cloth, leaving the remainder to hang free. This appears to be the practice of the Ait Lahsen too, though I have never seen a complete girth in their tents.

A rather similar but quite vestigial girth is used to protect the peak of the *velum* from the friction of the poles. It can be seen hanging down before and behind the point where the poles meet, decorated with long fringes of tassels. Such rubbing-girths are now rare, however; indeed I was only able to find two examples among some fifty tents. One of these was 15 cm wide, and 37 cm long, with tassels between 46 and 51 cm long, and the other was much the same size. The woven body of such girths is banded longitudinally, with a broad dark stripe at either edge, and a rather narrower white one down the centre. The weft is stopped at both ends with several strands of weft wrapping, and the remaining warp threads are divided into groups and twisted clockwise to form the tassels. In one case the wraps were of two red yarns, two white ones and then an alternation of single red and white yarns, six in all, to the end. There were fifteen tassels in

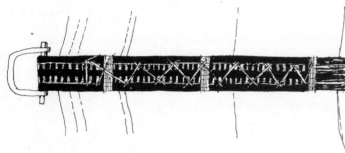

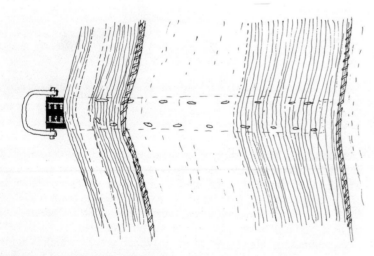

Top: *tag girth and prop at entrance of tent. Detail of tag girth near the end.*
Centre: *view of same girth on underside of* velum.
Bottom: *view of upper side of* velum *with stitching. Lansãs, Oulad Bu 'A̓sra, near Taidelt.*

three groups of five, black, white and black. Each tassel end was wrapped in a small bag of cotton held on by a whipping around the neck, so as to make a pompon. Each little bag was a different colour, red, yellow, blue or green, though they had faded even in the shade. In the other case the weft floating was broader, 8 cm at one end and 10 cm at the other, and at one end the floating was interrupted twice by bands of plain weave in black, 1 cm and 2 cm broad. The same alternating colours were used for the floating at both ends, one sequence being orange, white, orange, black, magenta, white, orange, black, white and orange at the edge. Several of these colours were worked in two yarns. The tassels in this case were finer, with thirteen black ones each side and ten white in the middle. The ends were knotted in a half hitch, without the cotton serving.

No girths or fastenings are found on the rear edge of the tent.

GUY ROPES AND PEGS

The nomads, living on the commercial fringes of the twentieth century, have adopted its rope and pieces of its reinforcing bars or angle iron for holding up their tents, but industry has gone no further. Steel pegs are undoubtedly more suitable for the stony ground than the wooden ones used before. They are sold in the *souks*, cut in lengths of 30 or 40 cm, with the head bent over or flattened, and the tip cut or ground to a point. The traditional material was *ttalh* (*Acacia Raddiana*), which was, of course, much lighter, but it is not used very widely nowadays.

The pegs are struck in more or less vertically with a stone or a simple mallet, so that only the head shows above the surface. If long steel pegs are used, 25 cm or more may be visible, but the guys are fastened around them near the ground.

Though sisal ropes are now used almost everywhere, the Ait Ūsa still use guys plaited from three strands of the same wool and goat-hair mixture that they use for making the tent itself, to a section about 2 cm wide and 1 deep. All the parts of these plaits are the same brown colour. The Ait Lahsen sometimes use cords made up from strips of camel leather 3 or 4 mm wide. The skin is prepared by soaking in water for three or four days with a herb called *themmeth*, after which it is taken out and when it has dried a little, oiled. After another two days it is cut up into strips, and put in water to soften. It is then worked. The guys may be made up as laid ropes, when three strips are twisted anti-clockwise into strands, and three of these strands are twisted clockwise into the finished cord. They may also be plaited in four, five or more parts – I was told that plaits are made in as many as fourteen. The leather, which is dark brown, hardens somewhat in the sun. Guys are sometimes made up, too, from rags twisted together: it seems likely that this is a makeshift for the leather ropes.

KNOTS

The guy ropes are made fast to the peg, then led up through the becket, and down again to be held by adjustable hitches around the standing part, about half way to the ground. The length of the ropes is rather variable. They are in any case easily worn, damaged or eaten away, and guys are shortened to take account of these accidents until it is absolutely necessary to replace them. Nevertheless the relative lengths of the four guys do follow a general pattern: they diminish in length towards the rear. The hindmost is only a half or a third of the front one, but there is not very much difference between the others. The front guy is usually from 150 cm to 180 cm from becket to peg, and a typical Ait Ūsa tent had ropes measuring, from front to rear, 180 cm, 170 cm, 155 cm and 80 cm. In small tents, or tents pitched on restricted sites, the front guy may be as short as a metre, and the others reduced in proportion. The longer the guy rope, the slower the slope of the roof, and the higher off the ground the sides may be. In this climate, where breezes must be allowed to freshen the interior whenever the conditions are right, such openness at the sides is an advantage, but long ropes can be a nuisance, as they prevent free movement around the tent. It seems that these lengths represent the limit where airiness must give way to practicality.

Perhaps it is because the deterioration of the ropes is recognised that double guys are sometimes found. The rope is middled, and the bight noosed around the peg, after which the paired ropes are treated as though they were one in the usual way. Otherwise the end of a single rope is knotted to form a stopper and this is pulled hard up into a half-hitch around the peg. This fastening is made very close to the ground, and the knot is often covered by sand. After the free end has been passed through the becket it is half hitched twice around the standing part of the rope. Three or more half hitches, spaced out, are also common. Occasionally a rolling hitch is put on the rope before the half hitches, making a midshipman's hitch or an adjustable hitch according to the arrangement. The end is pulled through, and never caught as a bight.

POLES AND PROPS

The whole weight of the *velum* can be supported on the two main poles, which meet at the peak though they are set far enough apart on the ground to form a nearly equilateral triangle. They are straight and evenly rounded, with a diameter of from 5·5 to 6 cm at the widest part near the base, tapering gradually by a centimetre or less to the top. The upper ends taper rather more sharply to a diameter of 4 cm at the tip. There is no decoration, but the pole is a pleasant yellow-brown, and perfectly smooth.

A truly complete tent is provided with a ridge piece in which the tips of the poles lodge, holding them fast and protecting the *velum* from their pressure. This is shaped rather like a tortoise shell, rounded on the back, and longer than it is broad. The underside is flattened in two slopes set at an obtuse angle to one another on either side of the short axis, so that the edges of these surfaces form a shallow inverted V, when seen from the side. Each surface contains a hemispherical hollow about 4·5 cm in diameter to receive the tip of the pole, placed not on the long axis but diagonally one on each side of it. When the poles are set up, they are crossed about 10 cm from the top before they are engaged in the sockets, and this offset allows the feet to remain on the short axis of the tent floor. The faces of the underside slope towards one another so that they are normal to the poles. The whole arrangement is quite stable, with the ridge held in place by the weight of the *velum* and its slight stretching at the peak, the feet thrust hard against the ground, and the poles bearing against one another at the crossing.

Small as they are, these ridge pieces may be any size between 15 cm and 28 cm long. A specimen I bought in Goulimine was 15 cm by 10 cm broad, and 6·5 cm deep, the V being 2 cm deep, and the sockets 6·5 cm apart at the centres. A Lansãs specimen was 21 cm long with the sockets 12 cm apart, and one from the Ait Ūsa was 28 cm long by 13 cm broad, and 15 cm between the sockets. The curved back meets the planes of the lower surface at an acute angle, but this is cut back in a step up to 1 cm deep, which may run straight across each end from side to side, or curve around the edges in a crescent whose thinning arms reach almost to the short axis. I once saw a ridge piece (Ait Ūsa) swathed in a piece of leather: the edges were pierced with holes and drawn down over the edges of the ridge piece by a system of zig-zag lacing that ran across the lower face of the wood. This may provide the explanation for such stepped edges, for they could help to hold the leather and its lacing in place. The ridge piece is usually undecorated. At most there are lines carved across at the meeting of the two faces, and a few pairs of nicks regularly spaced out around the edge. The rubbing girth, if there is one, is hung over the top of the ridge piece. The poles are crossed for this arrangement so that the rear pole runs to the right of the other when seen from the front, and the fringes of the girth hang front and back, to the right of the front pole, and to the left of the rear.

The great majority of Tekna tents have no ridge piece nowadays. Instead, the ends of the poles are wrapped together in a cloth, usually a piece of the blue cotton *dira'a* which the men wear. This is enough to connect the poles and to protect the *velum*, but since the poles, if they cross at all, cross only at the tips, they are not quite so stable as those with the ridge piece. The disappearance of the ridge piece is due, almost certainly, to the difficulty of obtaining pieces of hardwood that are large enough, as well as to the decline in skills, evident where these tents are concerned.

The length of the poles is adjusted to the size of the tent, and the two poles are not always the same. The Ait Ūsa, it is true, use poles of equal length, but the Lansãs and Ait Lahsen use a longer pole at the front. In general the longer pole is about half the length of the rear lip of the tent, and the shorter is between 5 cm and 20 cm less. There are often considerable departures from this pattern though, and it is clear that poles are used as they are available at the market. The result is, in any case, that the front pole is between 290 cm and 350 cm long, with 220 cm for a very small tent and 440 cm for a very large one. The foot of each pole simply rests on the ground. Since there is so much sand about, the end often sinks in a little, and a stone may be placed under it to prevent too much subsidence.

The props are straight, or straightish, barked sticks about 3 cm in diameter and between 140 cm and 180 cm long. They are usually grooved across the top so that they can be engaged with the ring becket, or they may end in a very short fork. They are erected slanting outwards from the interior, the foot pushed out as far as it will go against the tension of the tent lip on the head. Although only two props can be regarded as permanent, with corresponding fittings

to receive them on the *velum*, a variety of others are used as auxiliaries. As a matter of fact the front props are not always engaged in the beckets, for they are often found under the front corners of the tent instead, still raking out towards the top, as do all the props. Another prop may be inserted under the centre of the front lip, of the same length, and three shorter ones of about 120 cm may be put in along the back at the corners and in the middle. Often just one prop is used in the rear at the centre, and the churn tripod, which is much the same length, may be used there as well. Sometimes a single rear prop is used half way between the centre and the corner on the mens' side of the tent, so as to give them ventilation while allowing the women privacy as they work. All these extra props are used in the summer, and then only when the climate or the occasion requires it: they are used as much to control the glare outside as the air inside, and they are shifted about at different times of the day.

A prop or the tripod may also be used to raise the body of the *velum* and give more headroom to one side of the interior, but this is done only in very small tents, or when some special activity, like weaving, is taking place. Normally one or both of the short sides are held up by the storage shelving beneath them.

Strictly speaking the shelving is furniture, but as by design or accident it plays a part in shaping the interior, it is worth consideration as part of the structure. Each shelf consists of two trestles, two poles and a long leather cord. The trestles which stand at either end are each made up of nine straight staves with the reddish bark left on them, notched around each end where they are lashed together with camel leather thongs. The top and the four legs are about 3 cm in diameter, the top 80 cm long, the legs 115 cm. The legs are lashed to the top about 60 cm apart, so that the ends of the top staff project a little, and they are set wider apart, 85 or 100 cm, at the bottom. They

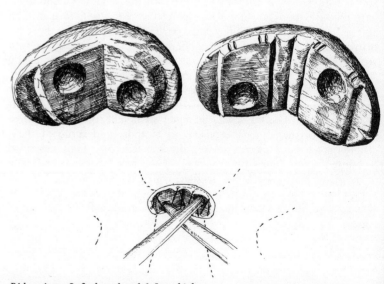

Ridge pieces. Left: *broad and 6·5 cm high.*
Right: *after Mlle due Puigaudeau: lower Dra valley, 21 cm long.*
Bottom: *as used by Ait Usa migrant to Mrirt in Middle Atlas. 28 cm long by 13 broad. Leather covering.*

are held firm in this position by a pair of diagonals lashed between each two legs. These are perhaps 140 cm long and 2 cm in diameter, fastened at the ends and where they cross each other in the middle. There are no base members. Each trestle can be folded like a pair of gates on the axle of the top staff. When in use, though, they are opened so that they stand about 110 cm high, and they are placed some 220 cm apart. The poles are about 250 cm long, and 4 to 6 cm in diameter. They are placed across the two trestles parallel to one another and 55 cm apart. The twisted leather cord is used to form the floor of the shelf between them, running from one to the other and back again in a continuous zig-zag, with a back turn made as it passes around each of them. This cord is itself quite a precious piece of equipment because of its length. It is made, like the leather guy ropes, to a thickness of 1 cm.

Another sort of shelving is found in tents belonging to nomads who migrate southwards, particularly among the Ait Lahsen. This is the *ameššáqqab*, one of the several kinds of litter used by the women on camel-back for travelling long distances. It is turned upside down in the tent, so that its base can form a platform. It then resembles the construction of the trestle gates, for there are two legs and a top bar braced by diagonals at each end, but these are held apart by top bars in the longitudinal direction instead of the poles, and two more struts are added from the feet to the mid points of these bars on each side. The legs are of blackwood in a flat section only 1 cm thick by 8 cm wide, beautifully and intricately carved in triangles, squares and arcs, and a kind of cross ribbing reminiscent of a banister. The whole litter is smaller than the trestle, standing only 70 cm high, with a top surface of 60 cm by 110 cm long. The work is Moorish rather than Tekna.

The timber used for the main poles of the tent is *Argan* (*Argania Spinosa*) and that for the trestles is *Ttalha* (*Acacia Raddiana*).

SIDE CLOTHS AND PINS

When the *velum* is stretched above the ground, uneven spaces are left around its edges. The front corners, lifted high by the props, are usually 70 cm or so above the ground, so the sides must slope down to the rear, where the height is only 10 to 30 cm. The tail cloth is lifted by the slope of the pole on which it rests, so that, without any props, there is a gap at the rear of about 60 cm in the middle. The spaces are generally filled by a sorry collection of faded patches, pieces and rags of cotton cloth and sacking stitched together to form a side cloth about 90 cm deep. The blue cloth used for men's and women's clothes is often prominent, and the whole motley is some-times oversewn in lines of running stitch at vertical intervals of 15 cm. Apart from this outer cloth there is often an inner lining of cotton. Nowadays cheap cotton prints are popular, with rather odd effects when pieces of six different 'regency' patterns are hung side by side along one wall. A more durable outer layer is formed from one or two old tent cloths, perhaps with a piece of cotton sewn along the lower edge to make the whole 1 m wide. These cloths are often weighted along the bottom with a row of stones holding the surplus to the ground, and they are pinned along the top. They are not

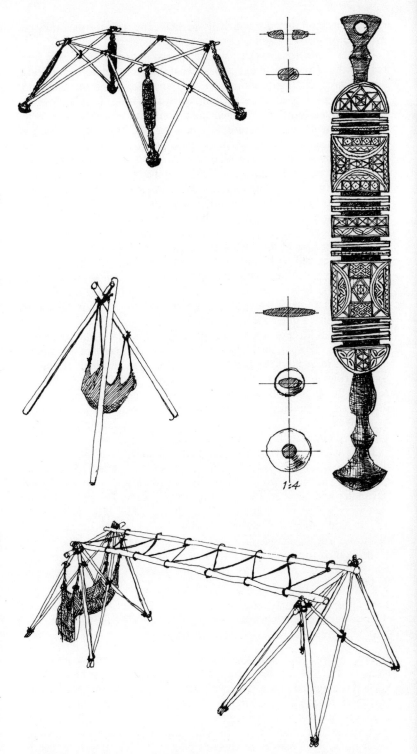

Top and right: *camel litter* (ameššaqqab) *upturned as shelving. Detail of leg carved in blackwood. Ait Lahsen, Ait Bū Meggūt, bought in Aiun.*
Centre: *Butter churn.*
Bottom: *Shelving with ditty bag hanging in trestle.*

135

continuous, and they are not really permanent either, for they may be dropped or thrown back according to the climate.

Richer tents are provided with a specially woven set of side and rear cloths. These are about 1 m wide, and up to 10 m long, but long as they are, this is not enough to surround more than one side and part of the back of an ordinary tent, so two are used. They are woven on the ground loom, like the tent cloth, but with more use of brown, black and white warp threads to create stripes. The weave is rather finer than usual, with 90 warps to the decimetre, and 22 wefts. The Ait Ūsa appear to use side cloths of this kind more than the other tribes; they are more noticeable in the smaller tents where the shelving elements are thrust against the *velum* so as to lift the sides of the tent until they are almost parallel with the ground. The multiple stripes attract attention because they run at right angles to those on the roof, though the colour is much the same overall. The warps are of pure goat hair in the dark areas, of wool in the white ones and of camel hair mixed with goat in the beige parts. The weft is a mixture of goat hair and wool. The wider stripes, up to 40 cm, are of the dark material; the beige ones are up to 7 cm only, but they are often defined with a line of two alternating white warps, which in turn may be picked out in dark ones.

The side cloths are lapped over the edge of the *velum* and pinned to it with iron skewers, every half metre or so. The skewers are round or square in section, with the heads beaten flat and bent round to form a ring, and 10 to 15 cm long. They are stuck into the fabric at right angles to the bolt rope, with the heads up or down, and they are usually strung together. The Ait Ūsa use a decorative string made up of a black, a white and a brown yarn twisted together clockwise; others a white one. Eight pins might be used each side.

I was shown an exceptional side cloth by some Oulad Bel-Lehwilat who claimed to have found it thirty years ago: it was 115 cm wide and 765 cm long, with a very fine weave of 33 weft shots per decimetre and between 150 and 180 warp threads. The stripes in this case were across the cloth, mostly an alternation of chocolate colour 12 cm and white 4·5 cm wide, with narrow stripes of the same colours bordering bands of beige 30 cm wide at intervals. The whole cloth seemed to be woollen, but there was probably some camel hair mixed in for the beige areas. It was fine enough to be used as spare bedding.[5]

LEASHES

About 75 cm from the peak, a collar is slung around the two poles, to hang in a gentle arc between them.[6] This may only be made from rope, but many tents are fitted with one worked elaborately in leather and dyed red, yellow, green and black. An eye is fitted at one end, large enough to receive the knob at the other end, which is perhaps 8 cm in diameter and 3 cm thick. The whole leash is 200 cm long and 2 cm thick. Thin leather thongs are plaited to form a surface sleeve around a rope core wrapped in cotton. Each thong passes over four and under four of its neighbours twice in the circumference; even the knob is covered. The leather is dyed after it has been plaited, in bands about 10 cm wide.

I was told that this leash prevents the poles from slipping apart, but it could quite clearly do nothing of the kind, unless it be that, loaded with bedding, it might help to stabilise the tent in a high wind. It is certainly used as a convenient hanging line for clothes, but it is more important as the means of furling the inner canopy of the tent up off the floor; the part of the cotton which would otherwise hang as a wall between the poles is thrown back over the line. It is also used to bind the folded tent for transport (q.v.).

Two smaller leashes of the same kind can sometimes be seen fastened around one of the poles about half way up. Each has a knob and an eye at either end, and the length from knob to knob is 70 or 80 cm. They are made with a soft leather covering in the same way, except that each thong passes under and over three others only, and the body of the leash is double, the two cords joining at each of the loops. These leashes too are used in packing the tent for transport, this time to bind the poles. They are also used for hobbling the forelegs of a rutting camel stallion.

Leash.

In the strict division of labour, the work of pitching and striking tents is largely womens' work.

Once the *velum* has been unpacked on a suitable site, the ground is cleared of the larger stones and brushwood, and the cloth is spread out flat over the poles which are laid end to end on the short axis. The knots and hitches on the guy ropes are made fast, and the women are able, from experience, to judge just the right distance from the edge of the *velum* for hammering in the pegs. The middle guys are stretched out in the line of the seams, but the corner guys are set diagonally, the front ones at an offset of up to a metre, and the rear up to half a metre from the position parallel with the others. Two women then grope underneath the *velum*, crouched down, to adjust the poles. They may be helped by the men in this. They engage the pole tips in the ridge piece under the peak of the tent, with the rubbing girth in place; if there is no ridge piece they wrap a piece of rag around the two tips to bind them together. They then lift the poles, crossed or bound as they are, so that the lower ends are dragged closer and closer together under the cloth. After some pushing and pulling against the tension of the guys and the stretch of the fabric, they are settled in their final position. The props are engaged in the lifting rings and under the front and rear edges to complete the tension. If any of the pegs show signs of pulling out they are made firm with boulders. Sometimes a stick is laid across the guys where they meet the ground and this is weighed down with stones: this device is used particularly on rocky ground. The floor of the tent is then cleared of any other uncomfortable stones, the shelving is put up, the mats spread out and the side cloths pinned on.

When it is particularly hot the two central beckets on each side may be lifted by forked poles 1 m long, against the pull of the guy ropes, to allow more air to circulate.

A tent can be struck simply by reversing this sequence. All the furniture is taken outside and packed, the mats rolled up tightly and the props removed. The feet of the poles have only to be dislodged for the tent to subside. A dramatic collapse can be produced just by tugging at the exposed end of the rear pole. The pegs are then pulled out.

The *velum* is spread out once more, and folded twice along the seams. The props are placed across this long bundle near either end, so that the ends can be folded over them to meet at the middle. Both sets of props are then lifted towards the middle to make another fold each side, and they are strapped together by the big plaited leash which hung around the poles in the pitched tent. Two smaller plaited leather leashes, each with two loops and two large buttons, are fastened at either end of the main poles which have been passed under the bundle, allowing them to be spaced about 50 cm apart. The folded tent can then be picked up by this shaft-like arrangement, and carried to the back of a kneeling camel, where it is fastened on top of the usual U-shaped bolster and pack saddle. One pole and half of the tent bundle hangs on each side of the camel.

If the tent needs only to be moved a short distance, it can be heaped on the two poles and carried shoulder high by four men to the new site.

Most of the ground inside a tent is covered with matting, which is stiff enough to form a smooth and comfortable floor over any small irregularities and stones that have not been cleared away. There are usually two long mats which are unrolled side by side between the main poles. They do not cover the ground where the shelving stands, or if there is none, the part close to the side cloth which is used for storage, so for an average tent they are 400 or 450 cm long by 85 to 125 cm wide. There is a special type of matting for tents which is distinct from another kind used in houses. It is made by some of the poorer tent-dwellers for sale in the market: the warp is of date palm fibre which is beaten out on stones and rolled between the hands into a brown anti-clockwise yarn. This is twined clockwise, and the warps are spaced out 2 cm apart. The weft is of pairs of twin esparto stems which are tucked one over and one under each warp alternately, with a half turn clockwise between each warp, to a count of about 56 per

Cushion.

137

decimetre. At the selvedge the stems are passed around the edge warp and then twisted around themselves one and a half clockwise turns. Hems are made at the ends of the mat by twisting the warps together clockwise [sic] and knotting them together. All the ends of the esparto are left on one side, which is therefore bristly. The upper side is smooth, with ribs running along the length where the warp yarns lie.

The mats are left out as a permanent floor running over both the halves of a tent, and their bland yellow ribbed surface gives every interior a pleasant simplicity. Even when animals are brought into the tent, when for instance newborn kids must be protected from the sun, they are tethered in a line at the side on the unmatted area, and the mats remain near by. Carpets are spread out on top of the mats for guests and for sleeping. There is one type used very widely, plain scarlet with a thick pile of about 2 cm, and about 180 cm wide by 500 cm long. The ends are usually finished with two blue and two yellow stripes, and the selvedges, which have no pile, with a row of black triangles. The pile is indeed very comfortable to sit or lie upon, and with the open mesh of the mat underneath it forms an excellent insulator against the cold ground at night. There may also be carpets with geometrical patterns, but only one is spread out at a time, unless someone needs to sleep outside the tent for politeness' sake, when a mat and a rug will be put out for him. Patterned carpets are imported from the Marrakech area.

The more nomadic Ait Ūsa and Ait Lahsen sometimes have a blanket made of dark brown lambskins sewn together, about the same size as the carpet. This is essentially a Moorish artefact, since the hairy sheep whose skins are used are not reared by the Tekna, but come from the Adrar hundreds of miles to the south. It can be used as a coverlet in cold weather. Both this and the carpets are kept on the shelf when they are not needed.

Comfort is completed with leather cushions. Since the tribesmen loll as often as they sit, these are useful for tender elbows. They are generally flat and waisted in shape, with no corners, up to 90 cm long and 45 cm across the wider parts with a 20 cm fringe all round, punctuated with broader tags. The ground colour of beige leather may show through the design, but it is often painted over to such an extent that the main colour is red, picked out in green and yellow. The leather is tooled a little to define the pattern. The style of such leatherwork may be Moorish, brought from the south, or slightly different local patterns.

THE CANOPY

Tents may be lined in several ways, partly for insulation, and partly to dress the interior with lighter surfaces than the dark tent cloth. Besides linings for the side cloths, which are quite common, one sometimes sees white cotton spread over the whole of the rear part of the roof, from side to side and passing behind the rear pole up to the peak. Linings of this kind are used in the south, near Tan Tan. The material is cotton sheeting or fine canvas, and the same white stuff is used for the more elaborate canopy which is hung from the roof for privacy and warmth.

This is really a tent within a tent. At the side of the tent the cloth is draped over the shelving, which holds it in place a metre above the floor. A small button is then made in the middle of the canopy by pinching a stone into a fold and binding around the neck. The button is fastened to one of the tags of goat hair yarn hanging from the central seam of the *velum*, some 10 cm below the surface. The remaining two corners are each tied around one of the poles about one third of the way up, so that the entire cloth is spread square in plan, with a single peak, and enough material left at the front, rear and middle of the tent to fall to the ground. A second peak may be formed by tying the canopy to the leash between the poles.

A married couple can retreat to this enclosure at night, to give them at least a little privacy from the others sleeping inside the tent. A single woman can resort to it to preserve decorum when there are visitors about (they would sleep outside the tent if she were alone). But during the day the sides are thrown up, and the part between the poles bundled over the leash, so that freedom of movement is restored. In winter the protection may be extended right across the tent.

Cloth for such canopies is bought in the *souk* in 4′ 6″ widths, three or even five of which are sewn together into a sheet about 4 m long to cover half the tent.

PLAN AND FURNITURE

The Tekna always pitch their tents so as to face southwards. In doing so they not only follow the Arab tradition, but they protect themselves by turning the streamlined tail of the tent into the prevailing wind. Tents are usually grouped in twos, threes and fours, roughly in line and about 12 m apart. Such neighbours are almost always related to one another; their camp may form part of a larger group which straggles without much order over a wide area if the pasture is good. The distance between tents is enough to keep the herds apart when they are brought close to each tent at night.

Those who stay on a site for any length of time build a hedge of brushwood out from each front corner in two curved wings, to enclose a semicircular forecourt 3·5 m across. This serves to keep the animals away from the tent at night, and provides a ready supply of firewood. The fireplace is simply a hob of three stones placed in the lee of one of these hedges at some distance from the tent. It is fed with sticks pushed in gradually from the outer side, with roots and even euphorbia cactus. The earthenware or aluminium *couscous* pot is set to boil here, or on more special occasions a brown glazed *tajine* dish with its conical lid. The lesser nomads, like the Lansās, use a different fire for baking bread. This may be a circular pit not far from the hob, about 40 cm across and 20 cm deep. When the embers in this are red hot, a metal plate is dropped on top of them, and the dough is placed on this; another metal sheet is drawn over the top of the pit to reflect heat on to the top of the loaf. I have also seen domed ovens outside Lansās tents. Kettles are brought to boil on the hob before being transferred to a three legged metal brazier for the almost perpetual tea making. Water is kept in goatskins with the hair left on them, each holding about 20 litres. These are hung by leather cords

138

oining the feet on trestles like those for the shelving, but only 90 cm high. A water trestle is usually placed outside the tent at the corner opposite to the kitchen; one or two skins are hung on it, and covered with rags to keep the sun off. Another goat skin used as a churn may hang on a rough wooden tripod just outside the tent on the kitchen side. At other times the tripod may be folded and used to prop up the tail of the tent. Cooking pots are left about in the kitchen area, and a black one may be turned bottom-up on one end of the hedge, for luck. A gazelle horn is sometimes stuck on top of a pole near the forecourt entrance. Pack saddles for donkeys and camels, and the crude bowed framework of a woman's camel litter are left outside.

A tentwife works in the side of the tent next to the kitchen. This is as often on the right as on the left, and it seems to be determined by the direction of the wind. If there is one shelving element it will be placed on this side; if there are two, this one will carry most of the household goods. The canopy is spread above.

The other side of the tent is the mens' side, and guests are received there. A second shelving element down the side may carry a carpet and a lambskin rug. Though there is no permanent division between the sides, and men may well lie or sit in both if the women are not there, the wife usually puts up a screen of the favourite sky blue cotton while she is working. This is made from two widths of a yard sewn together, one end being nipped between the front lip of the tent and the central prop, while the other is fastened to a corner prop at the back on the womens' side. Sometimes the screen is hung on a yarn from the *velum*, like the canopy, and sometimes there are even two screens at an angle to each other; in any case they form a barrier a metre high, enough to hide a sitting figure. Another piece of cotton may be hung along the lip of the tent to screen the front from passers-by.

The shelving is often hung with a cloth which hides it completely; sometimes a patchwork of different colours, sometimes a large piece of blue which is hung up to screen the women at night. Traditionally it was decorated with four pieces of decorated leather each about 60 cm wide and 90 cm deep, each slit into five hanging panels of unequal width. These were mainly red, worked over very minutely with incisions forming lozenges and squares picked out in yellow and green, in Moorish style. Such hangings are now very rare.

Leather hangings for shelving. Moorish work.

Apart from the rugs and a long striped blanket, which are kept folded on the top shelf, almost everything is kept in bags. A tanned goatskin bag (without hairs) is hung by leather cords on the trestle at the kitchen end, to hold flour. Another similar skin is slung in the trestle at the other end as a ditty bag. Then there are larger pouches (40 cm wide and 70 cm long), dyed red with Moorish ornament, a loop of leather cord at each end and a tassel at the bottom. One or two of these may hang on the trestles holding provisions and the woman's trousseau, all carefully padlocked. The big amber beads and silver jewelry on which these people set so much store, are kept in a little gazelle skin purse with a draw string. The other valuables are kept in a decorated leather pouch with an extravagant fringe, and the tea pot and glasses, which have an importance outweighing their value, are put in a basket with a leather neck. Clothes, sugar, tea and anything else of importance are put in a heavy leather travelling bag. It is made of thick tanned camel leather, folded and sewn into a rectangle 100 cm by 80 cm with a softer cylindrical neck 40 cm in diameter and 50 cm long protruding from the middle of one surface. It too is red, decorated with fringes and can be padlocked. It is kept on the shelf. There is often a small wooden chest under the shelf, and, alas, a suitcase or two.

There are several pieces of household gear that are too unwieldy to be packed up. The heaviest is the quern, which has a conical top with concave sides.[7] Then there are a tall cylindrical wooden mortar for

Mortar. Lansãs.

Brazier for tea-making. Moorish work.

Bread oven. Lansãs.

husking barley, the hemispherical wooden milk bowls, a round tea tray or table on three legs, a heavy wooden platter for serving meat, and coiled esparto grass plates. A well made brazier with brass mounts can be folded up for transport by undoing one screw. A pair of bellows is used to heat it. A small earthenware jar with ears and a lid is used to hold butter, and it hangs from the shelf near the kitchen. Some sieves and a huge wooden ladle are kept near by.

Tools on the other hand are kept on the mens' side. An adze, a bundle of sickles and a saw lie with the well rope and its leather bucket, a mule saddle and perhaps a bundle of skins.

The shelving trestles are sometimes replaced by a rectangular camel litter turned upside down to rest on its beautifully carved corner posts.[8]

An old-fashioned lantern is sometimes used at night, with a candle inside four glass walls and a pyramidal roof. Hurricane lamps are preferred. The light attracts insects, and even crickets come inside. Spiders are killed because they are 'bad for the tent cloth'. Women cook mainly by firelight if they have guests in the evening.

Tea-making is the mens' affair. The brazier is set up on the front of their mat, and the kettle brought to them. A guest is usually asked to make tea as an honour, and indeed the reception of a guest after the protracted greeting, which may consist of as many as forty responses, centres around the tea. If an animal is slaughtered it is hung from the side prop in front of the guests and skinned. The men roast the liver as kebabs while the women dress the meat for the main meal. This is the only cooking done on the mens' side. Meals are eaten on the mat, out of the platter placed inside a large esparto plate. The men sit in a circle around it, and are careful to leave enough for the women to finish afterwards.

When a ground loom is set up for weaving tent cloth, it runs through the tent from front to rear. The tentwife weaves inside the tent, with the heddle in front of her facing the light. As the weaving advances, she can wind in the finished cloth on its beam so as to bring the heddle back to the centre of the tent. Spun thread is stretched in front of the tent in the open.

No tent is complete without its watchdog; I once saw a small kennel built of stones. Cats are also kept.

Prayers are said outside the tent, at a discreet distance from anyone who is carrying on a conversation. At Assa I came across a line of boulders laid out straight on the ground for 4 or 5 metres, with a semicircle at the centre to represent the prayer niche of a mosque, and the direction of Mecca, so: ——————⌣——————.

SIZE, MAINTENANCE AND COST

These tents are all much the same in size. That is to say that the greatest number of them consist of seven or eight, or occasionally nine cloths besides the lip cloths, measuring between 450 cm and 550 cm. The length of the *velum* is not in a constant proportion to the width, but varies between 600 cm and 800 cm along the front. Widows sometimes have very small tents of only four cloths: in a Lansãs camp I saw two measuring 120 cm by 180 cm and 270 cm by 580 cm, but the smaller of them excited unkind hoots of derision. Such small tents are as rare as large ones. The largest Tekna tent I have seen was that of the Moqaddem of the Ait Ūsa at Assa, which

Quern.

Platter, ladle, spoon and sugar hammer.

had nine cloths and the lip cloth doubled at the back, measuring 579 cm wide and 1,060 cm long at the front. The entrance is always the same height of 150 cm, though the height of the peak varies.

A cloth lasts four or five years and new cloths are made as they are needed to replace old ones. A man rich in herds will keep his tent in constantly good repair, rather than expand it. The cloths at the centre wear out most quickly because of the strain of the poles against the peak, and tents often show dark new areas in the middle as a result. A new cloth is sewn in as soon as it is ready, but tents are not re-sewn regularly.

I was given figures for the weight of hair needed for weaving a cloth, which varied between 20 kilos and 10 kilos. People are evidently not used to thinking in these terms, but the second figure seems to be the correct one. This informant added that 8 kilos of goat hair could be mixed with 2 kilos of camel hair for the same result (Ait Lahsen). At the rate of about one pick a minute, a woman would take twenty-four hours to weave an 8 m *flij* if she worked fast and continually. In real terms, allowing for limited daylight, interruptions, and household chores, she would need a week to finish it, working hard.

A tent costs about £25 for the *velum*[9] alone. Other parts can be expensive, however: the two mats cost £6, and the carpet, depending on the quality, about £15 to £20 (1968 rates).

NOTES

[1] MONTEIL, V., *Notes sur les Tekna*.
[2] The measures used are the cubit, from the elbow to the extended middle finger of the same hand (about 50 cm); the span between the tips of the thumb and little finger (23 cm); the 'dog's gape' between thumb and index (17 cm); and the foot.
[3] I have not seen these, but judge from Baroja's photographs.
[4] It is interesting to compare this with the much more definite and symmetrical patterns shown by Mlle du Puigaudeau for Mauretania, which evidently play a decorative role, at least in part. See DU PUIGAUDEAU, ODETTE, 1967, Plate I.
[5] Another side cloth for sale at Goulimine was black (being new) with a ladder pattern in white down the edge, and a white stripe about 2 cm wide outside each of the narrower stiles of the ladder.
[6] Sometimes a longer leash is passed twice around the poles to form an arc in four parts about 60 cm long.
[7] This is very similar in shape to some found in the Canaries. The mill is used anti-clockwise, it being said that only the Jews grind clockwise.
[8] This pattern of litter is not to be confused with the ordinary kind, the lemsāma, of bent wood.
[9] A second-hand one.

Spinning, twining or twisting referred to as clockwise or anticlockwise results in S or Z yarns respectively.

BIBLIOGRAPHY

DU PUIGAUDEAU, ODETTE, *Arts et Coutumes des Maures*, Hespéris Tamuda, vol. VIII, 1967, Rabat.
MONTEIL, VINCENT, *Notes sur les Tekna*, Institut des Hautes Etudes Marocaines, notes et documents III, Editions Larose, Paris, 1948.
MONTEIL, VINCENT, *Essai sur le Chameau au Sahara Occidental*, Etudes Mauretaniennes No. 2. Centre IFAN-Mauretanie, Saint-Louis du Sénégal, 1952.
MONTEIL, VINCENT, *Notes sur Ifni et les Ait Ba 'Amrān*, Institut des Hautes Etudes Marocaines, notes et documents II, Editions Larose, Paris, 1948.
MONTEIL, VINCENT, *Les Tribus du Fars et la Sédentarisation des Nomade*
DE LA CHAPELLE, F. *Histoire du Sahara Occidental*, Hepéris, XI, 1930, Librair Larose, Paris.
MONTAGNE, ROBERT, *La Limite du Maroc et du Sahara Atlantique*, Hespéris, X 1930, Librairie Larose, Paris.
BAROJA, JULIO CARO, *Estudios Saharianos*, Consejo Superior de Investigacione Cientificas, Instituto de Estudios Africanos, Madrid, 1955.
U.N.E.S.C.O., *Nomades et Nomadisme au Sahara*, Recherches sur la zone Arid XIX, Paris, 1963.
Naval Intelligence Division, *Morocco*, vol. I, B.R. 506, Geographical Handboo Series, December 1941.
TROUT, FRANK E., *Morocco's Saharan Frontiers*, Bibliotheca Africana Droz Geneva, 1969.
MICHELIN Maroc (road map of Morocco), Paris

DRAWINGS

I am most grateful to Mr Anton Jansz for his generous help in preparing th drawings for this article.

Transport of a tent.

HOUSE FORM AND SOCIAL STRUCTURE IN BAKOSI

Michael D. Levin

'The process of artistic creation therefore consists in trying to communicate (within the immutable framework of a mutual confrontation of structure and accident) either with the model or with the materials or with the future user as the case may be, according to which of these the artist particularly looks to for his directions while he is at work.' (*C. Lévi-Strauss,* The Savage Mind, *p. 27.*)

'. . . the owner is his own builder, . . . the form-maker not only makes the form but lives in it.' (*Alexander,* Notes on the Synthesis of Form, *p. 49*)

Every man in an African society is an architect. His orientation is towards the balance of model, materials and user, the latter usually himself. In a closed, traditional society he acts unselfconsciously, regarding design within the cultural system of which he is part. With the transformation of his society under the pressures of modernisation, the stable equilibrium within the system is lost and the design process becomes one of selfconscious manipulation of new models, materials and new concepts of use. Each man is an architect for an uncertain future. But it is on the foundation of the traditional culture and in the frame of its symbolic order that these transformations are made.

The evolution of baKosi [1] houses and villages under the pressures of colonial policy and the new forces of modernisation, are structured

Location of baKosi in Africa.

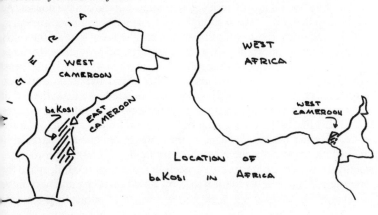

changes. Initially they were formed from the interaction of cultural and ecological inputs to the creative process, through which the traditional baKosi house is built, and was perfected. With the transformation under modernisation of this creative process from an unselfconscious one to a selfconscious one, the dynamics of social change were disruptive of the equilibrium state of culture and social structure, and of one of its concrete expressions, house form. Behind these innovations the continuing structure of baKosi culture can be discerned, while simultaneously one can predict changes in the expressions of that structure originating in the present interaction of past forms, new materials and new design and construction concepts.

In a relatively closed, politically autonomous, baKosi society prior to the imperially imposed *pax*,[2] one kind of building was adapted in form and building technique to the culture and ecology. This single, multifunctional form evolved as the outcome of the continuing, immediate and direct adaptation that is the result of '. . . a special closeness of contact between man and form', when the man who has shaped the form also lives in it.[3] The culture and ecology form the environment in which this design process has worked itself out.

The *ndab*, the conical roofed, circular house, is the outcome of this unselfconscious design process at the nexus of culture and ecology; of 'the universe as object of thought . . . [and as] means of satisfying needs'.[4] This is the fundamental form of all buildings, the different types being allocated among various culturally defined uses, each serving a range of differing functions. Whereas house form and groupings of houses seem primarily an adaptive expression in terms of materials, the demands of the day-to-day and annual cycles of work, subsistence needs and domestic life, the pattern of settlements is a spatial analogue of political relationships between kinship-defined political units. It is in terms of the parameters established by the concepts of baKosi culture and the ecological system of the baKosi territory, and their interaction, that the concrete expressions of house form and settlement pattern were determined.

The outputs to the culture of ecological relationships are made in terms of the defined cycles of agricultural work, the requirements of storage of food and firewood, the need for warmth and the preservation of buildings. Climax vegetation, rainfall, availability of water supplies, and fertility of soil are factors determining the availability of materials, limiting agricultural techniques, creating problems of storage, determining the duration of periods of use of a farm and of fallow, which in turn

Village chief's compound. Mound and pole in left centre is the site of the chief's old njeb. *The gable end of the Presbyterian Church can be seen at the extreme left.*

Round houses of Paramount Chief's compound. Large house with timber and cement walls and metal sheet roof is that of his deputy at the peak of his political power. Round houses are occupied by unmarried daughters of the chief and wives of the deputy.

in turn determine the ratio of population per unit area, the concentration of settlements and the permanence of settlement.

The inputs to the ecological system that maintain an equilibrium as established by these parameters are a given, unchanging technology, which includes tools, techniques and the range of crops and domesticated animals.

Cultural concepts: the conceptions of male and female, and especially, what maleness and femaleness consist of, the way the division of labour works itself out specifically in terms of tasks and prohibition of tasks, and the stratification of spiritual purity and knowledge, define the organisation of settlements. They also define the range of access to different kinds of houses and places, the uses to which they are put and the differing relationships of individuals to the houses and places in terms of ownership, custodianship and sharing in the collective interest the building or place represents.

BaKosi villages are sited along the eastern slopes of the Manengouba Mountains and the foothills linking Manengouba to Kupe Mountain and the surrounding foothills in the south. Most villages were at an altitude of 300 m in the south to 1500 m in the north near Manengouba. However, baKosi territory extended beyond the settled area—from the ridge of these hills into land at lower altitudes to the Mungo River in the east and its tributaries in the south. The soil of this area is composed of extremely fertile volcanic ash. During recent periods of economic and agricultural expansion, settlement spread into the unsettled area to the south under the political entrepreneurship of the new Paramount Chief of the colonial era. The southward expansion of the baKosi in precolonial times was limited by the lack of a reliable year-round water supply. Even in the rainy season stream beds were full only for a few hours after a heavy rainfall because of the high porosity of the volcanic soil. Some rain falls daily, with peak amounts from May to October, and very little during the dry season. There is a short dry period in August of one or two weeks. The high fertility of this soil and the continuous rainfall allows continual planting and rich yields. The agricultural cycle is not broken sharply into harvest and planting seasons, or periods of

plenty and scarcity. Coffee farms, at higher altitudes in the north, are harvested in the dry season, and cocoa farms, at lower altitudes in the south, are harvested in the rainy season. Until recently the absence of a regular water supply created a large-scale bi-annual migration between the southern cocoa farms and northern coffee farms. During the dry season the southern area depended on water sold by lorry drivers who brought it back in drums from their trips upland.

From this brief outline of ecological conditions we can suggest the outputs from the ecosystem to the cultural system, and the inputs to the ecosystem from the population, acting in terms of the cultural system. Continual rainfall throughout the year creates two problems which become most acute during the annual rainy season: the preservation of houses made only of vegetable material and the finding of dry firewood. The limitation on material is not a result of lack of ingenuity, but the absence of binding properties in volcanic soil which makes wattle-and-daub methods and mud blocks impossible to use without some additive as a binding element. The problem of finding dry firewood is a resolution of several factors, the high rainfall at some periods making newly cut wood unusable, the heavier demand on men's time for hunting in the rainy season and the need for large quantities to provide continuous fires in the rainy season for warmth and to reduce moisture in the houses. As trees are felled only by men, though women split the firewood and carry it from the bush, there would be severe conflicts for time in the rainy season. More important is the impossibility of providing the large quantities in demand during the rainy season, when working in the forest and carrying heavy loads is more difficult and dangerous. In fact, there are large quantities of firewood accumulated usually at the end of the dry season after the planting of new farms. If a store can be provided this limits the work in the bush to a minimum of farm maintenance, weeding during the lapse in the rains in August and harvesting according to need on the more favourable days. The design requirements of this environment are protection from high rainfall, space for storage of firewood, ventilation to allow firewood to dry and to remove moisture (at least avoid high concentration of moisture), sleeping

Lower half of a line village; note the modern buildings of concrete with metal sheet roofs among the traditional types of round and rectangular houses.

Round huts with temporary sheds between them built to house guests at funeral celebrations. Women are carrying jugs of palm wine for the celebrations in their baskets. They carry cocoyams and firewood in the same manner.

and cooking spaces, storage space for utensils and other general requirements of human settlements, such as waste disposal areas and drainage.

The high fertility of the soil allows several farms to be in production for every adult woman. Each farm can be of small area and the slash and burn cycle can be long because of the low demand for land to expand. The low ratio of population land within the limits of the given technology and range of crops allows for permanent settlement. The siting of the settlements is determined by the availability of good sites, level or suitable for levelling, which are also distant enough from streams to avoid flooding.

Distance between settlements seems to have been determined by these ecological outputs and the need for sight communication with one or two other lineages, sufficient land for a small farm close to the house site for each woman and grazing areas for cows and goats. Farms of one owner were scattered among different groups of farms planted in land cleared by different men of the lineage. One small farm was maintained near the clearing of the family group to provide an emergency source of food in the worst parts of the rainy season or for unexpected guests.

There appears to have been a low level of population to potential productivity even within given technological and agricultural limits. It is likely that the difficulty of clearing tropical rain forest, even during the short period of extensive use of iron axes, rather than low nutritional levels provided a check on agricultural expansion. Traditional baKosi agriculture, in contrast to modern cash crop farming, did not permanently alienate land from the farm-fallow cycle, and it would seem that the cultural outputs to the ecological system were few and tended towards a stable equilibrium. Man had not yet begun actively transforming his environment, but lived within it, as part of it. When land is permanently alienated from the farm-fallow cycle, and health and communications improve, man begins to transform the environment and population expansion puts pressure on the productivity of the available land.

In such a system, tending towards stable equilibrium, the cultural inputs to the form of house are more important than the inputs to the ecosystem. The unselfconscious design process described by Alexander has been adapting the cultural form to the day-to-day needs, variations in family structure and population, ecological changes and variations in site, to produce 'well-fitting forms', the necessary conditions to sustain this equilibrium. The equilibrium of well-fitting forms is at the nexus of the action of the generalised architect, that is *badbeKosi*, (people of Kosi), in this design process with the equilibrium of the cultural and ecological systems.[5]

It is the values of the culture, analog of the social structure, that have created the frame of concepts in which this design process has worked itself out. As Lévi-Strauss points out, except for war and child-bearing the distribution of tasks between men and women is culturally, not naturally determined.[6] Social codes, not biological codes, define the limits of the division.

The allocation of tasks related to house building and use in the division of labour in baKosi society is represented in the table below.

Allocation of Tasks in the Division of Labour:

	MEN	WOMEN
House	Building and repair	Maintaining fire in the hearth
	Gathering of repair materials	Regular use of fire to maintain the roof
Firewood	Felling trees, cutting logs	Splitting and carrying from the bush, drying and maintaining a stock
Agriculture	Cleaning farms, assistance in planting, planting plantains	Planting, weeding, harvesting, including carrying cocoyams from the bush
	Provision of meat by hunting or purchase	Cooking
	Provision of baskets for carrying, mortars for pounding, etc.	Carrying water

The reciprocal obligations and duties of marriage and kinship organise these tasks in interacting cycles of daily and seasonal activity in the context of the established relationships and spaces which form part of the environment. Each married woman has a right to her own kitchen and sleeping room, and conversely the husband is obliged to provide the kitchen, usually a new *ndab* if he has not inherited rights to that used by his mother. Other obligations as to cooking, eating and daily co-operation cement the day-to-day cycle of reciprocity between husband and wife.

The reciprocities of daily life change with the agricultural cycle: house repairs are done from February to May after the first heavy rains indicate the leaks; clearing and planting of cocoyams is done in March and April; hunting is at a peak in the rainy season, late May to October, and weeding is done in the break in the rains in August. The stock of firewood is built up throughout the dry season. Trips to the bush for building materials and clearing provide opportunities to locate suitable trees.

Benches built of bamboo along each side of the house serve as beds, sitting places or storage racks for pots. If both are in use as beds, small children may sleep on woven mats on the floor near the hearth. Cooking utensils such as wooden mortars are hung on the wall, others, such as knives, are wedged into the space between mats. A water pot is kept to one side of the entrance, convenient for setting down the full pot when returning from the stream and for emptying a half-full cup by throwing the water outside. This is only a sketch of the interior of an *ndab*. The actual appearance will vary greatly with the position and status of the owner and family who use it.

An *ndab* is built for a woman, though her husband builds it and owns it. As long as she remains his wife, she may stay in the house. The interior of the house, the house as kitchen, reflects the period of the woman's life and the wealth of her husband. The wealthier the husband the more clay pots, grinding and pounding mortars of various sizes and other kitchen utensils will line the walls. When she is very old these things will occupy much of the house though they will be infrequently used. A still active woman with grown children is likely to have extra firewood in spaces along the walls which she rotates to the attic for final drying. Usually she keeps a large quantity visible for display. When care of her children occupies most of the woman's time, firewood stocks will fluctuate with the season. The biggest stock is accumulated at the beginning of the rains. A part of the wood, stored in right-side and left-side stacks in the attic, will always be reserved for ceremonial use.

A woman's status in the community of women of her husband's lineage – mothers of the men and their wives – depends on her success in bearing children and on the store of firewood she can display. The mundane explanation is that the wood is an insurance against bad times, sickness of long duration and old age, but it also reflects on her status as a responsible, hard-working wife which is symbolised by the use of wood in reciprocal exchanges and ceremonies. Symbolically, firewood is the focus of women's work and is frequently a gift, or contribution on occasions when consumption is high, celebration of a birth, the death of a member of the family, and other feasts. The wood will be heaped in front of the house to display the giver's generosity and the high regard in which the receiver is held. At the death of a woman, firewood will be carried back an[d] forth in front of her house by her friends to show that she ha[s] worked hard. At the same time, half the wood in the store, the left, o[r] woman's side, will be burned in fires in front of the house and used i[n] cooking fires. On her husband's death the right, or man's side, will b[e] burned through the night in three fires in front of his houses. Th[e] amount burned is an indicator of virtue in hard work and reflects o[n] the prestige of the living spouse and the memory of the deceased.

The store of firewood takes up all the space under the roof of th[e] house. A platform is constructed within the house which forms [a] low ceiling and creates an attic in which firewood is stored. Th[e] particular needs of the environment are well served despite th[e] obvious inefficiencies in the location of the storage space. New fire[-] wood must be carried up a ladder and stacked in a cramped space[.] Once fully dried it must be brought down a few pieces at a time. Th[e] drying process, however, is most efficient. The smoke of the cookin[g] fire from the hearth in the centre of the floor of the house passes u[p] through the floor of the attic blackening the wood with soot an[d] drying it, making it very smooth burning fuel. At times of pea[k] accumulation the volume of dry wood stored in the attic may reac[h] five square metres. At such times just at the beginning of the rain[y] season, the cycle of storage is: initial drying in stacks on the floo[r] along the wall, final drying in the attic, then removal to a bench o[r] the top of initial drying stacks for convenience when needed for [a] fire. New firewood will be rotated into the rows stored in the attic fo[r] ceremonial needs, but only those species that dry and burn well wi[ll] be kept. Other species will be consumed without such extensiv[e] drying.

The locus of men's activities, visiting, drinking, eating and seden[-] tary work is in the *njeb*, the men's house. It is usually made with a[n] old roof from a kitchen and has relatively open walls and no door. I[t] is sparsely equipped and used only during the day.

The basic compound population comprises one man, and one o[r] more women and their children. The underlying relationships ar[e] those of a man and his son, a man and his wife, a man and hi[s] brother, and a man and his brother's wife. Variations in the popula[-] tion of a compound reflect different sets of these relationships, that is[,]

Section of round house.   *Floor plan.*

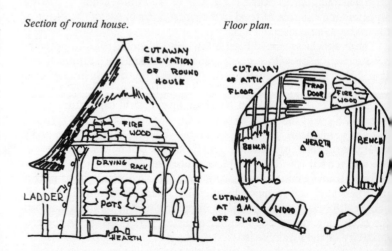

a man and his wife or wives; brothers and their wives and father's wives; fathers, their sons and their wives. While an ideal genealogical structure defines relationships, the actual biological relationships are more complex and more distant than a European would think from the terminology. The defining aspects of the common group, the lineage, are corporateness, that is, a share in the rights to property, and the rules of exogamy. Both the tracing of descent and an acknowledged right of access to land by virtue of membership in the lineage, establish and maintain the social boundaries of the group. One of the first sources of a division in such a group is population pressure which would necessitate a separate compound site.

A typical compound reflected this set of relationships and this allocation of tasks among the population. There was a men's house, the *njeb*, and kitchens and sleeping houses, *ndab*, one for each woman, wife, father's wife or father's brother's wife, for whom the head of the lineage is responsible. Less permanent rectangular houses used for sleeping by male youths might also be present. Larger groupings would be extensions of this basic set of combinations of relationships of agnatic kin. The extension of these relationships in terms of new buildings would be more kitchen/sleeping houses, *ndab*, and perhaps a second *njeb*, dividing the focus of male activity.

The status of the highest ranking male in the compound determined the status in baKosi of the *njeb* of the compound. If a man was wealthy enough he might build a 'house of two doors'. He would keep his, and other men's, sacred items and costumes, which he owned as a member of a secret society, in the house and use it for meetings of family members. Only freeborn women would be allowed to cook in the house, for those descended of slaves might see and contaminate the ritual objects. If his house became the focus of political activity for the village it would become known as the '*njeb* of so-and-so' and that name would continue to be used by his descendants. It was in the *njeb* also, that youths ate and slept with their age mates during the period when they were recuperating from circumcision. If the head of a family was regarded as the highest ranking headman of the clan, then his *njeb* became an *esam*, the focus of political activity for all the clan, the place where members of other clans came to consult the clan heads, where disputes between villages within the clan were settled.

The *esam* of a clan, or the *njeb* of a village, each 'owned' or in the custodianship of the chief of the village, was not in the full control of the chief, but ultimately in the control of the politically most powerful secret society and the council of elders. These men would all be free men, without slave ancestry as traced through three generations, just as the women who occasionally cook in these houses to allow smoke to maintain the roof, are of free descent.

Such a politically important *esam* or *njeb* had one or more poles between the two front doors carved in a representation of a totemic or spiritually powerful reptile or animal, or a stylised human figure. The houses were surrounded by stones, five, seven or nine, which served double duty as sitting places and symbols of the ancestral spirits.

The only extant 'house of two doors' in baKosi is the one in the accompanying photograph. The others have been destroyed by community action led by Christians of the community and encouraged

'House of two doors.' The only extant house of this type in baKosi. Newly cut firewood is heaped in front.

by European missionaries. Only mounds, usually overgrown with grass, occasionally the poles, now rotting, and the stones remain.

This group of houses was usually surrounded by a 'living fence', that is, a fence of saplings which regenerated and continued to grow. They were first tied together with bamboo thongs or vines and then further strengthened by their own branches intertwining. But with the increasing hunting ability following the introduction of firearms which reduced the wild animal population, and with the reduction of inter-group conflict under the European *pax*, the fences were limited in size or disappeared. With the decision in the mid-1950s, to eliminate cows in some areas because they damaged coffee trees, fences were unnecessary altogether.

At the entrance to this compound along the path bisecting the compound and leading to the next compound is an open space, around which are scattered large, round stones and broken pots. It is here that the annual fertility ceremonial is held. Here also on other occasions that supplications to the ancestors are made with offerings of food and drink. This clearing, called by the same word as the verb 'to eat', represents the continuity of the living members of the lineage with the deceased members.

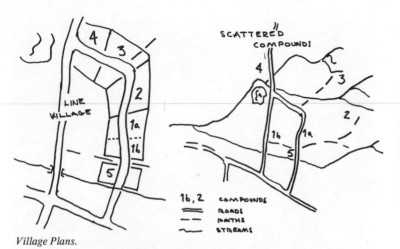

Village Plans.

Tying palm-mats to rafters.

Doorway detail; the black poles between the lighter load-bearing poles are giant ferns. Volcanic rocks and inverted beer bottles serve the same function at lower edge of wall. Two baskets of cocoyams and a bunch of plantains have been brought to celebrate a birth.

The selection of a site for a settlement in terms of ecological limits, level or potentially level places, and away from streams, is only the beginning of a continuing process. Prior to clearing and levelling the desired area, an oracle is consulted and if results are positive, work goes ahead. The process of preparation of the site is accompanied by rituals paralleling each stage. The time between building and final construction is needed to gather all the materials. Uninterrupted ritual and building processes bode well for the house. Failures or disruptions at any step may lead to abandonment of the site. Once a compound site is established, locations for additional houses involve only the ritual aspects, not the broad ecological aspects of the process. Once this is complete the building begins.[7]

There are two independent load-bearing systems in the house: that of the roof and walls and that of the floor of the attic, which serves as a firewood storage area. The load-bearing uprights of the walls and of the attic floor are hardwood, shaped to suit their use and notched at the top end to hold the roof or cross beams. The rafters are of bamboo or the spines of oil palm leaves. The first step in making the roof is the tying of a circle of heavy vines and resting it on pegs about 20 cm off the ground. Four poles are tied at the peak and to the ring. Other poles are then fitted on to the cone, the upper ends tied in by vines in a special weaving-like method at the peak and lashed at the base to the ring, until the ends on the ring are about 4 inches apart. Then palm leaf mats are tied to the roof, starting with 6–8 mats per row at the lower edge of the cone, making a kind of eave and proceeding with 2 mats per row on the main slope of the roof. The ends of the leaves are pointed upward leaving a short edge of 5–10 cm left exposed. After a season or two the sides of the leaf rot away leaving the spines along which water runs down. Continuous use of fire in the new house seals the roof with soot, coating and drying the exposed surfaces and preventing rotting of the mats. The use of fire continuously during the rainy season is necessary to slow the rate of decay and preserve the roof. A space between the wall and roof created by the rafters allows for more effective ventilation than the limited flow allowed by the roof and walls. Adult men of about forty years of age estimate that roofs still fully effective were there when they were children. During my stay of over a year only one such house was built in the northern part of baKosi where building

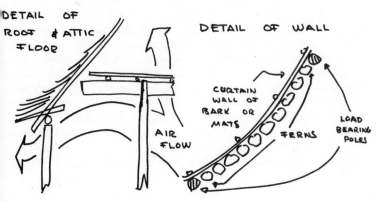

Construction details: roof and wall.

Palm-mat weaving. On roofs of round huts and lower edge is downward. On roofs of rectangular houses the edge towards craftsman is down as on the edge of the roof at the top of the photo.

materials are more readily available. The cash cost of such a roof is now in excess of one hundred U.S. dollars, if a specialist to tie the peak can be found and if the materials can be gathered.

The walls, made of mats or tree bark, are tied to the load-bearing poles on the inside in a technique similar to a modern curtain wall. The stems of giant ferns are fitted in the outside between the load-bearing poles to insulate the house and strengthen the wall.

As is shown in the map, the compounds were sited within short distances of each other. Usually one or two other compounds could

be seen from the compound, the conical roofs clustered at the end of the paths. Narrow footpaths linked the compounds of the village, and those of the village to other villages, and led to farms in the bush. The distribution of these units of settlement, the compound or the lineage, is within a territory occupied by persons all of whom trace descent to a common ancestor, in this case the founder of the village. The village shown on the map consists of five exogamous units, four of which are descended from the founder or father of the village. The fifth is a section of a lineage of blacksmiths whose members had

Exposed curtain-wall of a round hut and gable end of a rectangular house. Beer bottles and pieces of metal roofing sheets are used to seal the lower edge of walls. Bottles are also used to form a porch. Note the lap joint on the 2nd post from the door.

settled at one end of various villages throughout baKosi. They formed six compounds: four for each lineage, and two segments of the chief's lineage, one segment having split off on the basis of common descent from one wife of the founder of the lineage.

During their period of colonial rule, 1886–1914, the German authorities initiated a move to consolidate villages from the settlements of patrikin that existed on their arrival. One of two types of villages, cluster and line, developed depending on the terrain. Cluster villages tended to be formed in the hilly northern part of baKosi area, while line villages were built in the southern, heavily-forested areas. Cluster villages are essentially compressed versions of the original village form of fenced compounds, grouped together, with small gardens and rubbish heaps separating them. In cluster villages, fences are usually maintained to keep the domesticated dwarf cows away from the houses. The same conditions which make the cluster form more adaptive require wider spacing of coffee trees which in turn reduces the conflict between animal husbandry and cash crop farming. Fundamental spatial reorganisation does not appear to be an important aspect of this reorganisation, though increased density and greater proximity is. The reorganisation brought significant changes in social behaviour through increased frequency of interaction and a wider, regularly communicating community of more distant kinsmen. The basic settlement pattern of closed compounds of lineage segments was maintained, and the spatial separation, and to a lesser extent, the limitation of communication and interaction continued to follow the social units defined by corporateness and exogamy.

A line village, however, did transform the village spatially, turning compound groupings, or clusters of houses into a street-like arrangement of side-by-side houses. The social consequences of reorganization were much the same as in a cluster plan, but spatially the common spaces, specifically the path running the length of the village, were expanded greatly and transformed, and the lineage/compound grouping was no longer socially and spatially isolated. The bush no longer surrounds the family group but the village. A villager can see and be seen by his more distant kinsmen and perhaps his in-laws as well. But, as is shown in the diagram of the new village one cannot see the whole length of the village. The right angle formed by the path at one end of the village and that at the other end does not live up to the straight-line ideal of the German colonial authorities. The accommodation was between this European ideal and the baKosi insistence that one should not be able to see both ends of the village at once. Escape in time of war is made possible and an open vista for the eyes of witches, and consequently their power, is interrupted.

The line village represents the first transformation of traditional concepts into new forms. Its shape and the consolidation of functions of the central path as commons, and as avenues of communication for the whole village changed the patterns of interactions. In addition, the easy communication between kin groups across social boundaries of exogamous groups imposed new restrictions on behaviour within the group; the movement of land-owning groups from the centre of their land to a common settlement changed patterns of work and upset the easy identification of kinship and land. Marriage, once between spatially separated groups, now took place within the new spatial unit, the village. The unit of common identity and ownership of land were separated as the village became more important as a political unit. Although the political unit of solidarity became the spatially united village, each lineage maintained a limited spatial identity by building together along both sides of the central path. Boundaries of the housing areas have come to be identified with the furthest extensions of the houses of the lineage. No fences mark these boundaries and adjustments are easily made to accommodate new houses if land is available. If it is not, space can be made by clearing areas behind the line of houses and forming a U-shaped compound grouping opening on the central path.

The transformation of the village from a scattered set of patrikin settlements to a unified, open village was only one of the changes of the concepts of space and design. The German colonists in Cameroon built monumental stone structures and large frame buildings for their own use. To build these they trained carpenters, sawyers and stone masons, and imported European tools and materials. The dramatic changes in technology and potential use of stone, lumber and other techniques spread rapidly. In short, they produced a revolution in technology and in design concepts.

The house-types that evolved from these new concepts express many of the concepts that can be found in the single tranditional house-form. The new forms can be distinguished by the materials used for the walls: palm-mat, caraboard, plank and cement block. Caraboard, which perhaps is uniquely Cameroonian,[8] is an overlap siding split from several species of deciduous trees and nailed directly to the roof-bearing wall studs. It is more or less desired as a wall-covering depending on its resistance to termites, which varies with the species of tree. Roof coverings are palm-mat and metal sheeting; metal sheet roofs are desired for their permanence and freedom from frequent repair. They are used on the latter three more durable types of houses (caraboard, plank and cement block) though mat roofs are common on caraboard houses. Palm-mats may be used as temporary walls, tied to the lumber frame supporting a metal roof. Such unlikely combinations of temporary and permanent materials reveal aspirations and plans for more permanent dwellings. In order to make most effective use of savings and to avoid dissipating them, materials are often bought piecemeal, one kind at a time, and because of the danger of rotting, or misappropriation, they are put to use as soon as possible.

Open frames supporting metal roofs, partially walled frames, walls of two kinds of materials and unroofed concrete block walls complete with window and door frames are common sights. A range of modern solutions is then possible, but all converge at the requirements of a minimum of repairs and durability. Indirectly, other design characteristics become desired: spaciousness, good natural lighting, greater privacy and smoke-free rooms. The complexity of the design process is vastly increased. Specialists, carpenters and cement workers become involved in the construction process. Designs are a set of understandings and decisions made by owner–users and specialists. The beginnings of the selfconscious design process,[9] movement away from stable equilibrium and longer delays in the feedback between error and craftsman which extends this movement, appear in the results of the increasing complexity of the stages of design and building.

Lower half of the largest line village in baKosi. Large house on lower left is that of the Paramount Chief of baKosi. The procession of school children is escorting visiting officials to ceremonies at the school grounds.

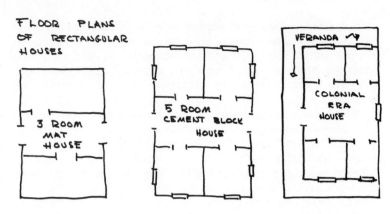

FLOOR PLANS OF RECTANGULAR HOUSES

3 ROOM MAT HOUSE

5 ROOM CEMENT BLOCK HOUSE

VERANDA

COLONIAL ERA HOUSE

Floor plans of modern houses.

For most of baKosi the solutions to the incorporation of these new materials, in terms of the continuing similar goals of the user, reveal much the same model as the traditional house. If the floor plan of the round hut is viewed as a central passage which is a working–sitting area, and the spaces to each side as storage areas and sleeping areas, then all versions of the rectangular house can be analysed as incorporating this same basic spatial structure and giving it expression in different forms. A mat house usually consists of three rooms arranged across the length of the house, which is parallel to the roadway of the village. The entrance is into the central room which is a sitting–working–eating place. Guests are entertained here and if a fire is necessary in colder weather this is where it is built. The most common location for the rear entrance is directly opposite the front door, in the rear wall of this room. It may, however, be in one of the side rooms. To each side of the central room there is a sleeping or storage room. One room, or section of one room, in such a house

may serve as a kitchen. In such cases a wood-drying platform, built in the same way as that in the round hut and similarly structurally independent, is built over, and defines, the hearth. This is the basic floor plan of all baKosi rectangular houses. All other types are only elaborations of this basic conception.

The larger caraboard, plank houses may follow exactly this pattern (even to the limit of three rooms), or sleeping–storage rooms may be added along the sides. The type built of more permanent materials most frequently found is a five-room house with four sleeping rooms, two on each side of the central room. This five-room plan is changed into six by partitioning the central room to make a storage area, and giving private entrance to the rear sleeping rooms.

There have been two phases of building in baKosi. The first was in the early British colonial period in the 1920s when some enterprising men became traders and took advantage of the high demand for, and limited knowledge of, imported trade goods. Clan and village chiefs who exploited this entrepreneurial niche built large frame and concrete houses raised on poles three to five feet off the ground. This

Tower and north entrance of the Paramount Chief's house. Palm leaves are temporary decorations to welcome official visitors.

Round hut in front of modern wood house with sheet metal roof. Coffee beans are spread out to dry at right. A men's society dancer is being escorted by the members of the society to the welcoming ceremony for official visitors.

form is distinguished by a veranda on three sides. The Paramount Chief's house and the house of his deputy are examples of this period of construction. High ceilings, wide overhangs and good circulation under the floor make this form highly successful in reducing moisture and allowing ventilation. Repairs of uprights, however, are frequent.

The post-war cocoa booms of the late 'forties and early 'fifties have been the main source of income for the modern cement block and plank-walled houses. They follow the basic form of the three side-by-side rooms with additions and variations. Ceilings may be installed to reduce the radiation of heat from the metal roofing sheets and to create more air circulation. Cement floors are usually installed in most rooms, the rear storage passageway being the last done, or permanently left unfloored. This allows water to run off in the house without sweeping it away. The flooring of a house is also done piecemeal in accord with available funds. In the piecemeal building process, the most expensive finishing touches, carpenter-made windows and doors and cement floors, are usually left to last, and then done one room at a time.

Once a house of modern materials is begun the kitchen is removed to a separate building, usually of palm-mat construction, or palm-mat roof with caraboard walls. If a man has more than one wife, each will have her own kitchen with an entrance, separated from her co-wife's by a partition. The interior will be similar to the round huts, but usually with more sitting space and more wood-storage space along the walls. The most permanent kitchens are metal-roofed with caraboard walls and cement block foundations. The floor is left unfinished, though cement pads may be used as the base for the poles supporting the wood-storage attic. Investments in kitchens are only made once the shell of the house is complete.

The new village form has easily accommodated the expanded use of lorries as taxis and the central path has been gradually widened by increasing the set-back of new houses from the path. The use of the path as a roadway has led to the building of low fences and planting of hedges in front of houses in order to define the roadway and protect children playing, livestock and coffee spread out to dry. But, these are minor innovations in a situation where those involved in the design process are not fully aware of the contingencies that their planning implies.

The major transformation of techniques and materials, requiring heavy investments and a high degree of permanence, has created a fixed spatial arrangement of the village. Many contemporary considerations – the best location for transportation, the best location for simple water supply systems, the convenience of present-day schools although recognised – become secondary in face of the high costs that would result from an attempted move of the village. It is within the context of the existing village plan that new house forms will be tried and innovations in design tested.

The present trends in house design are towards the building of larger houses. Techniques for building durable houses are known, and the goal has shifted to increasing size to enhance prestige and to accommodate the entire lineage segment. One justifies the size of the house in terms of the immediate kin who must be housed; a large family and a large house both enhance one's position in the commun-

ity. The waves of construction will follow the periods of economic boom in cash crop prices, though some modern building will continue to be paid for by the savings of salaried sons of the lineage, working in commercial or government jobs. It is during the waves of new building that the new forms will spread, perhaps derivative of the innovations in the houses of those with steady incomes. These innovations are often transmitted from the experience of living in cities and perhaps, from architect-designed houses. That one is building for an unknown future is recognised, but every man's aspirations and needs will continue: permanent housing for a large family.

Today the form of the house is based on minor adjustments to conventional forms and the affect of this reorganisation on family life is minimal, if observable at all. The creation of housing units which provide greater privacy and which separate segments of the lineage, may lead to a transformation of the family through a structuring of communications and interaction. The wide range of contemporary house forms in baKosi, from the *ndab* or round hut, to the modern multi-roomed cement block building represent a transformed set of materials adapted to essentially unchanging models for a continuing population of users. An open ended design process has begun: how the experience of these new forms will affect future social interaction and transform conceptions of the model of house form is at the moment an unanswerable question.

ACKNOWLEDGEMENT

My field research in the Federal Republic of Cameroon was supported by a fellowship from the Foreign Area Fellowship Program.

NOTES

[1] The term *baKosi* is used here in two ways: to refer to the people and to their territory. This usage accords with that of native speakers. At times it is used as an adjective when the referent is emphasised.
[2] *Pax:* With the imposition of colonial rule, the indigenous political systems were effectively 'decapitated'. In particular, control of and punishment of crimes was taken from indigenous peoples. Punitive or revengeful raids and executions were suppressed. As a result, protection was eliminated as a design requirement. See FALLERS, L., 'Are African Cultivators to be Called Peasants?' in *Current Anthropology*, Chicago 1961, Vol. 2, pp. 108–10.
[3] ALEXANDER, CHRISTOPER, *Notes on the Synthesis of Form*, Cambridge, Harvard University Press, 1964, p. 49.
[4] LEVI-STRAUSS, CLAUDE, *The Savage Mind*, Chicago, Chicago University Press, 1966, p. 3.
[5] ALEXANDER, CHRISTOPHER, op. cit., pp. 50–1.
[6] LEVI-STRAUSS, CLAUDE, 'The family' in H. L. Shapiro, (ed.), *Man, Culture and Society*, New York, Oxford University Press, pp. 274–8.
[7] A detailed study of the rituals of building and the beliefs about the steps in these rituals, the hearth and care of the house as found in ITTMAN, VON J: 'Das Haus der Kosi in Kamerun', in *Afrika und Ubersee*, Hamburg, 1960, No. 3, pp. 11–13.
[8] ARDENER, EDWIN, et al., *Plantation and Village in the Cameroons*, London, Oxford University Press, 1960, p. 92.
[9] ALEXANDER, op. cit., pp. 55–70. The independent maladaptive process described by Alexander has not yet a life of its own, but many aspects such as delayed feedback in design errors and deviation from an adaptive equilibrium between requirements and solutions are in evidence. Common recognised errors in design are wide steeply sloping veranda roofs which shade windows cutting off light, windows that are too small, omission of openings for ventilation in walls or between wall and roof or in the form of louvres in doors.

ASHANTI VERNACULAR ARCHITECTURE

Andrew F. Rutter

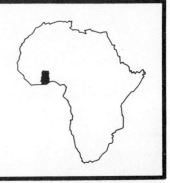

The visitor arriving by air in the forested Ashanti region of Ghana cannot fail to be struck by the very regular courtyard form of the houses, laid out in grid-iron fashion in settlement after settlement. A drive from the airport through the city of Kumasi and out into the surrounding countryside will only serve to reinforce this impression, since the majority of houses conform to a characteristic norm, both in form and detail.

The typical house consists of a group of rooms arranged on four

Aerial view of Central Kumasi, Ghana. Population in 1960: 180,642.

The village of Fumisua, population in 1960: 1,245.

Recently completed cocoa farmers' houses, Onwi.

Drinking bar, Onwi, with decorated exterior.

sides of a space to make buildings some eighty feet square, separated by lanes of bare laterite some twenty feet wide. The principal feature on the main frontage is likely to be a gaudily painted recessed balcony, reached by steps from the street, creating a sitting and viewing platform for special occasions. This does not form the main entrance since the inner courtyard and the rooms off it are entered from a door inconspicuously set on a side wall. In the central districts of the city many of these houses may be two to three storeys high containing upwards of eighty people, with an inner concrete staircase, balconies decorated with intricately patterned concrete balustrades, red painted corrugated iron roofs and plastered, colourwashed walls.

In the market towns and villages, the houses are mostly single storeyed containing fifteen to twenty people, the principal ones finished and colourwashed in the same way as the city houses, with contrasting colours for the base and upper parts of the walls. The rest show the basic red laterite earth construction of the walls externally, with extra details of finish being added according to the economic situation of the owners, starting from the inside. In both cases many houses on the principal streets incorporate 'stores', craft workshops or drinking bars. These are often decorated with naturalistic oil paintings depicting anything from large size Coca-Cola or Star Beer bottles to well-dressed middle-aged women or political figures, providing a mirror of daily life. Some suitable proverb or gaudily lettered inscription such as 'Moonlight Bay' or 'Freedom Chop Bar' would complete the decoration. Taken together all these elements add up to a vigorous vernacular style that is quite distinctive within the forest area. Furthermore, it spreads outside it wherever the Ashantis live, suggesting a society that has achieved a considerable measure of equilibrium.

It is significant that travellers to Ashanti throughout the nineteenth century reported a similar consistency of form in the settlements they passed through, though the details were different because the materials used then were derived entirely from the bush.

'Kumasi is very different in its appearance from any other native town that I have seen in this part of Africa', wrote William Winniett in 1848. 'The streets are generally very broad and clean, and orna-

mented with many beautiful banyan trees, affording a grateful shade from the powerful rays of the sun. The houses looking into the streets, are all public rooms on the ground floor. . . . They are entirely open to the street in front, but raised above its level from one to six feet, by an elevated floor consisting of clay polished with red ochre. They are entered from the street by steps made of clay and polished like the floor. The walls consist of wattle-work and plastered with clay, and washed with white clay. The houses are all thatched with palm leaves; and as the eaves of the roofs extend far over the walls, the front basement of the raised floors which is generally covered with rude carvings of various forms, have their beautiful polish preserved from the effects of both sun and rain. The mode of building gives to the streets a peculiar aspect of cheerfulness. . . . The apartments of the royal premises are of the same order and style as those of the native dwellings generally, consisting of a number of square court yards, connected with each other by doors at the corners, and having, on one, two, three, or all sides, a room entirely open on the side looking into the yard. . . .'

Characteristic shop sign – in this case for Ladies Dressmaking.

'An ordinary house has one court-yard; a large house three or four; the king's palace had ten or twelve,' Winwoode Reade observed in 1874. Henry M. Stanley wrote in more detail the same year, that 'In the King's Palace . . . Court after court opens to view, expanses of ochre washed walls and lengths of white plastered walls and columns, arcades, deep alcoves, lattice work and great catherine shaped circlets in plaster. No two of the courts were ornamented alike. The prevailing design of one court is an involved and complicated coil pattern, while another affects the square within a square work.'

The only other major building type to be found in Ashanti settlements at that time was the *abosomfie*, which contained the shrine of a god. This was built to the same courtyard pattern as the houses, but decorated externally with designs incorporating some strong animal, like the crocodile or lion, as a principal motif. The roofs were thatched, and cut into distinct layers in a stepped form. Inside the *abosomfie* there were two courtyards: one for the ceremonies and one for the priests. The one in which the ceremonies took place consisted of three open-fronted *paito* in which the drummers, priests and worshippers gathered facing the shrine room itself, which closed the fourth side with its very richly decorated front.

These public and private buildings were organised to provide a dignified and intimate setting for religious and political activities and family life. They produced an informal sequence of spaces, and a subtle variation in decoration, to complement the extraordinary richness of dress, and profusion of ornament, that was characteristic of the Ashanti Court.

In his *Mission from Cape Coast Castle to Ashantee*, 1819, Bowdich gives some idea of this in his description of a meeting with the *Asantehene*:

'Today . . . we were conducted to a large yard, where the King, encircled by a varied profusion of insignia, even more sumptuous than that we had seen before sat at the end of two long files of counsellors, caboceers, and captains; they were seated under their umbrellas, composed of scarlet and yellow cloth, silks, shawls, cottons, and every glaring variety, with carved and golden pelicans, panthers, baboons, barrels, crescent, etc., on the top; the shape generally a dome. Distinct and pompous retinues were placed around, with gold canes, spangled elephants' tails to brush off the flies, gold-headed swords, and embossed muskets, and many splendid novelties.'

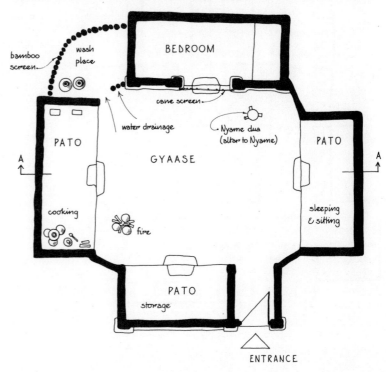

Plan of the courtyard house. The pato or paito, open-sided rooms, give on to the gyaase, or court. The entrance is unobtrusively placed on one side.

Section through a traditional Ashanti courtyard house.

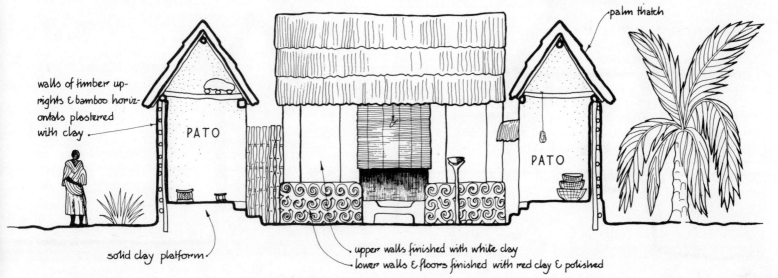

155

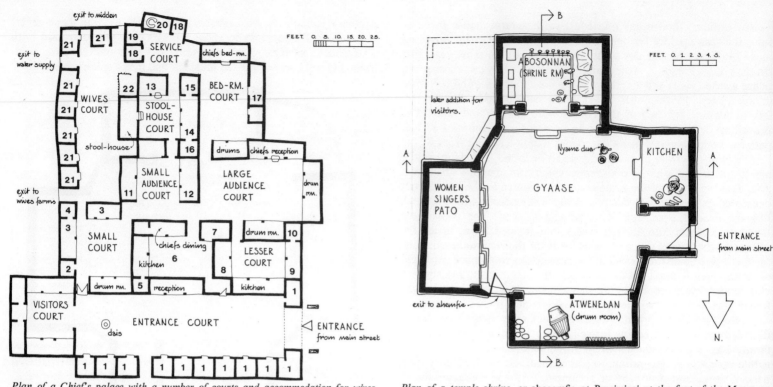

FEET. 0. 5. 10. 15. 20. 25.

Plan of a Chief's palace with a number of courts and accommodation for wives, visitors and their retinue.

FEET. 0. 1. 2. 3. 4. 5.

Plan of a temple shrine, or abosomfie at Bawjwiasi at the foot of the Mampong Scarp.

Section through the shrine at Bawjwiasi, at A–A.

FEET. 1. 2. 3. 4. 5.

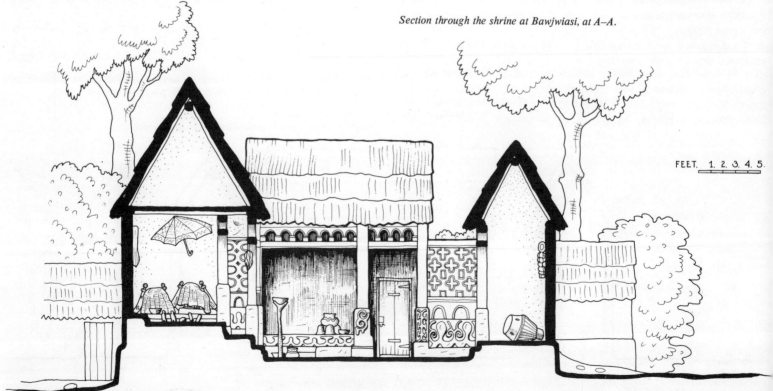

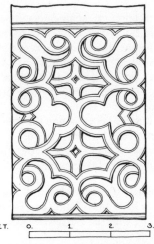

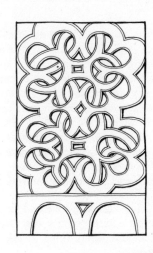

FEET. 0. 1. 2. 3.

Strapwork and crocodile motifs from a shrine wall.

This society was supported by an economy based on the intensive exploitation of the natural resources of the forest, a system of agriculture that made use of plantations, gold-mining and an extended trading system that reached from the European trading posts on the coast to the important inland market centres of the grasslands, located at the end of the desert trade routes. Cola nuts were in great demand from the Muslims of the north. The Europeans were anxious to obtain gold dust, ivory, slaves and animal skins. By exchanging these commodities the Ashantis were able to import guns, ammunition, spirits, fine cloth, leather, salt and other commodities to complement the production of their own craftsmen.

The difference between the Ashanti vernacular in the two centuries

Section through the shrine at Bawjwiasi, at B–B. In the abosonnan, *or shrine room, the sacred stools are covered and* afona *swords rest against them.*

can be accounted for by the direct introduction of European methods of organisation, economic development, and culture through the period of colonial rule between 1895 and 1957. This started with a series of wars in the middle of the nineteenth century which weakened indigenous leadership, interrupted court life and eventually led to the destruction of Ashanti architecture.

These events were followed by the introduction of the railway from the coast, in 1903, and the motor lorry in 1908, which altered the economy. They made possible the export of a bulky commodity like cocoa, in return for equally bulky imported manufactured goods like corrugated iron sheets and cement which by virtue of their prestige value, and longer maintenance-free life, replaced local materials in the evolution of the current vernacular style. Colonial

SINGERS

KITCHEN

Government also led to the reorganisation of settlements, house types and decoration to accord with European medical thinking, although the 'model' plans issued to the new corps of sanitary inspectors were to some extent based on local traditions. The energy and initiative of the Missionary bodies, and the introduction of academic education into the area, also challenged the authority of local religion, customs and artistic forms. It was not until the 1950s and 1960s with the securing of independence within the state of Ghana that sustained interest in indigenous culture was revived.

From a comparative study of the vernacular forms of the nineteenth and twentieth centuries these significant features emerge:

(a) The persistence of the rectangular courtyard form of house even where entirely new settlements have been built, despite the introduction of other forms of housing with the European occupation.

(b) The continuing importance of the gradation of spaces, from public to private, which occurs within the settlement.

(c) The retention of the principal entrance off a side street in a strangely modest way, despite its psychological significance to the inmates.

(d) The reintroduction of the showy external raised balcony, despite the fact that lengthy processions are no longer a significant part of community life.

(e) The re-emergence of a lively form of decoration and the formation of a precast concrete industry. This now provides pierced and moulded decorative features to replace the modelling of the hand-made plasterwork, after the forced austerity of early colonial days, when walls were tar painted at the base and lime-washed above, and balconies were prohibited.

To understand the roots of this vernacular, the persistence of these ideas and forms, and the assimilation of other, newer ideas, it is necessary to consider the environment, social organisation and daily life in Ashanti.

THE ASHANTI COMMUNITY

The Ashantis established their powerful state on an inland plateau that was forested and damp, with 60–70 inches rainfall annually, concentrated into two rainy seasons. Until only sixty years ago this forest consisted of a main canopy of trees 150 feet high and an undergrowth of bush some 20–30 feet high. The bush grew particularly densely in the numerous river valleys where the sunlight could penetrate, and harboured a profusion of wild life. This produced a dominant but gloomy environment, misty in the morning and evening, and penetrable only on foot, which must have been almost overpowering to a fairly sparse human population, equipped principally with cutlass, hoe and firearms. Psychologically, this created a need for a strictly controlled man-made environment, for which the courtyard houses, grouped together along a street in a brilliantly sunlit clearing, devoid of growing things except for a few shade trees, was a logical answer. Some idea of this setting is given by Freeman writing of Kumasi in 1898. 'After six days' stay in the open spaces of

the town it seemed very strange to plunge suddenly into the gloomy twilight of the Forest. One minute we were marching through the glaring streets of the city, the next we passed into a narrow opening in the lofty wall of dense forest that on all sides surrounded it and were shut out from the light of day.'

Politically, the Ashanti nation was made up of a group of states, each governed by a paramount chief, which had joined together to form a Union in the eighteenth century. This Union was based on common allegiance to the *Asantehene* who had authority on matters relating to the affairs of the whole nation, and the 'Golden Stool' which acted as a religious symbol of their unity and independence. Each state had its own Court, complete with linguists, treasurers, musicians, craftsmen, executioners and military organisation. In time of war the chiefs and their contingents had their allotted places in the different 'Wings' of the Ashanti army, whose organisation mirrored that of the State armies.

Within each State, apart from the town of the paramount chief, which was a market centre, there would be several farm settlements of varying size, formed by groups moving out from the original town into the forest in search of fresh land to cultivate. Depending on their size, each of these would be governed by a chief or headman who owed allegiance to the paramount chief of the State.

These population movements have continued up to the present day, though now it is trunk road construction or improvements that are exerting the most powerful influence on location. For example, on the twenty-four miles of road between Kumasi and Konongo, realigned in 1951, nine out of fourteen settlements have moved up to it from other sites. As a result of these movements there is now a somewhat uneven pattern of main nucleated settlements scattered at 2–3 mile intervals on the higher ground, with the greatest population density of 279 persons to the square mile close to Kumasi, to the south and east. Within the past fifty years these main settlements have been augmented by smaller hamlets and the scattered houses of immigrant families employed as 'caretakers' by the Ashanti Cocoa farmers, on the fringe of the region where good land is available.

This pattern is shown up by the statistics derived from the 1961 National Census for the Kumasi North district of Ashanti. This covers a wedge of 1,086 square miles, of which the Northern part has only been settled sparsely until recently, when the area has been opened up with a new trunk road.

Settlements over 5,000	0	—	—
Settlements 2,500–4,999	8	30,712	24%
Settlements 1,000–2,499	22	36,541	29%
Settlements 0–999	80	36,800	29%
Small Hamlets 200 or less		23,390	18%
Total population		127,443	100%

From this breakdown it can be seen that the small village is the norm. The majority of Ashantis still live a life related to agricultural production with an overall average of 76% employed in farming in the rural districts, dropping to only some 60% in the Service Centres

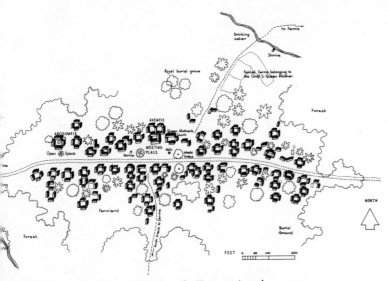

Plan of an Ashanti village, Ahinsai on the Kuntenasi road.

with a population range up to 8,000 people. To illustrate further points of detail, reference will be made to the village of Kwamo which is situated some eight miles east of Kumasi. This had a resident population in 1962 of 726 and was in the process of moving up to the main road, so that it contains examples of houses built from 1900 up to the present day.

Within each settlement there are several matrilineal clan or descent groups, *abusua*, who own the land belonging to it. (In Kwamo there were seven.) The affairs of each *abusua* are regulated by an elder (*Abusua Panyin*) who is responsible among other things for deciding which part of the land will be cleared of bush for farming in each year, and for settling any demarcation problems. The households forming the clan groups normally live in compound houses, adjoining each other, a feature which was still found to be true when the people of Kwamo moved to a new site in the 1950s. The clan elders also hold specific responsibilities in community life, derived from the traditional Ashanti social and military organisation. One of these clan groups represents the Royal group or stool, from which the chief is chosen to provide political and judicial leadership for the whole community in concert with the clan elders. The chief is also responsible for maintaining the continuity between the Ancestors and the present generations through performing various customs in accordance with religious tradition. This system has produced a democratic organisation with considerable checks and balances on the use of power, and a strong sense of community discipline.

Although the chief is responsible for the distribution of land between the clan groups, he would not dare to show strangers over the land belonging to another clan, without the consent of the *Abusua Panyin*. Again land ownership is vested in the community to be managed on their behalf, not in individual titles. No chief can be appointed without the consent of the Queen Mother and although selected by a group of elders, he can be destooled by the ordinary people if they can substantiate to the elders sufficient grounds for complaint.

Within the village there is a strong tradition of communal labour, organised by the chief for work projects affecting the community, such as the maintenance of footpaths, clearance of water sources, and the erection of public buildings. This is carried out on certain days set aside by religious tradition for a rest from farming. Special occasions, like funerals, affect the whole community and not just near relatives of the deceased, and farming is suspended until the public ceremony has been held. Members of clan groups have particular responsibilities to each other, and also for providing hospitality to visitors from other settlements who may be members of the same clan.

Within each clan group there is a varying number of domestic groups of which the largest number consists of a female head and her children of both sexes. In Kwamo this proportion was 61%, confirming the proportion found by Meyer Fortes for Agogo. In a typical situation husbands do not live in the same compound as their wife, or wives, but have their food sent over to them. Wives visit their husbands in the house in the evening, and if there is more than one wife living in separate houses they eat together to show that they are on friendly terms. Husbands are in turn expected to visit each of their wives and her parents every day, and deal with the discipline of their children. The children may be expected to perform certain household duties in his compound even though they live with their mother.

As a result, the compound house is a family house providing

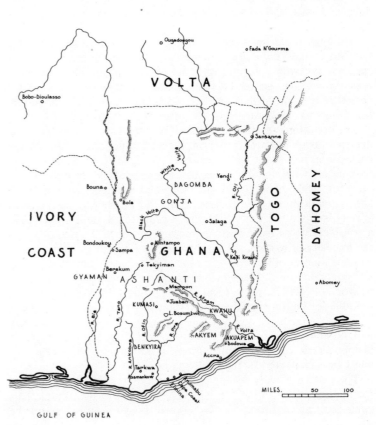

shelter for a group of people of varying ages, from very young children to elderly people, who provide mutual assistance. They are connected by a complex web of relationships to people in adjoining compounds, creating the need for a flexible system of communications between houses and an entrance that is informal in location.

At festival times like Christmas and Easter, and at funeral or marriage ceremonies, the whole family group, including those normally resident elsewhere, will gather together, making it desirable to have extra sleeping rooms available. This strong family loyalty, coupled with the mobility of the cocoa farmers who go on extended visits to distant farms, accounts for the fluctuating occupancy of the houses, making it difficult to assess the resident population on Ashanti settlements.

The village economy has always been based on the exploitation of the animal and vegetable resources of the bush to provide for the daily necessities, from building materials to medicines, in addition to food. The Ashanti farmer operates a type of subsistence agriculture consisting of a rotation of crops with intervening periods of bush fallow based on a minimum cycle of 7–10 years. For example, in Kwamo the residents of 66 compound houses own collectively 2,427 acres of land of which 9% was used for permanent tree crops, 64% farmed for normal food production and a further 16% farmed only occasionally for food. The importance of the subsistence farming is shown by the fact that 67% of the 107 households produced all their food requirements from this land, 21% supplemented their own produce and only 12% relied exclusively on purchases from outside markets.

Although the bush is cleared in the dry season between January and March, and there are set times for planting the staple crops of cassava, cocoyam plantain and maize related to the twin rainy seasons, there is no set harvesting time. Because of the constant period of growth throughout the year farms require daily attention, but the crops can be stored on the plant and used as required.

The traditional division of labour between men and women still persists though in a modified form; the women are responsible for the cultivation, harvesting and preparation of food, fetching water and looking after the children. The men are responsible for clearing the bush for farms, hunting, housebuilding and maintenance, craft work and cocoa farming. This division, coupled with the way that Ashanti society is organised, has meant that in practice men and women have a considerable measure of economic independence. To reinforce this the majority of women sell surplus food and engage in petty trading of some kind or other, which is valued for its social contact as well as its economic return. Many also organise extensive trade through the network of retail markets, local shops and chop bars. This makes it possible for both men and women heads of households to be responsible for the financing and construction of the compound house; they will of course call on their relatives, including those resident in distant places, to make contributions when major work is required, and this is facilitated by the family gatherings.

The pattern of daily life is based upon a rhythmic cycle occupying the daylight hours, which remain very constant in the tropics. This cycle is most consistent for the women though it will of course be

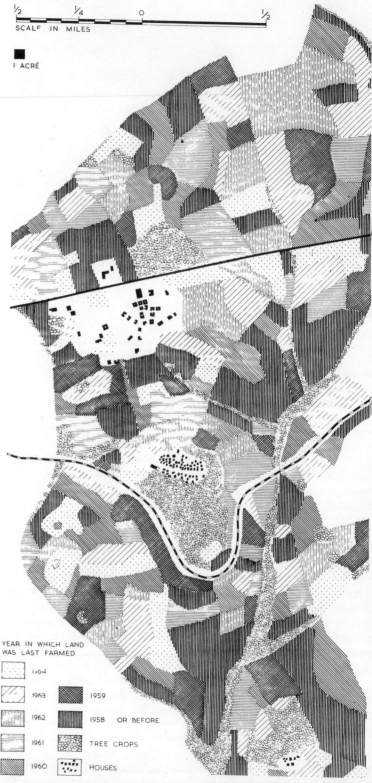

SCALE IN MILES

1 ACRE

YEAR IN WHICH LAND
WAS LAST FARMED

1964

1963   1959

1962   1958   OR BEFORE

1961   TREE CROPS

1960   HOUSES

Farming pattern of the land around the village of Kwamo. The cluster of Old Kwamo lies towards the south; the open spaces of New Kwamo are to the north-west.

ABUSUA GROUP	Number of Houses in Old Kwamo	Proportional percentage
Asenie	13 Chief and Queen Mother + four Elders	44% (4 Sub-divisions)
Asakyere	10 Chief's Deputy + three Elders	22·8% (3 Sub-divisions)
Asona	11 Three Elders (one who looks after Stool property) & Linguist	14·6% (3 Sub-divisions)
Ekuona	14 Priest	5·2%
Aduana	5	6·3%
Peretuo	3	5·2%
Agona	3 One Elder (Head of Stool carriers)	1·7%

59 Houses

Total Acreage : 2,427 acres
Total cultivated by 107
Households in 1963, 229 acres.

Land cleared and planted in Kwamo in 1963. The lands worked by the seven principal lineage groups are indicated.

varied in detail on market days, festivals and during funeral periods when farming is not allowed by tradition.

In the early morning there are night slops to empty at the communal pit latrines on the edge of the village; water to fetch from the stream involving three or four round trips of half a mile each carrying a three gallon kerosene tin; the central courtyard and the space round the outside of the house to be swept with a handbroom, the fireplaces to be relined with red clay, and numerous other household chores.

These activities are followed, about ten o'clock when the sun has driven away the early mists, by a visit to one of the current farms — anything from half a mile to a mile and a half away — to weed with the hoe, collect and bundle firewood and harvest some food. The latter items are then transported home by headload in the early afternoon. After taking a bath and preparing hot water for the menfolk it is time to cook the evening meal. First the root vegetables, then the ingredients for light soup are prepared and placed in heavy iron pots to cook over the open fires. The final process of beating up the starchy vegetables into *fufu* in wooden pestles and mortars takes place at the end of the afternoon. This rhythmic pounding occurs almost simultaneously in every compound making a symbolic prelude to the main meal of the day, which is eaten by the household sitting together round a communal pot in the central courtyard. Cooking utensils are cleared up before sundown and the arrival of the mosquitoes, when it is customary to retire to bed.

The men have a more varied pattern of activities based on their economic function as general handymen, and their social function as husbands or elders. The former may take them to bush, farm or market or require them to ply some craft like trap-making or weaving close to home. Fifty per cent of the residents of a small village like Kwamo will be children and they are expected to help fetch water, collect food from the farm or cook in addition to their schooling which may involve a three-mile walk to another village.

Every member of the household is responsible for looking after his own clothes and sweeping out his sleeping room, which will contain either a traditional sleeping mat or a bed, plus enamel pots or chests for the storage of their clothes.

Leisure is spent in playing games like *oware* or draughts, hairdressing and dressmaking, talking and drinking palm wine, all activities which take place between the houses in the afternoon. On special occasions there is also drumming and dancing when gay cloths will be worn and this may go on far into the night, when the moon is full.

ASHANTI VILLAGE AND HOUSE TYPES

Planning Principles

Not much is known about the traditional planning of Ashanti settlements though it is clear that there was a deliberate organisation based on:

A main street pattern whose axis east—west or north—south had religious significance.

The location of the Chief's Palace and the main clan groups, plus the suburbs for strangers.

Functional requirements arising from the retailing of food and the processions that accompanied formal visits, religious festivals or the return of an army from battle when the chiefs were carried head high in their palanquins.

These features were much more explicit in the principal settlements of the paramount chiefs, than in the smaller settlements where a simple pattern based on a single main street was sufficient.

From an architectural point of view the layout and grouping arising from the Ashanti social organisation has always been very undemonstrative, with the forest setting being the dominant feature. Unlike the farm compounds and walled towns of the grasslands to the north there was no need to relate the houses to an architecture of fortification, since the military organisation of the Ashantis was such that battles were fought in the bush and mostly outside their territory. Neither was there any need for an architectural form related to the storage of crops or animals, since food is collected daily and domestic animals don't thrive in the forest. Public buildings were not required to dominate their surroundings by any formal means of massing or elaborate outline since the political organisation was democratic rather than feudal, and shrines were designed to enclose the ceremonies of local gods and their attendants, rather than to demonstrate the authority of the supreme god or the power of a heirarchical priesthood. It is the location and use of the community buildings, and the fact that they were the only buildings with a direct entrance from the main street which gave them importance.

Similarly there is no architectural enclosure of the open spaces used as markets or for festivals, since both these activities were informal in organisation. Sellers in the markets create an organic pattern of twisting lanes designed to catch the eye which alters with the number of sellers present, most of whom have a dual role as buyers and sellers. During festivals it is the large colourful umbrellas of the chiefs, and the way that the court is arranged in a semicircle that creates any formal setting required. The people join in as participators rather than as spectators, changing their dress according to the mood of the occasion, with dark browns, reds and blacks for funerals, multi-coloured *kente* cloths for festivals and white or gold cloths as a symbol of victory on religious occasions. This change in dress creates a striking symbolism in an area that is so predominantly green.

A typical village of five hundred to a thousand people like Kwamo consists of a broad main street in which the principal buildings of social significance, the *Ahenfie* (chief's palace) the clan elders houses, the *abosomfie* (shrine) and the royal cemetery plus the open space for funerals, and one or two shops, are in pride of place on either side. The other houses are grouped behind them with the newer houses being added at right angles to the main street in rough clan groupings, provided that enough flat land is available. The long, low school building with its external verandah, formal garden plots, clipped hedges and football park will be located adjacent to the road at one end of the village, with perhaps a church building, complete with tower, near by. Neither of these building types have been influenced by the vernacular style since they are an alien introduction. Also located in a prominent position at either end of the village are the

Village festival; the Chief in his palanquin.

The Adaekese *ceremony in Kumasi with a group of Chiefs beneath ceremonial umbrellas.*

Map of the village of Old Kwamo showing detailed land use.

roofed, but generally open-sided, pit latrines for men and women, placed so that they can easily be reached from any compound without having to pass down the main street, in accordance with local etiquette.

In Kwamo the *Ahenfie* still retains the basic housebuilding form of the early 1900s and consists of three courtyards, with virtually no external windows. The outer courtyard made up of four open-fronted rooms contains the state drums and the chief's palanquin, and is used for public assembly. The inner one contains the 'Stool room', the chief's private apartments and the veranda where he receives visitors, holds meetings with the elders and performs the ceremonies connected with the blackened stools of the dead chiefs. This private courtyard is linked at the back to a service courtyard in which his food is cooked. In this case the Queen Mother's house is built on the east side with a common party wall, a practice which became common when houses became bigger on reconstruction in the period between the 1890s and 1920s.

The sequence of spaces within the settlement is very important to daily life even though its significance has tended to be disguised by the regularity of modern layouts. The main street in a small village, whether used as a through road or not, is valued as a place of public display. Although the arrival and departure of people in gaily painted Mammy trucks, taxis with yellow painted wings or the large cars of cocoa farmers and district officials is not as dramatic or colourful as when the Chiefs were borne in on their palanquins, it is still a matter of great importance. It is here that surplus food is exposed for sale, and communal activities, film shows and political rallies take place. Temporary shelters of bamboo or palm nut fronds are frequently built at a focal point in the street to give shade to these activities, but the valuable shade trees which were a feature of the traditional layout have mostly been removed with the advent of motor traffic. In large settlements special spaces are set aside for these purposes, the principal requirements being a prominent location and a multiplicity of connections to the houses on all sides. Between the houses there is a network of passageways to accommodate the criss-cross movements between relatives in the different compounds and to give access to the main paths leading out of the village to the streams and the farms. The areas adjacent to the entrances form significant semi-public spaces used for craftwork, hairdressing and other occupations in which people value contact with others passing by. Shade is appreciated when cast by the walls of adjacent properties, and in this respect the irregular layout of the older settlements is more successful than the grid-iron layout introduced by Europeans for ease of development control.

The courtyards are semi-private areas used for activities that members of a household share in common like cooking, eating, discussion of domestic affairs and for access between sleeping and bath rooms. This requires visual enclosure, a controlled entrance, a level floor surface and roofed spaces overlooking the courtyard to give shelter during the sudden and violent storms of the rainy season. It is only the sleeping rooms that are really private, requiring complete enclosure, good ventilation, sound insulation, and subdued light.

Domestic activity between houses in Kwamo.

Courtyard of a traditional Ashanti house showing painted dado, sacred bush, fine detail in openwork screens. The corrugated iron roof has replaced the original thatch.

'Fetish' priest officiating at a dance of worship in the shrine at Ayija.

THE COMPOUND HOUSE

A modern compound house consists of a group of 15–20 sleeping rooms arranged on three sides of the open courtyard, with the entrance, open fronted kitchen and small enclosed bath rooms on the fourth side, making a building some eighty foot square. The individual sleeping rooms are reached from an internal veranda by a single door, and ventilated by narrow louvred windows, mostly located on the external walls. Many houses have a larger sitting room on the main frontage, with doors leading into it from the courtyard, and the recessed balcony which looks out on to the street. This room is a special one for the use of the head of the household, containing prestige objects such as low easy chairs with cushions, photographs and souvenirs, crocheted table decorations and so on. In some cases this room is connected with sleeping rooms on either side, forming a 'suite'.

The development of the Ashanti house.

PAITO

SLEEPING

EXTENSION FOR RELATIVES

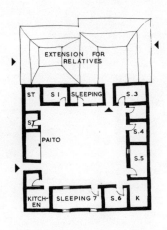

EXTENSION FOR RELATIVES

ST | S I | SLEEPING | S.3
ST | PAITO | S.4
| | S.5
KITCH-EN | SLEEPING 7 | S.6 | K

S.1 | SHOP | S.3 | S.4
S.2 | | S.5 | S.6
| | SITT-ING
| KITCHENS | S.7
| | SLEEPING
BATH
TOIL-ET | PAITO | S.9 | S.10 | S.11

TYPICAL   FLOOR   PLANS

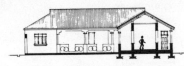

36'-0" SQUARE
BUSH STICK FRAME PLASTERED
PALM-NUT THATCH
BAMBOO-MAT SCREENS
DECORATED-RED BASE WHITE ABOVE
HOUSE ERECTED BY OWNER

1800 — 1880's

60'-0" SQUARE
SOLID SWISH WALLS
SHINGLE ROOF
INTERNAL NAILED DOORS & WINDOWS
DECORATED-BLACK BASE-WHITE ABOVE

1920 — 1930's

80'-0"×70'-0"
BLOCK OR SOLID SWISH WALLS
CORRUGATED IRON ROOF
LOUVERED WINDOWS & FRAMED DOORS
ASBESTOS CEMENT CEILING
CEMENTED COURTYARD
DECORATED IN MANY COLOURS
EXTERNAL DRAINS

1950 — 1960's

0 8 16 24
SCALE FT

TYPICAL   CROSS   SECTIONS

PLASTER WORK

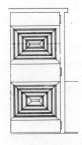

NAILED JOINERY

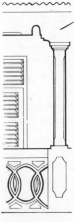

CONCRETE WORK

On most of the newer houses, like those built in new Kwamo, the details are very consistent.

Roofs of corrugated iron have a pitch of 25 degrees with hipped corners and a small gable at either end of the ridge on the main frontage to give it emphasis. This is supported on a light timber framework of 4 × 2-inch rafters and tie beams. The eaves project some 9 inches or a foot with a hardwood fascia board and flat asbestos–cement soffit. The more important rooms may also have ceilings made of flat asbestos cement sheets fixed to the ties with battens.

Balconies are recessed with massive concrete beams introduced to support the roof. These have cut-away scallops on the underside adjoining the column heads betraying their largely non-structural function. The columns are usually made up of round or square precast concrete sections decorated with imitation Classical Greek or Roman caps and bases. Precast concrete balustrades fill in the spaces between the columns, incorporating a variety of pierced geometric designs, many of which have a high standard of detail and finish.

Windows of vertical proportion are made of crudely detailed hardwood joinery with closely spaced louvres in fixed and opening casement frames. These wooden louvres provide permanent ventilation and a muted light inside though they do not let a large volume of air through.

Doors are of solid panelled hardwood set in chunky 4 × 3-inch frames to resist the warping effect of the dry *harmattan* winds in January.

Walls are plastered with a hard, smooth cement and sand rendering, and are decorated externally with a dark colour for the bottom three feet.

Above this, pale yellow, blue, pink, green or white are the norm with the recessed balconies picked out in brilliant red, purple, dark blue or green in very daring combinations.

Internally, the courtyards are more subdued in effect, with the verandah separated off from the large area of concrete surfaced floor by dwarf walls and one or two steps. The most interesting space is the open-fronted kitchen, blackened by wood smoke from the row of highly polished red laterite hearths. These are built against the outer wall with vents over to help the smoke to get out. These courtyards are a working area with one or two tar barrels containing the day's water supply in one corner, and open hearths surrounded with a miscellaneous collection of firewood bundles, stools, baskets and other chattels in daily use. Often there are red peppers, palm nut kernels, or items of washing spread out to dry in the yard and maybe a dog or turkeys moving in and out in addition to the movement of children and adults.

Rainwater run-off is usually allowed to drain away between the houses, without construction of any special channels, although some owners do construct gutters at the base of their walls, to prevent erosion at this vital spot. Similarly the water from the courtyards and the bathrooms is directed to the outside of the building.

View through the side entrance of a house showing the courtyard and kitchen area.

The basic shell of a new house being constructed in laterite.

The addition of decorative features being applied to a balcony.

BUILDING METHODS

The majority of houses are built of laterite earth dug up from large borrow pits adjacent to the building plot. These are later filled in again with household refuse over a period of years. The laterite is broken up, mixed with water, trodden under foot and made into balls which are then built up into layers eighteen inches deep by the thickness of the walls, which is usually nine inches to a foot. These layers are left to dry for about two weeks before another layer is added, so that the shrinkage cracks are distributed throughout the wall. No foundations are used and openings are left for doors and windows, spanned by wooden lintels. This produces a wall with good sound and heat insulating properties, which is durable and stable on cellular buildings provided the proportion of window to wall is not too great, the surface is protected, and the base of the wall is not undermined. This can be a very serious problem on the sloping ground at the edge of the village where the combination of daily sweeping and rapid rainwater run-off is very erosive, producing gullies up to five feet deep.

It is now common practice to employ Ewe *Attakpame* labourers to build the walls of a house at a fixed cost per room (between £6–£8 in Kwamo in 1964). For the roof structure a carpenter would be employed who might also nail on the corrugated iron sheets, though this is often undertaken by male members of the household.

This basic method of construction affects the timing of building operations since it is advisable to roof the walls before the rainy season commences to avoid their total collapse. Once this is achieved windows and doors may be purchased one or two at a time from the city, or made up by a carpenter on the site. Rendering is applied to the walls as money becomes available to purchase the cement.

The principal defects to be found on these houses arise from the lack of foundations on sloping ground, a skimped roof structure, difficulty in fixing the roof adequately to the walls to withstand the ferocity of some of the afternoon line squalls, and unsuitable mix-

tures of cement and sand in the renderings and floor screeds, leading to their premature breakdown.

Better quality houses are built with concrete strip foundations, sand/cement or laterite and cement blocks, concrete lintels and ring beams at the eaves. Door and window frames would also be built in as the work proceeds. These houses are usually built by individual masons and carpenters organised by the building owner rather than a building contractor. As a result, blocks would be made on site in simple moulds by hand, rather than by machine. Attempts to introduce simple block-making machines and concrete mixers by the Department of Social Welfare and Community Development have not caught on in housebuilding because of the need for continuous operation by a small team of semi-skilled men. The organisation of this is something beyond the reach of the normal house owner, who has his routine business to attend to.

A new street showing successive stages in building. The joints in the laterite wall and gradual addition of finishes may be seen.

Two- and three-storey courtyard houses in Central Kumasi.

A tomb of recent date, near Domiabra.

FINANCIAL CONSTRAINTS

The present method of building is geared very closely to the fact that finance for investment in rural housing comes in irregular amounts, depending on the success of the crops. It also depends on the absence of any competing demand for the money, such as treatment in time of sickness. Although food farms provide subsistence, they are not likely to provide the householder with more than about £40 cash income in a year. A palm wine tapper might earn between £50 and £100 in a year, but it is only cocoa farming that can be relied on

A new building type: hotel near Konongo.

for a greater income. Because of their small size the original cocoa farms provided income for the purchase of only one or two bundles of roof sheets at a time. It is only since the 1940s that the newer larger farms on the fringes of Ashanti have enabled a greater investment in housing at one time. This fact, and the social requirement that houses are built for a family group who will want to move in as a group, make phased construction of completed rooms unacceptable. This encourages the heads of the households to reckon the cost of a house in terms of a standard roof, with the minimum expenditure on supporting walls. This will remain so even though other methods would, in the long run, produce better results.

The comparative cost of building a similar house eighty feet by seventy feet, in either laterite or sandcrete block walls, shows this up clearly.

	LATERITE WALLED BUILDING		SANDCRETE WALLED BUILDING	
	Capital cost	% of total	Capital cost	% of total
Stage 1				
Basic roofed shell	£340	20·8	£1,684	52·3
(cost of roof	£232)		(roof £232)	
Stage 1 plus 2				
Shell plus windows and doors	£624	38·1	£1,868	58·26
Stage 3 only				
Finishes	£916	61·9	£1,354	41·74
Total cost	£1,540	100%	£3,222	100%*

* These costs are approximations based on a survey in Kwamo carried out in 1963/5 supplemented by calculations based on unit costs supplied by the Kumasi Technical Advice Centre. Heads of households are reluctant to divulge financial details and do not keep written records of all the items of expenditure in a house built over a 5–10 year period.

Note how low the initial investment is in the shell of the laterite walled house compared with the other, and what a high proportion is subsequently spent on the finishes, like rendering, cement floor screed, precast concrete elements, painting, etc.

The gap between the two forms of construction cannot readily be filled by borrowing money, since the source of finance is so unreliable that interest rates are exorbitantly high, 50% interest is not uncommon. The Government introduced an excellent 'Roof Loans' scheme in 1956, in which members of a village society were given a revolving loan so that the cost of the roof could be paid back over four years at a very low interest rate. Even so, this does not help family groups who lack a considerable income from cocoa, since they would be unlikely to be nominated for a loan.

Many of the houses built with the better standard of construction have been commissioned either by very wealthy cocoa farmers, or by people who have migrated to the towns and made money in business or accumulated savings as Civil Servants. They build the house for the benefit of their family group and as a place to which they can retire.

Plan and elevation of a tomb at Ahwia on the Mampong Road. The tomb has the date of completion inscribed upon it.

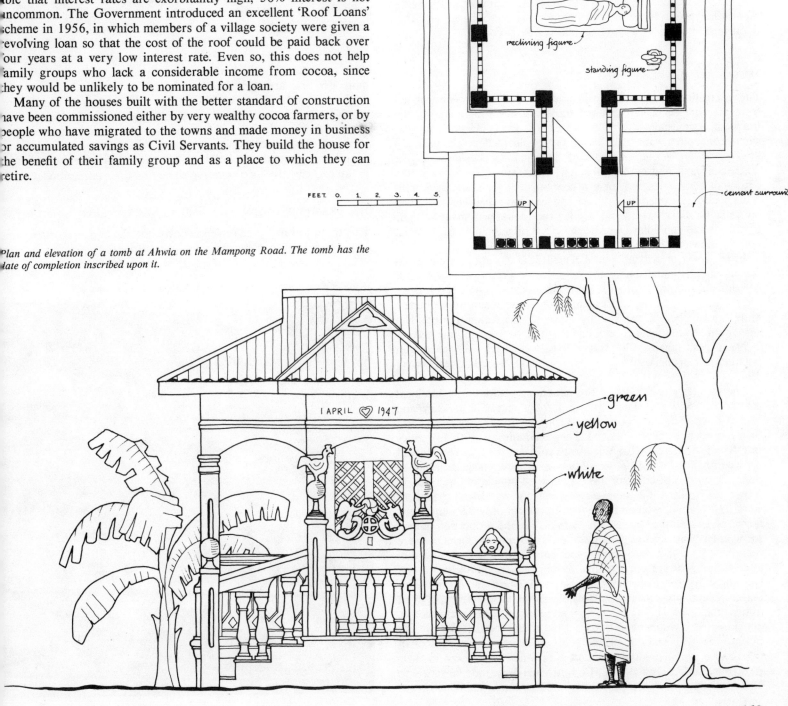

THE FUTURE OF THE VERNACULAR ARCHITECTURE

The social, economic and cultural forces outlined above which have combined to produce the current vernacular architecture are powerful and will remain so for a long time in rural Ashanti. Furthermore, the investment made in the houses built in the 1950s and 1960s is much greater than the comparable investment made in the 1930s so that the possibilities for a rapid change in the character of the buildings is not great. Nevertheless there are signs of change and it is important to consider what effects these may have.

AGENTS OF CHANGE IN RURAL AREAS

The inspiration for more richly decorated houses has probably arisen from the rich cocoa farmers and those who have emigrated to the towns, in a conscious desire to impress people. It is significant that such people often want to build on prestige plots adjacent to the main roads, and are proud of items of conspicuous consumption like American cars, and even tombs. The latter are to be found in the Christian cemeteries and form a new building type, complete with roofs, elaborate concrete sculpture and even have their cost inscribed on a plaque. This ostentatious display runs counter to many of their traditions and could have a profound effect on the buildings, if social constraints were to weaken.

In the heart of Ashanti round Kumasi the growth of the population is already outstripping the potential of the present system of rotation agriculture to provide sufficient foodstuffs. As a result there are indications that the farmers are progressively starting to undermine the fertility of the soil by reducing the fallow period. The survey in Kwamo suggested that with a population increase of 1·9% a year (against the National rate of 2·6%) the maximum population that their land could support (900) would be reached by 1973.

The men have responded to this situation by adopting a duo-local pattern of residence. They live in Kwamo between January and March to provide the labour for clearing the food farms, which are then looked after by the women. They then migrate 100–150 miles into Brong-Ahafo or Sefwi Wiawso to cultivate the cocoa which will provide finance for the housebuilding in the new village adjacent to the main road. The effect of this on the adult population was clearly shown up in the 1962 social survey, when it was found that there were 210 resident women to 82 men (of whom only 23 were cocoa farmers). In a similar survey ten years earlier, the proportion of men to women was evenly balanced and 129 cocoa farmers were recorded. It is also a common experience in this area to find that able-bodied men are not available to work on the self-help projects sponsored by the Department of Social Welfare and Community Development: projects for Schools, Community Centres and street drains that were so successful in the 1950s. Cocoa farms require considerable investment to develop, and it may be that this pattern of farming will produce pressure for a change in the system of inheritance, so that fathers can pass on their investment to their own sons. Such a change may also be needed if the food farms are to be reorganised on more productive modern lines, since the invest-ment required to clear the ground of roots for cultivation by machinery is enormous.

This change could not come about without the active co-operation of the women, since it would have a revolutionary effect on their role and daily life. Although they are not likely to give up their economic independence, the prospect of exchanging the present drudgery of water collection and work on distant farms for a system of highly productive vegetable gardens close to home, and water piped to taps in the village, might prove attractive. It would give them more time to spend at home caring for their children and themselves. This would fit in with the aspirations created by primary education, and visits to their more sophisticated relatives in the large towns. A desire for more personal accommodation and a higher standard of finish and furnishing in the home would be a natural corollary to this, having repercussions on the plan form details and layout of houses. The courtyard principle may still be valid, though it would appear to need breaking down into smaller units to give greater privacy. Alternatively, privacy might be increased without departing from the family group principle by incorporating some first floor accommodation.

THE URBAN CONDITION

This trend towards greater sophistication in the home can already be seen in the large settlements, which are attracting young adults who

Detail of a wall in a traditional Ashanti building, Adakwa Jachie.

have received some education away from the rural area, as the pace of Urbanisation increases. Within the towns the way of life, and the pattern of relationships between people, are bound to vary from that established in the villages. In a large compound house it is likely that many of the sixty or so residents will be unrelated, because they are occupying rented rooms. This creates problems of responsibility for cleaning and compatibility, in houses where water has to be fetched from a standpipe, washing dried on balconies, cooking done on charcoal pots and slops emptied into the communal septic tank latrines which serve the whole street block. An increasing number of the residents are being educated at secondary schools, or in various types of further education, creating an added desire for a high standard of environment. This trend affects the women as much as the men since many of them have now entered jobs in banks, hospitals, schools, commerce and social services, where a far greater sophistication of appearance is required than is possible in the villages. These changes in economic opportunity and values may well produce a significant alteration in the attitude to marriage, again leading to a desire for more specialised accommodation. It is noticeable that inside the compound houses greater emphasis is placed on the sitting rooms, and many people own radios and high-life records which are put on when people call, automatically improving the degree of aural privacy.

Most of the newer housing put up in these larger towns through Government initiative has been built to a European pattern of flats or houses with gardens. It remains to be seen whether this will become accepted as the norm or whether the high cost of living in urban areas and the traditional responsibility to elderly members of the family will restrict this type of accommodation to professional people.

The Building Industry

Parallel to these economic and social trends the building industry is beginning to become better organised. The young men trained in Technical College will be keen to use improved techniques, but not at all likely to be attracted to work as itinerant craftsmen in the rural areas. This suggests the possible growth in the number of organised workshops located in the 'service centres' to produce a new range of standardised components using simple machinery. The current vernacular already makes use of a range of components from roof sheets to precast concrete panels, because they suit the method of investment. There is no reason why this range should not be extended to include better windows, doors, roof trusses, lintels, sanitary fittings and drainage channels, designed to meet both the needs of the individual housebuilder and the programme of urban development. The speed with which this happens will depend to a great extent on how seriously the building industry is taken as a major factor in economic growth, requiring adequate funds for investment in plant, development of managerial skill, research and the marketing of products.

Design Attitude

The final factor influencing the future of vernacular architecture will be the outlook of the designers trained at the University. If they are intellectually prepared to tackle the problem of large-scale investment in mass housing, schools or welfare buildings, and integrate traditional sources of expression into modern techniques of production it may be that a new vernacular will be created. With the possibilities that exist for plan evolution, structural innovation, the design of wall reliefs and pierced screens on both traditional and new building types this could be artistically more vigorous than the past, and yet be disciplined by the consistency that is a characteristic of Ashanti Society.

BIBLIOGRAPHY

ABRAMS, CHARLES, BODIANSKY, VLADIMIR and KOENIGSBERGER, OTTO, *Report on Housing in the Gold Coast*, New York, United Nations, 1956.
BOAHEN, ADU, *Topics in West African History*, London, Longmans, 1966.
BOWDICH, T. E., *Mission from Cape Coast Castle to Ashantee*, London, John Murray, 1819.
FREEMAN, R. A., *Travels and Life in Ashanti and Jaman*, London, Constable, 1898.
FORTES, MEYER, 'Ashanti Survey 1945–46' in *Geographical Journal* Volume cx, Nos. 4–6, October–December, 1947. London, John Murray, 1947.
KYEREMATEN, AAY, *Panoply of Ghana*, London, Longmans, 1964.
LAWSON, ROWENA, *Social and Economic Study of Kwamo*, Kumasi, College of Technology, 1952 (mimeographed).
RATTRAY, R. S., *Religion and Art in Ashanti*, London, Clarendon Press, 1927.
RATTRAY, R. S., *Ashanti Law and Constitution*, London, Clarendon Press, 1929.
STANLEY, HENRY M., *Coomassie and Magdala, The Story of Two British Campaigns in Africa*, Low and Searle, 1874.
SWITHENBANK, MICHAEL, *Ashanti Fetish Houses*, Accra, Ghana Universities Press, 1969.
TETTEH, AUSTIN P., and RUTTER, ANDREW F., *Kwamo: A Study of Rural Evolution in Ghana* (to be Published).
WILLS, J. B. (Ed.), *Agriculture and Land Use in Ghana*, Oxford University Press, 1962.
WOLFSON, FREDA, *Pageant of Ghana*, London, Oxford University Press, 1958. This includes quotations from Winwoode Reade's *The Story of the Ashantee Campaign* (1874), and William Winniett's *Journal of a Visit to Ashanti* (1848).

ALGERIAN OASES

David Etherton

The Sahara covers about a third of the total surface of Africa, and a quarter of this area, two million square kilometres, lies within the national boundaries of Algeria. Although these boundaries are in many ways meaningless, the varied geography and climate and the different types of traditional oasis found in Algeria are representative of the Sahara as a whole. Sixty years of European colonisation and the discovery of oil and gas in the desert have transformed many of the oases, and now a new government is faced with the thousand-year riddle of developing the Sahara. Ninety-five per cent of Algeria's population lives in the fertile coastal strip between the Atlas Tellien and the sea. The pastoral nomads of the north occupy the Hauts Plateaux: red stony plains studded with clumps of halfa and *armoise*, reaching four hundred kilometres inland to the Atlas Saharien and the Aures mountains. Below this is the Algerian desert, four times the size of France.

There are more people living in the city of Algiers than in the entire Sahara and the average Arab from the capital could no more withstand the desert life than would a city dweller from any part of the world. Those who remain in the desert are the last survivors of a society which has adapted itself over hundreds of years to the rigours of the Sahara. The nomad has extended his senses to a degree which enables him to smell water and to hear movement over enormous distances, and his sense of orientation is uncanny. If you offer a nomad a ride in a car, don't expect him to tell you where he wants to go. It may be two hundred kilometres between one village and the next on a road which is the only mark on the landscape, but suddenly you must stop and he will stride off into what you think is still a completely flat and empty space.

To the western anthropologist, the ethnic autonomy and social qualities of the Nomad are cherished; to the newly independent government they are an embarrassment and a mark of underdevelopment. To the nomad the anthropologists are freaks, and the governments a nuisance; but plastic buckets, detergents and transistor radios are duly accepted by him as useful additions to his entourage.

The ecological balance which enabled the Saharan to live 'with' the desert has been upset, more than anything else, by modern communications. The technological possibility of compressing a thousand years of adaptation into an air conditioned capsule means that anybody can now live 'in', rather than 'with' the desert.

KEY TO PHYSICAL MAP

MOUNTAIN RANGES   (Tone/names marked on map)
The Hoggar and the Tassili n'Ajjar are part of a centra Saharan mountain range extending from the Adrar des Forha to the Tibesti in Chad.

The '*Tassili*' is a massive sandstone plateau 1,900 m high, an the 'Hoggar' a dome of cristalline rocks culminating in a series of volcanic peaks of which the Akator 3,500 m are th highest.

SAND DUNES   (Tone/names marked on map)
'*Erg*' covers only about a third of the Algerian Sahara. The Chech and Iguidi are part of an uninterrupted region of dunes covering Mauretania and Mali.

ROCKY PLATEAUX   '*Hamada*'
(Tone/names marked on map)

GRAVEL PLAINS   '*Reg*'. The Tanezrouft is the largest and most desolate in the entire Sahara.
(Tone/names marked on map)

STEPPE   '*Chotts*'. A series of open depressions, sometimes below sea level with a surface deposit of salt.
'*Daya*'. Small fertile depressions; the only areas in the Sahara where cultivation is possible without irrigation.
(Tone/regions marked on map)

RIVERS   '*Oued*'. Usually dry river valleys, but extremely fast and dangerous after rain.
(Main 'oueds' named and marked on map)

KEY TO COMMUNICATIONS MAP

PLACE NAMES   Principal Oases/towns marked giving administrative classification.
i.e. All names mentioned in text.
Oil-towns marked showing pipelines.
RAILWAY   Indicated.
ROADS   Surfaced roads and 'pistes' indicated.
Caravan routes indicated.
BOUNDARIES   National and Departmental boundaries indicated.

KEY TO POPULATION MAP

DENSITY   Oases and regional population indicated graphically.
ETHNIC   Main tribal areas indicated graphically.

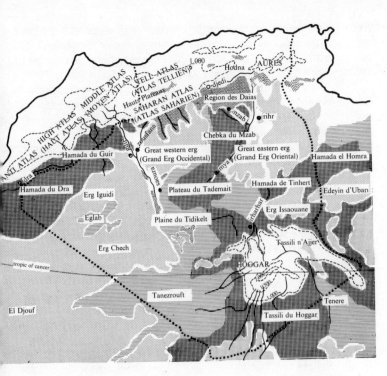

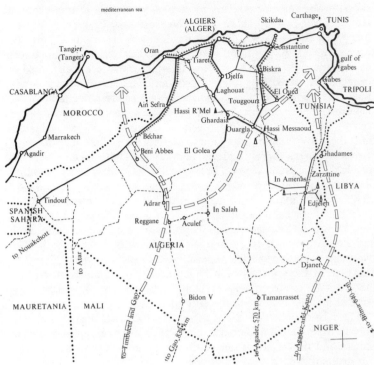

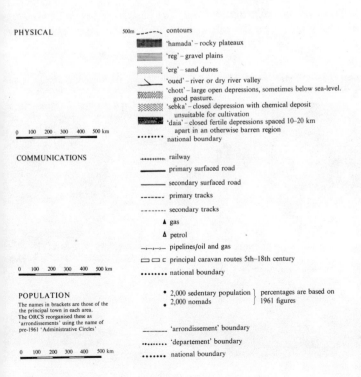

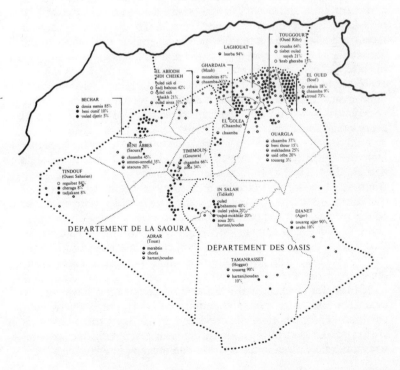

PHYSICAL

500m - - - contours

'hamada' – rocky plateaux

'reg' – gravel plains

'erg' – sand dunes

'oued' – river or dry river valley

'chott' – large open depressions, sometimes below sea-level. good pasture.

'sebka' – closed depression with chemical deposit unsuitable for cultivation

'daia' – closed fertile depressions spaced 10–20 km apart in an otherwise barren region

·········· national boundary

0 100 200 300 400 500 km

COMMUNICATIONS

++++++++ railway

———— primary surfaced road

———— secondary surfaced road

– – – – primary tracks

- - - - secondary tracks

▲ gas

△ petrol

pipelines/oil and gas

principal caravan routes 5th–18th century

·········· national boundary

0 100 200 300 400 500 km

POPULATION

The names in brackets are those of the the principal town in each area. The ORCS reorganised these as 'arrondissements' using the name of pre-1961 'Administrative Circles'

• 2,000 sedentary population
· 2,000 nomads

percentages are based on 1961 figures

———— 'arrondissement' boundary

·········· 'departement' boundary

·········· national boundary

0 100 200 300 400 500 km

Today the ratio of nomads to settled population in the Algerian Sahara is about 3:7. This proportion must have been reversed at a time when the oasis was little more than a well serving the Berber trade caravans. As the trade routes became established, certain tribes claimed the right to use familiar wells which they were then forced to protect. The oasis is as much a product of its surroundings as any other indigenous settlement. Yet the resources are more limited, the conditions more hostile, and the ingenious results contrast more sharply with the surroundings, than elsewhere. The first settled tribes built their towns on high ground in densely packed clusters of courtyard dwellings, surrounded by high walls. These *ksour* form the nucleus of almost all oases. The original wells made a certain amount of cultivation possible and the oases were soon able to offer refreshment, security and trade to the great trans-saharan caravans.

In the ninth century Ghadamés was the most important oasis in the Maghreb. Here merchants from Carthage exchanged salt, cloth and arms for gold, ivory and Negro slaves from the south. The two main routes across the Sahara have always been from Timbuctu and Gao at the source of the Niger, across the Tanezrouft and up the *Oued* Saoura to the Moroccan coast; and from Kano, through Agadez and the Hoggar to the Gulf of Gabés.

The idea of a settled life suggested by the oases appealed at first only to the pastoral nomads of the north. The Touareg of the central Sahara and the Reguibat remained aloof, preferring to leave cultivation to their Negro slaves and visiting, or raiding, other oases only when it pleased them. Even today national independence and international boundaries mean absolutely nothing to the Touareg or Reguibat tribesman. The contrast between the life of the nomad who lives, not so much in a tent but in the desert, and the oasis dweller hardly needs emphasis. Shelter to the nomad might mean the shade of a rock or tree, and even when he visits the oasis his tents will be pitched at a respectable distance from it. To the *ksourien* shelter means a house, but in a sense which is unfamiliar in Europe. In the Sahara the house is a commodity which, until a money economy was introduced, cost no more than the effort to make it. Wealth is expressed in the number of wives you have; in camels, or in goats. If your wealth increases you will build more rooms or enclose more courtyards, but they will be built the same way and look the same as every other house in every other oasis.

Traditionally in the Arab world, the courtyard house ensures that from the age of fourteen women may be seen only by their husbands and children. Only one door opens on to the street and the small windows of each room face inwards towards the miniature oasis of the courtyard itself. Although it may appear to be restrictive, the courtyard is a cool and beautiful place, a protected world for women, children and young animals. Most courtyards are interconnected so that women can pass from one to another without having to walk in the streets. Where there is more than one storey, these connections often cross the streets transforming the *ksar* into a private upper-level town for women, and a lower-level commercial town for the men. The use of rooms surrounding the courtyard is fairly standardised. The man entertains and eats in his own room which is always placed next to the courtyard entrance. Cooking and weaving sometimes take place in the courtyard, although there is often a loom fixed to the wall of the women's room. Also since the settled life brings more possessions, separate rooms are built for storage. None of the rooms is connected, although there may be an arcade passing each room which opens on to the courtyard. Except where there has been European influence, and in places where scorpions made it dangerous to sit or sleep on the ground, there is no furniture. If you are European you might have the dubious honour of sitting on the one broken, secondhand, upright chair in the house, while your host sits comfortably crosslegged on a superb carpet, which you have dirtied by forgetting to take off your shoes.

With the exception of the Souf, each *ksar* has a modular appearance arising out of a standardised roof plan limited by the length of date-palm trunks. These are supported by thick walls of masonry, or mud and straw bricks, and rendered with the same colour of plaster. Unlike the chateau forts of the Haut Atlas and the great oases of Mali and Niger, there is rarely any external decoration to be seen; the tight grid of courtyard houses is broken by an arcaded market and by the mosque, which is the only building in the *ksar* likely to be given a distinctive form. It is unusual to see vegetation of any kind in the narrow streets and public spaces of the *ksour*. The *palmeraie* is always clearly defined as a separate part of the oasis and provides an acceptable point of contact between the nomad, who often owns a garden, and the *ksourien* whom he employs to look after it. In the central Sahara this has resulted in a situation where the population of most of the oases are decendants of the original Negro slaves, *harratin*, bought from Niger by the Touareg.

Perhaps the greatest paradox of the Sahara is the quantity of water below it. A subterranean reserve known as the *Albien* covering an area the size of France, lies between seven hundred and two thousand metres below the desert. Other supplies are trapped in the rocky galleries of the *hamada* and *chebka*. The best water lies under the *erg* where the sand filters the salt and harmful chemicals which it often contains.

Typical 'balance' well on the edge of an oasis. Small whitewashed shrine in the background.

Two types of cultivation are possible in the Sahara. Dry culture or *bour* is confined to the few areas where plant roots reach the water table two to three metres below ground level. Otherwise some form of irrigation is necessary. Of the many ingenious methods used to bring water to the surface the medieval *foggara* are the most audacious. These make use of the reserves of water trapped in the fissures of the rocky plateaux. The water runs by gravity through underground channels linking the plateaux with the oasis. Holes at ten to twelve metre intervals above the *foggara* provide access for excavation and ventilation, and cylindrical walls are built around them above ground to prevent sand and dust drifting into the *foggara* and to cut down the loss of water through evaporation. It took four men one year to tunnel one kilometre and there are four thousand kilometres of *foggara* in the Sahara!

In Arabic they are called 'the fingers of light' and it is no wonder that date palms have become the object of special rites and festivals in the Sahara. The palm is well adapted to soil and climate variations and is unaffected by the sharp temperature changes of the desert. Apart from its fruit it provides essential shelter for cultivating other crops in the oasis. Wheat, sorghum and maize are the principal cereals and a more exotic variety of fruits including pomegranate, fig, peach and apricot may be grown, thanks to its protection.

Apart from cutting off direct sunlight, the palm provides a windbreak, induces humidity, and retains a blanket of warm air close to the ground at night, when the temperature would otherwise drop abruptly. Palm wood is far too valuable to burn. The trunks are sometimes sawn into planks for door construction, but more often used whole as roof beams, since the wood has a dense, fibrous texture which makes it hard to cut.

The thick ends of the branches are cut and often packed together between roof beams to form a base for a stone and plaster roof. The thinner portion of the branch is resilient and strong enough to be bent into a circle without splitting. In the Souf, branches are used to construct simple furniture, and in the Mzab as permanent centring for arches. Palm leaves are woven into baskets and even the felt from the base of the trunk is made into shoes. A kind of palm wine, is fermented from the sap and date stones are used as game counters.

The *ksar* with its mosque and market, the *palmeraie* and its wells, and the necropolis were the original clearly defined elements of the oasis. They were planned in clusters around the oldest settlement and the number of separate oases in a group varies from two or three in the Hoggar to over a hundred in the region of Touat. The important oases are located in the Saoura valley and along the north-eastern edge of the Sahara where the rainfall is highest and the underground water supply fairly easy to reach. Over half the population of the Algerian Sahara is concentrated around three oases: Ouargla, Touggourt and El Oued, each with a few days' march of the other. In the really arid area on either side of the Tropic of Cancer the oases are small and extremely isolated.

The greatest changes in the traditional structure of the oases are a result of European influence in this century. Phoenician, Roman, Byzantine, Arab and Turkish domination of North Africa preceded the arrival of the French in Algiers in 1830. Twenty years later the area between the Saharan Atlas mountains and the coast became part

Fort Mirabel. Deserted Compagnie Saharien *fort in the Plateau de Tademait between El Goles and In Salah.*

of *la France Metropolitaine*. The military adventurers whose job it was to 'pacify' the Sahara met tough opposition, and their success was made possible only by enlisting local tribes and forming efficient camel mounted units, later known as the *Compagnies Sahariennes*.

In 1902 the French were able to define the *Territoires du Sud* within approximately the present boundaries of the Algerian Sahara between the AOF and AEF*. The *Territoires du Sud* were administered by military and civilian officers with the help of the *Compagnies Sahariennes* now reorganised into six units with headquarters in Beni Abbes, Adrar, In Salah, Djanet, and two in Morocco. The *mehari* racing camels used by these units could cover two hundred kilometres of any kind of terrain in a day and the French invented a propellor-driven, rubber-wheeled contraption for crossing sand dunes. However, the really significant effects were to come as a result of new methods of communication set up to link these administrative headquarters. *La mission civilisatrice* began to change the appearance and significance of the traditional oasis. First came barracks, medical centres and an airstrip, and later European houses and schools grouped together on flat ground near the *ksar* with a simple pattern of roads and water supply from a reservoir. Bidon V was the first oasis of the twentieth century. Installed in 1926 as a refuelling station for aircraft and motor traffic on the Imperial Mauretanian *piste* from Bechar to Timbuctu, it was originally no more than a petrol tank placed next to a well. Now there is a small village depending on the petrol tank in the middle of the flattest, most desolate part of the desert, the Tanezrouft.

Geological expeditions, made possible by new means of communication, gradually revealed the mineral riches of the Sahara and renewed France's interest in its development. In 1947, the old *Territoires du Sud* were divided into two Departments, but it was ten

* AEF, *Afrique Equatoriale Française*, 1910–58 (French Equatorial Africa) originally included Niger, Chad and the Central African Republic. AOF, *Afrique Occidentale Française*, 1895–1958 (French West Africa) originally included Mauretania, Mali, Ivory Coast, Guinea, Upper Volta, Togo, Dahomey and Senegal. A referendum of 1958 attempted to make most of these countries member states of the French *Communauté*.

years later that *L'Organisation Commune des Régions Sahariennes* (*OCRS*) was formed as a serious attempt to tackle its economic development and to reorganise the administration. By this time oil had been drilled in Hassi Messaoud and the war for independence had begun in the North. *La France Metropolitaine* extending from Dunkirque to Tamanrasset was a dream which never came true. As the war became more bitter in the north, petrol exploration continued in the Sahara, and by the time Independence was gained in 1962, 158 million tons of oil had been released from the principal oilfields of Hassi Messaoud, Edjeleh and Zarzatine.

The *OCRS* had divided the Algerian Sahara into two Departments, one on either side of a two-thousand-kilometre line drawn due south from Algiers, with a more logical northern boundary defined by the Atlas Saharien. Apart from border disputes between the three countries of the Maghreb, the frontiers of the two Departments have remained unchanged with their *Préfectures* in Bechar and Ouargla. Touggourt; Adrar and Laghouat remained *Sous-Préfectures*. The effects of colonial development make it easy to distinguish the productive from the subsistence oases, which have an average population of only two thousand five hundred.

Region Des Ajjer

The paradox of these picturesque but declining oases is that they are overpopulated. Still relying on primitive methods of cultivation, they are unable to support a steadily growing sedentary population and with a dwindling number of caravans to serve, the economic foundations have collapsed. The oasis of Djanet is a good example. Its three *ksour* and *palmeraie* grew around sixty springs at the foot of the great escarpment of the Tassili n'Ajjer which reaches two thousand kilometres. It is as though the grey shale from the plateaux had

Djanet. A cluster of houses at the foot of the Tassili n'Ajjer not far from the oasis.

Djanet. View of the valley from the old French fort. The buildings are fairly recent with the traditional grass huts, zeriba, *constructed behind them.*

Djanet. Part of one of the old ksour *showing masonry houses and* zeriba.

formed itself into the crumbling hollow cubes of the *ksar* at its foot. Both the Touareg nomad and the *ksourien* have used a type of elephant grass from the *oued* to construct light shelters in which they sleep during the summer. These yellow *zeriba*, scattered among the more permanent buildings of the *ksar* and in the *palmeraie* completed the picture of Djanet before it became the headquarters for the *Compagnies Sahariennes*. Although they built on flat ground, the administration followed the simple shapes and courtyard pattern of traditional housing, using local materials in their new buildings which were dominated by a fort. For about twenty years the pre-medieval society of the Ajjer was overawed, but never much affected, by European technology. The trucks were unable to compete with camel transport in negotiating the mountainous country, and overland communications remained a great problem in the Ajjer. For this reason the OCRS moved the administrative centre to Tamanrasset, a

town which had grown up around an insignificant oasis after 1930, because of its favourable climate and position on the Trans-Saharan land route. Since then, Djanet has fallen back on its own resources which include the attraction of tourists to its magnificent landscape and the famous *rupestrian* cave paintings of the Tassili.

Region Du Tidikelt

A similar story can be told of the Tidikelt and the oases surrounding Aoulef and In Salah. It is the hottest, most exposed area in the Sahara and you will still find an air-conditioned office and a chilled-water fountain in what used to be the administrative headquarters of the Tidikelt and Hoggar regions. At In Salah both the three *ksour* and the Quartier European are plastered like iced cakes with the same red mud and a pattern of scooped vertical lines. The lines are supposed to carry water off the face of buildings into drain channels, but with an

In Salah. Mud rendered water reservoir, possibly built under French direction.

The oasis of In Salah. Town centre and mosque.

Touareg in front of a zeriba in Djanet. The blue veils or litham *of the Touareg are imported by camel caravan from Kano.*

177

average annual rainfall of 14·1 mm there is no danger of the houses dissolving. (By comparison, Algiers has an average rainfall of 762 mm per year.) Geographically the Tidikelt is important because the road from Reggane to In Salah is the only link between the two trans-saharan land routes. That the caravans still operate is partly due to an old colonial law which forbade the transport of salt by lorry, but by now the Touareg, who are too busy posing for photographs, prefer to send their *harratin* servants on the annual trek. (The blue veils make it hard to tell the difference in any case.) Aoulef and In Salah still form the trading bridgehead between the silent caravans from the south and the oases of the Saoura valley.

Region Du Touat

This important group of oases extends along the Saoura Valley eight hundred kilometres from Bechar to the plateau of Tademait. The region of Touat includes one hundred and thirty-five *ksour* strung out two hundred and fifty kilometres along the Rue des Palmiers. The harvest from about a million date palms (the second highest production in Algeria) is exported south direct to Mali or via the Tidikelt to Niger. The *foggara* in this region are exceptionally long, a single gallery sometimes extending thirteen kilometres. The region of Touat can still be described as productive although most of its population lives at subsistence level. The oases which are linked by surfaced roads to the northern urban centres are in a healthier position. The average population of these is 14,000.

Bechar has an exceptionally high population of twice this figure, due to its importance as *Préfecture*, and to coal-mining. After Independence it was agreed that the French army stationed in Bechar should remain there for a further five years to continue their nuclear experiments in the Sahara. This also meant that the local population continued to receive the only medical services available.

Hauts Plateaux. Part of a village most of which was built since 1900 around a French military outpost. On the top of the hill is a shrine. Farther down on the left, a water reservoir built by the French, and below the houses, wrecked cars.

Nomads on their way to Touggourt. Young wives and babies, water, firewood and the tent are all carried by camel. A light wooden frame, covered with cloth provides the traditional privacy for the women. Rubber inner-tubes from car tyres are a common addition to the goatskin guerba *used for carrying water.*

Rhoufi, a small hillside village on the southern slopes of the Aures Mountains. A sophisticated type of gourbi *with the living room open on one side, placed above a closed basement 'store'. All the living rooms overlook a spectacular gorge.*

Rhoufi, Aures. Detail showing roof construction reminiscent of tent structure.

The problem of attracting indigenous professional people to work in rural areas is the same everywhere. In the Sahara it is almost impossible.

Hauts Plateaux

In describing the other important oases in the north, something should be said about the Hauts Plateaux which forms a geographical buffer between the desert and the fertile coastal strip. The OCRS boundaries excluded Aïn Sefra, Djelfa and the oases of Biskra from the two Saharan Departments and like the small towns and scattered hamlets in the Djebel Amour and Hodna regions, they are commercial centres for the large semi-nomadic population of the steppe. Depending on the rainfall, the area around the salty depressions of the *chott* is reasonable grazing land. In the 1920s a million sheep were exported annually to France from the Hauts Plateaux. This tradition of sheep-rearing which encourages soil-erosion, is a threat to any serious agricultural development in the area. Nowadays, the nomads often travel north by lorry to the outskirts of Constantine and Oran for the wheat harvest, and south to the large oases of Touggourt and the Souf for the date harvest. Their sheep and part of the clan usually remain near good pasture in the steppe. This tendency to settle has led to the building of small mud and stone shacks, *gourbis*, next to the tent. The simplest type of *gourbi* has two adjacent rooms, each with only one opening and usually without a door, facing a corral of piled stones, or dried thorn clumps. Flat or sloping roofs imitate the tent construction with a central post supporting beams and purlins of oleander or *laurier rose*. Even the more sophisticated courtyard houses of the Hauts Plateaux are no more

Nomad tent, Hauts Plateaux. Interior view of the male side of the tent showing the secondary row of wooden supports. A rope is tied to the poles at ground level and is used to tether lambs at night.

than improved *gourbis* based on the two-cell plan of the tent. One section is for men, saddles and weapons, and the other for women, children, young animals, spare clothes and cooking material.

Region De'Oued Rirh

The oases of Touggourt still provide seasonal work for a large number of semi-nomads from the Hauts Plateaux. Intensive cultivation of dates for export was instigated by the French and the vast regimented plantations stretch one hundred and twenty kilometres from the north to south. The original *palmeraie* soon exhausted the superficial layer of water and it was necessary to drill artesian wells (1,700 m) to irrigate the oases. Today the plantations are run by co-operatives and continue to produce and export the best dates. Touggourt is linked by road and rail to the northern ports and has a population of 17,000. Early in this century two English ladies passed through Touggourt. Evidently they were not feminists, but were appalled at the brutal treatment of animals. The society for the

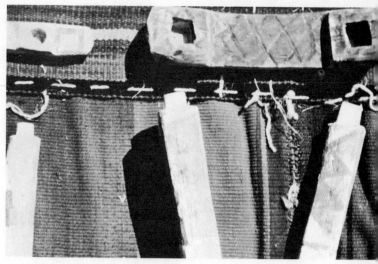

Interior detail of Ouled Naïl tent showing the crossed central poles and the wooden block into which they are morticed. A woven strip reinforces the tent along the line of the pole supports.

Ouled Naïl tent showing the male side of the open end of the tent with part of a thorn bush corral in the foreground.

protection of North African animals which they founded, still has a dispensary in Touggourt and they have patented the design of a painless bit for donkeys. . . .

The industrial Palmeraie of Touggourt.

Region Du Souf

Although separated by only a hundred kilometres of sand dune, the industrial oases of Touggourt are removed by centuries from El Oued and the nineteen smaller oases which make up the region of the Souf. Its main tribes are the Troud, who settled in the fourteenth century and the Rebaia who have maintained their nomadic life since their arrival from Libya three hundred years later. Together with a number of smaller tribes they make up the largest regional population in the Sahara (100,000). Although a small quantity of dates and tobacco are exported, the Souf is another overpopulated region relying on a subsistence economy. Until Independence there was a tradition of migration from the Souf to the region of Constantine and to France. These emigrants, who returned annually for the date harvest,

Aerial view of El Oued in the Souf, showing the courtyards and cumulative cell structure of the houses.

The deep depression of a ghout *in the Souf on the road between Touggourt and El Oued in the Grand Erg Oriental.*

assisted in bolstering the economy rather than in reducing the population.

Two conditions determine the unique ecology of the Souf. First, water, only a few metres below ground level, which enables dry culture, and second its situation in the dunes of the Oriental Erg. In order to maintain the relationship of the gardens to the water level they are grouped in the middle of deep circular depressions (*ghout*), which must be constantly cleared to keep back the sand. To give extra protection from a wind a more permanent sand well (*djerid*), is piled around the perimeter. El Oued, although an agglomeration of courtyard houses, is atypical, both because of the methods of its construction and, since it is neither fortified nor built on high ground, in not being a ksar. The town is grouped around a market place and divided into separate areas each with its own mosque. Individual rooms surrounding each courtyard are covered by a plaster dome, *dar* of about 2 m radius. The modular planning of El Oued and its system of incremental expansion is a delight. Prevented by the domes from settling on the roof, sand forms an acoustic carpet on all the streets. The ingenious method of dome construction relies on a setting-out rod which determines the radii of diminishing circular courses of plaster blocks laid one on top of the other to form a hemisphere. The rod, which is equal in length to the radius of the dome, is revolved about one end which remains on the centre point at the base.

Region D'Ouargla

Like Ghadamés, Ouargla was a northern terminus for the medieval caravans from Agades and Timbuctu. Whereas Ghadamés has decayed with some dignity, Ouargla has taken a severe social and environmental battering. Developments associated with the colonial administration, the military and now the petrol companies have combined to transform the original oasis town. What look like Hollywood Foreign Legion forts turn out to be churches, hotels, cinemas and a museum. As well as the usual collection of indigenous crafts, the museum has a superb permanent exhibition describing the workings of the oil fields at Hassi Messaoud. Discarded oil drilling-bits are a favourite gatepost ornament, and the outskirts of the town are littered with wrecked cars and military debris. Ouargla has unique evidence of the way in which nomadic tribes have recently adapted to a sedentary way of life. On a smaller scale this is an example of urbanisation such as is experienced in all African capitals, and is due to Ouargla's new role as a service centre for Hassi Messaoud sixty-five kilometres away. Three new settlements have grown up about two kilometres outside Ouargla in areas where the Saït Otba, the Beni Thour and the Mekhadma nomads have traditionally camped.

These new villages differ from the traditional *ksour* not only in density but also in the type of house which is eventually built. The process is gradual and begins with the tent and its enclosed corral, spaced at the usual distance from the neighbouring tent. As materials become available individual rooms are built inside the corral and soon the tent is folded for the last time. The buildings may begin with the familiar materials of the squatter settlement but are soon replaced by more substantial constructions of stone and plaster with domed or vaulted roofs similar to those of the Souf.

These three new villages were built in anticipation of employment in Ouargla or in Hassi Messaoud itself. The work offered to local people can only be accepted by men, and is limited to labouring and domestic service. The nomad tends to treat his wage as a subsidy rather than as a means of abandoning his traditional way of life. In contrast, the oil-technicians are either foreign or Algerians educated in the north. The kind of environment they demand, and will continue to demand, has to be transplanted in the desert. Hassi

Hassi Messaoud oil field and artificial oasis.

The valley of the Mzab looking north. Ben Isguen, the Holy Town, in the foreground. Melika, the 'Queen' to the right and Ghardaïa, the capital, in the background. Each ksar is dominated by the tower of its mosque. Dark patches of date palm conceal the 'summer towns'.

Messaoud has its air-conditioned offices and flats, a cinema, and secretaries in bikinis decorating the swimming pool.

Now that the Algerian Government has greater control over the oil-companies, the foreign employees feel less secure and their life in the desert has lost some of its luxury. There will still be cold beer in the ice boxes, high salaries with 'hardship' allowances and frequent leave, but the days when ladies were flown to Rome for their monthly shopping are almost forgotten. Much is known of the oases which served the ancient caravans and of the modern towns and additions built as a result of colonial interest and mineral exploration, but the oases of the Mzab Valley are unique. They represent the culmination of human effort and enterprise in the Sahara and their original social and physical structure can still be identified.

Region Du Mzab

The rocky plateau which divides the oriental and occidental *erg* is known as the *chebka* (Arabic: net). Rising once every thirteen years, the *oued* Mzab traces a dry course through this eroded maze of clefts and ravines. One thousand years ago the valley of the Mzab was chosen by the Ibādites as the site for seven new towns.

The Ibādites were descendants of the Kharijites (*khariji*: dissenter) whose fundamentalist brand of Islamic puritanism led to their expulsion from Iraq in the ninth century. Ibn Rustem, the leader of the Ibādites had a quick following of sympathetic Berber tribes when he arrived in the Maghreb. He founded the kingdom of Tiaret and as its theocratic ruler advocated an austere life devoted to study and trade. As his popularity grew so also did the opposition from orthodox Muslim fanatics and in A.D. 909 Tahert, the capital, was destroyed and the Ibādites fled to Ouargla. Sedrata was built near by as the first new Ibādite town. It was well situated for trade and quickly attracted other persecuted Ibādi communities. However, it was unprotected and the need for expansion demanded a new site located away from the main caravan routes (Sedrata was destroyed by Berber tribes in 1071). Of the seven Mzab towns, five are situated in the valley itself. El Atteuf was founded in A.D. 1011 and the other four valley towns before A.D. 1052. Guerrara and Berriane were built in the seventeenth century, fifty kilometres north of the valley.

Those Ibādites who settled in the valley became known as the Mozabites (Ghardaïa). Almost half the total population of 38,000 live in Ghardaïa, the capital, 13,000 in Guerrara and Berriane and 4,000 in Beni Isguen. Metlili, Bon Noura and El Atteuf each have a population of about 2,000.

The Mzab has more in common with the modern artificial environment of the petrol companies than with many traditional oases. The *chebka* is an unfavourable site from almost every point of view; water is far below ground level and communications are difficult. Rain falls on an average of twelve days a year and in the hottest months temperatures reach a maximum of 45°.

The physical planning of the valley follows a consistent pattern. Each of the five towns is made up of the same three elements: a fortified *ksar* or winter town, an oasis and summer town and a necropolis. The five town groups are linked by an elaborate hydraulic system which follows the course of the *oued*, but are separated visually by rugged, open areas of desert. The hydraulic system consists of barrages built across the *oued* to create surface and subterranean reservoirs. Rainwater is guided from the barrage into the crevices of the *chebka*, sometimes 80–120 m deep, or straight into the gardens through an ingenious network of irrigation channels – *souagui*. Over three thousand wells are connected to the underground reservoirs and the above-ground structures supporting the well-pulleys are a characteristic feature of the Mzab.

Except in the common need for fortification, the *ksour* of the Mzab differ fundamentally from the Berber *ksour*. Whereas each Berber town was occupied by blood relations of the same tribe or clan and was dependent on a higher authority, the Mozabites founded each town with a number of family groups. While retaining their individual identity, these groups surrendered juridical and executive power to a common higher authority, the *Quabā il*. Elders elected from the *Quabā il* of each town in the pentapolis, formed a higher assembly known as the *Jum'a* which held its meetings in the mosque. The church was supreme and had the power to excommunicate clans or individuals. All five *ksour* are built on high ground with concentric bands of courtyard houses falling away from the central mosque and its dominant tower. Originally the limits of each town were set by a fortified outer wall. The close texture of streets, ramps and steps is broken only by an open market and alcoves sheltering the public wells.

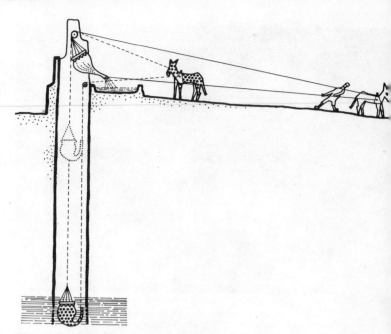

Diagram of well operation. The tirest *(skin containers holding about 10–13 gallons of water) are drawn in rotation by two donkeys. A pull on the cord releases the neck of the* tirest *and discharges water straight into the irrigation channel.*

The western wall of Beni Isguen, the 'Holy Town'. A paved prayer surface can be seen in the necropolis on the opposite hill.

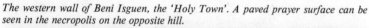

Houses in the 'Summer town' of Ghardaïa.

184

Ghardaïa market, showing the south-west side of the ksar.

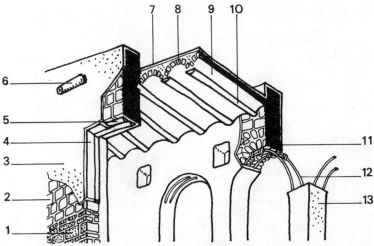

1 Masonry foundation and plinth
2 Mud block wall (15 × 15 × 35 cm 'toub')
3 'Timchent' rendering, coloured or natural
4 Reveal with smooth rendered finish.
   Colour contrast with 3
5 Double palm-wood lintel.
   Inner member continued around opening as door-frame
6 Baked clay gargoyle

7 'Timchent' roof covering
8 Small-stone vaults consolidated with 'timchent'
9 'Timchent' internal rendering often painted blue
10 Split palm-branch beams (2 m span @ 0.7 ccs)
11 Stone block arch
12 Permanent centering of palm nervures tied together
13 'Timchent' rendering

Typical well-house plan in the Mzab.

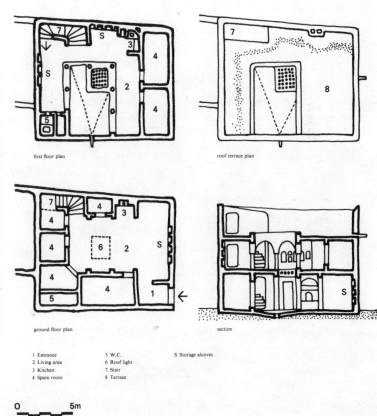

first floor plan

roof terrace plan

ground floor plan

section

1 Entrance
2 Living area
3 Kitchen
4 Spare room
5 W.C.
6 Roof light
7 Stair
8 Terrace

S Storage alcoves

0   5m

A roof terrace showing the stair exit and an opening over the courtyard below.

Palm wood house door and lock-opening. The Mozabite lock is an ingenious sliding wooden mortice which is released by inserting a stick about 30 cm long with a pattern of protruding nails at one end. The nails correspond to holes containing loose wooden pins in the lock. The door and key are symbolic of Mozabite society. The key stick is also an effective weapon.

A niche for prayer and meditation in a koubba. *The protected opening always faces east.*

There is no vegetation in the *ksour*. Their location on high ground deliberately leaves the flat areas close to the *oued* for cultivation. The whole valley has about 180,000 date palms grouped in separate plantations around each town. These are less productive than the palms of most oases but they play an additional role in protecting the summer towns and their gardens from the sun. At the hottest time of the year it was the custom for most of the population to leave the *ksour* and to move to the summer towns. During these months the *ksour* remained silent and parched and a new life of cultivation began in more pleasant surroundings. Today the annual exodus is less marked and the summer towns are treated more as a second home for prosperous Mozabite traders. Shaded by the foliage of apricot, pomegranate and date palm, the streets and houses of the summer town are cool, and a sense of refreshment is heightened by splashing water in open channels and the constant noise of well-pulleys. Until the beginning of this century, the life of the Mozabites was centred on the agricultural exploitation of the valley. There is still enough fruit and wheat grown to serve local needs. Each town has its own necropolis in the open desert area near the winter town and occupying about twice its area. Separate burial grounds for each clan are grouped around the tombs of famous saints. The individual gravestones are unmarked and large whitewashed areas are left open for prayer meetings.

The physiognomy of the Mzab towns was achieved during the first forty years of their existence – the time taken to build all seven towns. The original conditions imposed two guiding principles of speed and economy and these formed the basis for construction and planning. A clear policy for expansion and growth of the towns anticipated the steady influx of population during the first half of the eleventh century. The best use of land dictated that when one winter town reached its optimum size, a new one should be added on high ground. There is no hierarchy of building types in the Mzab. The same materials and methods of construction were used for hydraulic work, houses, public buildings and the mosque. The size of family determined the size of house and public buildings were no more than a number of typical houses joined together to provide extra space.

The individual house plan reflects a pattern of life which has hardly changed since the Ibādites first settled in the Mzab; an austere and secret life, proud of its early hardship and achievements and highly regulated in every detail. Until 1878 no stranger had set foot in a Mzab town, and even today visitors to Beni Isguen, the Holy Town, must leave before sunset. Women remain locked in their houses and are forbidden to leave the valley. Only women, children and old men remain in the towns for more than a few months at a time.

The traditions of Mozabite trading go back to the days of Sedrata, and today, they are the most astute and successful merchants in the Maghreb. A Mozabite general store will be found in almost every town and village of Algeria. Boys are sent from the Mzab to learn the trade with relatives and return home to marry at the age of 14–16. They leave the valley again, and only settle permanently in the Mzab when enough capital has been made to retire and continue house building.

The implacable blind walls of streets and narrow alleys express only the secrecy and austerity of the Mzab. Seen from above, the buildings take on a new meaning and the subtle organism of courtyard dwellings becomes clear. On all but the south-facing slopes of the winter towns, houses are open to the top with a central courtyard diminishing in area through two or three storeys to a small roof-light over the lowest floor. This is either at ground/entrance level or one floor below ground. It is the coolest part of the house during the day and consists of a large living space surrounded by small rooms on two sides. The next floor provides a more open living area with arcades around a central court. After sunset a violent drop in temperature changes the function of the roof terrace from parasol to sleeping area.

On the southern slopes of the winter towns the walls which usually surround the terrace on all four sides are left open to the south. The arcades efficiently cut off the vertical rays of summer sun and admit winter sun. The very small openings in external walls are limited to the south. There is evidence of Andalusian ornament in the ruined town of Sedrata yet no applied decoration appeared in the building of the Mzab. The only feature which is repeated is the semicircular arch and the four-pronged termination of the mosque towers. Otherwise the shapes and sizes of walls and openings were determined by orientation, privacy and the irregularities of the site.

Building materials and constructional details were the same for all buildings. A hard quick-drying plaster (*timchent*) processed from river silt was used for making building blocks, as mortar and for rendering. The external rendering of buildings is still applied in the traditional way with palm branches, giving an energetic surface texture to the wall. Stone was used only as rough reinforcement for wall openings, arches and vaults, and for foundations. Woodwork was limited to the ingenious use of palm; large planks sawn from the trunk for doors and shutters, branches cut in two as initial support for vaulted roofs, and the nervure bent and tied to form permanent centering for arches.

N

'Ksar' winter town

Necropolis

Palmaraie/summer town

Barrage

Trunk road

Secondary road

Ouargla 190 km

Tamanrasset 1,439 km

0   ½   1 km

The Valley of the Mzab. The outline shape represents the area of the valley given protective classification by the Service des Monuments Historiques, *Algiers.*

Bou Noura, 'The Town of Light', built up to a rocky edge of the oued *on the western slope of the hill.*

Discussing the ways in which dwellings can be tailored to suit the particular requirements of the individual while at the same time satisfying agreed common criteria, Christopher Alexander makes a distinction between 'mass' and 'fine adaptation' (to the environment). In the Mzab, a common solution is found in building for climate and for privacy, and at the level of 'fine adaptation'; the interiors of houses are literally moulded to suit the individual family. This is achieved partly by carving out a variety of storage alcoves from thick walls and also by taking advantage of the speed at which *timchent* partition walls can be dismantled and rebuilt within the basic plan.

In the 1966 'Review of the Algerian Ministry of Tourism', M. de Maisonseul suggests that Le Corbusier's work and thinking were deeply affected by visits which he made to Algeria in the thirties. He points out similarities in the forms of several buildings in Ghardäia and the Chapel at Ronchamps, and observes that Le Corbuier's interest in curved planes dates from the time of these visits. This quite common attitude to indigenous buildings seems to ignore the fact that their forms are an unselfconscious and inseparable product of social, geographical and climatic conditions. Of an aeroplane flight which he made over the Mzab Valley in 1935, Corbusier himself writes, '. . . every house a place of happiness, of joy, of a serene existence regulated like an inescapable truth, in the service of man, and for each'.

Recently, through the influence of industrialisation, under political pressure and through a slackening of religious practice, Mozabite society and its environment show signs of change. Inevitably the beginnings of change go back to the early days of colonisation. Ghardäia became the military centre of an area stretching about six hundred kilometres from Djelfa in the Hauts Plateaux to El Golea on the edge of the oriental *erg*. Gradually the effects of an alien culture took shape in a variety of administrative buildings, missions, a military camp and hospital and schools. One of the most damaging effects was the introduction of water-borne waste disposal. Traditionally, naturally decomposed waste proved a useful fertiliser and was regularly collected from each house for the purpose. Due to the infrequent rising of the *Oued* a large area outside Bou Noura has become silted-up, resulting in a vast stagnant pond of accumulated waste from Melika and Ghardäia.

The discovery of oil at Hassi Messaoud, two hundred and fifty kilometres east of Ghardäia, has had a profound effect on the whole region, including the Valley of the Mzab. The trunk road from Algiers branches at Ghardäia, making it an important relay town for traffic on the Tamanrasset route and for the eastern oil-towns. There is an airport-twelve kilometres from Ghardäia and the valley is beginning to attract a large number of tourists.

The extent to which the fabric of the Mzab towns can accommodate change is significant. Since the arrival of the petrol companies, the desert interstices between the towns have become disorderly but the untouchable cemeteries around the *ksour* have helped to retain a degree of legibility. To the modern Mozabite the acquisition of wealth is still seen as a means of fulfilling a moral obligation to maintain and improve the community. With his Citroen DS parked under the shade of a date palm, he may see no reason why the

Detail of the fortified western edge of Bou Noura.

building in which his family has lived for three generations should not easily accommodate the most up-to-date technological equipment, nor why his wives should ever want to leave the Mzab Valley.

The Mozabites are now on the point of expanding their towns and re-modelling their environment with full awareness of twentieth-century technology. There seem to be a number of choices open to them: either, a continuation of the *laissez-faire* pseudo-oriental building which is already blunting the clear definition of the original towns; or an attempt to encourage the traditional use of craft skills and materials still practised by small builders and to restrict the siting of new projects; or a complete freeze on new buildings in the old towns and the creation of a new separate town following the original expansion principle of the old winter towns. In reality this kind of planning speculation is academic and the future of the valley depends very much on the reaction of the Mozabites to the economic restrictions imposed on them by the government since Independence. Now that it is more difficult for them to invest money abroad, they may well grasp the opportunity of developing the Mzab.

Many possibilities for the development of the Sahara as a whole have been dreamed about, written down, and some worked out in great detail. New explorations will uncover more reserves of minerals and oil, and, provided that the underground supplies of water are tapped, agriculture is possible on a large scale. In 1870 Ferdinand de Lesseps was asked to solve the technical problem of creating an inland sea, linking the region of the *chotts* to the Gulf of Gabes. Mussolini was attracted to the idea fifty years later, but still it came to nothing. Another ancient project was revived in 1964 when the governments of Algeria, Tunisia, Mali and Niger met to discuss the construction for a trans-saharan road, linking in effect, the Maghreb with the seaboard countries of West Africa.

All these projects are technically possible and their realisation would provide new reasons for living in the Sahara – reasons which would be hard to find in what remains of the ancient oases.

REFERENCES

RAVEREAU, ANDRE, 'Vallée du Mzab', in *Cahiers du Centre Scientifique et Technique du Batiment*, No. 64, Paris, October 1963.

'Comment Construire au Sahara?' *Cahiers du CSTB* Paris, July 1958.

Atlas Regional des Departements Sahariens, Commandement en chef des Forces en Algérie, April 1960.

BATAILLON, CLAUDE (Ed.), 'Nomades et Nomadisme au Sahara', in *Rechérches sur la Zone Aride XIX*, UNESCO.

DESPOIS, PAUL, 'Le Hodna', in *Publications de la Faculté des lettres d'Alger*, XXIV, Algérie, 1953.

LHOTE, HENRI, *Les Touaregs du Hoggar*, Payot, Paris, 1955.

GAUDIO, ATTLILIO, *Les Civilisations du Sahara*, Marabout Université Verviers, Belgium, 1967.

ALPORT, E. A. A., 'The Mzab', in *Journal of the Royal Anthropological Institute*, Vol. 84, Part 1, June 1954.

RAVEREAU, ANDRE, and MANUELLE ROCHE, *Revolution Africaine (Alger)*, Nos. 61/62, March 1964.

Les Guides Bleues, *Algérie et Tunisie*, 1923.

BOUZDRIU, P., *Sociologie de l'Algérie*, Presses Universitaires de France, No. 802.

LE CORBUSIER, 'Aircraft', *The New World Vision*, London, 1936.

ALEXANDER, CHRISTOPHER, 'Thick Wall Pattern', *Architectural Design*, July 1968.

URBANISATION IN MALAWI

Ralph Mthawanji

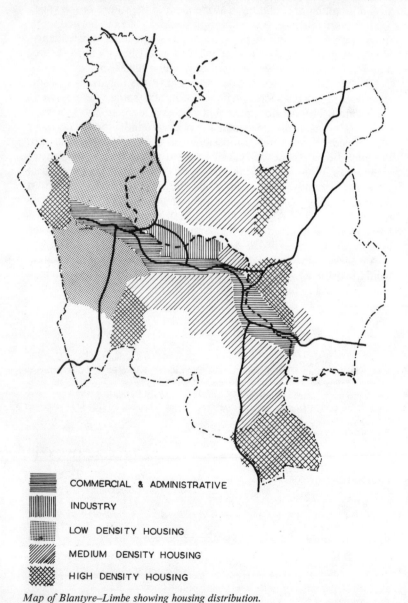

COMMERCIAL & ADMINISTRATIVE

INDUSTRY

LOW DENSITY HOUSING

MEDIUM DENSITY HOUSING

HIGH DENSITY HOUSING

Map of Blantyre–Limbe showing housing distribution.

Urbanisation in Malawi is determined by the availability of employment outside agriculture; implying change in the way of sustaining one's own environmental needs, in respect of food, shelter, clothing etc. Prior to 1891, when Malawi, then Nyasaland, was declared a protectorate in the British Empire, the essentials of life were met locally within the family or kinship unit. The socio-economic structure is hierarchical, in that the nuclear family deals with only those problems which it can manage, and the extended family of grand parents, uncles and sisters completes the welfare security of the nuclear family. The extended family in turn has its undertakings such as defence (if necessary), ceremonies, etc., in which as many members of the tribe as are within reach of the settlement join.

Unfortunately, since 1891, this self-sufficiency came to an end. Since then, the communities of Malawi have been tantalised by the existence in the same locality of two economies. The two economies are interdependent, but because financial capital is limited, the money economy is not ready to absorb the kinship group into its domain, and hence the romance between the two is one-directional, and only exists when the money economy needs labour. Therefore, in order to understand the degree of urbanisation in Malawi, it is necessary to analyse the two communities and economies, their areas of interaction, the physical translation of these interactions into the city plan of Blantyre, and finally what could have been the logical step towards urbanisation in Malawi.

Before 1891, Malawi settlement patterns were characterised by clusters of huts, scattered randomly across the countryside, possibly as near to a river as possible, and with agricultural land and a forest reserve within reach. This random scatter was in physical layout; admittedly there was a social organisation, but this only indicated how close one was to one's neighbour, or how dependent one was on the other members of one's kinship group. The settlement was based on a kinship unit, with either an elder brother or elder sister having supremacy over the younger sisters and brothers. Whether a sister or a brother led the settlement was dependent on whether the original tribe was matrilineal or patrilineal in inheritance.

The main differences in the tribes of Malawi are the form of marriage and the composition of the extended family settlement cluster.

In the extended family settlement cluster illustrated (p. 192), of a patrilineal tribe, the settlement would consist of the patriarchal head, is wife or wives, his unmarried children and his married sons with their wives and children. The sons obtain their wives by paying a bride-price in cattle to the bride's parents; whereas the daughters are married to a bridegroom from another cluster, in whose settlement, on agreement of the bride-price they eventually reside. The *lobola* (bride-price) is supposed indirectly to determine the future of the other daughters in the family, i.e. if the bride is barren the bridegroom is free to select one of her younger sisters for the same bride-price.

But in matrilocal extended families, the bridegroom does not pay a bride-price but performs bride-service (*chikamwini*) for the bride's parents and resides with their parents.

Since Malawi attained a nationhood status in the early 1960s, it is more difficult to draw a distinction among the tribes; and the urban areas are being built as though the prospective tenants had no differentiated background.

	Northern Region	Central Region	Southern Region	Matrilocal Extended Family	Patrilocal Extended Family	*Chikawini* (Bride-Service)	*Lobola* (Bride-Price)
NGONI	●	●			●		●
TONGA	●				●		●
NYANJA		●	●	●		●	
CHEWA		●		●		●	
YAO			●	●		●	
LOMWE			●	●		●	
SENGA		●			●		●

The basic unit of land holding of the indigenous economy was the family farm. On settling, the male member of each family played the major role in clearing up the forest and building a family hut within the region that the kinship unit had selected. After the clearance, the female members were responsible for sowing and weeding the staple crops, maize, cassava, rice, millet, etc., and besides were responsible for feeding the family unit and for general tidiness round the hut of their offspring. The girls followed their mothers and learnt the trade that they eventually would be doing; whereas the boys, instead of following their fathers in hunting or handicrafts, (such as mat- and basket-making, weaving or wood carving), went shepherding, but in so doing they were also picking up all the knowledge that their fathers possessed. Economically, the unit was self-sufficient and very little bartering trade existed between families.

The extended family situation is within the grasp of one or two generations; but when the link goes farther back, the relationship between settlement groups becomes a kinship; in fact to a certain extent all the settlements have a common root. And if two people from two different settlements meet, it is quite an interesting experience for them to go back in time until they find a common ancestor, which will establish the type of relationship between them.

Socially, the indigenous community, that is the kinship group, indulged in mutual co-operation to accomplish tasks the execution of which was too demanding for one individual household. The men always hunted in groups, and the clearing or weeding of individual family farms was also done on a group basis, with the female owner acting as a hostess to the rest of the group. After the day's work, the male members gathered at a *bwalo*, or forum, to discuss any matters of mutual interest; the women with children sat round a fire, and here the story-telling went on.

Politically, the elder of the kinship group was the village 'headman', and he arbitrated over all feuds within the village; those which were too intricate or involved members of different villages were referred to the area chief, who was responsible over a range of settlements. If any member of a group was in disagreement with the group headman, then he, and any supporters that he had in the village, formed a splinter group and negotiated resettlement with the area chief, either within the chief's area or outside it.

The base of indigenous society was agriculture. The family unit was economically self-sufficient, while socially it related itself to the parent unit. This in turn was related on a hierarchical basis to the area chief, who was the supreme power. The survival of this system depended on unlimited supply of land. Thus in each settlement, besides discontent developing as a consequence of the 'generation gap', there was a limit to (*a*) the number of people a piece of land could support with a given technology and (*b*) the number of years that crops could thrive on the land without preventive measures in the form of soil and water conservation, and rejuvenating the soil food values. So from the beginning the agricultural technology of shifting cultivation presupposed a degree of mobility.

As defined above, urbanisation in Malawi is the assimilation of the indigenous community into the money economy. Barter, or exchange of one commodity for another, started with the Arab slave trade, long before Dr. David Livingstone discovered Malawi for the British; when slaves were exchanged for beads or cloth, the slave trade exploited the differences between area chiefs, the winning chief in a tribal dispute or war, selecting the best manpower from the losing side. Worse still, any members of a kinship group found socio-economically or politically non-acceptable were dropped this way, much like the convicts who were shipped to Australia. When Dr. David Livingstone came to Malawi, as a good missionary he was appalled by this, and embarked on bringing a stop to the slave trade and intertribal wars.

But then the money economy was re-established, although admittedly under a more acceptable guise. From the beginning, the British administration wanted to inject Western values into the indigenous society; there was need for services (health, education), and to avoid perpetual subsidies from Britain, the administration felt it necessary to improve the quality and the quantity of agricultural production in order to produce an exportable surplus. And because the money from the sales was not forthcoming, they introduced a poll/hut tax, and a fine on failing to comply with agricultural or health inspector's instruction. Every male of 18 years or over was required to pay the poll/hut tax. When instituted it was a very low sum, but by 1968 it had risen to £1 17s 6d for anyone earning less than £61 per year. All this was an attempt to monetise the indigenous economy; of course overlooking the fact that the only place where the peasants could earn money from the sale of their agricultural products or the sale of their labour, was where the settlers themselves had opened some form of business: agricultural, mining or construction work. Concurrent with the monetisation of the indigenous agriculture, was the educational programme, whose curriculum was typically alien to rural life; those children who underwent the course were shattered to find that rural life did not quite offer them satisfaction in their newly acquired values. Finally, the health programme meant more children could survive and hence increased pressure on the land. The three reasons: economic, alienation from, and pressure on, the land speeded up the rural-urban migration in Malawi. Thus in a nutshell, a disturbance was set up within the traditional way of life; and the question is, how was the money economy able to accommodate those who were alienated from the land?

The British Administration realised the huge social and economic cost they would have to encounter, if they tried to integrate the indigenous society into the money economy; and besides, the alternative to the *status quo* had to be positively better before the indigenous population could decide to sacrifice their traditional way of life. But within the indigenous economy there were built-in redundancies; that is, the male member whose task it was to open up new fields for the family unit, could easily be dispensed with without reducing the overall productivity of the unit for one or two years. And when the administration introduced taxes and other penalties for failure to

comply with the new legislation, it was this male member whom the aimed at. He was absorbed into employment from about one month to two years, and then was repatriated from the short-lived romance with the money economy to the indigenous economy. What applied to this one man, applied to thousands of other men; the employer provided sites for the employees to build themselves mud huts. The monetisation of this indigenous economy which started before the end of the nineteenth century, meant that the whole indigenous population could not afford to live on the land that they owned. And because the Administration realised that socially and politically it was difficult to gain access into the indigenous society, they recruited the area chief, later called the 'native Authority', to register all the people living in his area, and take the responsibility of enforcing the administration's legislations: taxes and fines. Therefore, nearly every male over 18 in the kinship village had to get out of the village and hunt for a money-income, or otherwise he could end up in a prison camp. The prison camps were places where the defaulters were kept for the duration of their sentences: from there they were sent to work either for the Town Council or for the Native Authorities – in a way it was a means of getting labour without quite meeting its full cost.

The main characteristic of any economic activity is the concept of getting more benefits with less costs in any resource combination that one makes. One can imagine the time when the two economic systems (indigenous and money) existed side by side, the latter needing the former to perform some of its productive operations, and yet not quite accepting the former to enrol as a full member of its own system, because the economic costs would have been severe on the part of the administration. But given a situation in which the administration absorbed the redundant member of the family, the administration did not need to pay full costs for sustaining subsistence in the whole family, but only a token wage, which was regarded as extra to the unit productivity. This summarises the interaction between the two economies in the two communities. To integrate the family unit would have necessitated the resettlement of the whole unit (family

Organisation of a typical extended family settlement cluster.

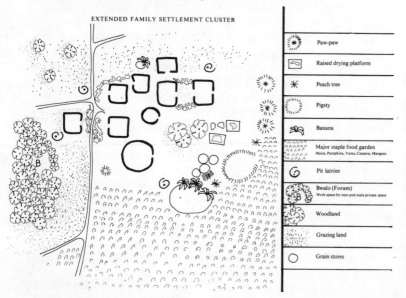

EXTENDED FAMILY SETTLEMENT CLUSTER

✺	Paw-paw
◠	Raised drying platform
✳	Peach tree
✺	Pigsty
✿	Banana
⬡	Major staple food garden Maize, Pumpkins, Yams, Cassava, Mangoes
⚲	Pit latrine
Ⓑ	Bwalo (Forum) Work space for men and male private space
❀	Woodland
∴	Grazing land
○	Grain stores

Settlements in rural Malawi, showing random scatter.

unit plus redundant male) in the urban area, and paying the male member enough wages to be able to buy shelter, food and clothing. This would have entailed less disruption in the indigenous social values, but would have required a high capital outlay to start with.

Urbanisation in Malawi went on in this manner: the indigenous population were drawn into money economy work places, which they helped to build, but no sooner had they got used to the new environment than their term of office expired, and they found themselves repatriated. Hence, in writing about urbanisation in Malawi, one has to recognise that the two ideologies co-existed, and that, in a way, the administration was unwilling to disrupt traditional society. But whether unknowingly or otherwise, the fact remains that traditional society has irreparably been disrupted.

Blantyre is typical of the settlements with money economy. It

started towards the end of the nineteenth century as a missionary station; almost immediately, two business-minded Scotsmen, formed there the African Lakes Corporation, which was eventually nick-named 'Mandala' by the indigenous population, because one of the partners wore a pair of spectacles, *mandala* meaning 'glass' in the local language. So by the beginning of the twentieth century, Blantyre – as the settlement later became known, after David Livingstone's birthplace in Scotland – was well on the way towards 'providing an alternative to the wretched traffick in human flesh'. In the words of *Welcome to Blantyre*, today Blantyre is not only the sole settlement with city status in Malawi, but also the only commercial and trading centre in the country. It is also the only urbanised settlement which has today an indigenous population of more than 100,000: 5,000 Asians and 3,300 Europeans, compared to that of 1896, when there were 130 Europeans, 26 Asians and 12 others. It

Projection showing the construction of a family hut.

Detail of the roof construction showing apex.

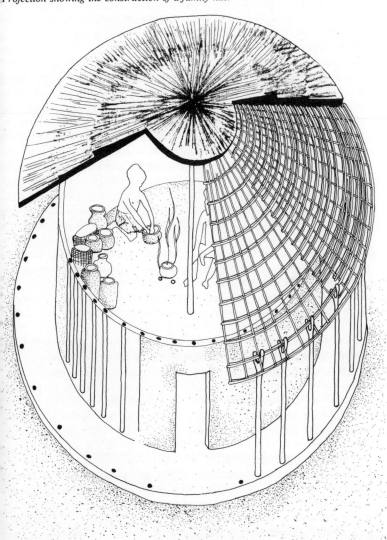

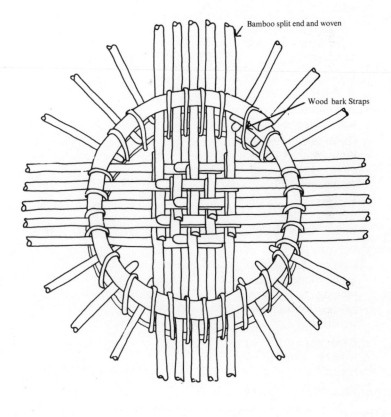

Bamboo split end and woven

Wood bark Straps

can clearly be observed that there has been a strong rural–urban migration.

Now the question arises as to what degree the indigenous population has been urbanised. To answer this I will quote extensively from a field survey done by the Zambian Institute of Social Research, (formerly the Rhodes–Livingstone Institute) of seventeen pari-urban villages round Blantyre, which shows the way in which the indigenous society is adapting to the monied society. In the table that follows, all percentages are based on the zone itself: i.e. (a) of all persons living in the peripheral zone, 70% have got a direct relationship with the founding family of the settlement. The remaining 30% are accretions: primary families which sought affiliation to the central group.

REMARKS	PERIPHERAL ZONE (0–4 miles)	EXTRA-PERIPHERAL ZONE (4–8 miles)	RURAL ZONE (8–15 miles)
(a) Percentage of persons in central lineage	70	55·8	67·2
(b) Percentage of resident males in paid employment	72	43	46
(c) Percentage of absent husbands	12	18	35
(d) Percentage of men who make a living from other sources than paid employment or self-employment	19	37	38
(e) Percentage of women who brew beer.	48	36	35
(f) Percentage of women in regular trade (pottery, mat-making, frying cakes, selling firewood, etc.).	22	18	5
(g) Percentage of women purchasing maize.	73	40	30
(h) Percentage of women from central lineage purchasing maize.	67	38	35
(i) Percentage of home-grown maize to the total.	47	79	89

(a) shows that despite the disturbance, socially, the composition of the villages round Blantyre is still traditional, in that the majority are related directly to the central lineage. This type of composition is also known to be the most stable form of settlement.

(b), (c) and (d) show that the majority of men employed and staying with their families are those near the employment centre, and that further away from the urban centre, more men engage in other forms of occupation.

(e) to (i) show that near the urban centre more women engage in other occupations to make up the husband's wage to an acceptable subsistence level; and finally that women nearer the urban centre purchase most of their daily supply of food.

So far, I have shown how the indigenous economic system is adjusting to fit into the money economy; I have already said that in order to absorb the indigenous economy into its domain, the money economy exploited the redundancy in the composition of the former. This meant that as long as the employees lived on the company or government estate, it was possible to do without any of the services that a complete family unit would have required. In Blantyre–Limbe, there are broadly four types of accommodation: (a) Executive class: very high standard, but its market is limited to the western or neo-western orientated cultures. (b) Residential family type, comparatively high standard, supplied by the Government, but application only through employer, and normally with a high rate of over-crowding. Both (a) and (b) although of a high standard, bear no relationship between the number of rooms provided and the household size. In particular, the (b) type has a higher overcrowding rate than: (c) Traditional structure in the peri-urban customary land, where the individual household can build as many rooms (a series of huts) as is socially acceptable within the family. The advantage of traditional layout and structure is that the number of dwelling units (huts) focusing on the parents' hut can increase or diminish, depending on how many people feed from the same pot or grain store. Protecting walls are non-existent in present-day Malawi; there are some communal play or work spaces both for men and women. Normally the women's working space is near the hut, while the men's is out of sight.

This must suffice for the purpose of establishing the changes that have occurred through the introduction of a money economy in the provision of shelter for the indigenous population. The main traditional building materials were mud and wattle for walls, thatch for roofs and earth stabilised with cow dung for floors. In Blantyre, 56% of all houses built for, or by, the indigenous population is of this construction, and only 33% is built of burnt brick walls, tin roofs and concrete floors. As for the water supply, traditionally, all toilet and washing-up were done in an adjoining stream. The city of Blantyre provides piped water to 12% of the households, 21% have a water tap within 100 m, another 23% walk farther than 100 m, and 3% are near a well. The lighting of the hut used to be effected by a fire in a centrally located fireplace within the dwelling. In Blantyre, 13% of the households are connected to electricity, but as many as 85% use candles or paraffin lamps for lighting.

Women near the urban centre purchase most of their daily supply of food at the market.

An example from Lusaka: urban areas are being built as though the prospective tenants had no differentiated background.

Traditionally, the cooking fuel was wood. In Blantyre 90% of the households still use this, while 8% use paraffin stoves. The kitchen was very flexible, in other words it was possible to cook indoors or in the *khonde* (verandah), or under a tree, depending on the weather. But in Blantyre 52% of the households have no kitchen, and even worse there is no verandah nor a tree where these households could cook in the shade.

The next analysis in the urbanised indigenous population is the relationship between home, work and leisure, if any. A glance at a land use map of Blantyre–Limbe shows that all the commercial, administrative, industrial and social services are located along, or near, the main road connecting the municipalities of Blantyre and Limbe. Immediately behind this complex are located the low-density, executive type housing with recreational facilities: golf courses, yacht

clubs, etc., and the medium density housing, either government or company built, with tenancy tied to employment. And finally, beyond this zone comes the high density housing which is equivalent, on a lower level, to a mixture of the unauthorised housing and 'site and services' schemes in Lusaka. The latter require some explanation. In the city of Lusaka in Zambia, the housing of urban workers was left to employers, who were allocated sites where their workers could build huts for themselves. These settlements, due to their lack of basic services and amenities were later referred to by the city council as 'unauthorised settlements'. Because of the cost involved in housing the workers in Lusaka, the Government decided to allocate plots of land 40 × 70 feet to the urban settlers and provide the basic services on each plot, so that the settler could build a healthy dwelling unit: this allocation of plots is termed the 'site and services'

Resettlement scheme outside Zomba.

A Maize-mill in Fort Johnston: an example of an effort to improve the quality of rural life.

The new entrants to the city build huts from any material that they can find in the urban areas. These are made of corrugated iron, plywood and 'mealies'.

A home of a recent arrival to the city, made from cardboard boxes, scrap timber and roofing felt, held down with iron pans and rocks.

scheme. Like their equivalent in Lusaka, the inhabitants of the Blantyre road settlements, in the absence of public transport, commute on foot to the workplaces in Blantyre–Limbe, where they man the industries and maintain the services that their better-off friends use in the centre. Distance, let alone their low incomes, is enough to stop them from using these services effectively. It is within these high density settlements that a lot of the rural villagers come to join their relatives, while waiting for some form of employment.

With the increasing growth of literacy in Malawi, and the decline of faith in the traditional kinship villages, more Malawians, particularly of the younger generation are drifting into the urban areas where they believe their future lies. If they cannot find employment in Malawi, they emigrate to South Africa, Zambia, Rhodesia or Portuguese East Africa, where they play nearly the same role as they would if they had stayed and worked in the Malawi urban areas: the urban areas only extract their power, they have nothing to do with their well-being.

The introduction to a counter-argument to 'urbanisation' of the form described above was made by His Excellency, the President of Malawi, Dr. Hastings Kamuzu Banda, when he was arguing the case for moving the Administrative capital from Zomba to Lilongwe: that the building of the capital is going to offer employment to a lot of people, meaning more money will get into more pockets. The people whom we will be employing there will have to eat. They will be buying food from our farmers. That means money in the pockets of farmers. When workers and farmers have money in their pockets, they want dresses for their wives, shoes for their wives and children, suits and shirts for themselves. That means money in the pockets of shopkeepers, money in the pockets of businessmen. In other words, money will circulate in the country more and more. That means more factories will have to be built up; so, more development. Monetisation or urbanisation of the indigenous people could be made

without disruptive consequences. Urbanisation could have operated within the traditional institutions of the indigenous society; so far urbanisation has implied too much reorganisation, and I do not personally believe that Malawi has the resources to absorb the whole of its population of 4,300,000 people in an economy based on urban concentration.

In a sense, an economy based on urban concentration is the result of a particular attitude of mind on the part of industrialists and developers. Their tendency to concentrate all development in the areas where the infrastructure of communications, education, health services, electricity and water supply and so on is already fully established, means that the rural areas which have none of these services will never be developed.

As the population continues to grow there will be more people seeking to cultivate the same acres of land until a possible limit of cultivable land is reached. Unless the farming technology is changed the yield per person will gradually fall, with a consequent fall in the standard of living of the rural communities. The strain on the land will also place a strain on the territories of the chieftaincies. Traditionally area chieftaincy boundaries are only definable by, and between, the chiefs, with rivers and mountains being the physical characteristics which normally are chosen to define the chieftaincy, in all tribes in Malawi.

To recapitulate, the indigenous population migrates from the rural areas because:

(a) their standard of living is falling, because the traditional method of farming assumes unlimited supply of land;

(b) the educational programmes inculcated in the young, values which call for an exodus from agricultural activities;

(c) conscious monetisation of the rural areas has demolished the traditional securities of rural life.

'Site and services' in Lusaka; an attempt to help the new urban entrants to fit into modern society. A water stand-pipe is in the foreground.

Temporary shack using an adapted traditional technique in the background and a concrete block house being erected beside it.

Therefore, to be less disruptive it is necessary to go back to the three hierarchies: the family unit, the kinship group and the area chief or the Native Authority. A parallel plan to this was implemented in the Lachish Region in Israel, where the family unit is the economic unit, the *moshav*, or the smallholder's co-operative is equivalent to the kinship group and the rural centre, a group of villages, is equivalent to the area chief. The advantage of thinking in the above way is that like the Israel experiment where they were dealing with people from different cultural backgrounds, Malawi area chieftaincy boundaries encompass all the villages within an area which are from the same tribe, or who at least can trace their history to a common event. Not that there were as many tribes as there were area chiefs because it is possible to have people from the same tribe living under different chiefs; but this could be a localised planning unit, which would not involve disintegrating the traditional communities.

The question is, how does one integrate urbanisation within the traditional kinship groups, so that they, and their institutions, can evolve organically into an urbanised pattern? The first point to examine is that agricultural products need processing before they become consumer or export goods, and that the urban population is fully dependent on the farmers' products for survival. But at the moment, these goods are sold either directly to the market by individual farmers at prices which are very low (because, if he does reach the market, due to lack of storage facilities, the farmer is just too delighted to dispense with his goods as quickly as practicable), or if lucky, he sells them directly to wholesale traders, who play the farmers against one another, forcing them to put their prices down. In my view, a more reasonable proposition would be to re-organise the kinship villages into co-operatives, so that their production and marketing are done on a shared basis.

Each family farm unit would be free to produce as much as is possible and be able to become richer than its neighbour, depending on how much labour the unit invested in its farm. This is unlike the African Socialism of President Nyerere of Tanzania; African socialism as defined in Tanzania, is that in the extended family economy no one is allowed to make personal gains. It is more or less an African version of the Israeli Kibutzim. But what I propose is some form of collectivization in the productive factors, with no limit to what each family can produce, and hence gain, because this is the incentive to work. To plan for this type of fluid urbanisation, it is

Children making mud bricks to serve the new building industry.

necessary to decentralise the decision-making process; that is, to establish a hierarchy of decision-making, more or less as was previously practised in the indigenous society. There are three levels in the hierarchy: macro-planning, working out national demands and supply resources; micro-planning, planning of the individual farm; and the two co-ordinated on an intermediate or regional level, at which level the planners (economic, social, physical and administrative) themselves are fairly autonomous.

The type of planning that has emerged in Malawi, is one where each Ministry has its own way of locating its priorities. At a local level, each departmental representative is directly responsible to the Minister in the administrative capital, and is not involved with any other departmental leader, although both might be aiming at solving the local problems. So that in the finalised plan one gets an educational programme which is not related to the health, or agricultural, or social programmes. The link between the various sections is at the top level only. In the autonomous planning unit here proposed, the various sectional leaders would form an integrated planning team at a regional level, and they would be responsible to the Ministry, in so far as the national inputs are concerned.

To date, there are two encouraging precedents to this proposed resettlement scheme. The first is that the kinship village was itself mobile as long as there was fresh land available; the second, the Young Pioneers, who are trained by the Malawi Government and resettled in rural areas as model farmers. Young Pioneers are trained by a team of specialists: agricultural extension officers, administrators, educators, dieticians, etc., and resettled in the rural areas so that they can act as spearheads of development. On resettlement they build themselves a traditional type of structure, but it is assumed that as they manage their farms better, they will require a more permanent type of shelter.

The national inputs involve the computation of the demands both within and without, and finally this production target is distributed equally to the farmers. Internal demands of agricultural produce could be worked out by the requirements of a balanced diet, taking account of traditional habits of consumption (for example some people in Malawi refuse to eat eggs for fear of becoming sterile), people's income, the climate (which dictates whether people should eat food stuff with high calorific value), etc. Based on such information, a *per capita* food basket could be worked out; this, multiplied by the total population could give the capacity of the internal market

The main shopping street in Blantyre.

The export market involves examining outlets outside Malawi; at the moment it looks as though most of our maize, rice, fruit and other food commodities could easily be exported to the neighbouring countries. The sum total of these two, internal and external demands, gives the size of the target for each agricultural commodity. Also on a national level the productive factors could be analysed, involving physical, technological and organisational, and finally, the human resources.

As for physical resources, because of its elongated shape on the north–south axis and because of its mountainous nature, Malawi offers a variety of climates, and is thus capable of supporting a lot of crops which could bring in the foreign exchange so badly needed. Technological and organisational resources are a matter of policy. Human resource is abundant; the present chaos is not because of lack of know-how, but because of ill-developed infrastructure (communications) services, which means it is difficult to reach the people who need the information.

On a local level there would be the people whose productive capacities one wants to rationalise. This can be done on four levels; economic, social, physical and administrative. The economic plan involves allocating to each family unit its quota of the national target, as defined above; and relating this to the fertility of the soil. The farmers' productive resources should, on full exploitation, be able to earn them an income at least equal to that which his counterpart in town earns. This will be an incentive for the farmer to stay on the land. Again, because most of the production factors require heavy initial investment, the farming units should be organised in a way that would make it possible for a group of farmers to jointly hire equipment such as tractors, combine harvesters, etc.

The social and political plan would work within the traditional hierarchies of the family unit, extended family or kinship group; but in the higher hierarchies, the economic number of people required to support a primary school, a health centre, a cultural hall or a co-operative store, will determine the number of families or kinship villages required to cluster round the service centre; in other words, if one kinship group comprises too few people to support such a centre, two or more kinship groups would have to get together and share it.

On human resources and organisation, it can be observed that at the moment the flight from the land is speeded up because of lack of alternative employment in the rural areas, and lack of amenities. The socio-economic model described above gives a framework in which non-agricultural employment can be provided. Economically, each rural family is going to be encouraged to produce a surplus, which if processed locally, would be sold to the non-agricultural workers. The returns resulting from this would enable the farmers to produce more, they would demand better and bigger processing plants, which in turn would absorb the surplus labour force result-ing on one hand from the natural population growth, and on the other hand from the redundancy created by more efficient means of production.

Such a scheme would encourage the growth of urban communities in the rural areas; the physical move from rural to urban Blantyre would not be necessary. This is a form of resettlement scheme, but as pointed out above, it is not as radical as it sounds for Malawi, because (a) the survival of the present system depends on locational change due to inefficient means of cultivation, (b) the current growth of urban areas (Blantyre, Lilongwe, Mzuzu, Zomba, etc.) implies that the rural population which resided on these areas has to be resettled somewhere, and this has to be decided by the Central Government; (c) the population is growing at the high rate of 3·7% per annum, which means that unless Malawi raises the standard of living of rural population, she will remain a source of cheap labour to South Africa, Zambia, Rhodesia and even Portuguese East Africa, and finally because Malawi, like the countries of the rest of the world, wants to develop, it would be much better if every able-bodied man or woman were to be productively employed.

BIBLIOGRAPHY

APTHORPE, R. J., 'Present interrelations in Central African Rural And Urban Life', being the proceedings of the Eleventh Conference of the Rhodes–Livingstone Institute for Social Research held at Lusaka, Zambia. January 4th–17th 1958.

BETTISON, D. G., Communication Number eleven: 'The demographic structure of seventeen villages,' Blantyre, Malawi. Rhodes–Livingstone Institute, Lusaka, 1958.

BETTISON, D. G., Communication Number twelve: 'The social and economic structure of seventeen villages,' Blantyre, Malawi. Rhodes–Livingstone Institute, Lusaka, 1958.

BETTISON, D. G. and RIENBY, P. J., Communication Number twenty: 'Patterns of income and expenditure,' Blantyre–Limbe, Malawi. Part I: The peri-urban villages. Part II: The urban households. Rhodes–Livingstone Institute, Lusaka, 1961.

KAY, GEORGE, 'Social aspect of village regrouping in Zambia.' University of Hull, Department of Geography. Miscellaneous series No. 7. 1967.

LUNDGREN, THOMAS, SCHLYTER, ANN, and SCHLYTER, THOMAS, 'Zambia, Kapwepwe Compound: a study of unauthorised settlement.' University of Lund. Department of Architecture IIB. Sweden.

MAIR, LUCY, New Nations.

HUNTER, GUY, 'Modernising Peasant Societies.' Institute of Race Relations, 1969.

WEITZ, RAANAN and ROKACH, AVSHALOM, Agricultural Development: Planning and Implementation. D. Reidel publishing company, Dordrecht, Holland, 1968.

DEPARTMENT OF CENSUS AND STATISTICS, 'Malawi Population Census.' Malawi Government, 1966.

DEPARTMENT OF CENSUS AND STATISTICS, 'House-income survey for major urban areas.' Malawi Government, 1967.

DEPARTMENT OF CENSUS AND STATISTICS, 'A Sample Survey of Agricultural Small holdings in the Southern Region of Malawi.' September–November 1965.

DEPARTMENT OF CENSUS AND STATISTICS, 'A sample survey of Agricultural Small holdings in Central Region–Malawi.' April 1966–June 1967.

THE CANIÇOS OF MOZAMBIQUE

Amancio d'Alpoim Guedes

Every city and small town in Moçambique is surrounded by *caniços*. They are the out-buildings of the towns – the places where the servants and the labourers live.

The word *caniço* means reeds; in Southern Moçambique reeds are the traditional building material most frequently used for walling and screens wherever they are available in the rural areas. The reeds are grown, cut and tied into bundles in the river plains and marshes and brought into town by truck. The sight of a loaded reed truck is quite awesome – as the *caniço* is light the volume becomes enormous, and almost hides the truck.

The *caniços* range from villages scattered around small towns, to vast slums and shanty towns made up of many quarters surrounding the larger towns and cities. In the small towns the *caniços* adjoin land where maize, manioc and other crops and fresh vegetables are grown. The sites they occupy are as close as possible to the town. Some are even within the towns occupying land which has not been developed because it was low-lying and

subject to flooding, or because of its irregular or steep configuration.

In Lourenço Marques some of the *caniços* occupy the edges of an old lagoon, an area which floods with any heavy rain, but which is quite close to the main part of town. The hillside above the docks and railway yard is the area where those who work in the port prefer to live. At João Belo, a country town near the mouth of the Limpopo River, the *caniço* occupies the remaining area between the town on the edge of the river and the high ground, and continues along the hillside squeezed between the town and the new residential suburbs. At Inhambane, a district capital on the site of an old *feitoria* (a Portuguese fortified trading post) in Southern Moçambique, the *caniço* has developed along the main road into town and the dwellings are in the palm tree groves.

At Beira, which is very low-lying, the *caniços* are separated into islands occupying whatever ground is slightly higher than the vast marsh, but at Tete, on the Zambeze River they have occupied an area

Air view of a rural village settlement.

View of the Joao Belo caniço *showing a group of traditional huts.*

Rural village house on the mainland near Moçambique Island.

A street on Moçambique Island showing variety of treatment in the traditional style.

parallel to the town on what remains of the high ground. The 'Linguri' quarters in António Enes, the site of the Sultanate of Angoche, are at the side of the town in a low-lying area close to the bay, while in Porto Amélia, the *caniços* are on the beach up against the old part of the town and scattered all around the new town.

In the towns close to the borders to the north and the west, the war has caused people to be brought from the bush to settle in and near to the towns. These settlements are built by the people themselves in the traditional local manner but their density is much higher than that of any traditional rural group.

The layout of the *caniços* is irregular and consists of a system of main access streets and tracks usually wide enough to allow a car or a small truck to pass, and which feed on to many subsidiary narrow passages and short-cuts. Sometimes a street will turn off into a *cul de sac* to form a small communal court-yard or it will widen into an irregular square with a shop on one side. The dwellings consist of huts, shacks and houses. The huts and shacks are often built on the

traditional tribal plan, some using the traditional materials while others are improvised from the scrap and rubbish thrown away from the adjoining city or bought from the scrap dealers. The houses are mostly built out of corrugated iron and wood, but the range of improvised walls and roofs is very great, imaginative use being made of any material available – flattened out tins and drums, old tarpaulins, packing cases, cardboard boxes, plastic sheeting.

Fires are frequent as most of the cooking is done with wood, charcoal or paraffin, and lighting is by candle light or paraffin lamp, and once a big fire gets under way it often spreads and burns down thirty or forty homes before it is put out, for the building materials are very inflammable.

Dotted throughout the *caniços* are the many *cantinas*, as the general stores are called. They have a multiplicity of functions, selling flour, rice, salt and other food-stuffs, lengths of cloth, hardware – and vast quantities of imported wine and local beer – in their dank and roughly furnished bars. One or two tailors or dress-makers

Street in a Beira caniço.

Screen wall and reed shacks in a Lourenço Marques caniço. *The wall is made of flattened paraffin tins.*

Street in a Lourenço Marques caniço *with reed screen walls of court-yards facing the street.*

Three corrugated-iron houses of different status. The girl on the left is on her way to fetch water.

Corrugated-iron house in a Lourenço Marques caniço *with cement block foundation walling.*

Street life in a Lourenço Marques caniço.

Owners' cars parked outside their houses in a Lourenço Marques caniço.

A cantina (*general store*) *in a Lourenço Marques* caniço *with women gathered round the water tap. A cart with bundles of reeds goes past.*

A cantina *at a street crossing in a Lourenço Marques* caniço. *The water tank is on the right.*

generally sit at their sewing machines in the front verandahs making up clothes to order. The *cantinas* are used as local post offices and public telephones, and act as a sort of community centre. They are also the haunt of prostitutes, and some *cantineiros* (shopkeepers) put up rows of rooms at the side of the *cantina* which they let to facilitate this trade and increase their bar sales. Adjoining the *cantina* there is usually a water tap at which water is sold to fill the bottles, tins and old barrels of the inhabitants. When they are provided the municipal water points, which are very few and far between, draw enormous crowds, because the water obtainable from them is free.

Fresh food-stuffs, cloth, reed mats, clay pots, baskets, discarded tins made into mugs, mirrors and all sorts of other things are sold in open markets which spring up off main roads and often occupy vast areas. The market shacks range from open stalls, made from packing cases and sticks, to elaborate boxes in hardboard – always very light and mobile since they often have to move because the land-owners wish to develop the ground on which they stand. Some municipalities have put up organised markets, but these do not have the popularity of the traditional ones because they are not central and the stalls are covered by a large roof, which makes them impersonal. Also, the

Method of wall framing in a traditional house in Northern Moçambique.

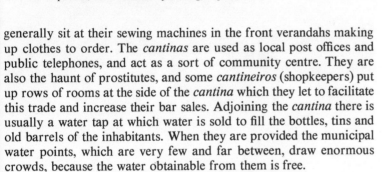

A caniço *depot in Lourenço Marques with sticks and reed bundles for sale.*

rents, licences or dues to be paid are beyond the means of the woman with a little pile of tomatoes, chilis, sweet potatoes or peanuts to sell.

Scattered through the *caniços* are many other shops and workshops, usually attached to dwellings. They are owned by the shoemenders, carpenters, paraffin tin-stovemakers, motor mechanics, basket weavers and many others. The reeds for building are sold in bundles at depots which also stock sticks, cut timber, corrugated iron, both brand new and very old, second-hand windows and doors, hardware and all sorts of scrap. The used materials are extracted from old corrugated-iron buildings in the town which are sold to demolishers.

On arrival at a *caniço* from the bush, the newcomers will either stay with relatives or friends or put up a precarious, temporary shelter made out of scrap, sticks, reeds and mats – a place in which to sleep, wash, cook and keep belongings. Authority to put up even a temporary shelter has to be obtained from the *régulo* or local African chief, and payment has to be made to the chief and to the owner of the ground if it is privately owned. The next step from the temporary shelter is the traditional hut.

A street in the Linguri quarter of António Enes, showing traditional huts and unfinished houses in various stages of construction.

Façade of the house shown on puge 232.

Traditional huts at Linguri with cement blocks being collected for new walls.

206

These are predominantly round in the south of Moçambique and roofed with thatch, and rectangular and roofed with palm leaf tiles or thatch in the centre and in the north. The huts are traditional in plan and section, even if they differ with regard to doors and windows. They open on to a court-yard with a cooking porch and a fenced-in washing area, enclosed by reed walls or some other kind of screening material. The screened court-yard is the real living area of these houses; it is here that the children play, that the wife cooks, where the visitors are received and the pets and chickens are kept.

The walls of the huts are made of reeds, sticks or screens of sticks with stones between them, or of woven mats, depending on what is available in the countryside near by or what is brought into the *caniço* for sale. This walling is often plastered over with earth or earth mixed with a little cement to make the wall proof against water and wind and reduce pests.

These traditional huts are buildings which almost every one knows how to make. The only complex work is the making of the roof structure and this is done by gathering together friends and neighbours to help out with it. Each hut costs approximately 700$00 (£10) which is the equivalent of an unskilled labourer's monthly salary.

From the round or square hut follows the rectangular corrugated iron house with a sawn timber frame and a lean-to corrugated iron roof. These houses usually have a narrow front porch facing on to the street and a central entrance door. They consist of three or six rooms with access through the central room or rooms and a back veranda, and open at the back on to a screened court-yard with a kitchen shack and washing room. The houses are often raised on a cement block base three or four steps high, and some of them have an inner lining and partition walls of cement blocks to fireproof them and to make them cooler and more comfortable.

Great status is attached to the better houses and many Africans who could afford to move into a house or an apartment in the city prefer to remain in the *caniço* and enjoy their high social position and influence. Some owners of even the more modest huts build them with great care and decorate them with painted doors and gates and are very house-proud. Many well-off inhabitants of the *caniços* put up rows of rooms and shacks or have houses built which are let for extremely profitable rents. The shack, the reed or stick hut and the corrugated iron houses are the only kind of dwellings allowed by the authorities in most *caniços* because they are considered temporary and easy to demolish. Most *caniços* are in areas which have not yet been planned or have purposely been zoned for future development in those towns which have a definitive plan. Frequently the land belongs to private individuals who charge a monthly ground rent.

The inability to own the ground on which the house stands is the most negative aspect of life in *caniço*. This gives the people a feeling of insecurity and anxiety and often leads to economic disaster when a house, or group of houses, have to be pulled down because the owner of the ground has managed to obtain authority to develop it or because of road building.

In the few *caniços* and other areas where individual land ownership has been made possible and encouraged, the inhabitants have to build permanent buildings in cement blocks and concrete to be granted full ownership of the ground. The cement blocks are cheap and easy to put up but concrete foundations, beams and slabs are expensive and require some specialised labour. Some municipalities provide cheap transport and some free sand and stone for the foundations as well as a choice of building plans as an encouragement to build.

Completed house in Linguri, made of cement blocks with reinforced concrete slab, roofed in corrugated asbestos.

Rectangular house meticulously built with partly plastered reed walls and corrugated-iron roof. The gate and door are decorated in various colours and fake panes are drawn on to the shutters.

At António Enes, for example, in the African quarter called Bairro Linguri, the municipality has given help and encouragement and has much relaxed building regulations. This has caused the *bairro* to undergo a rapid alteration. Many streets have buildings at various stages of construction and most are being lived in as the building proceeds in fits and starts as the owner can afford it.

Often an existing house in stick and reeds undergoes a metamorphosis into a construction of cement blocks, remaining occupied throughout the operation. These houses, and those in the other *caniços* of Moçambique, borrow their forms and decorations from the houses in the predominantly European suburbs.

It is interesting to compare the *caniço* houses on Moçambique Island with those around the more modern towns, because this island, until very recently, has been an almost untouched monument to the past. Here, therefore, the African houses are derived from the palaces built by the Portuguese merchants, slavers and adventurers of the eighteenth and nineteenth centuries. These houses, like their models, have symmetrical plans and elevations and sometimes have the typical plaster mouldings around the doors and windows as well. They are built of stick screens, filled with stones and plastered over.

The permanent houses in the *caniços* around the modern towns imitate other styles of architecture and a different method of construction. The one traditional feature that remains, however, in all but the most sophisticated dwellings, is the screened courtyard where cooking is done in the open air or in a little lean-to shack. The house proper is built of cement and concrete; the walling, pillars, beams and slab being done by skilled or semi-skilled labourers with the help of the owner and his relations and friends. In this way every one is gradually learning to handle and mix these materials, and cement

Opposite page

Another completed house in Linguri.

Double storey building in Linguri with living quarters above and shop below.

Partly reconstructed house in Linguri, made of cement blocks with reinforced concrete pillars and beams.

blocks have become so desirable that quite a few houses in the bush are being built or rebuilt with cement block walls. So much so that cement block walling and concrete slabs with some kind of roof on top will eventually become the accepted way to build and will in the future replace the old traditional techniques.

But it is a pity that these changes are taking place so rapidly. For at present, when walking through the *caniços*, one is struck by the lack of the usual 'slum' atmosphere so evident in the poor quarters of most cities. These people are certainly as poor as their counterparts in other parts of the world, and their areas lack most of the facilities considered necessary for a good standard of urban living. Perhaps the reason for the difference is that the *caniço* dwellers know how to make their own houses which are very economical and suited to the climate. Indeed, many of them are proud of their homes and put a lot of effort into their decoration and improvement. They do not have water-borne sewerage and electric light in their rural villages, and their daily trek to fetch water is often much longer and more laborious, so the lack of facilities in the *caniços* do not make for a way of life that they are not quite used to. Also, most of the tribes whose members live in the *caniços* have a natural appreciation of cleanliness and tidiness, and the municipalities in Moçambique have provided good cleaning, rubbish collecting and sanitary services. All these things contribute to the quality of life in these quarters, and the spirit of degradation and hopelessness, the filth and neglect found in so many slums are missing here.

The situation is changing, however, especially in the big towns and cities. Rapid expansion attracts increased immigration of workers from rural areas, but also encourages the development of the now valuable land where the *caniços* were situated – meaning more and more people, and less and less convenient land. And in some places the stricter control of building for those who wish to secure their plots enforces a standard far beyond the means of the vast majority of urban workers. The Linguri quarter in António Enes could serve as the example for a workable solution – encouragement of more permanent dwellings, use of the people's own skill and pride in home building, but tolerance and relaxation of standards for the time being. If the bigger cities would apply some of these ideas much misery could be avoided – but it would need imagination and the kind of attitudes not usually held by bureaucratic town planners and municipal authorities.

KOIDU, SIERRA LEONE'S SECOND CITY

Guy Gervis

This is a report from what is probably the only reasonable-sized town in the world growing, with comparatively few restraints, on top of a diamond mine. Koidu, in Sierra Leone, is a town with a present population of about sixty thousand. Economically dependent on diamonds, which are mined both legally and illegally with slight administrative controls, the town is usually tense and interesting. Diamonds symbolise exotic wealth. They are far more valuable than gold, weight for weight, especially large gem stones. So it is at first rather confusing to find that the buildings in the town are rather prosaic, and the place as a whole is rather a mess, despite the numerous Mercedes parked around. While the limited late-night bar life sometimes displays an exotic West African butterfly quality, the buildings themselves do not. But despite this visual flatness, and the not very apt label the journalists have offered of 'Wild West Town', it is fascinating, and worthy of study.

Koidu is on the Guinea Plateau, which is a bumpy one about a thousand feet up in the Kono District of Sierra Leone. It is some two hundred miles east of Freetown, the capital, and thirty miles west of the Guinea border. The climate fluctuates under the influence of the dry *harmattan* air from the desert, especially during December and the following two months, and the humid 'monsoon' air from the Atlantic, giving an annual rainfall of about a hundred inches.

Until the 1930s when diamond-mining started, it was a subsistence farming area, with shifting cultivation, much of it on the hills. On the maps showing economic activity during this period, it appears as a blank. No main trade routes passed through it, and the railway runs across sixty miles to the south. Even now few Kono have settled elsewhere in the country, and until diamond-mining started, few members of other tribes had settled in the Kono District.

The original mining concession to SLST, Sierra Leone Selection Trust, a wholly owned subsidiary of Consolidated African Selection Trust, had covered most of the country. In the 1930s and early 1940s, if children found diamonds lying around, and this certainly happened, they took them to the District Officer, or one of the Europeans working on the mine. It is a period to which some Konos look back with nostalgia, but it was possible because there was no local market for diamonds, a fact which affected the behaviour of Europeans as well as Africans.

Koidu was started in the 1940s. Mr. Koi built the first house, and he is still building with his own hands. *Du* means town, in Kono. The house was on a rise just to the north of the Woyie Stream, which was then being mined. The gravel was being treated in 2/4 Plant, nearer to the Stream. Farther away on the other side was the SLST compound. Two or three hundred yards to the east of Mr. Koi's house a side stream had been dammed up to supply water to the plant for the washing process. This formed Gbensan Lake, and across the dam was a 'dumper line' to take the trucks loaded with gravel to the plant. By 1951 the continuation of this dumper line beyond the dam was the main street to a village with eighty-four houses. The village of Yengema, near the main plant, six miles to the west, where the gravel concentrate was, and still is, taken for the extraction of diamonds, was slightly larger, having one hundred and twenty houses.

The original settlements were similar to those that spring up all over the world next to labour camps in the bush, whether they serve dam sites, road works or mining operations. The wages paid to the labour probably represents the first sizeable cash injection into the area, and the settlements aim to sponge it up by trading.

As soon as an internal market for diamonds developed the growth rate accelerated. Important among the factors responsible for the development of this market was the existence of the Liberian border, about fifty miles to the south-east, across which a fairly liberal view is taken of diamond operations. Another was the spread of mining skills and knowledge concerning diamonds, as a result of the growing number of people who had been involved in operations, mainly as employees of SLST. The last major factor was that the Lebanese spotted an excellent business opening. They already ran most of the medium-sized stores throughout the country, and when they moved into the diamond areas were well placed to operate. These operations were illegal, because SLST had rights over the diamonds throughout the country, but evidently they were profitable.

By the middle of the 1950s there were many hives of illegal digging activity up and down the rivers and streams where the alluvial deposits were to be found. These extended well to the south of the Kono District, and were too widespread for effective police action. It was estimated that in some years more than ten million pounds worth of diamonds were smuggled out of the country. Negotiations between SLST and the Government, which at that time was

Colonial, with a Sierra Leonian Minister of Mines, resulted in a reduction of the concession to two limited areas. Koidu is in the middle of the largest and richest of these concessions. New legislation established licensed mining in the remainder of the deposits, to give an outlet to local initiative, and also to safeguard the Company operation, which produced a substantial part of the national revenue. A Government Diamond Office was set up, to which the licensed dealers could sell.

In terms of easing pressure on SLST these policies were not a long-lived success. Illegal Diamond Mining, IDM, within the concession, especially around Koidu, was increasingly accompanied by subversion within the Company. Diamonds which had already been mined were taken at various points in the processing. These turned up on the internal market, and were either sold eventually to the Government Diamond Office, or smuggled, usually to Liberia, although this traffic had been substantially reduced. An added confusion was that extensive licensed mining developed just outside the concession, and some of the miners lived in Koidu. Nor did the permit system which was established within the concessions succeed in preventing growth of population.

This growth was in fact dramatic. The 1963 census, the first and only national one gave Koidu a population of 14,000. This was almost certainly below the true figure because some people involved in IDM would not have wished to be counted. Yengema had slipped behind with 7,000. The present population of Koidu has been estimated at 60,000, with an urbanising population in the area around it, including Yengema, of at least 30,000, giving a total of around 90,000. On the Koidu-Yengema road, one of the few tarred roads in the area, taxis make more than 2,000 journeys every day, and comprise about a half of the total traffic.

So much for the conditions under which this growth has taken place. Apart from diamonds, and their tremendous economic effects, any view of the town as it is today is dominated by three curiously contradictory aspects. These are the widespread mistrust of SLST, the 'stranger drives', under which non Konos are sometimes driven out of the area, and lastly the imminent completion of the Massingbe Road, on which it will soon be possible to travel direct to Freetown on tarred road. A discussion of these aspects will serve as a framework for a brief examination of economic and social factors, before taking a look at the buildings themselves.

There is nothing unusual in a large foreign company coming under attack in a newly independent country. SLST's annual expenditure in tax, and the cost of the operation in Sierra Leone, excluding capital expenditure, is equivalent to about 40% of the Government's revenue.[1] But diamond-mining companies have always required co-operation with the governments of the countries where they operate. Illegal mining in Sierra Leone has produced enormous amounts of loose money, some of which has been used to engender mistrust so that the illegal operations may continue, and some fairly extreme incidents have occurred.

At the time of writing negotiations have just begun between SLST and the Government who intend to take a 51% share in the Company. The Konos have objected that they are not sufficiently well represented in the negotiations. They have long maintained that they do not get their rightful share of the diamond wealth coming from their land.

The holding of land, or perhaps it should be described as territory, forms a vital part of tribal tradition. SLST's rights to mine diamonds places them in a position of obligation towards the Konos. Paternalism is no longer fashionable, partly because of the lack of initiative it induces, but it does match, to some extent, the tribal system. SLST has remained paternalistic, but in a slightly tetchy way, and certainly not to the extent that the Konos would like. Seen from SLST's viewpoint a large part of the vastly increased local population are stealing their diamonds. To the Konos it is not possible to 'steal' from one's own land. Members of other tribes are of course brothers to the Konos rather than to SLST.

Vast areas of land have been messed up by the mining process, and very little has been rehabilitated for farming. The diamonds are almost entirely alluvial and the mining process consists of the removal of the overburden, which can be up to twenty feet deep, and piling it to one side while the pay gravel, which contains the diamonds is taken out and away to the plants for treatment. The cuts are therefore usually left with piles of earth alongside them, and in addition there is often a water problem. Cuts have to be made for the diversion of streams, to enable mining to take place, and large areas of the mined-out land consists of semi-stagnant lakes, in addition some areas are flooded to protect them from IDM while others provide water for the plants. It is true therefore that large areas of land have been taken out of the farming sector, but it is also true that traditional farming methods have been partly overtaken by the cash economy. When communal and family labour is replaced by labour requiring wages, certain traditional crops are grown at a loss. The changeover to intensive fruit and vegetable farming, which could pay well with the large local market has only just begun, and there are in fact considerable areas of land around Koidu which could be farmed, but at present are not.

The routine and rates of compensation paid, when SLST takes over land being farmed, in order to mine it are well established, and although these rates are ample, friction and misunderstanding continue. But the conflict having the most direct bearing on the town itself is that between building and mining. If it is possible to acquire land bearing diamonds by building on it, this will obviously be done, there were even a few cases where the house itself was used as a shield for a mining operation.

It was along both banks of the Woyie Stream that the main disputes arose, for another settlement had started around the labour compound to the south of the Stream as well as the original settlement to the north, and these two have now fused to form Koidu Town. It was unfortunate that the bed of the Woyie Stream had two unusual characteristics. The distribution of diamonds was such that the plant used during the original mining left quite a number of stones, including large ones, in the tailings. SLST intended to re-mine at a later date with better equipment, but not unnaturally the area became well favoured by IDM, and in fact the whole of the Stream valley is reminiscent of a First World War battlefield. The other problem was that tests on the rock strata below part of the Stream gave incomplete results of a kind likely to make diamond prospectors, with thoughts of the Great Hole of Kimberley, cautious. SLST were thus holding land which they had already mined, and which could be extremely useful to the town's development because it adjoined the central area.

In Kono, land is held in trust for the people by the chiefs. They organise the use of land for both farming and building purposes, and receive gifts when granting the right to use land. Translated into the middle of a prosperous town, this system represents a considerable business for the chiefs, with no accounts to be kept, and the chiefs were unlikely to be co-operative in trying to reduce the growth of population. The multiplicity of chiefdoms increased this difficulty; the town proper covers two, Gbense, the most favoured, to the north and east of the Woyie Stream, Tankoro to the south and west. This has led to the town's official and rather clumsy title of Koidu/New Sembehun. Until recently it was generally known as Sefadu, which is the small village where the District Headquarters are sited, half a mile away. This is in another chiefdom, while Yengema is in a fourth one.

The 'stranger drives' have been adopted as a policy by successive governments because, by coincidence, they give satisfaction not only to the Konos, who feel that their position within their own 'nation' is being weakened by the influx of other tribes, but also to SLST. The drives take place at varying intervals, and take the form of a build-up of troops and police, who not only check on illegal mining, but also evict from the concession those who do not hold the necessary permit. These drives are often carried out with zest because many of the participants raise considerable sums of cash by way of sales of permits, and release after arrest. In fact they represent a form of unofficial, although at times extensive, taxation of the area. The population figures alone give a fair idea of how ineffective these drives have been.

Drives against strangers have recently become common in tropical Africa. The justification for them is often based on the theory that outsiders keep jobs from indigenous people. This is often quite false because outsiders, with fewer family ties, are likely to show more economic initiative, sometimes creating employment rather than taking it. In Kono it is true that many strangers are more successful than the Konos themselves.

SLST has been blamed for the influx of non-Kono people, and with the exception of the Lebanese there is some truth in this. When they started mining in the area they needed skilled workers of various kinds. The Konos were subsistence farmers of restricted experience, and many people were employed from other tribes because they required less training to become useful. This meant that when the diamond rush started there were many Temnes and Mendes, in particular, who had relations in Kono, and who therefore had somewhere to stay when they first came there.

At the 1963 census there were still a majority of Konos in the Chiefdoms throughout the District. This is unlikely to be so any more in Gbense and Tankoro, and in the urban areas of these Chiefdoms it is possible that the Konos have been outnumbered by one of the other tribes, the most likely being Temne. Inevitably this

Open land near the centre of Koidu, undeveloped in the squalid sprawl of the town.

Old 2/4 plant and the bed of the Woyie Stream, where extensive illicit mining has taken place.

situation has led to a weakening of the authority of the local Chiefs. This has been increased by the decline of the Poro societies in the urban area, because it was through these that the Chiefs retained their traditional power over the young men of the tribe. The custom of other groups appointing headmen, who were acknowledged by the local Chief has also lapsed, except among the Fulas. The power of Chiefs throughout the country had already been weakened when they were removed from their traditional position of President of the Native Courts. These are now appointed by Government.

This weakening of the traditional authority has not been accompanied by a corresponding strengthening of the local Administration, which has remained much as it was at the end of the Colonial period, and it is not altogether surprising that the local Members of Parliament are trying to obtain greater local influence. A Town Council was set up in Koidu early in 1969, but this was done under an old ordinance, and it does not at present have the power to achieve much more than a tidying up operation. Much of the control is held by the Ministries in Freetown, but the administrative machinery is awkward, and communication difficult in the extreme. It is virtually impossible to telephone out of Koidu, and there are very few lines within it. The Town Council, for instance, has no telephone.

This is part of a serious lack of investment in the area for which the Konos blame alternately the Government and SLST. There is still no water supply, although SLST donated sufficient funds over four years ago. The funds 'ran out' when the project was two-thirds completed. The electricity supply is woefully inadequate. There has been a recent increase in non-government schools, but many Kono children board at the better schools in Kenema, Bo and Freetown. The few tarred roads in the town are badly pot-holed; the remainder are bumpy and dusty, which brings us to the last of the three contradictory factors dominating the town today.

The Massingbe Road will be completed at about the same time as the railway is phased out. The only road connection from Koidu used to be south on a laterite road, to the line of the railway which served the coffee and cocoa area, and it was reasonable enough to regard the life of the town as a main centre to be limited by the diamond period. There are a number of towns around Sierra Leone which have suffered sharp declines, mainly in connection with changes in the transport network. But the new road is a major change for the better. It cuts straight across country bridging in particular the Sewa River, which was a major barrier, and it makes it certain that Koidu will remain an important town, and quite possible that it will retain its present position of second by size in the country, although it is at present behind both Bo and Kenema, 27,000 and 7,000 at the last census, in terms of provision of facilities. The fact that there will be diamonds found in the area long after the main mining operation has been completed is important, because this is an obvious attraction, but so also are the constrictions on the growth of Freetown. Sierra Leone needs another growth point for the provision of urban employment.

But investment in the town at present is limited, mainly consisting of housing. Much of it is rented, and a fair proportion mortgaged in order to raise capital for mining operations. The other main investment is transport, both taxis, and small pick-up lorries known as poda-podas. These have generated filling stations, and repair garages. There are two branches of Freetown firms and over thirty small units struggling with very small technical knowledge. There is no technical training available in the area outside SLST. There are a few bakeries, two cinemas, one small rice mill, and many sewing machines. The agricultural station is hardly operating in terms of encouraging and advising local farms, although some small vegetable and poultry units have started recently on more forward-looking lines.

Koidu is notoriously expensive. Rents and most goods cost more than in other parts of the country. The standard fare for a 'collective' taxi is 4s. As a result goods travel to Koidu from all over the country. Vegetables come from Freetown, and chickens, and on occasion cattle, are trucked equivalent distances. This is despite high transport charges. At present it costs 10s to transport a bag of cement from Freetown.

The future will depend very largely on whether more diverse investments are made in the area. The vast majority of the cash made at present goes out. There are three reasons for this: most of the people making money come from outside the area; the difficulties placed in the way of outsiders in securing any investment, mainly through land tenure; and the high rate of unofficial taxation which has already been mentioned. But whatever happens the new road will ensure Koidu's future as an important trading centre.

With the bad roads, dust, heavy traffic, heat and activity in the middle of Koidu, the town often seems a mess. But viewed from one of the hills around, it can be seen to be set in a fair and pleasant valley. With the eyes half closed, perhaps somewhere near Florence, no dramatic hills near by, and an undulating valley floor. When rain has cleared the air, the Tingi Hills which go over 6,000 feet, twenty-five miles to the north-east, stand up clearly with a rather fine craggy outline.

The town has grown out along the four main roads in a fairly regular way, with a constriction around the bridge across the Woyie Stream. The two Mosques are the only noticeable break in the pattern of low pitched roofs. The pattern of infilling between the roads becomes more confused, further away from the centre, and the existence of swamps, lakes and stream valleys add to the irregularities, but also break up the areas of housing. The main stores which are two-storey buildings do not extend very far beyond the original main street. The smaller stores line the main streets further out and are also fairly widely scattered. The market is squashed into an area immediately adjoining the centre, which has become quite inadequate for the volume of trade that is now transacted. Trading also spreads along the main streets. A wholesale section to the fruit and vegetable market has developed just across the road from the main market, in front of the local lock-up. The Government Hospital, which has far less equipment and staff than the SLST Hospital at Yengema, is sited beyond Gbesan Lake, rather unfortunately next to the town electricity generating station. The Casino, which is rather a dreary little building, is perched on one of the hills.

Sefadu, the District Headquarters is organised on rather more colonial lines, with a scattering of larger houses on the hills for senior officials.

Obtaining the right to build on land involves dealing with both the

Chiefdom Authority and, until recently the Health Superintendent. Some of the greedier chiefs will obtain money from two people for the same land on occasion, and the Health Department, who were administering the Health Rules, also reckoned to run the business at a profit. As a result by no means all land disputes involve SLST. The Town Council, which was set up early in 1969 has not yet succeeded in regularising the situation, partly because at the time of writing, there is some doubt concerning its legal right to do so.

The main provisions of the Health Rules establish a 'town lot' of 70 feet by 90 feet, which must adjoin a street. One third only of this may be built on, giving a built area of 2,100 square feet. Normal occupancy varies between twenty to thirty people, giving between 70 and 100 square feet per person. At the 1963 census 37% of the local population were under fifteen years of age.

The Rules also enforce minimum distances between buildings, 10 feet between corrugated iron roofs, 20 feet to a latrine. Pressures are greater in the centre, and in some areas extra extensions, and 'temporary' buildings, have created some very confused and confined spaces. But if these rules were administered properly they would enable the growth of Koidu to be kept under reasonable control until it become possible to introduce more sophisticated regulations.

Sierra Leone has no very developed indigenous building tradition. Around the country traditional house types vary, being predominantly circular in the north and rectangular in the south. Compound plans with enclosing walls exist in the north, but not in a sophisticated form. In Kono, as a result of the Mende wars, hilltop villages are one of the traditional types, and a number of these survive. There is usually a mixture of circular and rectangular mud walls, the houses being close together with steep, thatched roofs.

Creole houses around Freetown are quite different, going up to two and three storeys, with a rather special line in dormer windows in the upper storey. The chief's house at Kayima, 30 miles from Koidu has used some of the Creole motives to make an imposing building, but only one house in Koidu has attempted anything like it. The other noticeable type comes usually from the north where the Muslim influence is stronger. The house in Kabala is a good illustration. Nothing as extreme as this has been built yet in Koidu, although the general form, and many of the details do occur.

Until four years ago there was virtually only one plan for single-storey houses in Koidu, which was the same as that of the larger houses in many parts of the country. It consisted of a large central parlour, running from front to back of the main rectangular house, with bedrooms opening off both sides, and a verandah to the front. Variations included projecting the bedrooms on one or both sides into the verandah, giving rooms with external entrances, or turning one of the bedrooms on the verandah side into a store, with big double doors. The kitchen block which used to consist of a verandah where cooking could take place under cover in the rains, with a store and

Typical street, ending in a dried up swamp.

The chief's house at Kayima, thirty miles from Koidu.

house in Kabala in the north of Sierra Leone.

An 'H'-plan house in Koidu, a form which is becoming increasingly common.

bedroom or two beyond, added more bedrooms as the pressure on accommodation increased. In the main house it also became common to add an additional room in the back corner of the parlour, reducing through ventilation, but adding to the number of rooms available. It was at this point in the development that the only Kono architect and contractor, S. L. Matturi, started building what became known as 'H' plan houses, with the intention of improving ventilation. This form of building has now become part of the vernacular, and there are even examples out in bush villages in mud construction. One of the main reasons for the success in Koidu it seems, is that the plan is easy to subdivide into three units consisting of a parlour with a bedroom each side of it, and this makes it very profitable for letting.

There are no thatched roofs now in the town; nearly all are of currugated iron, with a few of fine gauge corrugated aluminium. The majority of new buildings have walls of sandcrete blocks, often with a pattern or 'stone' texture cast on one side. Fancy projecting pointing is sometimes used, which can be picked out in paint in a different colour to the blocks. Mud blocks are still made in the dry season, but they tend to be used on the edges of the town. The shortest construction time is achieved by timber pole and lattice construction, with mud ball infill. Some of the 'illegal' buildings are constructed in this way in addition to some in outlying areas.

Most buildings are on laterite which gives a good foundation, and trenches do not often go down more than a foot or so. Concrete footings are unusual, blocks layed flat being the normal procedure. Good sands and gravel are available, floors are raised at least 6

One of the smarter small stores.

An 'H'-plan house in a village twenty miles from Koidu.

Looking over Koidu from the hill to the north of the town.

Main Kainhardu road, principal shopping street.

inches, and blinded before screeding. Ready-made doors and win-dows are available, but many are still made on site. Blockwork wall are mainly 4 inches throughout. The $3 \times 1\frac{1}{2}$-inch wall plate is bolte to the top of the wall, and roof joists and purlins, are often of th same section, with heavier members at the ridge and hips. Fascia commonly 9×1 inch. In some work the roof joists are made of pole of from 2 to 3 inches diameter. Internal finish is usually cement san render, with hardboard ceilings as an optional extra. Latrines are the pit type, and in Koidu they tend to be dug deep.

Plans have to be drawn for building permit purposes, and these ar usually carried out by SLST surveyors, or members of the Healt Department. Such plans do not always determine what gets buil There are only two contractors who keep any record of their opera tions, and getting a house built is often arduous. The usual pro cedure is that the building owner buys the material and pays th contractor in four stages. These are at commencement of the work when the walls have been completed, when the roof is on, and a completion.

While diamonds last in any quantity around Koidu, there wil probably also be some element of confusion. At present a 'strange drive' has left the place looking empty, although it is said that th outlying villages are now rather full. Large numbers have been take down to help build some barracks, which is a new technique, and number of busloads of 'single girls' were collected to cook for them At the same time work is at last starting again on the installation o the water supply, a new electricity generating station is under con struction, a new telephone exchange is to be installed and approva has been given for a timber mill and woodworking plant, some mile down the new road.

Across the lake, beyond the verandah where this report is being written an SLST helicopter has just buzzed an energetic little grou on a Saturday afternoon dig. Most of them ran off, but the chance are that they will be back again soon.

NOTE

[1] Sierra Leone Government, *National Accounts*, Central Statistics Office, Freetown June 1969 and *Daily Mail* (Sierra Leone), February 4th, 1970, p. 3.

BIBLIOGRAPHY

CLARKE, J. I., *Sierra Leone in Maps*, University of London Press Ltd., 1966.
LAAN, H. L. VAN DER, *The Sierra Leone Diamonds. An Economic Study covering the years 1952–61*, London, 1965.

ACKNOWLEDGEMENTS

The Ministry of Housing and Country Planning, Freetown.
Sierra Leone Selection Trust.
J. M. Dent, Agricultural Consultant to the project.

PATTERNS OF HUMAN ENCOUNTER IN MOROCCAN BIDONVILLES

Badi G. Foster

The rapid and continuing growth of shantytowns in urban Africa offers an overt manifestation of social change. The movement of people from rural to urban milieux underlines a far deeper process of transformation in the new nations of Africa. The sight of thousands of shacks crowded together evokes responses which range from embarrassment on the part of host country officials to romantic illusions of 'modern citizens in the making' by the visitor. These responses contribute little to our understanding of the reality of life in shantytowns and the social dynamics which distinguish it from surrounding neighbourhoods.

The literature available on African urbanisation and the growth of shantytowns suffers from two competing views, both of which are inadequate. The first treats the existence of shantytowns as if they were communities of pathologies which endanger an otherwise healthy society. Residents of these communities are seen as being irresponsible, lazy degenerates, beggars, pimps and prostitutes. Family life is considered unstable and destructive of the better qualities of human beings such as cleanliness, the desire to work and a willingness to collaborate with others. The lack of community institutions and spirit is used to explain the social pathologies which run rampant. Inhabitants of shantytowns are classified as occupying the bottom rung of the social ladder because they have an inadequate orientation towards the future. They have an extremely difficult time imagining a future and an even more difficult time disciplining themselves to sacrifice the present for future satisfaction. In other words shantytowns are lower class or *lumpenproletariat*, which means that they represent a burden which the more progressive and responsible classes must support. Shantytowns are problems that must be solved; problems that require vast quantities of time and resources that could be better spent in other areas of human concern. *Bidonvilles* must be removed by assimilating their residents into a healthy mainstream of the larger society. The paramount questions of this school of thought are (a) How do you absorb, eradicate or bulldoze shantytowns? and (b) How do you turn degenerate people into useful and productive citizens?

The other dominant view on shantytowns in Africa derives from the independence struggle of such nations as Algeria. Frantz Fanon best describes the belief that shantytown dwellers will provide the revolutionary force necessary to liberate Africa from the bonds of colonialism and neo-colonialism. 'The men whom the growing population of the country districts and colonial expropriation have brought to desert their family holdings circle tirelessly around the different towns, hoping that one day or another they will be allowed inside . . . For the lumpen-proletariat, that horde of starving men, uprooted from their tribe and from their clan, constitutes one of the most spontaneous and the most radically revolutionary forces of a colonised people.'[2]

In this context, the masses of people moving to the cities and finding shelter in the mushrooming shantytowns represent the emergence of new citizens necessary to build new societies. Rather than depict these inhabitants as the dregs of life, this view holds them as the forerunners of a liberated people.

There are two major assumptions which underpin the view that shantytowns are unique repositories of revolutionary forces. The first assumption is the belief that recent urban migrants have suffered from profound trauma as they were uprooted from their rural setting. This trauma has made them more susceptible to fundamental transformation of human relationships than the urban middle and upper classes. *Bidonville* residents in search of new life styles are prepared for sacrifice in the building of a just and coherent society because they have little to lose and much to gain. The second assumption holds that shantytowners, having lived on the periphery of urban life, are less likely to rush blindly to imitate the folly and cruelty of the colonial and post-independence urban bourgeoisie.

These dominant views of shantytowns are inadequate and misleading for understanding the realities and dynamics of *bidonvilles* in Africa, and Morocco in particular. The first view stresses the pathologies of shantytown life which forces the reader to conclude that *bidonvilles* have little of positive and creative resources that can be used to rehabilitate them. *Bidonvilles* are considered unique in their lack of stable social institutions and human relationships. Employing this viewpoint, it is impossible to explain the stability and regularity of life in Moroccan shantytowns. It is unrealistic to believe that thousands of people can live in close proximity and engage in a struggle for survival, without some forms of order and predictable behaviour. This is not to say that the social institutions of shantytowns are perfect or totally adequate but it is false to suggest that these communities are devoid of the variety of social mechanisms found in other communities. It is clear that the inadequacy of this view of shantytowns stems from the class and cultural bias of its authors. If one holds a western middle class community as the model and standard for comparison, then it is not surprising that a non-western, lower-class shantytown should be viewed as pathological.

The 'radical' view of shantytowns is inadequate because it tells the reader what the authors would like to see, rather than what actually exists. This view assumes that urbanisation is the key variable in explaining the social and political transformation of *bidonville* inhabitants. Other factors such as education, length of residency, religion, may be of more importance. No attempt is made in this viewpoint to outline the process of transformation and revolutionary consciousness which are said to exist in shantytowns. There is little evidence to support this viewpoint, either in Moroccan shantytowns or in shantytowns in other parts of Africa. The reality of *bidonville* life suggests that its residents are more prone to adapt rural life styles and values to urban conditions in an effort to acquire the material comfort of the urban working classes. Traditional and 'non-revolutionary' political and social symbols are mixed with demands for justice and compassion. It may be true that justice and compassion can only be achieved after the revolution, but such consciousness is rare among people lacking in formal education and leisure time for analysis. Finally, the processes of rapid urbanization and the resultant creation of shantytowns, have existed for over forty years, yet the residents of shantytowns have not played a significant role in the numerous political revolutions that have taken place. The question must be, therefore, where were the revolutionary *cadres* of the shantytowns?

The phenomenon of rapid urban growth in Africa and the resulting shantytowns that mushroom in the major cities cannot be understood unless it is placed in the context of a more general revolution of modernisation. This revolution goes beyond what many describe as a 'revolution of rising expectations' normally associated with the developing non-western nations. The hallmark of modern life is the rapidity, persistence and pervasiveness of change. What we see in the events that bombard us daily is the largely unconscious attempt of man to deal with change, especially in the ways the self is related to others. The patterns of human encounter which have been used to relate man to other individuals, groups and ideas are proving to be inadequate for coping in any lasting fashion with the crucial issues of conflict, collaboration, change, continuity and justice. What is unique to this revolution of modernisation is that it affects western and non-western, white and non-white; in short it is universal and there is no evidence that any one culture, nationality, ethnic group or economic class has any inherent advantage. In this context, shantytowns in Morocco simply offer a case study of the revolution of modernisation. However, it is important that one realises that the issues which confront the *bidonville* resident are fundamentally no different than those faced by the urban middle and upper classes or those faced by rural communities in Morocco or in other societies.

A new framework of analysis developed by Manfred Halpern has proven to be most encouraging in the study of Moroccan *bidonvilles*.[3] Briefly summarised, Halpern maintains that the patterns of encounter which have bound individuals, groups and concepts and which give man the capacity to deal with the most basic issues of life, are being rendered incoherent. This incoherence, i.e. the lack of agreement as to which pattern of encounter should be used, between self and others, prevents any satisfactory resolution of the five central issues of all human relationships: How do men bind each other in collaboration yet free each other for conflict from opposing positions; assure continuity in their relationship with each other yet allow for change in the balance of costs and benefits in their relationship; and thus produce justice? The breaking of connections between the self and others is the hallmark of the revolution of modernisation. Persistent and permanent change which characterises this revolution is often unintended, owing to a lack of perception and action. The price of incoherence is described as repression of the self and others; deprivation; apathy and normless violence. Finally, Halpern has developed a typology of eight different patterns of encounter, two of which will be discussed later. Before moving to the definition of patterns of human encounter and their empirical examples, a brief discussion of the origins and present realities of Moroccan *bidonvilles* is in order.

Beginning with the successful pacification of Morocco by the French in 1934, the movement of people from the countryside to the city became noticeable. The destruction of traditional institutions such as the *agadir* (communal storehouses to be used in times of drought, floods or insurrection) by colonial forces and the conscious efforts to force Moroccan peasants into the money economy of the protectorate, contributed greatly to the flow of migrants to the large industrial areas on the Atlantic coast.

Historically, population movements in Morocco have followed a south-to-north pattern which persists today. However, today's migrant arrives in the city alone or at best with a few male friends. No longer does one witness large numbers of people from the same tribe descending on a city to establish a *homogeneous community* within the city limits. These *douars* were prevalent in the 1930s and 1940s and they constituted the first *bidonvilles* in the modern era. The homogeneity of these *douars* was crucial to the economic and psychological adjustment of the new migrants. It is accurate to refer to these communities as urban villages.

As the number of migrants increased, and as suitable housing became scarce, the homogeneity of existing *douars* decreased. While many of the newest migrants sought shelter in the traditional quarters, e.g. the Old Medina and the New Medina, those migrants who desired to establish a household had little choice but to look to the shantytowns. This pressure for housing in the shantytowns and the resulting fortunes made from real estate speculation slowly transformed older *douars* into heterogeneous communities in terms of tribal origin, education and economic status. One may still find streets or sub-sections that are surprisingly homogeneous in these terms, but the urban villages, with their characteristic institutions and values, no longer exist. One unfortunate consequence of this change has been that the literature, social theories and public policy do not adequately reflect these developments. A time-lag in our analysis of shantytowns in Morocco explains, in part, the misleading images of these communities.

The major cause for continued migration from the countryside to the shantytowns of the cities, stems from a crisis in agriculture. This crisis is the result of numerous factors such as (*a*) unequal distribution of land ownership, (*b*) a land tenure system which places the

Typical residential street. Freshly dyed yarn is put out to dry on the side of houses. Weaving blankets is a widespread cottage industry. At the end of the street, one can see the more prosperous working-class neighbourhoods.

burden of innovation on the shoulders of the sharecropper, (c) abuse of the land by shallow ploughing, over grazing, de-forestation and soil depletion, (d) lack of fertilisers and other modern techniques in addition to few credit facilities for purchasing equipment, (e) laws of inheritance which frustrate economical production and (f) a peasant mentality of caution and uncertainty as to the future. This crisis of agriculture has meant, in simple terms, that the land cannot support the population. That percentage which cannot be supported moves to the city even though it may be common knowledge that life in the city may prove to be equally harsh. Realistically, one cannot expect the rate of migration to decrease until some satisfactory solution is found for the crisis in agriculture.

Of the fourteen million people in Morocco over 30% live in urban areas. With an annual population growth of over 3%, it is estimated that one-fourth, approximately 600,000, of the rural population increase, migrated to urban areas each year. This influx, when added to the natural urban population growth, accounts for an overall annual rate of urban growth of 6%. The national population has doubled in the last twenty-eight years while the urban population has done the same in sixteen years.

The number of shantytown residents ranges from 1·5 to 2 million people. The vast majority of these people is found in the cities of Casablanca, Rabat, Sale, Kenitra and Fez. Casablanca ranks first in number of *bidonville* residents with over 400,000. Although the Government has embarked on a policy of eradicating shantytowns it is unclear whether the number of *bidonville* residents has decreased. Aerial photographs taken periodically testify to the silent growth of new dwellings in established *bidonvilles*. Indications are that government policy priorities may shift to the countryside where efforts will be taken to retain people on the land and thereby reduce the rate of migration and shantytown growth. What is clear, however, is the fact that substantial numbers of people will continue to live in *bidonvilles* for the foreseeable future. Therefore it is crucial that one avoids the ostrich-like posture of pretending to ignore that which exists.

The realities of life in Moroccan *bidonvilles* can be described in a number of ways, although no one way will convey in the fullest sense the view from below. On first contact the visitor is struck by the sheer number of people compressed into a small area. During the day bands of young children play in the streets and vacant areas making sure that they do not fall into large puddles of drainage water. Women of all ages move about to complete their chores before the men arrive in the early evening. Those men who have employment return on bicycles while those unsuccessful in their search for gainful employment return on foot. The smells of urine, garbage and decay are mixed with the hot sun, blowing dust and millions of flies. The universal burden of poverty is apparent and the visitor can hardly wait to escape the reality of human despair.

The physical location of *bidonvilles* is more a result of real estate speculation than government planning. The immediate consequence is that too often shacks have been constructed on land that was ill-prepared for this use. Drainage is a serious problem not only during the rainy season but also throughout the year, due to the absence of sewerage systems. There is no electricity and the number of public fountains and toilets is totally inadequate. Efforts of individuals to make improvements in these services are discouraged as a result of government policy to avoid making *bidonvilles* too attractive, for fear that this would attract more migrants.

It is estimated that at least 60% of shantytown residents own their shacks. In most cases the land is owned either by the Government or by private real estate interests. No rent is paid for government land. The shack normally consists of two rooms and an open patio which is used for cooking and cottage industry works. The total area covered by the shack is approximately 20 square metres and it rises to a height of around 2·5 metres. The Government calculates six residents per shack although the average may be higher. For those who do not own their shacks, rents may run from 5 to 20 dollars a month depending on size, location and condition. It is estimated that 400,000 cannot pay a monthly rent of 4 dollars.

The concern for housing among *bidonville* residents is greater than might be expected. Their desire is for a home, made of brick or concrete, which belongs to them and which is impregnable to fire, flood and government. With this form of security they reason that survival would be ensured. This concern for housing runs counter to government policies aimed at absorbing existing *bidonvilles*. The amount of new housing being built to absorb the *bidonvilles* is totally inadequate yet the Government cannot sanction private efforts to make wooden, tar paper and tin shacks more permanent. To do so would turn *bidonvilles* into permanent communities and thereby signal to large numbers of rural peasants that migration to the cities is the path to a better life.

The ambiguity of government policy and implementation creates a tension in the lives of *bidonville* residents that exemplifies the general tensions they experience in most areas of human life. They are betwixt and between in social categories and benefits. Although they desire adequate and secure shelter, their own efforts to attain such an objective must be tempered and subsequently thwarted by government actions. An example can be found in the elaborate procedure the resident must go through in order to make necessary repairs to his shack. Official permission must be obtained from the local official for a 'repair permit' before any repairs or additions are made to the exterior of the shack. The bureaucratic red tape involved in the request for a repair permit is sufficient to discourage most from applying. Clandestine activities are the logical alternative; however it is virtually impossible to be clandestine in such a densely populated community. Your business is your neighbour's business and what your neighbour knows the local officials will know. Thus the *bidonville* resident must contend not only with public officials but also with his peers. It seems as though the objective of government policy is to discourage *bidonville* residents so that they will eventually seek alternative housing, thereby gradually eliminating shanty towns. The problem is that there is no acceptable alternative and the result is the squeeze and tension felt by the *bidonville* resident. Public works projects in the general vicinity of *bidonvilles* must be guarded throughout the night so as to prevent residents from pilfering materials which can be used to improve the shacks. Recently materials for constructing a wall around a local football playing field disappeared within three days of delivery. A stroll through the nearby shanty town revealed that the residents had 'discovered' these materials and had proceeded to build concrete surfaces in front of their doors.

The educational situation reflects a similar ambiguity in the lives of *bidonville* residents. Shortly after Morocco received its independence from France, steps were taken by the Government to institute a policy of compulsory education. Rapid population growth and limited public funds have resulted in a situation where a space in the classroom is not as compulsory as might be expected. Under these conditions it should be no surprise that the educational opportunities available to *bidonville* residents are restricted. This restriction derives from (a) the nature and organisation of Moroccan education, (b) the prejudice of middle class oriented educators against the urban poor and (c) the failure to absorb recent graduates in a non-expanding economy.

Although Arabic is the official language of the nation, French as a vehicle of expression in the modern economic and social sector remains dominant. The dual importance of French and Arabic is reflected in the national educational system, where French is emphasised as a requisite for entrance into the better educational institutions and work situations. Those students who receive their education entirely in Arabic face the prospect of limited access to the few jobs open to recent graduates. The apparent second class quality of Arabic education in an officially Muslim state poses one of the fundamental issues in the development of Morocco. Finally, pedagogists argue that the majority of Moroccan students are stunted in their intellectual growth, because they must master not only literary Arabic but also French, while learning basic concepts of education. The result is a growing number of students who are proficient in neither literary Arabic nor French. This failure to develop students in language skills is most apparent among the children of the *bidonvilles*.

Bidonville parents have the following educational alternatives for their children: Koranic *Msids*, public schools and private schools. The Koranic *Msids* are schools of religious instruction for the young. Their nearest equivalent in western societies could be the

View of a business avenue. Horse-drawn carts are collecting used wood to be sold to the local bakeries. Public lighting, recently installed, is restricted to major streets within bidonvilles.

catechism classes of the Roman Catholic Church. *Msids* are directed by the *oufkihs* of each mosque where classes are held six days a week.[4] Curriculum is based on the Koran and tuition varies according to what each family can pay. The majority of students in the *msids* are pre-school age from 4–7 years of age. For those students who do not succeed in being admitted into the public schools and who cannot afford the fees of private schools, continued attendance of the *msids* remains the only alternative. Such a student after numerous years can look forward to becoming an *oufkih*.

The most widely employed alternative is the public school. Admission to these schools is limited to certified residents whose children have not passed their seventh birthday before November of the new school year. Proof of age under these circumstances is crucial but sometimes difficult for shantytown dwellers. There are no public or private schools within the *bidonvilles* so it is necessary for students to walk to adjoining neighbourhoods. The large number of school-age children and the limited spaces has made it necessary for public schools servicing *bidonville* children to operate on double shifts. Under these conditions students who have problems in a learning situation are often weeded out after several years of attendance.

The final alternative open to *bidonville* parents is to send their children to private schools. These schools are monitored by the Ministry of Education and follow a curriculum similar to that found in the public schools. Tuition averages ten to fifteen dollars a month which places this option out of reach for the very poor. Private schools are often housed in vacant buildings which were designed for single family residence. Overcrowding and lack of facilities characterise these schools and it is no surprise that these factors have an unfavourable effect on the learning process.

The performance of *bidonville* students in public and private schools is adversely affected by the bias of the education professionals. In general, students from shantytowns are viewed as coming from an environment which is vulgar and pathological. Words such as 'ignorant' and 'savage' are used frequently when *bidonville* students are discussed. Teachers complain that they receive little help from the parents in working with the children. The absence of parent-teacher contact is attributed to the ignorance of the parent. Parents seem to believe that their responsibility is simply to make sure that the children attend school. They consider it beyond their competence to assist their children in classroom assignments. While middle-class students may have a time and place set aside at home for study, the *bidonville* student must be content with the lack of privacy and space characteristic of *bidonvilles*.

The *bidonville* student who persists in his education faces additional barriers as he continues. It is clear to him that there are many walking the streets looking for work, even though they have been successful in their studies. Furthermore, as he progresses in his studies his material deprivation becomes more apparent to himself and his classmates which may cause him to reconsider his decision to remain in school. If he cannot be assured, or guaranteed, material progress at the end of his studies then it may be preferable to leave school in search of some mechanism which will allow him at least to acquire such outward symbols of progress as new clothes and a motorcycle.

The large number of shantytown youth who leave school prior to graduation points to a double loss. Not only do they lack the formal training and skills and diploma required for employment in the modern sector of the economy but they also lack the traditional skills which could provide some form of employment. It is too late for them to become apprentices in carpentry, blacksmithing or tailoring. These drop-outs from school are miseducated in the true sense and they are treated as such not only by outsiders but also by some within the community. Quite often the student has alienated members of his family or community in his struggle to remain in school. It is difficult for many to understand the strain and tension, as well as the special needs, of a student. Therefore, when requests are made for quiet by the student or when the student makes a statement criticising *bidonvilles*, those around him may resent his pretence that he is better, or requires special attention. Finally, the Government is aware of the growing dilemma facing the miseducated in the *bidonvilles*. Recent laws establishing compulsory military service have been promulgated and it is hoped that two years in military service will not only defuse a potentially explosive situation but will also provide an alternative method for teaching basic skills for economic success.

The employment situation of *bidonville* residents is one characterised by massive unemployment, and underemployment. There are no precise statistics which measure the degree of unemployment but government estimates range from 55% in Casablanca to lower percentages in the smaller cities of Kenitra and Fez. The majority of the employed occupy positions in the tertiary sector of the economy and generally involve clandestine selling of goods and services on a limited day-to-day basis. Within *bidonvilles* there exists a limited class of shopkeepers who service the daily needs of the population. Grocers, barbers, water carriers, public bath attendants, fuel merchants, bakers and cycle mechanics represent the range of shopkeepers and petty merchants within the *bidonvilles*. While the major-

ity of these merchants operate on a limited scale with few opportunities for expansion there exists a notable exception. Berbers, as a distinct ethnic group, control the retail grocery business in shanty towns as well as in other sections of the cities. A high degree of group solidarity and self-help has permitted Berber merchants to branch out into other business activities, such as real estate speculation and wholesale grocery. The consumer credit system operated by these merchants plays a major role in the survival of numerous *bidonville* families.

The ragged appearance of *bidonvilles* leads many to conclude that health and sanitary conditions must be the worst in the city. While it

Local merchant selling firewood by the kilo to local families.

cannot be denied that serious health problems do exist, other sections of the city, especially the older part of the *medina*, have higher rates of tuberculosis and trachoma. Unlike these older neighbourhoods, *bidonvilles* have an abundance of fresh air and sunshine, which decreases the breeding grounds of these diseases. The widespread ailments that affect *bidonville* residents are intestinal in nature and stem from low protein diets and lack of sewerage.

As with education, the major health problem is the serious overcrowding of facilities and the resulting paralysis in delivering health care to the community. The most serious overcrowding can be found in the district out-patient clinics, where minor treatment and medication is dispensed. For serious illness which requires hospitalisation the *bidonville* resident is treated at the central hospital. Proof of indigence relieves the individual and his family from the burden of medical expenses. Unfortunately there exists little public aid for post hospitalisation medication. The result is that the patient may suffer a relapse due to inadequate care while convalescing at home.

While it is important to grasp the social and economic realities of life in the *bidonvilles*, no description would be adequate if it ignored the bureaucratic apparatus that impinges in a direct way on the daily existence of *bidonville* residents. Only by examining the complex interaction between human concerns articulated by *bidonville* residents and the formal administrative institutions of government can we advance our understanding of Moroccan *bidonvilles*.

Upon receiving independence in 1956, the Moroccan government inherited the administrative machinery developed by France. Although slight modifications have been made, the basic administrative model remains the same. The King is the head of state and appoints all major officials. An example is the Ministry of Interior which has the major responsibility for day-to-day administration and co-ordination of government activities. The minister is appointed by the King alone with the governors of each province. The governors in consultation with the King appoint officials to administrative districts within each province. Each district is headed by a *khalifa* and is assisted by several *moqqademine*.[5] The hallmark of Moroccan administration is the high degree of centralisation at the local level and the direct line command from the King to a *bidonville* *moqqadem*.

A short list of the services and functions of each *khalifa* will provide a glimpse of the importance of this administrator to the *bidonville* resident. Birth, marriage, death, indigence and existence are the major certificates that must be acquired at one point or another from the local *khalifa*. Applications for public welfare, such as free foodstuffs, must be made to his office. Elementary school enrolment, household repair permits, military conscription and proof of unemployment come under his jurisdiction. The major instrument for keeping track of individual requests and status is the *carnet de Famille*, a family identity book in which vital statistics and records are kept. Loss of this document by the head of the household can jeopardise the continued 'official existence' of the family. Without this *carnet* ordinary requests for government services can be temporarily denied. Denial to the *bidonville* resident has a much greater impact because he has fewer alternative means for securing his needs.

The following example may better illustrate the importance of the

Interior photograph of bidonville *mother preparing the noon meal. A large earthenware container in the corner holds the daily supply of drinking water. Cooking is done in the patio area of the shack which has been covered with a corrugated iron roof.*

administrative world of the *khalifa* to a *bidonville* family. Mr. Bedaoui, a resident of a *bidonville*, was told at the out-patient clinic that his daughter must undergo a tonsillectomy. Although he was unemployed and therefore had no health insurance to pay for medical costs, Mr. Bedaoui learned from a neighbour that poor people with no money could receive free medical attention if they possessed a certificate of indigence. In order to acquire such a certificate it was necessary to apply in person at the *khalifa's* office, fill out the necessary forms and present his 'carnet de famille'. Once a formal request was made it was forwarded to the *moqqadem* for investigation.[6] Each *moqqadem* is responsible for a specific territory which consists of an average of 4,000 people. The investigation consisted of the *moqqadem* verifying that Mr. Bedaoui was a resident of his district and that he was indigent. The methods employed by the *moqqadem* included interrogation of the family and neighbours. Once the investigation was completed the dossier was returned to the *khalifa* for a decision. Mr. Bedaoui was then summoned to see the *khalifa* personally. Some five weeks after the initial request a certificate of indigence was issued.

General descriptions of *bidonville* life are important but they are limited in what they tell us about the ways by which people cope with their concerns in conditions of material deprivation. What is important to know are the patterns of human encounter employed by these urban poor as they experience the revolution of modernisation. What are the costs and benefits associated with the patterns employed? Do the patterns allow for the successful resolution of the basic human issues of collaboration, conflict, continuity, change and justice? To answer these questions it will be useful to focus on the relationship of *bidonville* residents and the bureaucratic world above them.

The most frequent pattern of encounter found between *bidonville* residents and the world above them is *emanation*. Emanation is a type of encounter in which (1) one treats the other solely as an extension of one's own personality, one's own will and power, as an embodiment of one's self, and (2) the other accepts his denial of a separate identity as legitimate because of the mysterious source or nature of the overwhelming power of the former. Such mysterious power may have as its source charisma, unfathomable competence, unanalysed or unanalysable power over vital resources, or covert manipulation. The mystery may lie within any power or competence whose roots or manifestations the other cannot fully understand. As long as change takes place solely at the command of the source of emanation, continuity of this form of relationship remains assured. Collaboration is unilaterally shaped at the cost of repressing conflict. Justice in this pattern of encounter means limitless security for the self, thanks to the limitless capacity of the other.

Morocco is a Muslim state with a constitutional monarchy. The King is not only the secular head of state but also the 'defender of the faithful' which results in a fusion of secular and sacred authority. In varying degrees the entire governmental structure reflects this dual nature. From the Minister of Interior to the *khalifa*, public officials are seen and treated as extensions of the King's personality. This has unintended consequences for the functioning of a supposedly modern rational bureaucracy in that no official has the autonomy to make decisions without being over-ruled by his immediate superior and so on until the decision reaches the King or his personal representative. More important for our purposes is what happens at the level of the urban poor. The *khalifa* is the representative of the King and therefore shares in part the King's charisma. In addition the *khalifa* seemingly manipulates a western bureaucracy inherited from the French, the logic of which escapes most poor people in *bidonvilles*. Finally, the *khalifa* controls some vital resources which are easily recognised by the poor.

For people living in *bidonvilles* housing is an important and immediate problem. To acquire a key to one of the new public housing units is viewed as extraordinary. As is the case with almost every important event or problem in life, the residents of *bidonvilles* must go to the district mayor for relief. If housing is desired, the applicant understands that he must submit to the *khalifa* by presenting himself as an obedient and faithful subject. In this case, Mohammed, a *bidonville* resident, prefaced his request for housing by appealing to Islamic principles of compassion and justice. Mohammed made it quite clear that he could not understand the complicated procedures for receiving housing and therefore had no alternative but to rely upon the mercy and benevolence of the *khalifa*. Since Mohammed could do nothing to alter the situation due to his ignorance and self-denial, it could only be the *khalifa* who could intervene and change the course of events. As might be expected due to the shortage of

housing and Mohammed's poverty, the *khalifa* discussed something concerning regulations, promised to consider the request and asked Mohammed to return next year.

A second pattern of encounter describing the relationship between the residents of *bidonvilles* and the world above them can be called *buffering*. In this pattern, the tension created by the changes in the balance of costs and benefits between the self and other is managed by intermediaries. Such a position may be occupied by a mediator, arbiter, broker or by a concept. Buffering allows for change by permitting indirect and limited forms of conflict and collaboration. Money, or certain forms of contract, may also serve as the nexus. Buffering depends upon shared, or at least convertible, values and upon a share willingness to pay commissions.

Mustafa the barber has devoted much of his life to developing his role as broker and intermediary for numerous residents of a Casablanca *bidonville*. He is well known in his neighbourhood and is frequently called upon to intervene on behalf of the residents. His success as a broker depends on continued good favour with the *khalifa* on the one hand, and continued respect from the community. Mustafa is useful to the *khalifa* and the *moqqadem* of the district because he is an excellent listening post and an effective mobiliser for government action. The *khalifa* grants special recognition to Mustafa as payment for his services. This recognition of being near to power strengthens Mustafa's reputation within the *bidonville* and encourages residents to bring their problems to him for resolution.

In one instance charges of assault and battery were filed against L'Hacen, the son, of a *bidonville* family. The mother approached Mustafa for advice and assistance. It was understood between both parties that the currency required in this pattern of encounter would be money, and an unspecified favour to be repaid in the future. The money would be used immediately in arranging matters with outsiders while the favour would be for Mustafa's services. The charges were eventually dropped and some months later Mustafa returned to the family for payment. In this case, someone had come to him asking if he could not arrange for a distant relative from the countryside to come to the city for medical treatment. Mustafa knew that the older brother of L'Hacen was an orderly in the city hospital and could possibly arrange such an affair. Upon completion of this task, the family of L'Hacen had paid in full for the original intervention by Mustafa.

The above illustration may seem unduly complicated but the point is simply that there are situations in which the *bidonville* resident can mobilise some resources and thereby employ buffering as a pattern of encounter. Finally, buffering is the dominant pattern of encounter describing relations among the urban poor within Moroccan *bidonvilles*.

Each of the two patterns described are no longer effective in providing the capacity to deal with the basic issues of life in *bidonvilles*. While the urban poor may feel that emanation and buffering are desirable and should be employed, it is clear to them that the political-administrative structure above them does not agree. Some in the *bidonvilles* have rejected both patterns for important reasons. Emanation is being destroyed because the mystery of reified concepts and sources of power to which others had bound themselves, is losing its magic as it becomes accessible to analysis. The capacity to eal with new qualities of change is being tested and found wanting y those once held in trusting embrace. The cost of emanation is ne's identity, a cost viewed by many as too high.

Buffering is being destroyed for three reasons. First, the poor lack ne very resources, specifically money, to make buffering effective. econd, buffering requires shared or at least convertible values. It is rystal clear that the non-poor have less in common with the poor nd therefore the nexus is more difficult to find for this pattern. inally, buffering is based upon a shared willingness to pay commis- ions. As modern, urban life presses even harder on the poor there is growing militancy among the young, which finds expression in the efusal to pay commissions because there are emerging new ideas as o what could be called inalienable rights. The situation in *bidonvilles* s moving closer each day to a pattern of encounter between the rban poor and the non-poor characterised by incoherence, i.e. an bsence of any shared forms of tension management.

In conclusion, what advantages can one claim for focusing on atterns of human encounter in *bidonvilles*? What does it contribute o our understanding of *bidonvilles* in the larger context of the evolution of modernisation? There are four immediate benefits in sing this framework for analysis. First, the framework focuses on oncrete patterns of interaction rather than on idealised systems of elief and behaviour. Secondly it is clear that although increased esources are needed for meeting the needs of *bidonville* residents, esources alone will not suffice. The actual pattern of encounter mployed in meeting these needs are as important as the material esources. It is imperative that the social innovator and the recipient oth agree as to the pattern of encounter to be employed. Failure to o so will result in chaos, distrust and eventual apathy because either party will be playing the game using the same rules. The cry

for justice heard in *bidonvilles* is for material comfort, but also for some degree of coherency in the ways by which men relate to each other. Third, this framework is substantially free from the cultural and class bias inherent in most theoretical models of social relations. The issues confronting *bidonville* residents are fundamentally the same as those found in other strata of Morocco, as well as in other societies. Finally, if *bidonvilles* are considered to be part of a city social system then it will be necessary to develop concepts and frameworks which will permit the observer to describe the ways by which the urban poor are connected to the other parts of the system. The issue of modernisation, as understood in this essay, requires that we talk about social connections and patterns of human encounter if we are to advance our understanding of such urban communities as the *bidonvilles* in Morocco.

NOTES

[1] Although the word *bidonvilles* (tin-can cities) is widely used by observers, the residents of these shantytowns refer to their communities as *carreenes* which is an Arabisation of the French word *carrée*.

[2] FANON, FRANTZ, *The Wretched of the Earth*, translated by Constance Farrington (London: MacGibbon and Kee, 1965), p. 103.

[3] HALPERN, MANFRED, 'A Redefinition of the Revolutionary Situation', in *Journal of International Affairs*, Vol. 23, No. 1, 1969.

[4] *Oufkih* is the title of the leader of the mosque and the ranking religious official within a subsection or neighbourhood of the bidonville.

[5] *khalifa* is the title of the governor's ranking administrative officer in each district within the province.

[6] *moqqadem* is the title of an assistant to a *khalifa* whose primary function is to provide a direct linkage between the citizen and the *khalifa*'s office.

View of a business avenue showing a cycle repair shop and the minaret of a local mosque.

SHELTER IN URBANISING AND INDUSTRIALISING AFRICA

Thomas L. Blair

LEGACIES OF THE URBAN PAST

'*L'Afrique est mal partie.*' This is the judgement of one of the fore-most European observers of African development, the French agronomist Rene Dumont.[1] And many urban sociologists familiar with the African housing situation would agree. The causes are complex but all of them are related to the colonial past and are evident in one way or another in the cities of industrially developing areas. Colonialism, and its companion imperialism, profoundly affected the habitats and economies of Africa and left a ragged scar of oppression on the bodies and the souls of black folk. It also established severe constraints on urban economic and social life which will bar the way of Africa's progress towards better housing and living conditions if they are not speedily resolved. Understanding these legacies of the urban past, and changing them, is crucial if future urban growth and its co-ordination with national economic development is to be accomplished in a positive and beneficial manner.

Pre-Colonial Cities

Africa has a long and varied history of human settlement. Its cities reach back to the thresholds of man's urban experience when the dominance of activities at sacred temples, armed camps, palaces, market places and caravanserai drew neighbouring peoples into complex productive systems. From the ninth century expansion of inland and ocean trade to the fifteenth century – long before the penetration of European slavers, factors and conquistadores – the port cities, market centres and city-states of powerful kingdoms enclosed large, densely populated permanent settlements within their boundaries.[2]

Large mining centres and stone-building civilisations prospered in the southern tier at Mapungubwe (Transvaal), Zimbabwe and Monomotapa (Southern Rhodesia and Moçambique), north to the Lunda-Luba settlements and beyond; they flourished in the kingdoms of the Rift Valley in East Africa and westward to the empires of Mali, Songhai, Kanem, Ghana, and the Kongo-Angola states.

Detail of a view of Benin City as recorded in J. Ogilby's Africa, *published in London in 1670.*

The city of Timbuctoo, drawn by René Caillié in 1828 and published in his Journal d'un Voyage a Temboctou et à Jenne, *Paris, 1830.*

Administrative and trade centres of Sudanic kingdoms were located in capital cities like Ségou and Gao. Timbuctu, Wagadugu, Kumasi and Kano were known for their affluence and power. Seaport towns grew along the East African coast at Mogadishu, Brava, Malindi, Mombassa, Pemba, Zanzibar, Kilwa, Kilimane and Sofala.

In West Africa the cities of Yoruba kingdoms rose to prominence as ruling chiefs expanded their control over trade routes. The chief's palace and the market-place dominated the central areas of well-planned cities like Ile-Ife, Ilesha and Ekiti. In the old quarters near by the houses of the guilds, traders and important families nestled between the major roads radiating to neighbouring towns. Newly-settled areas were laid out in a rectilinear pattern. The populace lived in compounds each of which had a large house set in a square-shaped space bounded by a high wall. Some were more than a half acre in size and provided living space for a large family and kinsmen. Groups of compounds were administered by elders and together they formed the basis of an urban council responsible to the princely authority.

African pre-colonial cities of the Great Iron Age grew out of the traditional past in response to self-generated political and techno-logical changes. They were urban expressions of emergent adaptive self-assured political states whose economies developed with the in-creased production of commodities for trade. Sociologists like E. Franklin Frazier and Gideon Sjoberg have classified them as 'pre-industrial cities'.[3] Unlike the rural hinterlands where men still wrestled with nature to claim the land, pre-industrial cities were theatres of competition for the symbols of power and material well-being. Cities had a wider range of non-agricultural workers, espe-cially craftsmen and traders, and an embryonic class structure rang-ing from nobles to commoners and dependent peoples. Kinship provided a firm basis for social organisation and social cohesion, and linked the rulers to the ruled in an intricate web of meaningful experience.

Colonial Urban-Industrial Growth

The vitality of African cities declined during the long dark night of slavery and wars with European invaders. Kingdoms fell, and colon-ial rule began. African societies, pinioned by the flag-staves of European nations, lay helpless while their material wealth was unearthed and exported, as their human populations had been cen-turies before, for Europe's benefit and to Africa's loss. The colonies became strategic suppliers of raw materials and outlets for European manufactured goods. Cities grew as peasants were prised from their grip upon their land and pushed towards employment centres. Later, when industrial innovations expanded production, new migrants were attracted to the city's breasts of steel.

Migration and settlement focused upon the major locations of economic activity: mines, plantations, cash crop farming, transport and processing plants. In West African and Sudanic states European enterprises accommodated themselves to pre-colonial patterns. Old towns, bypassed by economic change, languished or declined. In the new colonial capitals, export and trading centres, business and government districts were modernised while the debris of human

problems in the overcrowded African migrants' quarters were neglected. In the settler territories of north, east and southern Africa, by contrast, colonial towns were new towns: European in appear-ance, planning and organisation served by an itinerant class of land-less peasants, migrant black paupers, mine boys and domestic ser-vants.

Rapid urban growth, marked by deteriorating rural conditions and mass emigration, continued during the later stages of colonialism, 1947–60. Cities with more than 100,000 inhabitants grew at a rate of 9% per annum or double the rate of growth of the continent's entire population. By 1960, 8% of all the people in Africa lived in cities of 100,000 or more, and 13% lived in places of 20,000 or more inhabitants. Today there are 30 million urban-dwelling Africans in the larger cities alone and their numbers are increasing rapidly, mainly because of in-migration, at an astonishing rate of 3 million per year.

The Independence Building, Lagos. A prestigious, forbidding, western-styled monument to governmental bureaucracy.

Modern Underdevelopment

Rapid urban and industrial growth, initiated under colonialism, continued after independence. The problems it created are among the major indices of contemporary underdevelopment and can only be understood within the context of today's problems of demographic imbalance and political and economic dependence on European nations. The demographic situation, according to recent United Nations statistics, may be briefly summarised as follows:[4]

1. Variability of population distribution: 70% of the continent's population is contributed by twelve countries with 7·3 million inhabitants each; most nations are non-viable mini-states.
2. Rapid total population growth: due largely to falling, though still high, death rates among young and old.
3. Rapid urban growth: though Africa is the least urbanised major world region, its urban growth rate of 5·5% is among the highest in the world, i.e. double the world average.
4. High death and disease rates, and malnutrition, especially among infants and children: for each child that dies in France or Sweden, 4 die in Portugal, 24 in India and 50 in Africa.
5. High ratio of non-producers to producers: 40% of the population in the productive ages 15–44 years has to support the remaining 50% children and 10% older adults.

African economies are characterised by low national incomes, unskilled manpower, inadequate transport and misguided economic policies. Expatriates control most enterprises and decision-making. There is a reliance on the external trade sector and a restrictive range of primary commodities which are increasingly being displaced on the world market by synthetic goods. Finally there are sharp contrasts between the rural traditional sector in which most people live and the urban modern sector designed to meet the tastes of a minority elite of Europeans and African public functionaries.

The squalor of housing on the periphery of Lagos where immigrants from the surrounding area have settled.

Urban Parasitism

Colonial cities, like colonial economies, were parasitic. They were tightly organised and self-contained enclaves which skimmed off the cream of human and material resources from the countryside and oriented the bulk of its economic activity abroad. Colonial towns were indexes not of economic growth, but of retardation and deterioration. Demand stimuli, whose effects might otherwise have spread throughout the economy, leaked away through costly imports and the repatriation of profits abroad. Meanwhile the energies of the low-paid indigenous wage-labour force were diverted from productive tasks of benefit to the traditional rural sector.

Today's cities still reflect these trends. The functions they perform are crucial to external trade; but their regional ties are parasitic. Cities on internal transport routes are relatively unimportant, and despite the rapid growth of large cities there has been little change in their relationships to internal markets. In the interior the rural economy fails to meet even the subsistence needs of growing populations. The size of cropped areas is expanding, but food production is falling; rural populations increase but fewer persons can find employment. This rural decline is the corollary of urban parasitism. It takes place at the same time as urban growth, and the human link is mass migration; the only means of respite available to beleaguered people. Urban growth in Africa is, therefore, a symbol of the failure of agriculture to support fast-growing populations and of the inability of governments to decolonise and diversify their internal and external trade relations.

Social Problems

Together the migrating peoples of Africa constitute the most significant population movement since the slave trade. Impoverished unskilled migrants pour into cities at a faster rate than local industries, services and housing can absorb them. Many find a home in the overcrowded quarters or spill over into ever-widening enclaves of despair. In every city, thousands of migrants become illegal squatters, sleeping in the markets, streets and lorry parks, and under railway trestles and bridges. Slums flourish on swamps, marshes, airport roads, cemeteries, and factory sites. In makeshift huts, dugouts, stalls, cabins and shanties life grows stagnant with disease and few people are free from dysentery and parasitic infestations. Most urban workers live in houses of mud walls and corrugated iron roofs or squat in rude thatched-roof shacks on the periphery of cities. Most live far from work and transport and face long, tedious and costly journeys to work. All want better housing, a home of their own, but few can afford better housing. On incomes of less than £6 per month there is little left after paying for food, clothing, utilities and other essentials.

These facts give cause to wonder at the vicissitudes of life. Street minstrels sing about the pain and sorrow that befalls the country boy in the city, and poets, like Dei-Anang of Ghana, ponder the relative values of that which has been lost and gained in the process of migration.[5]

> 'Here we stand
> Poised between two civilisations.
> Backward? To days of drum
> and festal dances in the shade
> of sun-kist palms.
> Or forward?
> Forward!
> Toward?
> The slums, where man is dumped upon man?...
> The factory
> To grind hard hours
> In an inhuman mill
> In one long ceaseless spell?'

Lack of Civic Identity

In many cities, Africans do not feel a sense of civic identity; they do not feel the city and its destiny belong to them. This is understandable. All African nations inherit a racially segregated urban social structure. Colonial policies endorsed the segregation of human groups – African, European, Asian, Arab and 'coloureds' – into separate residential areas and limited their contact within the framework of European overlordship to the workplace, the market-place and a few public areas. Indeed, the colonial city was not a civic entity. It was not created to meet the needs of new urban dwellers and little provision was made for their social and cultural requirements. It was merely an administrative area built up and run by Europeans and incidentally inhabited by Africans. In the settler regions, where territorial apartheid is most severe, Africans are guests in town. They are closeted back-of-town to 'keep the night white' in the European areas, and are deported to their villages when their labour is no longer needed. The accommodation provided is temporary housing for transient workers, not homes for an African urban community.

The colonial city was a pastiche of zoned functions, land uses and populations. Six typical zones emerged. On the one hand Europeans controlled the modern commercial and administrative centre, the industrial, transport and military zones, and the well-kept residential compounds for Europeans and the African bourgeoisie; on the other hand, were the old city, the strangers' quarters and the sprawling zones of squatters – the trespassers of desperation – scattered in the city and on its outer edges. This inherited pattern of ecological segregation impedes the creation of healthy planned communities in new nations. In every city, occupational, religious, cultural and racial factors are volatile fire-brands of civil strife, ready to ignite the pile of existing urban problems. African cities harbour hundreds of differing allegiances, smouldering in recalcitrance and intolerance, flaring up unexpectedly in hatred and mass hysteria.

Algiers does not lack civic identity but its identity is almost wholly French. The mosque looks out of place in this context.

The Decline of Egalitarian Residence

With independence and the rise of a bourgeois class the pattern of social segregation hardened. As more Africans ascend to the ranks of power they take up residence in formerly European residential areas, or in isolated middle-income housing estates. As new African elites cross the residential ethnic-class line they foreshadow the decline of the egalitarian residential patterns typical of traditional local African communities, where on a street of ordinary houses a wealthy man lives next door to an artisan, farmer or labourer, and herald the rise of isolated one-class neighbourhoods common in Western nations.

Today, geographical mobility follows social mobility. The attainment of new status positions is expressed by dissociation from the traditional group and association with another group in better surroundings. Elite African areas are created and separated in distance as well as by income, education and standard of living from the masses of people. This exodus of elites has disastrous effects on social relations in the traditional community and deprives the community of leadership and taxable incomes.

The affluence of élitist groups contrasts with the poverty of African workers in an increasingly stratified society. Labourers in the truck, clerks on their bicycles, government employees in their cars.

The 'Socialism of the Rich'

Modern housing, like income, is not distributed equally or randomly across the urban landscape. Modern housing tends to cluster around those persons employed in the expanding industrial and governmental sectors. Employed workers live in subsidised homes, while the unemployed and unskilled workers bear the full brunt of the high rents and housing shortages.

In the housing estates, no resident pays an economic rent for accommodation, and some pay less than others. The higher the occupation, the greater the subsidy and the lower the portion of annual wages spent on rent. Lower income occupants may pay as much as 7–10% of their annual income on rent, while the upper ranks pay as little as 3–5%. There is emerging, as a result, a kind of 'socialism of the rich' whereby upper class status, income and privilege are subsidised by government at an annual cost of millions. It duplicates in the sphere of housing the increasing differentiation of a tiny, affluent and powerful urban-based section of the national bourgeoisie from the large mass of urban and rural dwellers. If these cubicles of urban privilege are not to become immortalised in mud and concrete, then present patterns of housing and of social segregation must be scrapped and the democratisation of urban African life accomplished. An independent nation should have a well-planned housing policy and a programme of public action that will not only be economic, but ensure a maximum of social justice.

In sum, Africa's urban legacy of colonialism, accounts, in large part, for the tendencies we see today: the urban centredness of political and modern life, the disparities between town and region, and the alienation of affluent carefree elites from the problems of migrants and slum dwellers. Urban residence is the only means by which citizens of new nations can hope to have access to literacy, mass media information, new products, and to broad political participation. And precisely because of the city's exclusive possession of political and economic power and the means of modernisation, it is a negative factor in extending the dream and the substance of freedom and progress to rural dwellers, who comprise the overwhelming mass of people in African nations.

CRISIS IN URBAN HOUSING, PLANNING AND ECONOMIC DEVELOPMENT

Africa is in the throes of the most dynamic revolution in its history – rapid and simultaneous urban and industrial growth. As new nations and their leaders mount massive economic development programmes, cities become the focal points of dramatic social change. Peasants seeking cash wages flee declining rural areas for urban centres of new industry. This unprecedented convergence of men, capital and industry places severe strains on the limited facilities of ex-colonial cities. In every nation therefore there is a crisis of urban affairs which exposes the contradictions in the economic programmes of newly-industrialising countries.

Housing Markets and Finance

Financing housing for Africa's new urban proletariat is not an easy task. The working man's meagre wage and the paltry assets of potential entrepreneurs are insufficient. Government spending on housing is limited by scarce financial resources and the more urgent demands for creating capital-producing industries. And private enterprise hesitates to invest in what they consider to be unproductive social benefits. Despite these difficulties slow progress is being made in overcoming housing problems with the aid of industry, foreign governments and international agencies.[6] The major target is mass housing for wage-earning industrial and government employees. But they are only a minute proportion of the able-bodied urban population. For every employee in large-scale enterprises there are scores of low-income salaried commercial workers, self-employed artisans and traders, and thousands of unemployed migrants and their dependants. These groups form the human core of the urban housing problems, and are, therefore, the major markets for low-income and 'no-income' housing.

MAJOR HOUSING MARKETS

Occupation–Status	Cash income	Need	Provision
1. Highest officials, administrators, parliamentarians, chiefs of large areas	£3,000 plus	Low	High
2. Professionals, rich large traders	£1,000–3,000	Low	High
3. Civil servants, teachers, clerical staff, administrative personnel	£700–1,000	Low	High
4. Self-employed: landlords, builders and contractors, lorry-owners, shop owners, big cash crop farmers, artisans who own cottage industries, lesser chiefs and clan officials, etc.	£600–2,000	Low	High
5. Skilled technicians, cash wage workers, seamstresses, cash crop farmers	£240–600	High	Low
6. Unskilled labourers, petty traders	£60–120	High	Low
7. Casual migrant labourers	£20–60	Moderate	Low
8. Small peasants and sharecroppers	£5–20	Moderate	Low
9. The unemployed and landless	less than £5	High	Low

Towards a Building Industry

Most new urban housing is built by the people themselves with the help of friends and relatives. The products of their labour range from a modest house with cement walls and corrugated iron roof to makeshift shelters in the shadow of public buildings and upper-income housing estates. Salaried and self-employed workers seeking homes are increasingly relying upon the services of local builders and contractors. In many nations there is a marked trend towards the creation of a local building industry. Housing by local builders has several advantages: less expensive local materials can be used; costs of building and maintenance are closer to the economic means of wage-earners; and buildings are capable of continuous improvement with modern materials. Local builders have a crucial

role to play. Workers cannot build and work at the same time and the replacement of housing requires a specialised cadre of trained personnel. With technical assistance, local builders can improve their techniques, learn the basic principles of business and costing methods, and be encouraged to design economical and convenient dwellings.

Slum Rehabilitation

The overcrowded quarters are the dwelling places of the large majority of unskilled workers and migrants. They are rapidly declining into slums. In the early days of independence every nation recoils from the sight of urban slums, especially those in capital cities, and seeks to banish them with the magic wand of slum clearance. It has become obvious, however, in Lagos, Tananarive, Cotonou and other places, that slums are much more than mere blemishes on the urban landscape. They are symptoms of the housing shortage, high rents, land speculation, insufficient municipal services and bad land use planning. What is needed are effective urban planning and land use reforms.

The raw material of a building industry – turnip-shaped mud bricks being manufactured for sale to builders in northern Nigeria.

Slum clearance does little good unless the forces which produce slums are eradicated. As long as there is no housing available, slum clearance only destroys existing dwellings (bad as they may be), dislocates thousands of families and crushes more people into adjacent neighbourhoods.

Slum growth can be curtailed, and the major negative effects of wholesale slum clearance avoided, by aiding workers to build homes and by improving existing housing. Aided self-help housing, a 'pull yourself up by your own bootstraps' philosophy, has captured the fancy of many nations; it is a way of mobilising and directing human investment in personal and community development. Lower-income workers are encouraged to build by instalments, i.e., to save small amounts of money and periodically convert savings into improved building materials. Another approach is to lay out the framework of roads and services for a new community, and then sell plots and allow workers to build their own homes.

Property rehabilitation programmes in densely populated areas have a useful function since a fairly large proportion of urban housing can be improved by re-roofing, enlarging windows, paint, landscaping and introducing better air circulation and sanitary improvements. Property rehabilitation is aided when governments subsidise the production of essential house parts, roofs, walls and elementary sanitation facilities and make them available through loan schemes and local building societies.

The Politics of Squatting

Squatters' settlements are, like slums, endemic to the urban socioeconomic and political system. Their problems have been duly

Self-help housing in Moçambique providing a simple, but acceptable standard of living.

recorded over the years in a variety of sources: annual reports of colonial administrators, the monumental African survey of Lord Hailey, the 1956 UNESCO survey of urbanisation and industrialisation in Africa, and in a recent book by the United Nations consultant Charles Abrams. Planners and municipal governments generally accept the fact that for a long time to come squatters' settlements will play a necessary role in the urban housing market and will continue to provide an elementary form of shelter for the urban masses. They feel that with adequate government assistance, public health and town planning measures the growth of healthy communities can be encouraged.

But this assumes that squatters and squatting is merely a transitory phase in urban development and that squatters are social dropouts prepared to wait until something is done for them. Contrary evidence is at hand. The peoples of shanty towns and *bidonvilles* are to a large extent productive workers, no different in their socio—economic composition than residents of other working-class areas. They want a stake in the city and are ready to seek more dramatic and effective ways of establishing their claim to the benefits of modern life. At the moment there are admittedly few examples of involvement by planners and architects working directly as advocates of squatter settlements in Africa. But models for import do exist in other Third World countries. Leaders of squatters' settlements (*barriadas*) in Lima, Peru, for example, made great strides towards self-help community development after they had effectively seized the land and organised themselves into a cohesive political force. The squatters' militancy has validity because it is a means of blasting their way into the twentieth century. A recent research document by Mangin and Turner confirms this view. 'Once they consolidate their seizure of the land, the *barriada* dwellers' stake in Peruvian society goes up. *Barriadas* are therefore not slums, because they become communities of people on the way up socially.'[7]

Housing, Urban Planning and National Economic Development

Housing is only one element in a complex of facilities and social amenities which constitute a city and make life endurable. Building and rebuilding African cities requires that more than half the total investment be made on the infra-structure of roads and service and the super-structure required for economic and social activities. The private investor will not spend money on these items; hence until the public sector provides them there can be little hope for the coherent progressive growth of cities. Recognition of these facts leads governments to consider a number of devices for urban development; the major ones are international co-operation, external aid loans and programmes of guided national economic development.

1. *Co-operation*

In the search for planned co-ordinated solutions to urban and economic development the governments of new nations encourage co-operation with the former colonial powers. In *Afrique francophone* for example, French agencies like the *Société pour l'Etude d'Aménagements Planifiés* (SETAP) have played a key role. Two of their major efforts to create new towns and rationalise workers' housing, industrial processing and port installations are located at Boké, Guinea and Port Etienne, Mauretania.

Co-operation of this sort has many problems, mainly because the major emphasis in these large-scale projects is on the economic activity, e.g. mineral exploration, and not town development. In many parts of French-speaking Africa workers' housing is provided in a *cité*, an ensemble of multi-storey dwelling units of a type preferred by French architects and builders. *Cités* are often segregated communities where the European and African senior service quarters are separated from low-income workers. Very rarely does a complete *cité* get built, and their cement slabs stuck in the cleared barren land are shadeless denuded sores on the nape of the African forest.

2. *External Aid*

Government-sponsored programmes depend to a large degree on external loans for building materials, mortgage credits and so on. It has become apparent that the economics (and aesthetics) of housing loans often retard recipient nations in their attempts to solve their housing problems. And future expansion of government housing based on external loans will require a re-analysis of the benefits and disadvantages of foreign aid contracts.[8]

African administrators are discovering some of the inadequacies of charity. Loans, as presently conceived, are not a satisfactory solution to Africa's housing needs because they too often rigidly determine the design, cost and type of materials used according to the donor nation's industrial interests and tastes – not to Africa's needs and climates. In addition, tied housing loans and deferred payments which involve credits for purchase of capital goods and services from contractors in the donor nation present crucial economic problems. These contracts often involve 'rigged' prices for goods and services and require loan repayment in foreign currency over a short period of time. As a result they place a heavy burden on African budgets. Not enough time elapses for the project to generate capital to service the credit loan and there is a drain on foreign exchange currency reserves, thus reducing the capacity of the nation to import more capital for development.

Squatter Housing.

There is some evidence that the etiquette of donor-recipient relations is changing, to allow greater freedom for the recipient to expend a larger percentage of a donor nation's aid on a multilateral basis for feasibility studies, pilot projects, personnel, equipment and materials. As these trends proceed, recipient nations will be enabled to shop on the world market for the building ideas and components required, and desired, and not have their housing programme dependent on donor nations alone.

3. *Development Plans*

Three out of every four African countries have published development plans. They are essentially transitional programmes to accomplish two goals: (1) to bridge the period of constitutional transition from internal self rule to independence; and (2) to cover the period of change from the rudimentary planning of the colonial public expenditure budget to full resource planning introduced by the new government. The plans heavily emphasise industrialisation, i.e. factories to process local raw materials for export and manufacture simple import substitutes, especially consumer goods for domestic use.

It is obvious, however, that until quite recently, little thought has been given to co-ordinating industrial and urban growth. A number of basic criticisms of development plans have been made by United Nations agencies. Where industrial growth occurs it encourages unplanned urban expansion and intensifies housing demand. New industry unleashes a backlash of powerful forces. Squatters and shanty towns follow factories into new locations. The rate of building of mud housing falls as the industrial use of scarce water supplies rises, and overcrowding results. And furthermore, for a variety of reasons, industrialisation does not resolve the problems it creates. On the contrary, the housing needs of a small élite section of the populace are met while the needs of the vast urban population go unheeded.

In Nigeria, for example, three years after the introduction of its development plan, a United Nations consultant, Dr. Otto Koenigsberger observed that: '. . . there were acute housing shortages particularly in the industrial and port towns: Lagos, Port Harcourt, Ikeja, Onitsha and Kano. Prices for urban land and rent for accommodation went up to unprecedented heights. Available accommodation became overcrowded, clandestine settlements sprang up on the outskirts of the big cities and squatters occupied open grounds near the city centres. I counted over a thousand squatter families in central Lagos in 1965. As there were no plans for urban expansion, cities sprawled outwards and journeys to work became longer. Traffic problems increased and standards of public health deteriorated. At the same time, a good number of houses were built for the exclusive use of the very rich, particularly the staff of large business houses, foreign embassies and international agencies.'[9]

Emergent Principles

Housing in Africa is a national question, and intimately connected with the desire for industrial and national economic development.

Most African governments recognise the need for a national housing programme based on six principles: (1) housing for all workers and their families; (2) modernisation of existing houses; (3) a central housing agency; (4) co-ordination of housing and economic development; (5) creation of a housing industry; and (6) co-operation with industry and the people.

Planners have begun to recognise the intricate relationships between economic development, urban growth, and housing. They recognise that most housing is utterly inadequate, in quantity and quality; this is due largely to reliance on market forces to solve economic and social problems. They also recognise that the creation of viable communities must complement, not negate, investment in

A concrete-lined open sewer – part of the infrastructure of an African city, which acts as a constraint on the spread of housing.

other sectors of the economy and society. There are major economic and political constraints on current simplistic urban planning solutions to decelerate and decentralise industry, for example. Deceleration of rates of economic development is not feasible nor desirable; and devices to relieve urban pressures, e.g. decentralising industry, must be based on sound economic planning principles.

The major question for the future is 'How to mobilise and co-ordinate the human, material and financial resources necessary to deal with urban planning and housing problems within the framework of economic development?' Some of the planning approaches receiving careful attention today can be summarised briefly as follows. Housing programmes, and the planned growth of cities, are essential elements of national economic development. The totality of activities in a city must pay for the costs of building, rebuilding and planning. Costs and responsibilities must be shared by private investors and industries, public authorities and community institutions. A central government organisation, affiliated with special bodies, is required to initiate and co-ordinate the mobilisation of financial and human resources, research and feasibility studies, design, specifications, information and training schemes and pilot projects. Housing should be seen, not as a social overhead, but as an essential objective and powerful tool of development planning. The achievement of these principles will require the resolution of conflicting pressures to develop urban facilities and to facilitate economic development.

BUILDING AFRICAN CITIES

African cities need not suffer through the same mistakes of western industrial societies. It is possible to preview many crucial problems in the crucible of today's arenas of change and to plan for urban development in orderly regulated ways. Africa can be the laboratory for a new science of planning human settlements. A science which will have at its core a liberating idea – building for people as humans, not as fodder for the mills of economic development; building for variety, access to amenities and for security; building for that stage of history beyond slavery and colonialism.

Study and Co-operation

African cities must find a way to opt for an urban physical structure which enhances and re-affirms the African presence in mankind. More study, widespread co-operation and planned action for change is necessary. There is a need for study of the forces which distribute persons across the face of the city. The most important are the factors which frame expansion and growth: size (some cities are 200–400 square miles), water for irrigation, drinking, housebuilding and electric power, army and police barracks, road systems and traffic and the siting of enterprises, markets, shopping and squatter's areas. Patterns of local government organisation, urban land tenure and the effects of customary, statutory and squatters' rights on urban growth must also be evaluated. Control must be established over house-plots, their prices, allocation and development; 'one man one plot' is a slogan with little meaning if the leaseholder cannot, or will not, build on the land. Land use charges, especially to industry, require rationalisation, for at present there are many urban industries who pay as little as £50 a year.

Basic demographic studies and population forecasts are required. In addition, there is a need for surveys of existing households and housing types, amenities, costs of building and maintenance, and ability to pay an economic rent for low-cost modern housing. Computers, based in large cities, can be programmed to solve a wide range of probability problems.

Migration is international. Increased co-operation between African nations and municipalities should have top priority; and an organisation of African town administrators is needed to co-ordinate solutions. Regional authorities must take responsibility for planning and financing rural development and village resettlement. The basic needs are for a good water supply, marketing roads, drainage, schools and housing.

Urban Planning and Development

The co-ordination and implementation of new approaches to problems of housing urban dwellers lies to a large extent in the hands of specialists. Architects, building engineers, sociologists and town planners are beginning to assume a crucial role in man's quest for shelter in urbanising Africa. They are part of the nation-building process and can together build adequate houses and plan whole neighbourhoods and cities. Their buildings will form the environment in which future generations will grow to maturity. What shall be the unique characteristics of African cities a century from now? How can African cities grow and develop, yet avoid the ills of Western industrialised nations, urban sprawl and squalor? Will African cities be cultural coffins or life generating stations along the path of healthy urban-industrial societies?

Surveys of existing households, amenities and user requirements can contribute to a valuable documentation of resource material for the urban planner in Africa.

Important housing research and action programmes are being conducted in Africa and Europe. The Department of Tropical Studies of the Architectural Association School of Architecture, London, is one of Britain's most important institutions providing training and skills for building in Africa.[10] Both the faculty and postgraduate students recruited from tropical areas have been directly involved in planning housing and urban development in Nigeria, Sudan, Zambia and Ghana. In *Afrique francophone*, French architects have also been concerned with housing development and urban planning. The *Société pour l'Etude d'Aménagments Planifiés* (SETAP) planned the construction of three urban sites in the bauxite mining areas of Guinea. The *Secrétariat des Missions d'Urbanisme et d'Habitat* (SMUH) has done urban re-development work in the Niari Valley towns of Congo Brazzaville, and in Malagasy, Ivory Coast and Chad.

Case Studies in Urban Planning

Planners are in action today in all types of cities in widely divergent climates, cultures and political situations. In Guinea, the United Arab Republic and Tanzania they are urged to plan within an African socialist framework. In Malawi, Liberia and Ivory Coast the planning parameters are set by neo-colonial capitalist *laissez-faire* concepts. In Sierra Leone, Nigeria and Congo Leopoldville civil-military regimes and revolutionary councils backed by international consortia establish the planning context. And in the Portuguese colonies, the white settler territories and South Africa, planners accept the constraints of *de jure* and *de facto* racial distinctions and apartheid.

The tools they use, according to the maxim 'Survey, Analysis, Plan,' are often mis-applied. European planners slap diagrammatic cultural poultices on decaying central areas while peri-urban squalor goes unheeded; they plan 'Garden Cities' in countries which have never known an industrial revolution, and force workers to make even longer journeys to work. Few of their plans show any depth of political and social analysis or recognise the necessity for an Afro-centric outlook. In general, they are journeyman-like jobs done as efficiently or inefficiently in Africa as in Covent Garden, New Haven, Lyons or elsewhere in the western world.

1. NIGERIA

Lagos

Lagos, Nigeria, the capital of one of the fast developing African countries is a case in point. In metropolitan Lagos, home of a million people, the twin forces of industrialisation and urbanisation have flung a chain of sprawling settlements along a highway and railway line. Industrial estates at Apapa and Ikeja may soon stretch to Agege 20 miles away. On Lagos Island skyscrapers jostle slum buildings for a place in the sun; on the mainland, industrial and housing estates are oases in a sea of sprawling, crowded human settlements. At Suru-Lere, a bustling worker community not long ago unsettled, three large housing schemes were built by the Lagos Executive Development Board in co-operation with the Federal Government.

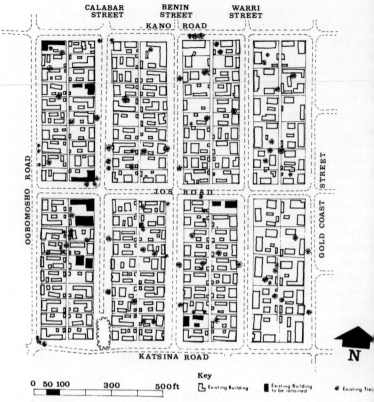

Section of the Sabon Gari, Kaduna, as existing.

The first project was a re-housing estate for displaced Lagos City slum families. Later, two subsidised worker housing estates, Obele Odan and Obele Oniwale, were built; they comprised 1,500 one- to four-room bungalows renting for 16s 6d per room per month. In future, two five-storey blocks of flats and single-room units are to be built.

In Lagos, as in other cities, solutions are also required to deal with urban expansion, overcrowded housing, transport, rising land values and the need for community facilities. A United Nations team in 1963 proposed a series of short- and long-term policies to plan the development of the city and its economic base. These included: drainage and reclamation of swamps, and the development of mainland settlements towards the north and west; a housing agency to secure land for low-cost housing; the expansion of water works and control over industrial waste and sewage; the creation of a metropolitan region co-ordinated by one supervisory agency; and the planned decentralisation of industry and the formation of peri-urban satellite towns.[11]

Kano

Kano, Northern Nigeria, is the ancient capital of a Muslim Hausa-Fulani kingdom. It grew rapidly following the introduction of British military administration (1903), the telegraph (1904), a dry season trunk road to the coast (1906) and the railway which reached Kano

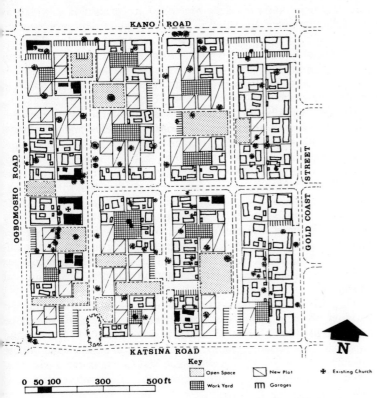

Section of the Sabon Gari, Kaduna, as proposed by Max Lock and Partners.

Key

▨ Open Space	◸ New Plot
▦ Work Yard	⫿ Garages
	✛ Existing Church

0 50 100   300   500 ft

N

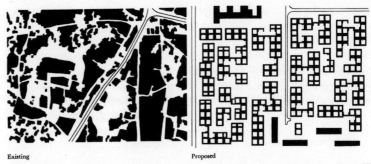

High Density Housing in metropolitan Kano, existing and as proposed by B. A. W. Trevallion.

Existing   Proposed

in 1911. As a result new foci were created around European trading companies, strangers' quarters, and a government centre; all were firmly established by 1930.

Kano's rich commerce and trade and expanding production of groundnuts, textiles, cattle and meat, hides and skins attract migrants and dependents from all over the northern region and Nigeria. The present urban population is estimated as 160,000 in the old Hausa walled city, 250,000 in all the major built-up areas, and 383,000 in metropolitan Kano. In addition, about two million people live within a 30-mile radius. These figures suggest that Kano is one of the most densely populated urban regions in all Africa.

Kano's residential zones are inhabited by particular ethnic groups. The *Kanawa*, or Kano Hausa, live in the old city. Fagge houses many Levantine, Arab and upwardly mobile Hausa traders. Low income migrant Hausa from other parts of the North find homes in Tudun Wada. Hausa and Ibo people, of both low and high incomes, reside in Gwagwargwa. The Sabon Gari or new town was, until the recent hostilities, almost completely inhabited by Ibos and other southern peoples. Finally, European and Levantines live in the township area, and expatriates and senior civil servants reside in institutional and governmental housing estates.

Migration to Kano occurs mainly for 'push' reasons: lack of opportunities, poor housing conditions and the lowly status of rural dwellers. Within a decade it is estimated that migrants in metropolitan Kano will outnumber the *Kanawa* old time residents. Migration

and urban economic growth has had negative effects on the social order of this once feudal kingdom. In the old town there is an increasing tendency for young people to reject religious and customary practices. The ledgers of Muslim courts are filled with family disputes as more youth leave their fathers' houses upon marriage, live outside the walled city and spend their leisure time in the strangers' quarters of Fagge, Gwagwargwa and Tudun Wada.

Meeting Kano's problems of sub-standard housing, unbalanced industrial and population growth and its social and community problems will not be an easy task. In November 1962, the Greater Kano Planning Authority was constituted to plan urban development. It proposed a programme of planned expansion of rural settlements, comprehensive system of development control and a public relations campaign to sell the city as a desirable place for private investment. Its major aims were to co-ordinate industrialisation and urban growth, and create an effective urban government without destroying the traditional Muslim base.[12]

Kaduna

Kaduna, Northern Nigeria, is an agglomeration of military garrisons, government headquarters and industry on the Kaduna River at the junction of trans-Nigerian rail and road lines. Rapid economic growth and population expansion have distorted the image of a peaceful colonial capital carefully planned by the British military governor, Lord Lugard. The city has grown, the centre is congested with traffic, residential areas and workplaces are mal-coordinated, and the majority of people live in overcrowded clusters of mud compounds and shantytowns along the main roads.

The Kaduna Plan by Max Lock and Partners, commissioned in the mid-1960s proposed the 'diagnosis, treatment and cure of environmental ills'. In the short term it proposed to tidy up the relationship between men and machines and halt urban sprawl. This would involve siting new owner-built housing near industrial estates, conservative surgery to reduce densities, improve uses and visual qualities, and the improvement of civic, business and housing areas. In the long term the plan proposed the stabilisation of peri-urban village populations and the settlement of a labour force near new agro-industrial enterprises.

Kaduna's future growth, they suggested, ought to follow a set of general principles. Kaduna should be an 'African city' developing

237

according to a 'balanced relationship of its three primary functions as capital, garrison and industrial town'. Growth should be encouraged within a 'city-region' composed of two parts: the central urbanised core increased to fifty square miles to accommodate a population of 350,000 at densities of ten persons per acre and a larger region of 4,000 square miles having a half million people and supplying the city's immediate living needs. To secure the viability of these innovations, the plan advocated 'open-ended planning' under 'one authority' so that 'circulation and land use can be rationalised,' 'wastefulness eliminated' and the 'city be enabled to pay for itself'.[13]

2. THE COPPER BELT, ZAMBIA

The Copper Belt mining towns of Zambia are a unique phenomenon: seven sprawling communities along a billion dollar mineral vein running from the Congo to the Zambesi River. Each has a European town centre and African workers' quarters and company-owned suburbs at the periphery.

At the tail end of this chain lies Lusaka, the chief administrative marketing and manufacturing centre. It occupies a strategic position at the junction of a complex road and rail network connecting East and Central Africa to world markets. Lusaka was laid out on the lines of a 'garden city'. The poorer sections are located on the fringes of an urban area as large as Liverpool and workers have to make long, tedious journeys to and from work.

Manpower, housing and residential location are all tied together as a legacy of the colonial past. It is based on induced cyclical migration: a pattern of rigidity and fluidity which involves migratory labour, a short spell of urban employment, and a return to home villages. Urban African workers earn low wages relative to whites; they have few opportunities for advancement in jobs and education, and live in jerry built segregated barrack hostels. Urban housing conducive to normal family life is open only to Europeans and a small privileged fraction of the labour force. Africans, until recently, were debarred from acquiring titles to urban plots, and must rely on accommodation provided in company-owned townships.

Copper Belt urban areas and housing problems were reviewed on the eve of independence by Dr. Otto Koenigsberger at the request of President Kenneth Kaunda, Prime Minister, and Sir Ronald Prain, a director of the principal mining company, Rhodesian Selection Trust. In his brief report Dr. Koenigsberger offered some guiding principles for the democratisation of urban human relations. He cited the inadequacies of segregated low-amenity workers' suburbs and called for the transference of local administration from the mining companies to elected urban councils. He also proposed a national housing board, and the co-ordination of housing programmes and economic growth.[14]

Technocrats, Artists, Social Revolutionaries?
What should architects and planners be?

More radical solutions than these are necessary if architects and planners are going to aid Africa effectively to end the gross inequa-

lities that exist, and diffuse the benefits of modernisation as widely as possible. Ultimately the solution to housing and urban problems lies not in technical expertise alone but in the arenas of political values commitment and action. Looked at from this point of view contemporary planning in Africa exhibits an impoverishment of both ideology and practice. Professionals go forth from the metropole to export know-how and import Pounds, Francs, Deutsche marks, etc. Plans are hurriedly put together without societal analyses. Few utilise a scientific methodology, propose hypotheses and alternative proposals for testing. Gradual change is sought within the *status quo*. These criticisms, levelled at planners both at home and abroad, highlight some basic questions: What are the goals of planning? How should architects and planners define their professional roles, responsibilities, actions and reactions? Who is the client, the servant and the master? Optimising benefits – for whom and why?

Young African architect/planners, on whose shoulders much of the future of housing will depend, are graduating in increasing numbers from faculties in Europe and America, and in Africa at colleges in Kumasi, Ghana, Zaria, Nigeria and in Algiers, Khartoum and Cairo.

They will be called upon to deal with a wide range of housing and building problems. They and their expatriate colleagues should be equipped to accomplish three tasks: (1) resolve conflicts of styles and materials; (2) encourage co-operation with local builders and initiate training schemes for local technicians; and (3) experiment with new forms of buildings and environment based on the objective conditions of the society.

But, in addition, they should also be ready to defend the people, the nation and themselves against neo-colonialist ideologies and practices on all levels. They should be able to say 'No' to plans which lack a social scientific base, which tie national economies adversely to metropolitan powers, which endorse residential segregation and the socialism of the rich, and which are not revolutionary enough to meet the rapidly rising expectations of the Arican people.

Laissez-faire open-ended plans conceived in tandem with unquestioned developmental motives will not ensure African cities against the mal-co-ordination of housing, services, labour migration and economic growth. Architects and planners must free themselves from servile adherence to dirigiste policies of governments, international consortia and industry. Plans must evolve from the conscious will of the people, and be based on shared participation and involvement at all levels. African students must be involved as colleagues and apprentices both in European offices and schools as well as in the projects taking place in their own countries.

Africa and the Third World can become a crucial laboratory of a new science/art policy of urban and rural planning. The question is what will it be? How can it be less than a philosophy and method allied to the desires of emerging populations for social reconstruction, which reckons its growth by the contradictions it overcomes, and whose inter-disciplinary practitioners feel impelled not only to understand, plan or replan industrialising urban socio-economic systems but to radically change them where necessary? And failing that, to set about re-examining their whole relationship with society.

NOTES

[1] DUMONT, RENE, *L'Afrique Noire Est Mal Partie*, Paris, 1962.

[2] DAVIDSON, BASIL, *Africa: History of a Continent*, Weidenfeld and Nicolson, London, 1966.

[3] FRAZIER, E. FRANKLIN, 'Urbanisation and its effects upon the task of Nation-Building in Africa south of the Sahara', in G. Franklin Edwards (Ed.) *E. Franklin Frazier on Race Relations*, University of Chicago Press, Chicago, 1968, and Gideon Sjoberg, *The Pre-Industrial City*, Glencoe, Illinois, Free Press 1960.

[4] United Nations Economic Commission for Africa, *A Survey of Economic Conditions in Africa 1960–64*, United Nations, New York, 1968.

[5] DAVIDSON, BASIL, 'The African Personality,' in Colin Legum (Ed.) *Africa Handbook*, Penguin Reference Books, London, 1969, p. 539.

[6] See for example, *Housing in Africa*, United Nations, New York, September 1965, and BLAIR, THOMAS L., *Africa: A Market Profile*, London, Business Publications Ltd., and New York, PRAEGER, F. J., 1965, Chapter Ten 'The Social Utility of Industry in Housing'.

[7] MANGIN, WILLIAM P., and TURNER, JOHN C., 'Benavides and the Barriada Movement', in Paul Oliver (Ed.), *Shelter and Society*, Barrie and Jenkins, London, 1969.

[8] BLAIR, THOMAS L., 'New Directions in African Development', *The Correspondent*, Harvard University, Cambridge Mass. No. 35, Autumn 1965.

[9] KOENIGSBERGER, Dr. OTTO, 'Housing in the National Development Plan', *Architectural Association Quarterly*, London, Vol. 2, No. 1, January 1970, p. 13.

[10] ABRAMS, CHARLES; KOENIGSBERGER, Dr. OTTO et al., *Report on Metropolitan Lagos*, prepared for the Government of Nigeria by a team appointed under the United Nations Technical Assistance Programme, April 1964.

[11] TREVALLION, B. A. W., *Metropolitan Kano*, a report on the twenty-year development plan, 1963–1983, prepared for the Greater Kano Planning Authority, 2 vols, Kano, Newman Neame for the GKPA, 1966.

[12] LOCK, MAX and Partners, *Kaduna 1917–1967–2017*, Faber and Faber, London 1967. See also the 'Kaduna Debate' following the criticism of the plan in BLAIR, THOMAS L., 'Kaduna! African City – Western Plan', book review *Architectural Association Quarterly*, Vol. 1, No. 1, Winter 1968/69; reply by LOCK, MAX, 'Dr. Blair Tilts at Windmills', Vol. 1, No. 3, July 1969, pp. 91–3; and 'Kaduna – An International Forum', Vol. 1, No. 4, October 1969.

[13] KOENIGSBERGER, Dr. OTTO, *Housing and Planning in Northern Rhodesia: A Reconnaissance Survey*, Architectural Association, London, April 1964.

REGIONS OF AFRICA

The United Nations has classified Africa into five major regions:

1. North Africa: Algeria, Libya, Morocco, Tunisia, the UAR, Sudan, Spanish North Africa and Ifni.

2. West Africa: Mauritania, Senegal, Mali, Ivory Coast, Upper Volta, Dahomey, Niger, Gambia, Guinea, Sierra Leone, Liberia, Ghana, Togo, Nigeria, Cape Verde, Portuguese Guinea and Spanish Sahara.

3. East Africa: Malawi, Zambia, Southern Rhodesia, Madagascar, Mauritius, Tanzania, Uganda, Kenya, Somalia, Ethiopia, Comoro Islands, Seychelles, Reunion, and French Somaliland.

4. Central Africa: Cameroon, Chad, Central African Republic, Gabon, Congo Brazzaville, Congo Kinshasa, Rwanda, Burundi, San Tome and Principe, and Spanish Equatorial Africa.

5. Southern Africa: Angola, Mozambique, Republic of South Africa, South West Africa, Botswana, Lesotho and Swaziland.

SELECTED BIBLIOGRAPHY

Cities and Regions

BARBOUR, K. M., and PROTHERO, R. M. (Eds.), *Essays on African Population*, London: Routledge and Kegan Paul, 1961.

LLOYD, P., MABOGUNJE, A. L., and AWE, B. (Eds.), *The City of Ibadan*, Cambridge University Press, 1967.

MABOGUNJE, A. L., *Urbanization in Nigeria*, London, University of London Press, 1968.

MINER, H. (Ed.), *The City in Modern Africa*, London, Pall Mall Library of African Affairs, 1967.

Continuity and Change

BASCOM, W. R., and HERSKOVITS, M. J. (Eds.) *Continuity and Change in African Cultures*, Chicago, University of Chicago Press, 1959.

FIELD, M. J., *Search for Security: An Ethno-Psychiatric Study in Rural Ghana*, London, Faber and Faber, 1960.

MALINOWSKI, B., *The Dynamics of Culture Change: An Enquiry into Race Relations in Africa*, New Haven, Yale University Press, 1961.

Politics of National Liberation

BLAIR, THOMAS L., *The Land To Those Who Work It: Algeria's Experiment in Workers' Management*, New York, Doubleday, 1969.

COLEMAN, JAMES S., 'The Politics of Sub-Saharan Africa,' in ALMOND, G. A., and COLEMAN, J. S. (Eds.), *The Politics of the Developing Areas*, Princeton, Princeton University Press, 1960.

FANON, FRANTZ, *The Damned*, Paris, Presence Africaine, 1963.

NKRUMAH, KWAME, *Neo-Colonialism: The Last Stage of Imperialism*, London, Nelson, 1965.

WORSLEY, P., *The Third World*, London, Weidenfeld and Nicolson, 1964.

History

DAVIDSON, BASIL, *Africa in History*, London, Weidenfeld and Nicolson, 1968.

DuBOIS, W. E. B., *The World and Africa*, New York, International Publishers, 1965.

OLIVER, R., and FAGE, J. D., *A Short History of Africa*, London, Penguin African Library, 1962.

Housing, Urbanisation and Industrialisation

ABRAMS, C., *Housing in the Modern World*, London, Faber and Faber, 1966.

BLAIR, THOMAS L., 'Man's Quest For Shelter in Urbanizing Africa', Report of the Proceedings of the Town and Country Planning Association Summer School, University of Keele, September 1966.

UNESCO, *Social Implications of Industrialization and Urbanization in Africa South of the Sahara*, Paris, UNESCO Tensions and Technology Series, 1956.

WALLERSTEIN, I. (Ed.), *Social Change: The Colonial Situation*, New York, John Wiley and Sons, 1966.

Economic Development

FRIEDLAND, W. H., and ROSBERG, C. G., *African Socialism*, Stanford, California, Stanford University Press, 1964.

LITTLE, I. M. D., *Aid to Africa: An Appraisal of UK Policy For Aid to Africa*, London, Pergamon Press for the Overseas Development Institute, 1965.

UNITED NATIONS, *Industrial Development in Africa*, New York, United Nations, 1967.

NOTES ON THE CONTRIBUTORS

ANDREWS, Peter Alford
Peter Andrews is Research Fellow with the Department of Development Tropical Studies of the Architectural Association. He is engaged in research into the tent cultures. His detailed study of Moroccan tents was sponsored by the Social Science Research Council and conducted with the help of the Moroccan Government.

ARCHER, Ian
Ian Archer was educated at the Architectural Association School of Architecture, the Kumasi University of Science and Technology, Ghana and the AA Department of Tropical Studies. He worked for the firm of McNab and Jamieson for two years, taught part-time at the Portsmouth School of Architecture and is now in private practice, being involved in industrial projects.

BIERMANN, Barrie
Barrie Biermann was educated at the Grey Institute, Port Elizabeth. He is a graduate of the School of Architecture at the University of Cape Town, Senior Lecturer at the School of Architecture at the University of Natal and maintains a practice. His publications include works on colonial and indigenous architecture.

BLAIR, Thomas L.
Thomas L. Blair is Senior Lecturer in Sociology, School of Planning, Faculty of the Built Environment, The Polytechnic, London. Dr. Blair is also a member of the Editorial Advisory Board of the Journal *Official Architecture and Planning*, and author of a number of publications including a forthcoming book *The Urban Crisis*.

DANBY, Miles
Miles Danby trained at the Architectural Association. He has spent many years in Africa. He was Professor of Architecture at the Faculty of Architecture of the Kumasi University of Science and Technology, Ghana, and was subsequently Professor of Architecture and Principal of the Faculty of Architecture at the University of Khartoum. He is now Professor of Architecture at the University of Newcastle.

ETHERTON, David
David Etherton studied architecture at the Architectural Association 1958–64. He worked mainly on educational buildings in London, Glasgow and Hull before going to Algiers. While in Algeria he designed and built a domestic science school near Djelfa in the Hauts Plateaux, and made a survey for the Algerian Ministry of Education for the building and organisation of school canteens in the Oasis Department of the Sahara. Now lecturer in Architecture at the University College, Nairobi.

FOSTER, Badi G.
Badi Foster is presently teaching political science at Livingston College, Rutgers University, while completing his doctorial thesis at Princeton University, where he is acting chairman of the Afro-American Studies Programme. Mr. Foster has resided in Morocco for several years and has recently returned from a year in field work on Moroccan *bidonvilles*.

GEBREMEDHIN, Naigzy
Naigzy Gebremedhin was educated at the University of Kansas and at the Massachusetts Institute of Technology. He is an Associate Member of the American Society of Civil Engineers and a Member of the Ethiopian Association of Engineers and Architects. Mr. Gebremedhin was formerly Principal of the Ethio-Swedish Institute of Building Technology and at present is Social Affairs officer for the Centre for Housing, Building and Planning, United Nations, New York.

GERVIS, Guy
Guy Gervis is carrying out a planning project in Koidu as Town Planning Associate with Kenneth Scott Associates, Architects and Town Planners. He has been to West Africa previously as a Visiting Lecturer at Kumasi, in Ghana, and his interest in this kind of problem began in Latin America where, after living in Brazil he made an extensive tour of other countries on the continent, studying the problem of housing.

GUEDES, Amancio d'Alpoim Miranda
Amancio d'Alpoim Miranda Guedes was born in Lisbon and spent his childhood in St. Thomas Island and Moçambique. He completed his high-school studies in South Africa, after which he graduated in Architecture at Witwatersrand University. After having his degree recognised in Porto, Portugal, he set up a private practice in Lourenço Marques, where he has been ever since.

LEVIN, Michael
Michael Levin studied at the University of British Columbia and at Princeton University, reading Anthropology. He spent some two years in field work and research in Nigeria and the Cameroon, and is now Lecturer in the Department of Anthropology at the State University of New York, Buffalo.

LEWCOCK, Ronald
Ronald Lewcock is an Australian who began his research on architecture in Africa in 1949, and has since published several books and many articles. He was a Howard Fellow at Columbia 1963–64, and has subsequently worked on research in West Africa, Persia, India, Ceylon and Indonesia. After lecturing at the University of Natal he is now at Clare College, Cambridge.

MTHAWANJI, Ralph
Ralph Mthawanji, born of Chewa and Ngoni parents is a native of Malawi. Astutely aware of his country's problems in urbanisation, and westernisation, he is at present in the Department of Tropical and Development Studies of the Architectural Association.

RUTTER, Andrew
Educated at the AA, Andrew Rutter was a United Nations instructor with the Research and Development Department at Kumasi University of Science and Technology, Ghana, where he participated in resettlement programmes in connection with the Volta Dam project. Later he worked in the Town Planning Department in Edinburgh, Scotland, and is now with the Hampshire County Planning Department at Winchester.

SCHWERDTFEGER, Friedrich W.
Friedrich W. Schwerdtfeger was born in Zittau, Germany. He studied architecture in Berlin and worked later in Greece and Iran. In 1965–66 he studied at the Department of Tropical Studies, Architectural Association. Recently he designed and built an International Training Centre for the World Assembly of Youth in New Delhi, and is at present working on a Ph.D. thesis at University College, London.

VERITY, Paul
Paul Verity is at present a student at the Architectural Association, having previously trained at Hornsey Art College. He has travelled widely in the Near and Middle East and North Africa carrying out various research projects.